P9-ARX-949

Parenting and Child Development
in "Nontraditional" Families

Parenting and Child Development in "Nontraditional" Families

Edited by

Michael E. Lamb

*National Institute of Child Health
and Human Development*

LEA LAWRENCE ERLBAUM ASSOCIATES, PUBLISHERS
1999 Mahwah, New Jersey   London

DISCARD Property of WLU
Social Work Library

Property of the Library
Wilfrid Laurier University

Copyright © 1999 by Lawrence Erlbaum Associates, Inc.

All rights reserved. No part of this book may be reproduced
in any form, by photostat, microfilm, retrieval system, or by any
other means, without the prior written permission of the publisher.

Lawrence Erlbaum Associates, Inc., Publishers
10 Industrial Avenue
Mahwah, New Jersey 07430

LIBRARY OF CONGRESS CATALOGING-IN-PUBLICATION DATA

Parenting and child development in "nontraditional" families / edited by
    Michael E. Lamb.
        p.   cm.
    Includes bibliographical references and index.
    ISBN 0–8058–2747–1 (alk. paper)—ISBN 0–8058–2748–X (pbk.:
alk. paper)
        1. Family.   2. Family—Psychological aspects.   3. Parenting—
    Psychological aspects.   4. Child development.   I. Lamb, Michael
    E., 1953– ⱅ1825
    HQ734.N68 1998
    306.85—dc21   98–18422
                                                                         CIP

Books published by Lawrence Erlbaum Associates are printed on acid-free paper,
and their bindings are chosen for strength and durability.

Printed in the United States of America
10 9 8 7 6 5 4 3 2 1

Contents

Preface

Nearly two decades ago, I edited a book entitled *Nontraditional Families: Parenting and Child Development* (Lamb, 1981). In that book, a distinguished group of researchers and scholars examined the empirical literature documenting the effects of "nontraditional" childrearing practices on child development. The nontraditional practices discussed, described, and analyzed involved deviations from the traditional two-parent, father-as-breadwinner, mother-as-careprovider paradigm. Contributors thus reviewed the effects of maternal employment, single parenthood, and increased parental involvement on children and families.

In the ensuing decades, researchers have continued to study nontraditional patterns of childcare and family structure, although many mainstream theorists and researchers have continued to write as though, in ideal circumstances, children are raised by full-time mothers supported by husbands/fathers who are breadwinners with minimal direct involvement in childcare. As a result, several chapters in this book are devoted to the analysis of the expanded literature on parental employment and child-care patterns, both inside and outside the family. The efforts of developmental psychologists and family social scientists are not only constrained by a preoccupation with traditional two-parent families, however. Scholars and researchers have also focused largely on middle-class White families in anglophone North America—in part, perhaps, because these families are most familiar to the majority of researchers and social theorists themselves. This preoccupation has become increasingly anachronistic in the face of demographic changes that have made traditional middle-class, White, affluent families increasingly unrepresentative of the population.

The goal of this volume is to discuss in depth the ways in which various "deviations" from traditional family styles affect childrearing practices and child development. Instead of dwelling on the "deviance" of these childrearing modes or styles, the contributors each attempt to illustrate the dynamic developmental processes that characterize parenting and child development in contexts that can be deemed nontraditional because they do not reflect the demographic characteristics of the traditional families on which social scientists have largely focused. Contributors thus deal with the dynamics and possible effects of dual-earner families, families with unusually involved fathers, families characterized by the occurrence of divorce, single parenthood, remarriage, poverty, adoption, reliance on nonparental childcare, ethnic membership (Black, Latino, or interracial), parents with lesbian or gay sexual orientations, as well as violent and/or neglectful parents. By so doing, the authors provide thoughtful, literate, and up-to-date accounts of a diverse array of nontraditional or traditionally understudied family types. All the chapters offer answers to a common question: How do these patterns of childcare affect children, their experiences, and their developmental processes? The answers to these questions are of practical importance, relevant to a growing proportion of the families and children in the United States, but also have significant implications for the understanding of developmental processes in general. As a result, the book will be of value to basic social scientists, as well as to those professionals concerned with guiding and advising clients and public policy.

Completion of this volume was greatly aided by my cheerfully competent secretary, Jenny Harbin Lake, and I am very grateful to her. In addition, Ranisha Patel prepared a thorough and accurate Subject Index.

—Michael E. Lamb
Bethesda, MD

Parental Behavior, Family Processes, and Child Development in Nontraditional and Traditionally Understudied Families

MICHAEL E. LAMB
National Institute of Child Health and Human Development

Parental influences on children's development have been the topic of speculation for centuries and the focus of theory and research for decades. Although efforts in this area continue to vary in the degree of sophistication, one consistent similarity has been the preoccupation with the superiority of "traditional" family styles and "traditional" parental roles. Thus, social scientists have lauded family dynamics, parental behavior, and child development in two-parent families in which mothers are full-time homemakers and care providers, while fathers are primary bread-winners with minimal direct involvement in child care. Although less often re-marked, scholars and researchers have also focused largely on middle-class White families in North America—in part, perhaps, because these families are most familiar to the majority of researchers and social scientists themselves. The ex-clusive focus on (and evaluative preference for) families of this type has become increasingly anachronistic in the face of demographic changes that have made tra-ditional families less and less characteristic of the environments in which most children are raised, and that have made, even in the United States, the White, affluent, educated families that are widely studied increasingly unrepresentative of the population.

The goal of this volume is to discuss in depth the ways in which various devi-ations from traditional family styles affect childrearing practices and child de-velopment. I use the term *deviations* advisedly, because it implies deviation from some established norm, and there is scant evidence that traditional families rep-resent a pattern of family life that has been normative historically or cross-culturally. As many commentators have observed, the traditional norm is some-what illusory, existing primarily in the conceptual models and assumptions of social scientists rather than in the societies and communities they observe and study. Instead of dwelling on their deviance, therefore, contributors to this volume attempt to illustrate the dynamic developmental processes that characterize parenting and child development in the various ecological niches that can be deemed nontraditional because they do not reflect the demographic characteristics of the traditional families on which social scientists have largely focused. With these considerations and implicit definitions in mind, in this introductory chapter I review the principal issues raised in the study of nontraditional families and their impact on child development.

Many discussions regarding familial influences on early socioemotional development implicitly assume that the traditional family constellation is normative and thus the most adaptive for parents and children. Consequently, most considerations of nontraditional families begin with the assumption that these families are deviant and are likely to have adverse effects—especially on young children growing up in them. Fortunately, some of these deviant forms of family organization such as maternal employment and extrafamilial child care have been in evidence long enough for researchers to assess empirically the validity of the assumption that "nontraditional is necessarily harmful." However, other deviant styles and practices are of such recent origin or have been studied so little that empirical research remains limited. In addition, evaluative judgments about traditional and nontraditional family forms abound, making it difficult to separate opinions from facts.

In this introductory chapter, I first explore some myths about the origins and history of the traditional family. Then I define the five principal assumptions that appear to form the basis of prevalent beliefs about the inherent superiority of traditional over nontraditional family forms. Finally, I present an outline of the volume, discussing the relationships between the individual chapters and the propositions mentioned in the second section.

ORIGINS OF THE TRADITIONAL FAMILY

The belief that traditional two-parent families are more likely to preserve marital harmony and raise psychologically healthy children has achieved widespread and almost unquestioned acceptance, even though this belief reflects an unwarranted equation between what was (briefly) common and what should be the case. Ironically, it also involves misunderstanding of both the origins of the traditional family organization and the social adaptability of the human species.

Contrary to the claims of its contemporary defenders, the traditional family is of relatively recent origin. Although it is true that women have always and everywhere assumed primary responsibility for the care of very young children, this responsibility has seldom precluded either their major involvement in subsistence provision or a substantial reliance upon other caretakers (Lamb, 1998). Consider, for example, the !Kung Bushmen, whose habitat and hunting-and-gathering ways constitute a modern representation of the ecological niche for which we probably evolved. Among the !Kung, gathering by women accounts for about 60% of the group's nutritional needs, and toddlers or preschool-age children are frequently left in the care of older children and siblings (Lee, 1979). The same occurs in a variety of other societies, whether they have hunting, gathering, pastoral, or agricultural economic bases. In many such "primitive" societies, furthermore, men are expected to assume a role in socialization (especially of boys) and so are more directly involved in childrearing than are most Western fathers.

Shared responsibility for economic provision and (to a lesser extent) childrearing appears to have been common throughout most of our history. It was the industrial revolution that brought it to an end. Instead of working in fields or workshops close to their homes, men now had to travel to mines or factories located some distance away, and instead of perfecting skills they could proudly pass on to their sons, men found that their only salable commodity was unskilled labor. Concomitantly, the subsistence economy gave way to a monetary economy, and thus the fathers' yield in the form of wages increased in importance while the ability of their wives to contribute significantly declined. Nevertheless, most women (only the well-to-do were exempt) entered the paid labor force and remained employed except for a brief interruption for childbearing and childrearing. Only when general increases in wage levels occurred around the turn of the century did it become unnecessary for some women to work. It was at this point that the traditional family form emerged—less than a century ago.

On the other hand, certain aspects of traditional family organization that are now being questioned by the proponents of alternative family style have been with us far longer. As noted earlier, first of all, women have always and everywhere assumed primary responsibility for early child care. Until the invention of the nursing bottle, only the availability of wet-nurses could free mothers of caretaking responsibilities, and this expensive option was available to relatively few. On the other hand, respect for the sanctity of childhood was limited, and so children were forced into paid employment at very young ages (Aries, 1962; Kessen, 1965). Child care was simply not accorded much consideration by either men or women. Similarly, single parenthood is considered deviant in Anglo-American and Western cultures, although the number of illegitimate children born to unwed mothers in the past appears to have been considerable, especially in medieval cities and towns, and the stigma attached to illegitimacy and divorce appears to have developed only in the Victorian era. Curiously, until the middle of the 1800s, children were customarily placed in the custody of their fathers (not their mothers) when marital dissolution occurred. Under common law, children were viewed as their fathers' possessions, and it was assumed that men could make satisfactory arrangements for their children's care until they remarried or their children reached adulthood. The traditional belief that custody should be awarded to mothers can be traced to judicial decisions in the 1830s, which gradually gained acceptance over the succeeding decades. In all, therefore, the belief that women should assume primary responsibility for childrearing has been with us for little more than a few generations.

The preceding paragraphs also reveal that human social behavior is highly adaptable in the face of changing ecological demands. To an extent unequaled in any other species, our behavior is highly flexible. Relatively few of our behavior patterns appear to be innately and immutably organized, and the evolutionary success of our species is attributable to our enormous adaptability. Furthermore, even when biologically based predispositions exist, they are usually tendencies that bias behavior in certain directions subject to environmental demands; seldom do we find humans biologically impelled to behave in one way or another. This realization appears not to have occurred to contemporary advocates of natural family organization. Presumably, beliefs in the superiority of traditional family forms reflect the limited perspective of many social scientists, as does their narrow focus on White and middle class families. Unfortunately, attempts to understand such families were seldom constrained by efforts to limit generalization. Instead, social scientists either assumed that all families functioned like those they studied or, when this assumption was untenable, that alternate family forms represented deficient processes with predictably detrimental effects on child development. As the contributors to this volume make clear, many nontraditional family forms have unique characteristics, strengths, and weaknesses that make them worthy of study in their own right and defy simplistic efforts to view them simply by disparaging comparisons with traditional families.

THE ASSUMED STRENGTHS OF TRADITIONAL FAMILIES

The assumption that the traditional ways of allocating family responsibilities and raising children are necessarily preferable is itself based on five principal axioms or beliefs, namely:

1. children need two parents, one of each sex;
2. family responsibilities should be divided between the parents, with fathers as economic providers and mothers as homemakers and caretakers;
3. mothers are better suited for childrearing and caretaking than fathers are;
4. young children should be cared for primarily by family members; and
5. White middle-class parents have superior parenting skills and have children who are more likely to excel.

Each of these assumptions are subject to scrutiny in the chapters that follow.

In the first three chapters, the focus is on two-parent families in which the two parents do not divide provisioning and child care roles in the traditional fashion. There are three sources of concern here. The traditional within-family division of parental responsibilities is altered when fathers share the responsibility for bread-winning, and so (it is argued) lose authority and status. In addition, some of the responsibility for child care is frequently shifted in such families to persons outside the family. These persons are said to be less reliable and consistent and to lack the commitment that parents manifest. As far as child development is concerned, harm is likely to result both because the developing relationships between parents and children are weakened and because children are offered substitute care of lower quality than they would receive at home. These issues have been investigated in two partially overlapping literatures, one focused on the effects of maternal employment (Gottfried, Gottfried, Bathurst, and Killian, chap. 2) and the other on the effects of nonparental care (Lamb, chap. 3).

One source of concern about maternal employment is that it may blur the roles of husbands and wives to the detriment of harmonious interaction within the family. This concern has its origins in the notion that male and female roles complement one another and permit couples to capitalize on these complementary areas of expertise. According to Parsons (Parsons & Bales, 1955), for example, women are more expressive, nurturant, and emotionally sensitive and thus should take responsibility for the management of relationships, child care, and so forth. By contrast, because men exhibit instrumental competence, they are suited for executive leadership of the family and for using their instrumental skills in the employment area. However, the Parsonian assumption that heterosexual interaction is more harmonious when the parties are "appropriately" gender typed has not received empirical support (Ickes, 1985) and the reviews by both Gottfried and her colleagues (chap. 2) and Lamb (chap. 3) reveal little empirical support for concerns about the inevitably harmful effects on children of maternal employment and extrafamilial care.

Studies of dual-earner families reveal that a traditional division of roles and responsibilities within the family often persists, even when both parents are equally involved in the paid labor force (Pleck, 1985). It could be argued, therefore, that the maintenance of traditional roles and responsibilities helps to protect children from the harmful consequences of their mothers' employment. Similar claims cannot be made about those cases in which fathers share in, or are primarily responsible for, child care, while their wives share in, or are primarily responsible for, the economic support of their family. The concerns expressed about role-sharing and role-reversing families are multiple, but two dominate: the belief that men are simply inferior to women in childrearing abilities and the fear that children will be confused about gender related social roles when they are not provided with gender differentiated parental models. The first of these concerns derives from the premise that women are biologically destined to be childbearers and childrearers. Proponents often point to the evidence that the female hormones (prolactin, progesterone, estrogen) potentiate parental behavior in nonhuman species and suggest that these hormones play a similar role in humans. Actually, there is no empirical support for this claim (Lamb & Goldberg, 1982) and the few relevant studies show that men and women are equivalently responsive to their own infants at least initially, although differential experiences over time seem to make fathers on average less sensitive than mothers (Lamb, 1997). The second concern depends on assumptions that the gender appropriate quality of parental behavior will be lost when men become primary caretakers and women become primary breadwinners, and that the psychological adjustment of children requires the acquisition of a traditional sex role. The first of these assumptions is challenged by the research reviewed by Russell (see chap. 4) on highly involved fathers as well as by evidence concerning the benign impact of growing up with two parents of the same gender (Patterson & Chan, chap. 10). The second assumption is faulty both because it implies a confusion between gender identity and gender role (the acquisition of a secure gender identity is developmentally important, but it need not involve conformity to a traditional gender role) and because it equates conformity to a traditional gender role with psychological adjustment. There is no justification for this assumed congruence; in fact, less traditionally gender-typed children are arguably better prepared should the future involve more egalitarian societies.

Despite the shaky bases on which they are founded, concerns about role-sharing and role-reversal remain. Until recently, unfortunately, no attempts were made to study role-sharing and role-reversing families and document the effects of parental role sharing on children and parents. These findings are discussed by Russell (chap. 4), who attempts to place parental role sharing in context by examining the motivations, the stresses, the effects on parental behavior, and the effects on child development. Patterson and Chan (chap. 10), meanwhile, explore the implicit assumption that children need parents of both sexes, noting that children raised by lesbian and gay couples seem to develop quite normally, with variations in their outcomes dependent on variations in the parents' behavior and circumstances.

Although concerns about maternal employment, extrafamilial child care, and role sharing or role reversal are based largely on parochial prejudices and enjoy little empirical support, concerns about single parenthood are better founded. Several large-scale studies have shown that marital disharmony and hostility are more likely than any other family variable to have adverse effects, and of course such disharmony is likely to precede family dissolution (Cummings & O'Reilly, 1997; Emery, 1994). Furthermore, divorce is a stressful experience from which all parties (mothers, fathers, children) take time to recover. Consequently, at the time when children are in greatest need of emotional support and reassurance, their parents are least capable of providing it. Even after the initial turmoil subsides, single-parent families are economically strained (partly because most are headed by women who still face extensive economic discrimination) and socially isolated (Hetherington & Stanley-Hagan, 1997). Although such prejudices seem to be declining, divorced parents and children suffer from their own and others' perceptions that their family constellation is deviant and inferior. In addition, single parents often have difficulty obtaining temporary respite from child-care responsibilities. It is a tribute to the resilience of human beings that the adverse long-term effects appear to be modest and extremely deviant outcomes quite rare.

Popular and legal prejudices also influence the composition of single-parent families. Until recently, courts upheld, in the form of "the tender years doctrine," the presumption that mothers should be awarded custody of young children following divorce because they were better suited for parenting than fathers were. Challenges by advocates of equal rights have led to removal of the legal presumption, and an increasing number of contested custody cases are now resolved in the fathers' favor, although the majority of single parent families are still headed by women. Three chapters—one each on single motherhood (McLanahan & Teitler, chap. 5), noncustodial fatherhood (Thompson & Laible, chap. 6), and stepfamilies (Hetherington & Stanley-Hagan, chap. 8) review the multifaceted effects of divorce on families and children, while Lamb, Sternberg, and Thompson (chap. 7) present a consensus analysis of the implications for public policy and legal decision making.

As researchers have moved beyond ethnocentric assumptions about the superiority of White middle-class families, they have begun to recognize the unique features—both strengths and weaknesses—associated with ethnic variations and socioeconomic variations. Gadsden (chap. 11) and Leyendecker and Lamb (chap. 12) thus discuss the status of Black and Latino families, noting that these represent the second and third largest subgroups, respectively, of the U.S. population. The special circumstances and challenges faced by families in poverty are then discussed by Brooks-Gunn, Britto, and Brady (chap. 14).

Poverty and socioeconomic status are associated with the incidence of both child neglect and family violence, yet these phenomena also appear much more complex than is often recognized. The effects on child development are nuanced, and the resilience of children exposed to such events is noteworthy in light of continuing beliefs in the fragility of developmental trajectories. Families characterized by neglect and violence are discussed in the final chapters (15 and 16) of the volume.

OUTLINE OF THE VOLUME

Dual-Earner Families

In the next chapter, Gottfried, Gottfried, Bathurst, and Killian (chap. 2) deal with the increasing participation of women—including mothers—in the paid work force. As developmental psychologists, these authors focus on the personal motivations for employment and the ways in which variations in maternal employment may affect child development.

The increased labor force participation of women undoubtedly represents the most common and most frequently mentioned deviation from the traditional pattern of family organization. Indeed, in the United States many more women are now employed than are not employed, and the rates of employment for mothers, including mothers with infants, are around 60% (H. Hayghe, personal communication, October 17, 1995). Strictly speaking, therefore, maternal employment is now normative, although developmental theorists still view dual-wage-earner families as deviant, and there remain many popular misconceptions about effects on the development of young children.

By and large, the evidence suggests that maternal employment often results in an inequitable distribution of chores and responsibilities within two-parent families. Even when they work as many hours outside the home as their husbands do, employed mothers typically retain primary responsibility for home care and child care, although fathers do participate in home care and child care more when their partners are employed (Pleck, 1997). Despite the potential dangers of role overload, however, maternal employment appears not to have adverse consequences on child development. Indeed, the sons and daughters of employed mothers tend to have less traditionally stereotyped attitudes about male and female roles than do children whose mothers are unemployed. Gottfried and her colleagues detail a number of other respects in which middle-class children today appear to benefit from their mothers' employment.

Extrafamilial Child Care

As increasing numbers of mothers with young children have entered the paid labor force, nonfamilial child care has become more important. The chapter by Lamb (chap. 3) is included in this volume for this reason. Clearly, if one is to understand how changing role assignments within the family affect child development, one must also consider the impact of experiences outside the family that are correlated with the intrafamilial variables. Most of the early research was concerned primarily with the effects of center-based care, even though a minority of the young children receiving extrafamilial care are enrolled in day-care centers (Lamb, 1998). The majority receive informal family day care, the effects of which have received much less attention. Representative samples of children and families are rarely studied, so even though enrollment in day care appears not to have adverse effects on socioemotional development (even in infancy), we can only conclude that nonfamilial care need not have adverse effects—we do not know whether developmental deviations are more likely to occur when it is received. Among the factors affecting the influence of extrafamilial care are the quality of care provided; consistency between the caretaking styles of parents and supplementary caretakers; the opportunity for interaction with other children; and the quality of parent–child relationships before and after enrollment. In addition, because different types of families may select different types of alternative care, there may be interactions between family and caretaker characteristics that need to be considered as we strive to determine how these factors affect child development. More generally, the effects of day care need to be studied and understood in the context of the broader social ecologies in which children are raised.

Increased Paternal Involvement

The next chapter (chap. 4) is concerned with a far less common characteristic of nontraditional two-parent families than maternal employment—major paternal responsibility for child care. Graeme Russell, who conducted one of the first studies concerned with the internal dynamics of families in which fathers assumed major responsibility for child care (Russell, 1983), reviews the growing literature concerned with these families and the effects of increased paternal involvement on child development. He argued that male sex roles need to change if women are to achieve equal opportunities in the educational, occupational, and social spheres because male and female sex roles are defined in relation to one another. As intimated earlier, for example, increased paternal involvement may be necessary if employed women are to be relieved of the role strain and overload under which many now suffer.

Divorce and Single Parenthood

We next turn attention to families in which children do not live with their two biological parents, either because the child's biological parents do not live together or because the child has been adopted by one or both parents. Census and demographic data show that the number of single-parent families has been increasing since the late 1960s (South & Tolnay, 1992; U.S. Bureau of the Census, 1992). Although these numbers appear to be reaching a plateau, the situation is such that about 50% of the children born in the United States in the late 1990s will spend at least part of their childhood with only one (usually female) parent. One third of the live births in the United States today are to unmarried mothers, although most single-parent families are created by divorce, and 90% of them comprise single mothers and their children. Economic discrimination ensures that single mothers have great difficulty finding jobs that pay them adequately, particularly when they have been out of the work force for several years and so do not have recent experience and skills. Further, many of the couple's friends have difficulty relating to single parents after the divorce, especially when (as is often the case) these were work associates of the fathers/husbands. Not surprisingly, therefore, social isolation is a frequent complaint of single parents. Further, single parents do not have partners to whom they can hand over their children when they are in need of "time out" from the incessant demands of parenting. The lack of concrete and emotional support in the face of severe socioemotional and economic stress combine to make the single parents' role an invidious one.

Five chapters in this volume deal with divorce, single parenthood, and remarriage. McLanahan and Teitler (chap. 5) and Thompson and Laible (chap. 6) deal with single mothers and noncustodial fathers, respectively; two aspects of the families created by parental divorce or separation. The authors of these chapters review large bodies of research, and the implications of this research for decision making that is sensitive to the needs and welfare of children are described by Lamb, Sternberg, and Thompson (chap. 7). Many divorced parents remarry, as Hetherington and Stanley-Hagan (chap. 8) note in their discussion of stepfamilies. Children in stepfamilies live with one parent to whom they are not biologically related, although many are adopted by their stepparents (Grotevant & Kohlar, chap. 9).

The effects of divorce and single parenthood on mothers, fathers, and children have been studied extensively, particularly since the late 1980s (Emery, 1994; Hetherington & Stanley-Hagan, 1997; McLanahan & Sandefur, 1994). Two bodies of literature have developed, one involving relatively small-scale, intensive studies focused on individuals and family processes, mostly in more affluent, educated White middle-class families that have experienced divorce, and another concerned with large scale demographic and survey-based studies of respondents from diverse backgrounds, many of whom became single parents nonmaritally. The two bodies of literature have converged on similar conclusions, as the consensus report reproduced in chapter 7 makes clear, but some differences have emerged, attributable either to differences in the researchers' disciplinary backgrounds (psychologists vs. sociologists and demographers) or differences in the populations sampled. In this volume, McLanahan and Teitler (chap. 5) focus primarily on the results of the representative large-scale studies, whereas Hetherington and Stanley-Hagan (chap. 8) emphasize the results of smaller sized psychological studies. McLanahan and Teitler show that children who grow up in single-parent families are disadvantaged psychologically, educationally, and economically. Statistical controls for the economic consequences do not eliminate the apparent effects, suggesting that the psychoeducational effects are not merely epiphenomenal or secondary to the economic effects. The same conclusions are supported by some of the findings reviewed by Hetherington and Stanley-Hagan; whereas stepfathers often improve the economic status of single mothers, their accession does not eliminate the effects of divorce or single parenthood on children. Hetherington and Stanley-Hagan note that stepfamilies differ from nondivorced two-parent families in many ways, with stepchildren often resenting their new "parents" and stepparents often avoiding the full exercise of their parental responsibilities. In addition, the entry of stepfathers often compounds the difficulties faced by noncustodial fathers, further weakening their often tenuous relationships with their children. The tendency of noncustodial fathers to drift out of their children's lives is noted in chapters 5, 6, 7, and 8, although only Thompson and Laible (chap. 6) discuss its apparent origins. They speculate that conventional visitation patterns (and the label itself) disenfranchise fathers and leave many feeling as though they cannot play meaningful roles in their children's lives. The psychological dilemmas of noncustodial fathers dominate chapter 6, therefore, just as the dilemmas faced by stepparents attain center stage in chapter 8.

Adoptive and Lesbian/Gay Families

Much has been written in the last decade about the effects of divorce and father-lessness on child development, and although controversies persist regarding inter-pretation, there is consensus regarding the effects themselves (Lamb, Sternberg, & Thompson, chap. 7). By contrast, controversy still characterizes discussions of adoptive and gay/lesbian families. Although adoption is widely viewed as a desir-able option for abandoned, maltreated, or orphaned children, critics have focused on some widespread aspects of adoption, including transracial adoption (viewed by some as being inattentive to the ethnic identities of vulnerable children), in-ternational adoption (viewed by some as exploitative), adoption by homosexual parents (viewed as a practice that places children at risk of maladjustment and even maltreatment), and blind or anonymous adoption (criticized for perma-nently denying individuals the opportunity to seek contact with relatives from whom they have been separated). The issues are discussed more fully by Grote-vant and Kohler (chap. 9), who also describe some unique characteristics of adop-tive families. Grotevant and Kohler further note that the traumatic histories of some adoptive children may place them at risk, but that adoption tends to promote better outcomes than might have been expected in their absence.

The controversies surrounding lesbian and gay families are more intensive, of course, as might be expected when disapproval of homosexuality remains so com-mon. As Patterson and Chan (chap. 10) point out, however, lesbian and gay fami-lies are quite heterogeneous. Some involve parents who had children in the course of heterosexual relationships, other families involve lesbian parents who conceived through sperm donation, and still other families involve couples who adopted children biologically unrelated to either of them. Contrary to widespread belief, children in such families do not appear to be at psychological risk, developing het-erosexual identities and well-adjusted psyches at the same rates as in straight families.

Ethnic Status and Poverty

The next three chapters focus on families that are nontraditional only by virtue of the unwillingness, until the 1980s, of scholars to study them seriously, other than as examples of deviations from the norm (that is, White, affluent, two-parent fam-ilies). In the first of these chapters, Gadsden (chap. 11) reviews past depictions of Black African American families (and, typically, of their weaknesses) by White social scientists. She then describes the many economic and social barriers to ad-vancement faced by Black parents and children, both historically and today, and the ways in which these have shaped and limited children's development and adjustment. More recent work on the characteristics of Black families illustrates adaptability and resilience while providing the descriptive basis for process-oriented studies of development in this rather heterogeneous social context.

Whereas Black families have faced and been shaped by several generations of discrimination and mistreatment in North America, immigration has been a central formative experience for Latino-American families (see Leyendecker & Lamb, chap. 12). With the exception of those whose native lands were annexed by the United States, Latino Americans or their recent ancestors immigrated to the United States from Central or South America, usually in search of better socioeconomic circumstances and better opportunities for their children. Unlike earlier waves of immigrants from Europe, however, Latino Americans have sought to maintain a bicultural orientation, cherishing the values and language (Spanish) of their native lands while accommodating the demands of their new cultural context. Among the values, the enduring emphasis on family bonds and responsibilities have provided supportive strengths during difficult periods of transition and hardship.

Multiracial families face somewhat different difficulties, attributable primarily to discrimination and prejudice rather than poverty (Rosenblatt, chap. 13). In part, this reflects the heterogeneity of multicultural families, which may be created either by transracial adoptions or by partnerships between parents from different racial backgrounds. Unfortunately, the developmental trajectories of children in multicultural families have yet to be studied empirically.

Whatever their unique characteristics and strengths, Black and Latino families in the United States are disproportionately likely to face the ravages of poverty (Brooks-Gunn, Britto, & Brady, chapter 14), and poverty or economic distress is widely seen as a prominent determinant of the difficulties faced by parents attempting to raise children alone (chap. 5 and 7) as well as ethnic minority families (chap. 11 and 12). As Brooks-Gunn and colleagues point out, however, poverty is not limited to these contexts; indeed, the majority of poor families are White, although many are single-parent families. In addition, research (Duncan & Brooks-Gunn, 1997; Mayer, 1997) showed that poverty alone does not explain the poor adjustment and school performance of many children from minority backgrounds, just as it does not explain the disadvantaged status of many children raised by single parents. Nevertheless, poor families face a daunting array of problems that impede their function and their ability to raise children, as Brooks-Gunn et al. chronicle in chapter 14.

Violent and Neglectful Families

The final two chapters in the book focus on violent (Sternberg & Lamb, chapter 15) and neglectful (Dubowitz, chapter 16) families. Both domestic violence and child neglect are surprisingly common features of families in the United States, and substantial—albeit halting—progress has been made in attempts to understand the internal family processes that characterize such families and the diverse effects on children. From a simplistic knee-jerk judgment that violence or neglect are merely pathological and pathogenic, we have now acquired a broader understanding of the complex and heterogeneous circumstances that complicate efforts to both understand and intervene. It is ironic that these efforts promise to advance our understanding of normative family processes, outcomes, and developmental trajectories at least as much as they inform our comprehension of violent and neglectful families. Indeed, this subliminal message runs through many of the chapters included in the volume—the more we examine the dynamics and circumstances of nontraditional and traditionally understudied families, the closer we come to a broader understanding of socialization and developmental processes, many of which may remain unexamined when we focus narrowly and exclusively on traditional families and their offspring.

SUMMARY

In sum, the contributors to this volume discuss a diverse array of nontraditional families. Although the specific issues dealt with in each chapter differ, the themes outlined in the second section of this chapter predominate, and all the chapters have implications for a common question: How does this affect children, their experiences, and their developmental processes? Because nontraditional family styles are being adopted or at least considered by an increasing number of parents, answers to this question are of manifest and growing practical importance. The chapters in this volume are of importance to students of social policy and applied issues. The study of nontraditional families has significant implications for the understanding of broader developmental processes. For example, by studying gender role development in children raised without fathers, we can appraise the necessity of having a male model within the family. Similarly, the relative significance of intrafamilial and extrafamilial influences can be explored by comparing the sex roles of children whose parents' roles deviate from those adopted by the majority of men and women in the society. In addition, studies of role-reversing and role-sharing families promise to reveal whether maternal and paternal roles have a biological origin or are largely the product of gender differentiated socialization. In general, absolutist statements equating what is or was normally the case with what should be the case are most readily evaluated by observing the consequences of deviations from the normative practice. The study of diverse family styles and childrearing practices helps to illustrate the complexities and potential variability of developmental processes.

REFERENCES

Aries, P. (1962). *Centuries of childhood*. New York: Vintage.
Cummings, E. M., & O'Reilly, A. W. (1997). Fathers in family context: Effects of marital quality on

child adjustment. In M. E. Lamb (Ed.), *The role of the father in child development* (3rd ed., pp. 49–65, 318–325). New York: Wiley.

Duncan, G. & Brooks-Gunn, J. (Eds.). (1997). *Consequences of growing up poor.* New York: Russell Sage Foundation.

Emery, R. E. (1994). *Renegotiating family relationships: Divorce, child custody, and mediation.* New York: Guilford.

Hetherington, E. M., & Stanley-Hagan, M. M. (1997). The effects of divorce on fathers and their children. In M. E. Lamb (Ed.), *The role of the father in child development* (3rd ed., pp. 191–211, 360–369). New York: Wiley.

Ickes, W. (Ed.). (1985). *Compatible and incompatible relationships.* New York: Springer.

Kessen, W. (1965). *The child.* New York: Wiley.

Lamb, M. E. (1997). The development of father-infant relationships. In M. E. Lamb (Ed.), *The role of the father in child development* (3rd ed., pp. 104–120, 332–342). New York: Wiley.

Lamb, M. E. (1998). Nonparental child care: Context, quality, correlates, and consequences. In W. Damon, I. E. Sigel, & K. A. Renninger (Eds.), *Handbook of child psychology: Vol. 4. Child psychology in practice* (pp. 73–133). New York: Wiley.

Lamb, M. E., & Goldberg, W. A. (1982). The father-child relationship: A synthesis of biological, evolutionary, and social perspectives. In L. W. Hoffman, R. Gandelman, & H. R. Schiffman (Eds.), *Parenting: Its causes and consequences* (pp. 55–73). Hillsdale, NJ: Lawrence Erlbaum Associates.

Lee, R. B. (1979). *The !Kung San.* New York: Cambridge University Press.

Mayer, S. (1997). *More than money.* Cambridge, MA: Harvard University Press.

McLanahan, S., & Sandefur, G. (1994). *Growing up with a single parent: What hurts, what helps.* Cambridge, MA: Harvard University Press.

Parsons, T., & Bales, R. (1955). *Family, socialization, and interaction process.* New York: Free Press.

Pleck, J. H. (1985). *Working wives, working husbands.* Beverly Hills, CA: Sage.

Pleck, J. H. (1997). Paternal involvement: Levels, sources, and consequences. In M. E. Lamb (Ed.), *The role of the father in child development* (3rd ed., pp. 66–103, 325–332). New York: Wiley.

Russell, G. (1983). *The changing role of fathers.* St. Lucia, Australia: Queensland University Press.

South, S. J., & Tolnay, S. (Eds.). (1992). *The changing American family: Sociological and demographic perspectives.* Boulder, CO: Westview Press.

U.S. Bureau of the Census. (1992). *Poverty in the United States, 1991* (Current Population Reports, Series P60–181). Washington, DC: U.S. Government Printing Office.

Chapter 2

Maternal and Dual-Earner Employment

Family Environment, Adaptations, and the
Developmental Impingement Perspective

ADELE ESKELES GOTTFRIED
California State University, Northridge

ALLEN W. GOTTFRIED
KAY BATHURST
California State University, Fullerton

COLLEEN KILLIAN
University of California, Riverside

Although families with nonemployed mothers and working fathers may be considered to be traditional, and maternal employment within dual-earner families is considered to be nontraditional, demographic data indicate that maternal employment is presently the norm. Statistics from the U.S. Department of Labor (1991) indicate that the majority of U.S. mothers were in the labor force in 1990. Rates of labor force participation by mothers vary with the age of the child, from 52% of mothers with children under age 2 through 75% of mothers with school-age children (ages 6–17). The Bureau also reported that whereas through the mid-1980s married mothers with children under age 2 were less likely than single mothers to be in the labor force, the trend is now reversed, and married mothers are more likely than single mothers of children under age 2 to be in the labor force (U.S. Department of Labor, 1991). Concomitantly, the proportion of traditional families (single-earner families with the husband in the labor force) declined from 61% to 25% from 1960 through 1990, as the proportion of children in two-parent families with both parents in the work force increased from 36% to 61% from 1970 through 1990 (U.S. Department of Labor, 1991). In this document, child care was described as the area of family life especially affected by mothers' employment (U.S. Department of Labor, 1991). Maternal employment not only has become the norm in the United States, but also is a growing phenomenon in Western and Third World countries (e.g., Engle, 1991; Lewis, Izraeli, & Hootsmans, 1992; Peng, 1993).

Although dual-earner families constitute the norm demographically in the United States, they continue to be considered nontraditional in that they deviate from the single, (male)-earner, two-parent family that has dominated cultural expectations and developmental theory (A. E. Gottfried & A. W. Gottfried, 1994a). This deviation from cultural norms may be especially salient with regard to the dual-earner family in which mothers' work may not be viewed as an economic necessity, as it may be so perceived for single-mother and minority households (McLoyd, 1993). Researchers continue to rely, regardless of their questionable relevance to contemporary families and children's development, on developmental theories that focus on maternal employment as detrimental to children (A. E. Gottfried & A. W. Gottfried, 1994b). Such theories have as their basic assumptions that families with employed mothers are deficient, and include the *maternal deprivation perspective* (i.e., mother is not available due to employment) and *compensation perspective* (i.e., that families may make special efforts to overcome the deficits inherent in maternal employment) (A. E. Gottfried & A. W. Gottfried, 1994b). Both deviation from cultural expectations and explanations of child development based on traditional views of the family (particularly psychoanalytically derived explanations) have provided impetus for the researchers' negative expectations regarding the "effects" of maternal employment on children's development (A. E. Gottfried, A. W. Gottfried, & Bathurst, 1995). Such negative expectations were especially prevalent in the early years (1950s) of maternal employment research (A. E. Gottfried & A. W. Gottfried, 1994b; A. E. Gottfried et al., 1995). However, the search for negative effects of maternal employment on children's development continues despite the absence of empirical support. For example, article titles perpetuate the expectation of negative effects of maternal employment. Armistead, Wierson, and Forehand (1990) entitled their report: "Adolescents and maternal employment: Is it harmful for an adolescent to have an employed mother?" Their findings show no differences in the functioning of adolescents with employed and nonemployed mothers, although the title produces the expectation of detriment.

A great deal has been published about the role of maternal employment in children's development. Research conducted across many domains of development, from infancy through young adulthood, cross-sectionally and longitudinally, and holding constant for pertinent demographic factors, as well as reviewed by many different individuals, all converge on the conclusion that maternal employment per se is not detrimental to children's development (Etaugh, 1974; A. E. Gottfried, Bathurst, & A. W. Gottfried, 1994a; A. E. Gottfried & A. W. Gottfried, 1988a, 1988b; A. E. Gottfried & A. W. Gottfried, 1994b; A. E. Gottfried et al., 1995; Hoffman, 1989; Lerner, 1994; Zaslow, Rabinovich, & Suwalsky, 1991). Although there have certainly been discrepant and contradictory findings, overwhelmingly, the literature, as well as well-designed research, supports this latter conclusion. It also indicates that maternal employment is embedded within a complex network of cultural, developmental, environmental, family, and socioeconomic factors.

Many authors have supported the view that the research questions about maternal employment need to be reconceptualized, moving from the search for negative findings to the elucidation of the complex relationships between family and work processes and benefits of maternal employment (Demo, 1992; A. E. Gottfried & A. W. Gottfried, 1994b; Greenstein, 1993). As we have noted (A. E. Gottfried et al., 1995), there is no research conceptualizing the benefits accruing from occupying dual roles. Further, it is clear that searching for "effects" of maternal employment is an inadequate approach as maternal employment exists within a complex network. The key to understanding maternal employment and its relationship to parenting and children's development is to study the processes and contexts within which maternal employment exists. We address such questions in this chapter.

Based on the key research finding that there is no main effect of maternal employment on parenting and children's development, we focus on the four conclusions offered in our previous work (A. E. Gottfried & A. W. Gottfried, 1988a, 1988b; A. E. Gottfried, Bathurst, & A. W. Gottfried, 1994; A. E. Gottfried et al., 1995). First, we have concluded that, if maternal employment were to have any impact on children at all, it would be necessarily through its impact on the child's proximal environment (i.e., the experiences to which children are directly exposed). Hence, any reports of significant differences, or lack of differences, between families with employed mothers and those with nonemployed mothers would not be interpretable without an analysis of the proximal environment. Second, we have proposed that a balance of roles and factors in dual-earner families exists, and that these parental (including fathers') roles change as a result of maternal employment. One needs to study these balances in dual-earner families to understand the processes that may mediate maternal employment, on one hand, and children's development, on the other. Third, we have proposed that there are adaptations within dual-earner families regarding responsibilities and activities that have implications for children's development. Hence, it is necessary to elucidate such adaptations. Fourth, and most importantly, we have proposed the *developmental impingement perspective,* to explain children's development in alternative families, but which actually applies to all families. In this perspective, one needs to evaluate the complex interweave of factors associated with particular family structures and children's development. Further, this complex interweaving must be studied longitudinally to establish the developmental trajectories of such influences over time; must include child characteristics, varying family ecology and contexts; and must assume a neutral (not a negative) value orientation. In this chapter, we focus on these four issues with regard to contemporary research.

PROXIMAL ENVIRONMENT

Proximal environment consists of the cognitive, social-emotional, and physical stimulation as well as family interpersonal relationships available to children in the home (A. E. Gottfried et al., 1995; A. W. Gottfried & A. E. Gottfried, 1984). Maternal employment is considered to be a distal, not a proximal, variable. It categorizes mothers on the basis of employment status but conveys no information regarding the nature or quality of the environment that impinges on children's development (A. E. Gottfried et al., 1995). An extensive literature indicates that children's development is significantly and consistently related to the quality of home environment and family processes across socioeconomic status (SES; Bradley et al., 1989; A. W. Gottfried, 1984; A. W. Gottfried & A. E. Gottfried, 1984; Wachs, 1992). Therefore, maternal employment is expected to play a role in children's development to the extent that it is related to home and family environment. In addition, to the extent that other distal variables, such as SES and ethnicity, impact the proximal environment of the home, they also may be expected to play a role in the relation of maternal employment to parenting and children's development (as we discuss later in the developmental impingement perspective section).

Data from our longitudinal study of maternal and dual-earner employment provided the foundation for our view regarding the role of proximal environment in understanding the impact of maternal employment (A. E. Gottfried, A. W. Gottfried, & Bathurst, 1988; A. E. Gottfried, Bathurst, & A. W. Gottfried, 1994). We provide a brief overview of results from our longitudinal study, as well as other research supporting this view.

Fullerton Longitudinal Study

Within the Fullerton Longitudinal Study, our longitudinal research on maternal employment and children's development studied proximal environment as a major component. This study began with 130 one-year-old infants and their families, comprising a broad middle-class range from skilled workers through professionals. Each participating child's history of maternal and paternal employment status has been collected continuously from infancy through adolescence. Additionally, children's development has been assessed across a broad array of domains, such as infant developmental status, cognitive functioning, intelligence, academic achievement, temperament, social competence, social-emotional development, behavioral adjustment, academic motivation, and self-concept (A. E. Gottfried et al., 1994; A. E. Gottfried, Gottfried, & Bathurst, 1988). Children were assessed with major standardized measures in the university lab and also with measures completed by parents and teachers. A cross-time, cross-context methodology was used. Extensive demographic data were collected throughout this study, including mothers' and fathers' employment status, education, occupation, and family socioeconomic status. Additional employment-related variables included parental work hours, flexibility of employment, parental attitudes towards employment, and role satisfaction.

Data regarding the proximal home environment have been continuously collected also and have included direct home observations as well as survey data reported by parents. Instruments included the Purdue Home Stimulation Inventory (Wachs, 1976) and the Home Observation for Measurement of the Environment (HOME; Bradley, Caldwell, Rock, Hamrick, & Harris, 1988; Caldwell & Bradley, 1984), which were administered during the infant, preschool, and school-age periods. Parent report data were collected using the Family Environment Scale (R. H. Moos & B. S. Moos, 1994) to assess family climate, as well as our Home Environment Survey, developed during the study, to measure parental involvement and cognitive and educational stimulation (Bathurst, 1988; A. E. Gottfried, Bathurst, & Gottfried, 1994; A. E. Gottfried et al., 1988; A. W. Gottfried & A. E. Gottfried, 1984). Additionally, mothers' and fathers' involvement with their children, including sharing activities and time, were measured throughout the study. Children were assessed semi-annually from ages 1 through 3.5, and annually from age 5 through age 17. Complete details regarding the methods can be found in A. E. Gottfried et al. (1988); A. E. Gottfried, Bathurst, and A. W. Gottfried (1994), A. W. Gottfried and A. E. Gottfried (1984), and A. W. Gottfried, A. E. Gottfried, Bathurst, and Guerin (1994).

Analyses have thus far been conducted from infancy through age 12. The data overwhelmingly show that maternal employment status per se (i.e., whether or not a mother is employed) is not significantly related to children's development across the child developmental domains, either contemporaneously, or over time. Analyses were conducted both contemporaneously and prospectively, and data were analyzed controlling for socioeconomic status, marital status, number of children in the home, home environment, and gender. There were no "sleeper" effects of maternal employment. Regardless of maternal employment status, proximal environmental variables have consistently been related to children's development (A. E. Gottfried, Fleming, & A. W. Gottfried, 1994; A. E. Gottfried et al., 1988; A. W. Gottfried & A. E. Gottfried, 1984). Hence, children's development was consistently, significantly, and positively related to the proximal environment. However, as reported later, aspects of maternal employment relate to the proximal environment, and these, in turn, relate to children's development.

Regarding the relation between maternal employment and proximal home environment, patterns of consistent relations exist across the study. Overall, where maternal employment status is significant, evidence indicates that employed mothers support developmental advance in their infants; have higher educational aspirations for their children at ages 5 and 7, and for boys at age 12; and provide more activities for their children, which include lessons at ages 5 and 7, having children involved in more activities at age 8, and providing a greater number of learning opportunities for boys at age 9. Some of these relationships were predicted by earlier maternal employment. For example, higher educational aspirations were predicted by earlier maternal employment at ages 3.5 and 5 to 5 and 7 year educational attitudes, respectively, and employment at age 1 to number of activities at age 8 and age 12 educational attitudes. These results were controlled for socioeconomic status, marital status, number of children in the home, and gender. However, other than these differences, there were no significant differences in the homes of employed compared to nonemployed mothers across many proximal environmental variables. The positive associations between maternal employment and educational aspirations and learning opportunities are significant inasmuch as they suggest that mothers who are employed have higher values for educational opportunities, which may be reflected in the types of activities that are provided to their children. In our research, then, whereas there were no significant relationships between maternal employment and children's development, there were significant relationships between maternal employment and certain aspects of proximal environment, and these aspects of proximal environment have been found to be positively related to children's development. Hence, it may be that maternal employment plays an indirect role in children's development through its relation to the proximal environment. For example, if employed mothers hold higher educational aspirations for their children, and if educational aspirations are related to achievement and behavior (A. E. Gottfried et al., 1988; Seginer, 1986), then children of employed mothers may have higher achievement to the extent that educational aspirations influence that relationship. This reasoning is consistent with the view that maternal employment may influence children's development only to the extent that it affects aspects of the proximal environment. Other aspects of proximal environment were also shown to be related to maternal employment, specifically father involvement, shared activities between children and mothers and fathers, and time spent with children on weekdays and weekends. These data are presented in the section on balancing roles and family adaptation.

Other Research

Other research has supported the importance of considering the proximal environment in maternal employment research. In A. E. Gottfried and A. W. Gottfried (1988a), results of five longitudinal studies, comprising a broad range of middle socioeconomic status families, were compared regarding the proximal home environments of employed and nonemployed mothers (Galambos, Petersen, & Lenerz, 1988; Goldberg & Easterbrooks, 1988; A. E. Gottfried et al., 1988; Lerner & Galambos, 1988; Owen & Cox, 1988). The results from these studies are consistent in supporting the overall conclusion that there is little difference in the home environments of employed and nonemployed mothers. Overall, the quality and quantity of stimulation and parent–child interactions tended to be equivalent in the homes of employed and nonemployed mothers. We interpreted these results as demonstrating that employed mothers were as capable as nonemployed mothers in providing a stimulating and nurturing environment, and that the home environments of children of employed mothers were not deficient (A. E. Gottfried & A. W. Gottfried 1988b). As we found in our longitudinal study, there were some specific results regarding maternal employment. For example, using path analyses, Lerner and Galambos (1988) found that role satisfaction of employed and nonemployed mothers was significantly related to mother–child interactions, which in turn related to child difficulty. More satisfied mothers had more favorable interactions with their children, and, consequently, children were less difficult. Goldberg and Easterbrooks (1988) reported that toddlers of employed mothers who had stable alternative care were more likely to have two secure family attachments, rather than one. These findings further support our view regarding the importance of the proximal environment for mediating the role of maternal employment in children's development.

Moorehouse (1991) found that, when mothers and children engaged in frequent shared activities, such as reading, playing, and talking, children whose mothers changed employment hours showed school competence equivalent to that of children whose mothers had more stable employment histories. Parenting behaviors, rather than employment stability per se, were important for children's competence. Crouter, MacDermid, McHale, and Perry-Jenkins (1990) found that parental monitoring rather than maternal employment per se was important for boys' school grades. In a study of the daily experiences of adolescents of full-time, part-time, and nonemployed mothers, Richards and Duckett (1994) found that children of part-time employed mothers spent more time in sports, children of full-time employed mothers spent more time doing homework, and that fifth and sixth grade boys and seventh and eighth graders, when mother was employed, spent less time in leisure activities, except for television viewing. The finding that children of full-time employed mothers spent more time doing homework is consistent with findings from the Fullerton Longitudinal Study regarding a greater emphasis on educational activities in the home environments of employed mothers. Because the children of full-time employed mothers do more homework, this research suggests that full-time employed mothers value educational activities more than part-time employed mothers. Research by Parcel and Menaghan (1994) suggested that the quality of a cognitive home environment is positively related to the complexity of maternal occupations. Similarly, A. E. Gottfried et al. (1988; A. E. Gottfried, Bathurst, & A. W. Gottfried, 1994), found that maternal occupation is positively related to educational aspirations and children's cognitive development and achievement. Both mothers' and fathers' occupational status significantly and positively related to features of the environment dealing predominantly with the provision of cognitive and educational stimulation, learning opportunities, cultural enhancement, intellectual focus, and educational aspirations. Also, both maternal and paternal occupation were significantly and positively related to children's intelligence, achievement, school performance, and academic motivation from infancy through early adolescence. It is interesting that social-emotional and behavioral adjustment were not related to parental occupation. Hence, these data suggest that parental occupation is associated with an academic and intellectual achievement orientation in the home, as well as the provision of experiences to foster such achievements.

Because these findings regarding the proximal environment come from diverse studies, they provide convincing and generalizable support for the importance of considering the proximal environment in understanding the role of maternal employment in children's development. Collectively, the studies included variation in family SES. Most studies reported in this section included a wide diversity of middle-class families, including skilled workers through professionals. The Parcel and Menaghan (1994) study included economically disadvantaged families. Moreover, the environmental measures varied across studies and included such methods as direct observations, interviews with parents, self-report surveys, use of standardized environment instruments, telephone assessments, and child report.

Where results regarding the proximal home environment pertaining to the social-emotional realm are significant, they tend to be modified by a host of variables, including, for example, consistency between employment status and attitudes toward employment, role satisfaction in employment and parenting, work–family conflict, and maternal separation anxiety (A. E. Gottfried & A. W. Gottfried, 1988b; A. E. Gottfried et al., 1995). Overall, the body of results regarding the proximal environment indicates that maternal employment not only is *not* a negative factor, in many instances, particularly with regard to educational aspirations and activities, there are positive relationships to maternal employment. It must be emphasized that that there is no evidence in the literature that maternal employment per se is a direct cause of a greater intellectual and cognitive emphasis in the home. Because it is possible that maternal and paternal educational and occupational values are associated with maternal employment, these factors need to be examined as possible causal factors.

BALANCE OF ROLES

Fathers' Involvement

One of the clearest significant trends indicating that there exists a balance of roles within dual-earner families is the increased participation of fathers in childrearing. Evidence indicates that this is not only true in middle-class, White families, which are the focus of many dual-earner studies, but also in families of varying ethnic background and across a wide occupational and income range. In an extensive review of research, A. E. Gottfried et al. (1995) reported that there is a replicated, large body of literature indicating that fathers are more involved and engaged in activities with their children, and more involved in child care when mother is employed, and this involvement increases as mothers' work hours increase from infancy through adolescence. This is true cross-culturally within the United States and cross-nationally. Findings are robust and have been obtained across a variety of indices including absolute (total) and relative (proportional) measures. Further, the types of measures used across studies reported in A. E. Gottfried et al. (1995), varied widely including observations, surveys, self- and other-report, and individual and joint parental report. The families represented a wide range of occupations and income levels generally falling within a lower middle to middle SES range. In a review of literature, Pleck (1997) reported that father involvement in the homes of employed mothers was greater with regard to relative measures, whereas support for absolute measures was less consistent. However, this does not diminish the changing emphasis of the paternal role in dual-earner compared to single-earner families. Whether considered in absolute or relative terms, the body of findings converge: fathers in dual-earner families have a greater opportunity to be involved with their children. Overall, we conclude that, whether considered in absolute terms or as a proportion, relative to families with nonemployed mothers, children with employed mothers are more likely to have a greater exposure to their fathers. Although there may be some families in which fathers' proportional involvement with children increases primarily due to decreases in mothers' involvement resulting from the demands of her employment, those children are being exposed to a more equivalent presentation of mothers' and fathers' balance of roles due to the demands of family and work responsibilities. Further, the content of the father's participation is likely to be responsive to the employment-related demands of a dual-earner family. In homes in which the absolute amount of fathers' interactions and child care is greater, it is clear that fathers are more involved. Future research will be needed to tease apart the complexities and nuances of role changes for dual-earner fathers.

Research with Hispanic families (Herrera & DelCampo, 1995; Valdez & Coltrane, 1993; Ybarra, 1982), in Sweden (Sandqvist, 1992), and in Singapore (Yuen & Lim, 1992) supports these findings cross-culturally and cross-nationally, indicating the pervasiveness of this trend. There is a qualification, however. Whereas mothers' employment tends to increase fathers' participation in childrearing and child care, women continue to bear the major responsibility. Although fathers' participation is greater when mothers are employed, mothers continue to spend more hours in such activities than do fathers (e.g., A. E. Gottfried, Bathurst, & Gottfried, 1994; Hossain & Roopnarine, 1993; Lewis, 1992; Peterson & Gerson, 1992). Further, fathers' increase in household work tends to be concentrated in child care rather than other household chores, which continue to be completed on gender based lines (such as indoor work being predominantly completed by women and outdoor activities predominantly completed by men; Fish, New, & Van Cleave, 1992). Hence, the overall burden of total indoor household work falls to mothers. Regardless, it is promising that children are apparently a priority in the balance of roles in dual-earner families, such that, when work is shared to a greater extent between mothers and fathers, it tends to be concentrated in the realm of childrearing activities.

A factor that appears to be related to fathers' greater participation in child care concerns gender role equality. Increased father participation in child-related activities within dual-earner households implies that, as egalitarianism increases in families, child care is likely to be increasingly shared between mothers and fathers. We recognize that time spent in role behavior may not be absolutely equal across mothers and fathers. However, compared to the traditional family, the frequency of fathers' involvement with children changes in the direction of less gender-based assignment of activities. Furthermore, father involvement is related both to gender role flexibility and egalitarian views (Barnett & Baruch, 1987; Herrera & DelCampo, 1995; Radin & Harold-Goldsmith, 1989) and to fathers' availability due to fewer hours of employment (C. P. Cowan & P. A. Cowan, 1987; A. E. Gottfried, Bathurst, & Gottfried, 1994). In nations with more traditional adherence to gender defined roles, fathers' participation in child care does not show the same trends, as reported for India (Chowdhury, 1995; Sekaran, 1992) and Malaysia (Peng, 1993). Indeed, Peng (1993) reported that 23% of Malaysian women were forced to leave the labor force due to lack of adequate child care and that there are quite low participation rates of fathers in child care activities. We suggest that, both within families, cultures, and nations, egalitarian gender role concepts are likely to be associated with an increasing balance of roles in dual-earner families.

Fathers' increased participation appears to have early developmental roots and benefits children and family functioning. In the Fullerton Longitudinal Study, we collected an extensive data base regarding fathers' participation with their children in dual-earner and single-earner families from infancy through early adolescence. In addition to greater participation of fathers in interaction with their children, more participation in shared activities, and more time spent with their children (A. E. Gottfried et al., 1988; A. E. Gottfried, Bathurst, & Gottfried, 1994), we also found that these patterns began in the preschool years. Maternal employment from the time children were as young as 3.5 years was significantly related to fathers' increased participation with their children through age 12 years. Early patterns of increased father participation had long-term predictability over the childhood and early adolescence of their children. For families in which mothers entered the workforce earlier, fathers established increased involvement with their children, which was consistent over time. We also studied patterns of fathers' time involvement with their children during weekdays and weekends. Fathers whose wives were employed spent significantly more time with their children on weekdays, but not weekends. This further exemplifies the balance of roles in dual-earner families. When mothers were less available (during the week), fathers played a complementary role by spending more time with their children. On the weekends, when mothers were available, fathers' time did not vary by mothers' employment status (A. E. Gottfried, Bathurst, & Gottfried, 1994). These findings are supported by those of Crouter, Perry-Jenkins, Huston, and McHale (1987), who observed that fathers in dual-earner families spent more time caring for their children than fathers in single-earner families, but that their leisure time did not differ.

Data on fathers' participation in child care and involvement activities also indicate benefits for children and the family. In our study, increased father involvement was significantly and positively related to children's social maturity, IQ, and achievement (A. E. Gottfried et al., 1988). Radin (1994) reported that children of highly participant fathers often evidence greater internal locus of control in her sample, as did Sagi in Israel. Hence, it is proposed that a network of factors exists in dual-earner families. When mothers are employed, fathers tend to be more interactive with their children. Hence, children's development may benefit from increased father involvement in intellectual, achievement, and social maturity realms. Maternal employment may have indirect relationships with child outcomes through father involvement, as discussed for proximal environment. Other research indicates benefits for a more egalitarian division of child care. For example, Deater-Deckard and Scarr (1996) found that in dual-earner homes, both mothers and fathers reported lower distress when fathers shared or provided most of the child care in the home. They concluded that a more egalitarian division of child care had benefits for both mothers and fathers. Wiersma and van den Berg (1991) found that family cohesion was higher when work–family role conflict was lower, and that domestic responsibilities related to role conflict more predominantly for women. Factors that should be examined more closely in future research concern the interplay between fathers' increased involvement with their children in dual-earner families, reduction of stress and role conflict, and enhancement of family functioning, including children's development.

Family Roles and Factors

There are many ways in which family roles and factors may balance each other. As we suggested (A. E. Gottfried & A. W. Gottfried, 1988), there is a network of factors that appear to balance each other in families with employed mothers. In the instance presented, fathers' increased participation with their children and in child care is a significant balancing factor to consider. Fathers' increased participation corresponds to mothers' increasing employment role. Children are exposed to a more equal presentation of mothers and fathers, which may influence their development. The balance of roles appears to contribute to the ability of families with employed mothers to function more effectively. It may be an adaptation that contributes to the maintenance of such families. The general similarity in the development of children of employed and nonemployed mothers may be inherently tied to the balance of factors that exists within the homes of all families.

FAMILY ADAPTATIONS

We proposed that family adaptation occurs in families with employed mothers (A. E. Gottfried, Bathurst, & A. W. Gottfried, 1994; A. E. Gottfried et al., 1995). Family adaptation, as we view it, concerns changes that support effective functioning within mother-employed families. One such adaptation—the increasing participation of fathers with their children when mothers are employed—was described in the section on balance of roles.

This increase in father participation should not be interpreted as compensation by fathers to make up for maternal absence due to employment (A. E. Gottfried & A. W. Gottfried, 1994b). Compensation perspectives presume a deficit due to maternal employment. That is, according to compensation views, the absence of the mother requires a special family effort to overcome the presumed deficit. However, our perspective regarding family adaptation views the changes in the family as a strength of the families and not as compensatory. Increased father involvement may be considered to be an adaptation that emerges from more egalitarian gender role conceptions. Maternal employment may be considered as a family adaptation emerging from the same source. Together, maternal employment and increased father participation form a family adaptation that successfully responds to the needs of dual-earner families and provides a nurturing environment that meets children's needs. These families are different, but are not compensating for a deficiency.

There have been many adaptations that have emerged in the context of increased maternal employment. In addition to increased father involvement, other family adaptations include nontraditional work schedules and flexibility, patterns of parental time availability and use within the family, child care, and child participation in the family responsibilities (A. E. Gottfried et al., 1995).

Nontraditional Work Schedules and Flexibility

Nontraditional work schedules and flexibility have emerged as family adaptations. Presser (1994) studied the variants of job schedules and shift work among dual-earner families. She found that the degree of nonoverlapping work hours in married dual-earner families was related to increases in housework completed by husbands and wives. As both husbands' and wives' nonoverlapping home hours increased while the other was at work, engagement in housework by both husbands and wives also increased. However, only wives' housework decreased when husbands' housework increased. Husbands' housework did not decrease as wives' housework increased. Presser concluded that husbands being home alone, particularly during the day, increased their participation in housework. Husbands' participation in housework also increased as their educational level increased, and if they engaged in professional and managerial occupations. Presser concluded that husbands' education may tap an egalitarian gender ideology for both husbands and wives. When children were present, both husbands and wives engaged in significantly more housework. However, the burden of housework was greater for women in the presence of children because the increase in housework was greater for them. Presser's research is significant: it indicates that the patterning of work and nonwork hours in dual-earner families plays an important role in the participation of spouses in household labor. Such research has not been conducted in relation to children's development, and this is an important direction for future study. It may be that it is not only the mothers' employment that is related to increases in fathers' involvement with their children, and subsequently to their development, but also that the patterning of time availability of mothers and fathers with their children may be important as well.

Similar research regarding correspondence between mothers' and fathers' work schedules was conducted by Brayfield (1995). In a study of dual-earner families with preschool children, Brayfield found that fathers were more likely to engage in child care when their work hours differed from those of the mothers. Fathers were more likely to be primary caregivers for preschool-age children if they worked nonday hours, but were more likely to be the primary caregivers for school-age children if they worked day hours. This probably relates to the correspondence between fathers' work schedules and children's child-care needs at different ages. It is interesting that, when mothers worked full-time rather than part-time, fathers were less likely to engage in child care. It may be that when mothers work full time, then supplemental child care is used, although this possibility was not measured in this research. However, Caruso (1992) reported that when mothers worked more than 35 hours per week, child care by fathers decreased and use of more formal child-care arrangements increased, supporting this possibility. Once again, this research indicates that the scheduling of work hours, not work hours alone, relates to fathers' participation in child care. These findings illustrate the complexity of family work situations and scheduling in modifying the balance of roles between parents, parental involvement, and family adaptations.

Another aspect of family adaptation concerns work restructuring and family responsive work policies, allowing for work behaviors to vary from typical expectations in order to meet family needs (Brett & Yogev, 1988; Cook, 1992; Hughes & Galinsky, 1988; Karambayya & Reilly, 1992). Work restructuring may take various forms, including flexitime, shift work, job sharing, part-time work, a compressed work week, work at home, shift of hours, personal days for family responsibilities, time bank, relocation assistance, and benefits (e.g., dependent care assistance plans, child-care benefits). In studies of dual-earner couples with children, Brett and Yogev (1988) and Karambayya and Reilly (1992) found that women engaged in more restructuring on a regular basis than did men. Men's restructuring was more likely to be in response to a special need and was more temporary (Karambayya & Reilly, 1992). It may be less acceptable for men to restructure their jobs, and supervisors may perceive work restructuring by men as an indication of lower work commitment, threatening job advancement.

In the Brayfield (1995) and Karambayya and Reilly (1992) studies, women worked fewer hours than men. Further, women tend to have less consistent work patterns over time and to have more periods of entering and leaving the work force (A. E. Gottfried, Bathurst, & Gottfried, 1994; Maret, 1983). To the extent that limiting work hours and exiting the work force to raise children represent work restructuring, then again, women are affected by work restructuring to a greater extent than men. Further research might examine how specific aspects of work restructuring relate to children's development and parental interactions.

Considerable research has examined the role of part-time versus full-time employment schedules of mothers (A. E. Gottfried et al., 1988, 1995; A. E. Gottfried, Bathurst, & A. W. Gottfried, 1994; A. E. Gottfried & A. W. Gottfried, 1988). In our longitudinal research, we analyzed children's development in relation to part-time versus full-time employment schedules of mothers. There were no significant differences between children's development, parenting, or home environment from infancy through early adolescence in homes of part-time and full-time employed mothers. These results have been confirmed in other longitudinal studies (Galambos, Petersen, & Lenerz, 1988; Goldberg & Easterbrooks, 1988; Lerner & Galambos, 1988).

Research on mothers' part-time versus full-time employment has been methodologically inconsistent across studies, that is, researchers have used different definitions of part-time and full-time employment. For example, no criterion number of hours defining part-time and full-time employment status has been adopted between studies. Further, full-time, compared to part-time, maternal employment may be associated with greater work involvement and commitment, and socioeconomic status may differ according to full-time or part-time maternal employment status. Differences in value orientations, for example, egalitarian orientation, are factors that need research, as part-time and full-time maternal employment schedules may be related to more or less traditional gender role values. Further, research by Presser (1994) and Brayfield (1995) implied that patterns of work schedules may be more important than actual hours of employment. We suggest that analyzing part-time and full-time maternal employment is not an adequate variable for analysis. Rather, specific variables rather than the broad categories of part-time and full-time employment need to be examined.

There has also been research on the relationships between number of maternal work hours and children's development. In the Fullerton Longitudinal Study, to provide a more comprehensive picture of family processes, we analyzed both mothers' and fathers' work hours beginning at the child's age 8. Our most recent research (A. E. Gottfried, Bathurst, & A. W. Gottfried, 1994) indicated that parental work hours were not significantly related to children's development or home environment from childhood through early adolescence. In our earlier research with infants through age 7, most relationships between maternal work hours and children's development were nonsignificant as well (A. E. Gottfried et al., 1988). Although some research reports inverse relationships between mothers' employment hours and certain aspects of parenting or children's development (e.g., Goldberg, Greenberger, & Nagel, 1996; Owen & Cox, 1988), future work needs to examine more closely the proximal home environment, the supportiveness of spouses, father involvement, and work schedules of husbands and wives in order to tease apart the issue of maternal work hours from the more comprehensive context of work and family in those homes.

Patterns of Parental Involvement

Another aspect of family adaptations has been studied by Crouter, Hawkins, and Hostetler (1992) and Crouter and McHale (1993) who found that there are seasonal changes in patterns of mothers' and fathers' involvement with their children. During the summer, patterns of involvement varied in relation to the continuation of parental dual-earner status over the summer, or whether the family became a single-earner family during this period (presumably due to vacation and changes in work schedules). Families that continued in the dual-earner mode continued their greater egalitarian sharing regarding child involvement. When families became single-earner over the summer, a more traditional sharing of activities occurred. Also, fathers' greater occupational prestige was related to greater involvement in housework. Because this research was longitudinal, the findings suggest a causal link between changes in mothers' work status and paternal involvement. Further, these findings also indicate that the ecology of dual-earner families may change over the course of a year.

Child Participation in Family Responsibilities

Children's greater participation in household chores in dual-earner families represents another family adaptation (Bartko & McHale, 1991; Goodnow, 1988). In their reviews, the overall findings indicate that there are modest differences in engagement in household chores between children in dual-earner and single-earner families (Bartko & McHale, 1991; Goodnow, 1988). The importance of considering both child's gender and mothers' employment involvement is illustrated in a study by Benin and Edwards (1990). In this research it was found that adolescent daughters in full-time employed families shouldered this responsibility, whereas adolescent sons in such families engaged in less housework than those in traditional families. Adolescents in dual-earner families in which the mother worked part-time spent the least time in housework. Benin and Edwards explained their findings as related to the mothers' perceptions of the importance of household tasks to their roles.

Child Care

Nonparental child care, of course, is a family adaptation for dual-earner families. Although it is beyond the scope of this chapter to examine child care in detail, it is interesting to note that studies indicate that a large number of dual-earner families resort to multiple forms of child care. This was found in our own research (A. E. Gottfried, 1991), as well as in research reported by Burchinal, Ramey, Reid, & Jaccard (1995), and Caruso (1992).

DEVELOPMENTAL IMPINGEMENT PERSPECTIVE

We proposed the developmental impingement perspective as an interpretive and heuristic framework with which to understand family functioning (A. E. Gottfried & A. W. Gottfried, 1994b, 1994c). This perspective is meant to apply to all family types, including what we term *redefined families* (families which differ from traditional family structure) as well as traditional families (A. E. Gottfried & A. W. Gottfried, 1994b). Maternal and dual-earner families fall within the rubric of redefined families. The developmental impingement perspective comprises four basic tenets:

1. There is no presumption of deficit, detriment, or benefit to children being raised in families with alternative structures.
2. The developmental level of the child must be taken into account. Child outcomes cannot be assumed to be the same for different kinds of development at different levels.
3. The multivariate nature of children's development across a broad array of developmental domains must be taken into account. Many published articles on alternate family types use a single, one point in time outcome measure of limited significance. Such articles often contain explicit statements based on restricted evidence regarding the negative or favorable outcome of the family. Only multivariate, longitudinal studies can address the breadth, cross-time, and developmental aspects of effects.
4. A multiplicity of factors must be investigated at various ecological levels, and these effects must be examined with regard to the spectrum of possible outcomes, including positive, negative, or no differences.

Nonpresumption of Deficit

We propose that there is no presumption of deficit to be associated with any alternate family type. With regard to maternal and dual-earner employment, the legacy of negative expectations with which this field of study began is clearly inappropriate, particularly in the context of the research results indicating the preponderance of no detriment.

The research on maternal and dual-earner employment clearly indicates that there is a complex interweave of factors at many ecological levels that relate to parenting and children's development. Although the large majority of research in the United States has concerned middle-class Euro-American families, there is a growing literature concerning families of differing socioeconomic status and culture. Evidence suggests benefits of maternal employment for children within lower socioeconomic status families (Cherry & Eaton, 1977; A. E. Gottfried et al., 1995; Heyns, 1982; Rieber & Womack, 1968). However, Wilson, Ellwood, and Brooks-Gunn (1995) suggested that maternal employment for mothers previously on welfare may be associated with many previously unencountered stressors, such as schedule changes, loss of welfare benefits and thus income, inadequate child care, and unavailability of the mother. From the developmental impingement perspective, it is essential to consider the context of maternal employment in low SES families in designing research and interpreting outcomes. Although the specific mechanisms mediating maternal employment and children's development in less advantaged families need to be elucidated, it may be speculated that increasing economic resources to poorer families allows a more enriched quality of environment, which, in turn, enhances children's development (A. E. Gottfried et al., 1995). This possibility is consistent with our view of the importance of the proximal environment in mediating the potential effects of maternal employment.

McLoyd (1993) suggested that, because of the greater instability of African-American men's support, employment of African-American wives is more essential to the economic stability of these families than is the employment of Euro-American wives. Therefore, Black women's income is more central to the economic well-being of their families than is White women's income for their families. These differences may relate to the more positive acceptance of maternal employment in Black as compared to White families. McLoyd reviewed evidence indicating that husbands' approval and support of wives' employment is more positive in African-American families. Within this context, relations between maternal and dual-earner employment and family processes must be conceptualized and interpreted differently. In Black families, work is viewed as compatible with maternal and marital roles (Bridges & Etaugh, 1994; McLoyd, 1993). This view contrasts with that of the existing body of research on maternal employment as a whole, in which mothers' work roles are most frequently viewed as conflicting with family roles. The role of maternal employment in varying ethnic and cultural groups appears to differ within the specific contexts. Children's development may be affected to the extent that such variations influence the proximal environment.

As dual-earner families adopt more egalitarian views, they are likely to increasingly view parental work and family roles as compatible, rather than as conflicting. The impact of maternal and dual-earner employment status on children's development and in families will be interpretable within the context of the values within these nontraditional families. The research cited earlier indicates that conceptions of parental and household responsibilities differ in dual-earner and single-earner families and in relation to egalitarian attitudes. Thus, the impact of maternal employment is likely to differ in families with more egalitarian gender role concepts than in families with more traditional views. The developmental impingement perspective is able to account for such differences.

There is an emergent literature on maternal employment in developing and third world countries (Desai & Jain, 1994; Engle, 1991). The issues with regard to child development differ dramatically from those dealt with in developed countries. Major issues with regard to the impact of maternal employment relate to child survival, health, and growth. In Guatemala (Engle, 1991) and rural India (Desai & Jain, 1994), maternal employment was not related to children's health when other background factors were controlled. Child-care quality was more important to children's height growth than maternal employment (Engle, 1991) and was viewed as essential to children's wellbeing in India (Desai & Jain, 1994). Again, the context of the society is important for framing the issues regarding the impact of maternal employment.

Multivariate Characteristics of Child Development

A host of child and parental characteristics have been and continue to be studied in relation to maternal employment, including child gender, temperament, security of attachment, maternal role satisfaction, role spillover from work to family, and maternal separation anxiety (A. E. Gottfried et al., 1995). The results of specific studies are interpretable within the context of the developmental impingement perspective and the role of the proximal environment. Additionally, different ecological contexts exist with regard to maternal employment in single-parent and divorced households, as well as any family structure that is nontraditional. The complex interplay of factors needs to be examined for each family context individually. We propose that the developmental impingement perspective provides the framework with which to formulate research questions and interpret such findings.

We recommend the use of multiple measures in research to determine the generalizability of results. Also, research results must not be based upon measures, such as ratings, that may be contaminated by raters' perceptions about maternal employment. If research depends on perceptions of respondents who are knowledgeable about subjects' maternal employment status, results may be biased. Maternal employment continues to be negatively perceived by college students and in popular magazines (Bridges & Orza, 1993; Bridges & Etaugh, 1995; Etaugh, Williams, & Carlson, 1996). Maternal employment is often viewed more negatively by other nonpsychology professionals and in the child development literature (A. E. Gottfried et al., 1995). It would be a mistake to believe that perceptions of raters who are knowledgeable about maternal employment status of the ratees are objective. It is essential that multiple measures, concentrating on more objectively collected data, be included in research. The developmental impingement perspective advocates a multivariate approach, which is necessary to determine the generalization of results across data and the limits of conclusions.

We implore researchers to create a new generation of research within which the family processes of maternal employment are elucidated. Searching for positive or negative findings simply perpetuates a competition for determining the best family type. In today's society, it is unlikely that any one family type will be the winner. Rather, each individual family will have particular characteristics that are more or less conducive to adequate family functioning and children's development. This is the charge for the next direction of research. It is necessary to determine the significant variables of family functioning that support the optimal development of children within their unique family circumstances. To the extent that maternal and dual-earner employment supports favorable developmental environments within varying contexts, cultures, and in relation to varying child and parental characteristics, then it will be a successful nontraditional family form.

REFERENCES

Armistead, L. Wierson, M., & Forehand, R. (1990). Adolescents and maternal employment: Is it harmful for an adolescent to have an employed mother? *Journal of Early Adolescence, 10,* 260–278.

Barnett, R. C., & Baruch, G. K. (1987). Determinants of fathers' participation in family work. *Journal of Marriage and the Family, 49,* 29–40.

Bartko, W. T., & McHale, S. M. (1991). The household labor of children from dual- versus single-earner families. In J. V. Lerner & N. L. Galambos (Eds.), *Employed mothers and their children* (pp. 159–179). New York: Garland.

Bathurst, K. (1988). The inventories of family functioning: A psychometric analysis. *Dissertation Abstracts International, 49,* 2918 (University Microfilms No. DA 88–22158).

Benin, M. H., & Edwards, D. A. (1990). Adolescents' chores: The difference between dual- and single-earner families. *Journal of Marriage and the Family, 52,* 361–373.

Bradley, R. H., Caldwell, B. M., Rock, S. L., Hamrick, H. M., & Harris, P. (1988). Home observation for measurement of the environment: Development of a home inventory for use with families having children 6 to 10 years old. *Contemporary Educational Psychology, 82,* 58–71.

Bradley, R. H., Caldwell, B. M., Rock, S. L., Ramey, C. T., Barnard, K. E., Gray, C., Hammond, M. A., Gottfried, A. W., Siegel, L. S., & Johnson, D. L. (1989). Home environment and cognitive development in the first three years of life: A collaborative study involving six sites and three ethnic groups in North America. *Developmental Psychology, 25,* 217–235.

Brayfield, A. (1995). Juggling jobs and kids: The impact of employment schedules on fathers' caring for children. *Journal of Marriage and the Family, 57,* 321–332.

Brett, J. M., & Yogev, S. (1988). Restructuring work for family: How dual-earner couples with children manage. *Journal of Social Behavior and Personality, 3,* 159–174.

Bridges, J. S., & Etaugh, C. (1994). Black and white college women's perceptions of early maternal employment. *Psychology of Women Quarterly, 18,* 427–431.

Bridges, J. S., & Etaugh, C. (1995). College students' perceptions of mothers: Effects of maternal employment-childrearing pattern and motive for employment. *Sex Roles, 32,* 735–751.

Bridges, J. S., & Orza, A. M. (1993). Effects of maternal employment-childrearing pattern on college students' perceptions of a mother and her child. *Psychology of Women Quarterly, 17,* 103–117.

Burchinal, R. R., Ramey, S. L., Reid, M. K., & Jaccard, J. (1995). Early child care experiences and their association with family and child characteristics during middle childhood. *Early Childhood Research Quarterly, 10,* 33–61.

Caldwell, B. M., & Bradley, R. H. (1984). *HOME observation for measurement of the environment.* Little Rock: University of Arkansas at Little Rock.

Caruso, G. L. (1992). Patterns of maternal employment and child care for a sample of two-year-olds. *Journal of Family Issues, 13,* 297–311.

Cherry, F. F., & Eaton, E. L. (1977). Physical and cognitive development in children of low-income mothers working in the child's early years. *Child Development, 48,* 158–166.

Chowdhury, A. (1995). Employed mothers and their families in India. *Early Child Development and Care, 113,* 65–75.

Cook, A. H. (1992). Can work requirements accommodate to the needs of dual-earner families? In S. Lewis, D. N. Izraeli, & H. Hootsmans (Eds.), *Dual-earner families: International perspectives* (pp. 204–220). Newbury Park, CA: Sage.

Cowan, C. P., & Cowan, P. A. (1987). Men's involvement in parenthood: Identifying the antecedents and understanding the barriers. In P. W. Berman & F. A. Pedersen (Eds.), *Men's transitions to parenthood: Longitudinal studies of early family experience* (pp. 145–174). Hillsdale, NJ: Lawrence Erlbaum Associates.

Crouter, A. C., Hawkins, A. J., & Hostetler, M. (1992). Seasonal stability and change in dual earner husbands' psychological responses to work and family roles. *International Journal of Behavioral Development, 15,* 509–525.

Crouter, A. C., MacDermid, S. M., McHale, S. M., & Perry-Jenkins, M. (1990). Parental monitoring and perceptions of children's school performance and conduct in dual- and single-earner families. *Developmental Psychology, 23,* 649–657.

Crouter, A. C., & McHale, S. M. (1993). Temporal rhythms in family life: Seasonal variation in the relations between parental work and family processes. *Developmental Psychology, 29,* 198–205.

Crouter, A. C., Perry-Jenkins, M., Huston, T. L., & McHale, S. M. (1987). Processes underlying father involvement in dual-earner and single-earner families. *Developmental Psychology, 23,* 431–440.

Deater-Deckard, K. & Scarr, S. (1996). Parenting stress among dual-earner mothers and fathers: Are there gender differences? *Journal of Family Psychology, 10,* 45–59.

Demo, D. H. (1992). Parent-child relations: Assessing recent changes. *Journal of Marriage and the Family, 54,* 104–117.

Desai, S., & Jain, D. (1994). Maternal employment and changes in family dynamics: The social context of women's work in rural south India. *Population and Development Review, 20,* 115–136.

Engle, P. L. (1991). Maternal work and child-care strategies in peri-urban Guatemala: Nutritional effects. *Child Development, 62,* 954–965.

Etaugh, C. (1974). Effects of maternal employment on children: A review of recent research. *Merrill-Palmer Quarterly, 20,* 71–98.

Etaugh, C., Williams, B., & Carlson, P. (1996). Changing attitudes toward day care and maternal employment as portrayed in women's magazines: 1977–1990. *Early Childhood Research Quarterly, 11,* 207–218.

Fish, L. S., New, R. S., & Van Cleave, N. J. (1992). Shared parenting in dual-income families. *American Journal of Orthopsychiatry, 62,* 83–92.

Galambos, N. L., Petersen, A. C., & Lenerz, K. (1988). Maternal typing in employment and sex early adolescence: Contemporaneous and longitudinal relations. In A. E. Gottfried & A. W. Gottfried (Eds.), *Maternal employment and children's development: Longitudinal research* (pp. 155–189). New York: Plenum.

Goldberg, W., & Easterbrooks, M. A. (1988). Maternal employment when children are toddlers and kindergartners. In A. E. Gottfried & A. W. Gottfried (Eds.), *Maternal employment and children's development: Longitudinal research* (pp. 121–154). New York: Plenum.

Goldberg, W. A., Greenberger, E., & Nagel, S. K. (1996). Employment and achievement: Mothers' work involvement in relation to children's achievement behaviors and mothers' parenting behaviors. *Child Development, 67,* 1512–1527.

Goodnow, J. J. (1988). Children's household work: Its nature and functions. *Psychological Bulletin, 103,* 5–26.

Gottfried, A. E. (1991). Maternal employment in the family setting: Developmental and environmental issues. In J. V. Lerner & N. L. Galambos (Eds.), *Employed mothers and their children* (pp. 63–84). New York: Garland.

Gottfried, A. E., Bathurst, K., & Gottfried, A. W. (1994). Role of maternal and dual-earner employment status in children's development: A longitudinal study from infancy through early adolescence. In A. E. Gottfried & A. W. Gottfried (Eds.), *Redefining families: Implications for children's development* (pp. 55–97). New York: Plenum.

Gottfried, A. E., Fleming, J., & Gottfried, A. W. (1994). Role of parental motivational practices in children's academic intrinsic motivation and achievement. *Journal of Educational Psychology, 86,* 104–113.

Gottfried, A. E., & Gottfried, A. W. (Eds.). (1988a). *Maternal employment and children's development: Longitudinal research.* New York: Plenum.

Gottfried, A. E., & Gottfried, A. W. (1988b). Maternal employment and children's development: An integration of longitudinal findings with implications for social policy. In A. E. Gottfried & A. W. Gottfried (Eds.), *Maternal employment and children's development: Longitudinal research* (pp. 269–287). New York: Plenum.

Gottfried, A. E., & Gottfried, A. W. (1994a). Demography and changing families: Introduction to the issues. In A. E. Gottfried & A. W. Gottfried (Eds.), *Redefining families: Implications for children's development* (pp. 3–8). New York: Plenum.

Gottfried, A. E., & Gottfried, A. W. (1994b). Impact of redefined families on children's development: Conclusions, conceptual perspectives, and social implications. In A. E. Gottfried & A. W. Gottfried (Eds.), *Redefining families: Implications for children's development* (pp. 221–229). New York: Plenum.

Gottfried, A. E., & Gottfried, A. W. (Eds.) (1994c). *Redefining families: Implications for children's development* New York: Plenum.

Gottfried, A. E., Gottfried, A. W., & Bathurst, K. (1988). Maternal employment, family environment, and children's development: Infancy through the school years. In A. E. Gottfried & A. W. Gottfried (Eds.), *Maternal employment and children's development: Longitudinal research* (pp. 11–58). New York: Plenum.

Gottfried, A. E., Gottfried, A. W., & Bathurst, K. (1995). Maternal and dual-earner employment status and parenting. In M. H. Bornstein (Ed.), *Handbook of Parenting* (Vol. 2, pp. 139–160). Hillsdale, NJ: Lawrence Erlbaum Associates.

Gottfried, A. W. (1984). *Home environment and early cognitive development: Longitudinal research.* New York: Academic Press.

Gottfried, A. W., & Gottfried, A. E. (1984). Home environment and cognitive development in young children of middle-socioeconomic-status families. In A. W. Gottfried (Ed.), *Home environment and early cognitive development: Longitudinal research* (pp. 57–115). New York: Academic Press.

Gottfried, A. W., Gottfried, A. E., Bathurst, K., & Guerin, D. (1994). *Gifted IQ: Early developmental aspects.* New York: Plenum.

Greenstein, T. N. (1993). Maternal employment and child behavioral outcomes: A household economics analysis. *Journal of Family Issues, 14,* 322–354.

Herrera, R. S., & DelCampo, R. L. (1995). Beyond the superwoman syndrome: Work satisfaction and family functioning among working-class, Mexican American women. *Hispanic Journal of Behavioral Sciences, 17,* 49–60.

Heyns, B. (1982). The influence of parents' work on children's school achievement. In S. B. Kamerman & C. D. Hayes (Eds.), *Families that work: Children in a changing world* (pp. 229–267). Washington, DC: National Academy Press.

Hoffman, L. W. (1989). Effects of maternal employment in the two-parent family. *American Psychologist, 44,* 283–292.

Hossain, Z., & Roopnarine, J. L. (1993). Division of household labor and child care in dual-earner African-American families with infants. *Sex Roles, 29,* 571–583.

Hughes, D., & Galinsky, E. (1988). Balancing work and family lives: Research and corporate applications. In A. E. Gottfried & A. W. Gottfried (Eds.), *Maternal employment and children's development: Longitudinal research* (pp. 233–268). New York: Plenum.

Karambayya, R., & Reilly, A. H. (1992). Dual earner couples: Attitudes and actions in restructuring work for family. *Journal of Organizational Behavior, 13,* 585–601.

Lerner, J. V. (1994). *Employed mothers and their families.* Newbury Park, CA: Sage.

Lerner, J. V., & Galambos, N. L. (1988). The influences of maternal employment across life: The New York Longitudinal Study. In A. E. Gottfried & A. W. Gottfried (Eds.), *Maternal employment and children's development: Longitudinal research* (pp. 59–83). New York: Plenum.

Lewis, S. (1992). Introduction: Dual-earner families in context. In S. Lewis, D. N. Izraeli, & H. Hootsmans (Eds.), *Dual-earner families: International perspectives* (pp. 1–18). Newbury Park, CA: Sage.

Lewis, S., Izraeli, D. N., & Hootsmans, H. (1992). *Dual-earner families: International perspectives.* Newbury Park, CA: Sage.

Maret, E. (1983). *Women's career patterns.* New York: University Press of America.

McLoyd, V. C. (1993). Employment among African-American mothers in dual-earner families: Antecedents and consequences for family life and child development. In J. Frankel (Ed.), *The employed mother and the family context* (pp. 180–226). New York: Springer.

Moorehouse, M. (1991). Linking maternal employment patterns to mother-child activities and school competence. *Developmental Psychology, 27,* 295–303.

Moos, R. H., & Moos, B. S. (1994). *Family environment scale.* Palo Alto, CA: Consulting Psychologists Press.

Owen, M. T., & Cox, M. J. (1988). Maternal employment and the transition to parenthood. In A. E. Gottfried & A. W. Gottfried (Eds.), *Maternal employment and children's development: Longitudinal research* (pp. 85–119). New York: Plenum.

Parcel, T. L., & Menaghan, E. G. (1994). *Parents' jobs and children's lives.* New York: Aldine de Gruyter.

Peng, T. N. (1993). Maternal employment and child care. In C. H. Keng (Ed.), *Securing our future: Proceedings of the conference on children—our future* (pp. 251–255). University of Malaya, Malaysia: Child Development Centre.

Peterson, R. R., & Gerson, K. (1992). Determinants of responsibility for child care arrangements among dual-earner couples. *Journal of Marriage and the Family, 54,* 527–536.

Pleck, J. H. (1997). Paternal involvement: Levels, sources, and consequences. In M. E. Lamb (Ed.), *The role of the father in child development* (pp. 66–103). New York: Wiley.

Presser, H. B. (1994). Employment schedules among dual-earner spouses and the division of household labor by gender. *American Sociological Review, 59,* 348–364.

Radin, N. (1994). Primary caregiving fathers in intact families. In A. E.. Gottfried & A. W. Gottfried (Eds.), *Redefining families: Implications for children's development* (pp. 11–54). New York: Plenum.

Radin, N., & Harold-Goldsmith, R. (1989). The involvement of selected unemployed and employed men with their children. *Child Development, 60,* 454–459.

Richards, M. H., & Duckett, E. (1994). The relationship of maternal employment to early adolescent daily experiences with and without parents. *Child Development, 65,* 225–236.

Rieber, M., & Womack, M. (1968). The intelligence of preschool children as related to ethnic and demographic variables. *Exceptional Children, 34,* 609–614.

Sandqvist, K. (1992). Sweden's sex-role scheme and commitment to gender equality. In S. Lewis, D. N. Izraeli, & H. Hootsmans (Eds.), *Dual-earner families: International perspectives* (pp. 80–98). Newbury Park, CA: Sage.

Seginer, R. (1986). Mothers' behavior and sons' performance: An initial test of an academic achievement path model. *Merrill-Palmer Quarterly, 32,* 153–166.

Sekaran, U. (1992). Middle-class dual-earner families and their support systems in urban India. In S. Lewis, D. N. Izraeli, & H. Hootsmans (Eds.), *Dual-earner families: International perspectives* (pp. 46–61). Newbury Park, CA: Sage.

U.S. Department of Labor. (1991). *Working women: A chartbook* (Bulletin 2385). Washington, DC: Bureau of Labor Statistics.

Valdez, E. O., & Coltrane, S. (1993). Work, family, and the Chicana: Power, perception, and equity. In J. Frankel (Ed.), *The employed mother and the family context* (pp. 153–179). New York: Springer.

Wachs, T. D. (1976). *Purdue Home Stimulation Inventories* (Sections I, II, and III). Unpublished manual, Purdue University, Lafayette, IN.

Wachs, T. D. (1992). *The nature of nurture.* Newbury Park, CA: Sage.

Wiersma, U. J., & van den Berg, P. (1991). Work-home role conflict, family climate, and domestic responsibilities among men and women in dual-earner families. *Journal of Applied Social Psychology, 21,* 1207–1217.

Wilson, J. B., Ellwood, D. T., & Brooks-Gunn, J. (1995). Welfare-to-work through the eyes of children. In P. L. Chase-Lansdale & J. Brooks-Gunn (Eds.), *Escape from poverty: What makes a difference for children* (pp. 63–86). New York: Cambridge University Press.

Ybarra, L. (1982). When wives work: The impact on the Chicano family. *Journal of Marriage and the Family, 44,* 169–178.

Yuen, E. C., & Lim, V. (1992). Dual-earner families in Singapore: Issues and challenges. In S. Lewis, D. N. Izraeli, & H. Hootsmans (Eds.), *Dual-earner families: International perspectives* (pp. 62–79). Newbury Park, CA: Sage.

Zaslow, M. J., Rabinovich, B. A., & Suwalsky, J. T. D. (1991). From maternal employment to child outcomes: Preexisting group differences and moderating variables. In J. V. Lerner and N. L. Galambos (Eds.), *Employed mothers and their children* (pp. 237–282). New York: Garland.

Chapter 3

Nonparental Child Care

MICHAEL E. LAMB
National Institute of Child Health and Human Development

This chapter is concerned with variations in the extent to which young children receive care from adults other than their parents and the effects that such care arrangements have on their development. Although it has traditionally been viewed by developmentalists as a deviant and thus potentially harmful practice, nonparental care is extremely common. U.S. Census statistics show that 55% of mothers with children under one year of age were employed or looking for work by 1994 (H. Hayghe, personal communication, October 17, 1995) and that rates of employment rise as children grow older. Approximately 66% of preschool children and 75% of school-age children had mothers in the work force by 1995 with few differences in the employment rates of married and single mothers (H. Hayghe, personal communication, October 17, 1995). Even higher proportions of children have employed fathers. The majority of children thus receive some form of nonparental care on a regular basis, although a surprisingly large proportion have parents who adjust their work schedules to allow the two parents to share child care responsibilities (Presser, 1986, 1988).

Rates of nonparental care have increased since the 1980s, leading many writers and commentators to view this as an anomalous and novel pattern. But, as I have shown in other work (Lamb, 1998), arrangements regarding nonparental care do not represent a new set of problems for the world's parents. In fact, decisions and arrangements about children's care and supervision are among the oldest problems faced by human society. Exclusive maternal care throughout the period of dependency was never an option in what Bowlby (1969) called "the environment of evolutionary adaptedness," and there are no societies in the 1990s in which it is the typical practice. Indeed, exclusive maternal care through adulthood was seldom an option in any phase of human society; it emerged as a possibility for a small elite segment of society during one small portion of human history. In 40% of the cultures Weisner and Gallimore (1977) sampled, more than half the time infants were cared for by people other than their mothers, and rates are surely higher where toddlers, preschoolers, and young children are concerned. Despite this, exclusive maternal care came to be labeled as the *traditional* or *natural* form of human child care, with all deviations from this portrayed as unnatural and potentially dangerous. Indeed, the misrepresentation of exclusive parental care as a species-typical pattern exemplifies well the ways in which definitions of the normal or natural, as opposed to the deviant and artificial, are often shaped by political ideology rather than by objective analysis.

In this chapter, I briefly summarize evidence regarding the effects of nonparental child care on the development of children whose exposure to nonparental care began in infancy or early childhood. As I emphasize in a discursive concluding section, the underlying issues are more complex than they appear, and thus our understanding remains quite limited. In particular, nonparental care experiences assume a variety of forms and are initiated for many different reasons in the context of various family circumstances. We are unlikely to find that nonparental care has predictable and universal effects regardless of these other circumstances and thus need to view nonparental care in its broadest context.

EFFECTS OF INFANT CARE

Effects on Infant–Parent Attachment

Most infants (and young children) initially respond with distress to enrollment in a new child-care setting, although this distress diminishes over time. Beginning in 1986, however, a series of reports in the popular media and in the professional literature suggested that early initiated nonparental care might adversely affect infant–parent attachment and related aspects of psychosocial development (e.g., Belsky, 1986, 1989). These reports, in light of renewed reliance on nonparental care arrangements by increasing numbers of parents in the United States, fostered widespread concern and extensive research. As detailed elsewhere, the available evidence now indicates quite clearly that nonparental care, in and of itself, does not harm infant–mother attachment (Lamb, 1998). Quality of care does not directly affect the quality of infant–mother attachment either, although rates of insecurity are disproportionately elevated when infants are exposed to poor quality (insensitive) or unstable care both at home and in nonparental care settings (National Institute of Child Health and Human Development Early Child Care Research Network, 1996).

After determining that infant day care per se is not harmful, researchers now need to specify what types of care are potentially harmful and potentially beneficial for specific subgroups of infants and families and to identify with greater precision those aspects of quality likely to be of particular significance in defined circumstances. It is obviously important not to exaggerate the potentially negative effects of nonparental care and to view out-of-home care in combination with other social and familial variables that may have important influences on infant–parent attachment. Because a variety of factors may interact to determine the effects of day care on infant development in general, and infant–mother attachment in particular, it is also important to obtain information about child and family characteristics prior to enrollment in day care.

Relationships With Care Providers

Instead of studying reactions to brief separations, several researchers have asked whether children in day care develop attachment-like relationships with care providers or teachers, and, if so, how these relationships compare with mother–child relationships. The evidence suggests that enrollment in day care allows children to form additional significant relationships but does not lead care providers to displace mothers as the primary objects of attachment. As in the case of infant–parent attachments, the quality or security of infant and care provider attachment is influenced by the care provider's sensitivity and responsiveness.

Children in day-care centers overwhelmingly prefer to be close to and to interact with their mothers rather than care providers (Ainslie & Anderson, 1984; Cummings, 1980; Farran & Ramey, 1977). Such behavioral patterns vary both over time and in relation to the quality of the relationships children have established with care providers. Anderson, Nagle, Roberts, and Smith (1981) reported more contact seeking, distance interaction, and exploration in the presence of highly involved than less involved care providers, and Barnas and Cummings (1994) found that toddlers similarly preferred long-term stable care providers. The security of infant and care provider attachment is not simply determined by the security of infant–mother or infant–father attachment (Goosens & van IJzendoorn, 1990; Howes & Hamilton, 1992a, 1992b; Sagi et al., 1985; Seltenheim, Ahnert, Rickert, & Lamb, 1997); as with parents, it is associated instead with the sensitivity, involvement, and quality of care given by the specific care providers (Howes & Hamilton, 1992b; Howes, Phillips, & Whitebook, 1992; Seltenheim et al., 1997). Galinsky, Howes, and Kontos (1995) reported that the security of infant and care provider attachment, assessed using a Q-sort rating, improved after family day-care providers participated in a training program that enhanced the quality of care they offered. Improvements in the level of teacher training also led to increases in the proportion of children who behaved securely (Howes, Smith, & Galinsky, 1995). Such findings are especially important in light of evidence that more than half of the infants in family day care are insecurely attached to their care providers (Galinsky, Howes, Kontos, & Shinn, 1994) and underscores the value of care provider training.

Secure infant-care provider relationships promote more advanced types of play (Howes, Matheson, & Hamilton, 1994) and more positive peer relationships (Howes & Hamilton, 1993) with the nature of the relationship with the primary teacher more influential than the number of changes in teachers experienced (Howes & Hamilton, 1993). Kibbutz-reared infants who behaved securely toward care providers in the Strange Situation were later less ego controlled and more empathic, dominant, purposive, achievement-oriented, and independent than those whose relationships were insecure-resistant four years earlier (Oppenheim, Sagi, & Lamb, 1988). Such findings suggest that, even though the quality of non-parental care does not consistently affect the security of infant–mother attachment, it does affect the quality of infant and care provider relationships, which in turn has a broad influence on child development.

Compliance With Parents and Care Providers

Researchers such as Belsky (1988, 1989) warned that early nonmaternal care may foster noncompliance, and although the evidence is mixed, several researchers reported findings that support the prediction (Belsky & Eggebeen, 1991; Finkelstein, 1982; Rubenstein, Howes, & Boyle, 1981; Schwarz, Strickland, & Krolick, 1974; Thornburg, Pearl, Crompton, & Ispa, 1990; Vandell & Corasaniti, 1990a, 1990b). Howes and Olenick (1986) found that compliance with adult requests at home and in the laboratory did not vary depending on the quality of out-of-home care or even on whether the children had any regular out-of-home care experiences. Their findings also cast doubt on the notion that compliance and noncompliance represent traits that are stable across contexts and relationships (with parents and care providers, for example) and further suggested that the association between child-care history and noncompliance may be more limited and narrow then it once appeared. Research on children who entered care later (discussed later) supports this conclusion. Nevertheless, the association between early experiences of nonparental care and subsequent noncompliance has been reported with sufficient frequency to merit continuing concern and further research.

Relationships With Peers

Initially, researchers reported that infant day care was associated with later aggression toward peers, although the aggression diminished over time (Barton & Schwarz, 1981; Farber & Egeland, 1982; Haskins, 1985; Rubenstein, Howes, & Boyle, 1981; Schwarz et al., 1974). Hegland and Rix (1990) reported no differences in the aggression and assertiveness of children who had experienced infant day care and those who had remained in the exclusive care of their parents, however. Similarly, British 6-year-olds who began family or center day care in infancy were no more aggressive or otherwise behaviorally problematic than peers who received care only at home (Melhuish, Hennessy, Martin, & Moss, 1990). Thornburg et al. (1990) reported that children in continuous part-time or full-time care and children who remained at home for the first two years had interactions of the poorest quality with their peers whereas Vandell and Corasaniti (1990a, 1990b) found that third graders who had begun extensive nonmaternal care in infancy had poorer peer relationships and were less popular than children who received no nonmaternal care or entered care later. Unmeasured differences in the quality of

care and in children's initial orientation—including differences in temperament—may help account for these inconsistent findings. In an intriguing exploratory study, for example, Volling and Feagans (1995) reported that socially
fearful infants developed more positive relations with peers when they received
high-quality care, whereas their social relations deteriorated when placed in centers of lower quality.

Howes (1988) reported that preschoolers were more sociable with their peers
when they began day care in infancy, although low-quality care beginning in infancy was associated with poorer relations with peers at kindergarten age (Howes,
1990). Howes, Hamilton, and Matheson (1994) later reported that the more secure
the teacher–child relationships, the more complex, gregarious, and less aggressive
was the play observed with peers at age 4 whereas dependence on teachers was
associated with social withdrawal and hostile aggressive behavior. Other studies
speak to the beneficial effects of high quality care (Field, 1991; Field, Masi, Goldstein, Perry, & Parl, 1988; Howes et al., 1995), although statistical interactions between quality of care and individual characteristics continue to receive little attention. The potential benefits of high quality care were also illustrated by Andersson
(1992), who found that 13-year-old Swedish children who entered out-of-home
care as infants were rated by their teachers as more socially competent than children without such experiences. These predictive relations parallel other reports
that, among preschoolers, children who have secure relations with their teachers
and care providers are more socially competent with peers (Howes, Phillips, &
Whitebook, 1992; Pianta & Nimetz, 1991; Sroufe, Fox, & Pancake, 1983). They
also suggest that the reliable associations between infant day care and later aggressiveness may be mediated via poor relationships with care providers, rather
than by the effects of separation on infant–mother attachment.

Effects on Cognitive Competence

Experimental research has documented that out-of-home care can have positive
and enduring effects on cognitive performance, particularly among children from
less stimulating homes. Nonexperimental studies paint a less impressive picture
of the benefits.

Ramey and his colleagues have continued to study a group of Black children
from impoverished backgrounds who were enrolled as infants in the Abecedarian
intervention project. Significant group differences favoring the children who received early enrichment persisted through 7 years of school (Campbell et al., 1995;
Campbell & Ramey, 1994, 1995), and similar results were obtained in the Infant
Health and Development Program (1990; Brooks-Gunn et al., 1994; Ramey, Ramey, Hardin, & Blair, 1995), which was modeled after the Abecedarian program.
Burchinal, Lee, and Ramey (1989) and Golden et al. (1978) showed that community day care can have beneficial effects on the cognitive performance of children
from impoverished unstimulating homes, although formal intervention pro-

grams were obviously more influential. The results of the Infant Health and Development Program, the Abecedarian Program, and Project CARE all underscore the importance of providing care and stimulation directly to children in out-of-home contexts.

By contrast with the results of intervention programs, the results of nonexperimental studies designed to explore the effects of community day care are quite contradictory and inconsistent. As summarized by Lamb (1998), some researchers have reported that child care has beneficial effects, whereas others have reported adverse consequences. The NICHD Early Child Care Research Network (1997) reported that the quality of child care was reliably though not strongly associated with variations in children's cognitive development, even after other factors were taken into account. Differences in the quality of both home and out-of-home care are likely to be critical, but unfortunately, these have seldom been measured.

In general, it seems clear—as it did in the late 1970s (Belsky & Steinberg, 1978)—that high quality educationally oriented programs have positive effects on cognitive performance, particularly for children from disadvantaged backgrounds. Unfortunately, few attempts have been made to evaluate the relative effectiveness of different curricula or pedagogical approaches, so we cannot identify the salient aspects of successful programs. Follow-up studies show that significant effects are often attenuated over time unless maintained by continuing care or education of high quality. Care of poorer quality presumably has effects that vary depending on its quality relative to the quality of care and stimulation that children would receive at home. As a result, the performance of some children from well-organized and stimulating families may be affected adversely by out-of-home care experiences.

EFFECTS OF LATER INITIATED DAY CARE

Effects on Mother–Child Relationships

Although Bowlby's (1951) work on maternal deprivation and separation had highlighted the effects of extended separation on infants, the same interpretive framework was initially applied by researchers concerned about the effects of day care on 2½- to 5-year-olds. Buttressed by attachment theory (Ainsworth, 1969; Bowlby, 1958, 1969), therefore, professionals warned that repeated daily separations might harm psychosocial development, and their initial research was designed to address the implicit question, Is day care bad for preschoolers? Initial reports (Blehar, 1974) that day care harmed the relationships between preschoolers and their mothers have not been replicated (e.g., Caldwell, Wright, Honig, & Tannenbaum, 1970; Kagan, Kearsley, & Zelazo, 1978; Moskovitz, Schwarz, & Corsini, 1977; Portnoy & Simmons, 1978; Ragozin, 1980). This suggests that the effects Blehar observed may have reflected temporary maladjustment because the children had only recently entered day care (Blanchard & Main, 1979) or were attributable to factors other than enrollment in day care. Roopnarine and Lamb (1978, 1980) showed that group differences in responses to brief separation were greater in preenrollment than postenrollment assessments, underscoring the need for preenrollment assessments: Group differences that are observed in a single post-treatment assessment cannot be interpreted as effects of nonparental care, and the absence of group differences in a posttest does not necessarily mean that nonparental care has no effects. Unfortunately, researchers still tend to ignore preenrollment characteristics in studies designed to assess the effects of day care on young children.

In more recent studies concerned with child–mother relationships among children in day care, researchers have focused on group differences in compliance, motivated by observations that infant day care may promote noncompliance and aggression (see earlier section). Ketterlinus, Bookstein, Sampson, and Lamb (1989; Prodromidis, Lamb, Sternberg, Hwang, & Broberg, 1995; Sternberg et al., 1991) found that individual differences in noncompliance at 40 months were predicted by the quality of both home and alternative care and by the amount of nonparental care received before age 2 in the Göteborg Child Care Study. Thornburg et al. (1990) reported that children who had been at home continuously since infancy were rated by their teachers as more compliant with adults, whereas Clarke-Stewart, Gruber, and Fitzgerald (1994) reported that middle-class 2- to 4-year-old children in day care, especially those in center care, were more friendly toward and more compliant with unfamiliar experimenters than those in the exclusive care of their parents. These children were most socially competent when they experienced intermediate amounts of care on a regular basis (10–30 hours per week) and when the care was of good quality. Taken together, these reports reveal a tendency for early enrollment in day care to be associated with noncompliance and less harmonious child–mother interactions, particularly when the out-of-home care is of poorer quality. Several contradictory findings and evidence that noncompliance does not constitute a coherent cross-situational trait (Sternberg et al., 1991) imply that the association is context-specific and poorly understood, however.

Peer Relationships

Howes, Matheson, and Hamilton (1994) reported no differences in peer interaction skills between groups of children who entered child care in infancy ($M = 5$ months), early toddlerhood ($M = 19$ months), and late toddlerhood ($M = 33$ months), whereas Harper and Huie (1985) and Clarke-Stewart and colleagues (Clarke-Stewart et al., 1994; Clarke-Stewart, Umeh, Snow, & Pederson, 1980) found that group care experiences indeed facilitated the development of children's social skills. Poor quality care was associated with more negative and aggressive behavior with peers.

The results of two retrospective longitudinal studies were more troubling, suggesting that the extent of out-of-home care was significantly associated with maladjustment in kindergarten (Bates et al., 1994; Thornburg et al., 1990), although in neither case were data available concerning either preenrollment differences in the children's characteristics and experiences or the quality of care received. Howes et al. (1995) found that changes in state regulations led to improvements in both the quality of care and the quality of peer interactions observed among toddlers and preschoolers and a correlation between quality and peer skills was also reported in a large, four-state study *(Cost, Quality, and Child Outcomes in Child Care Centers*, 1995). In the Göteborg Child Care Study, observational measures of social competence with both peers and unfamiliar adults were quite stable over time and were predicted by the quality of care received both at home and in the out-of-home care settings (Broberg, Hwang, Lamb, & Ketterlinus, 1989; Lamb, Hwang, Bookstein, et al., 1988a; Lamb, Hwang, Broberg, et al., 1988).

Overall, it appears that simple enrollment in day care during the preschool years does not reliably facilitate or impede the development of positive relationships with peers. Instead, it seems that the quality of nonparental care is important: Children receiving care of high quality have superior relationship skills, whereas children receiving care of poor quality have deficient social skills and may behave more aggressively than children without such experiences.

Personality Maturity

In the Göteborg Child Care Study, mothers' ratings of their children's ego resilience, ego control, and field independence were quite stable over time and were best predicted by observational measures of the quality of care received at home and in the alternative care settings (Lamb, Hwang, Bookstein, et al., 1988; Lamb, Hwang, Broberg, et al., 1988; Broberg et al., 1989). There were no differences between children in the home-care, family day-care, and center-care groups on any of the personality measures at 28 and 40 months of age. But, at 80 and 101 months of age, children who had been enrolled since toddlerhood in family day-care settings appeared less mature than those in the other groups (Wessels, Lamb, Hwang, & Broberg, 1997). The quality of home and out-of-home care did not moderate or qualify these effects. Howes, Matheson, and Hamilton (1994) found that children who had secure relationships with their care providers—presumably because these care providers behaved more sensitively and supportively—were more ego resilient and more appropriately ego controlled than those who had insecure relationships with their care providers. Reynolds (1994) reported that preschool and elementary school intervention were associated with improved teacher ratings on various indices of mature adjustment to school for children in the fifth grade.

Although the number of studies is quite small, the available evidence suggests that center care of high quality has positive effects on personality maturity, whereas children receiving care of lower quality tend to be less mature. Further exploration in large samples is called for, however, particularly in light of Wessels et al.'s (1997) findings that the effects of quality diminish over time.

Cognitive and Intellectual Competence

As in the case of infants, there has been considerable research on the association between nonparental care and intellectual development in preschoolers. Most of the research on the cognitive and intellectual correlates of nonparental child care has been gathered in the course of evaluating intervention programs designed to enhance the school readiness and academic performance of children from disadvantaged family backgrounds (Lamb, 1998). Interventions that begin after infancy tend to be less influential than those initiated earlier and the effects tend to fade over time when not supplemented by continuing enrichment. Several researchers have also examined the intellectual, cognitive, and academic performance of children in nonexperimental community programs; the results indicate that high quality out-of-home care has positive effects on intellectual development, at least in the short term (Broberg, Wessels, Lamb, & Hwang, 1997; Burchinal, Ramey, Reid, & Jaccard, 1995; Clarke-Stewart, 1984, 1987; Clarke-Stewart et al., 1994; Dunn, 1993; Vandell & Ramanan, 1992). Too few researchers have studied family day care to permit confident conclusions about the effects of this form of care, however.

Unfortunately, little effort has been made to specify the influential aspects of intervention programs so that attempts can be made to fine-tune their effectiveness. As a result, we can offer only the most general conclusions about the beneficial effects of high-quality care rather than empirically supported conclusions about the value of particular programs and approaches.

AFTER-SCHOOL CARE

The need for nonparental care does not end when children enter the formal educational system, particularly as parental employment rates continue to rise in association with children's ages (Lamb, 1998). The typical school day extends for only six hours, and in most European countries, children are expected to go home for lunch either at the end of or in the middle of the school day. As a result, many parents make provision for the care and supervision of their children in the periods that they are at work and their children are not at school. Since the 1970s, however, great concern has been expressed about the safety and welfare of unsupervised or "latchkey" children (Bronfenbrenner, 1976; Genser & Baden, 1980). Much of this concern was prompted by Woods (1972), who reported that unsupervised Black inner-city, fifth-grade girls scored more poorly on measures of cognitive/academic, social, and personality adjustment than did peers who were supervised after school. Richardson et al. (1989) later reported that eighth graders in the Los Angeles and San Diego metropolitan areas were more likely to abuse illicit substances when they spent more time in self-care. By contrast, Galambos and Garbarino (1983) reported no differences in achievement, classroom orientation, adjustment to school, and fear between fifth graders and seventh graders who were either supervised by adults or cared for themselves after school in a rural community. Neither did Rodman, Pratto, and Nelson (1985), who studied fourth and seventh graders. Steinberg (1986, 1988) criticized this study, arguing that researchers need to distinguish among children who stay home alone; those who go to a friend's house where they may be, but typically are not, supervised by the friend's parent; and those who hang out in the mall or some other public place. Suburban fifth, sixth, eighth, and ninth graders in fact appeared more susceptible to antisocial peer pressure when they tended to hang out in public places, whereas those who went to a friend's house were more susceptible than those who stayed home alone (Steinberg, 1986). Comparable results were obtained by Galambos and Maggs (1991) in a longitudinal study of sixth graders living with both of their parents in suburban Canadian communities. It is interesting that several researchers have found that children who stay at home unsupervised do not differ much from those under adult supervision (Galambos & Maggs, 1991; Rodman et al., 1985; Steinberg, 1986; Vandell & Corasaniti, 1988), although Vandell and Posner (in press; Posner & Vandell, 1994) found that children attending formal after-school programs received better grades for math, reading, and conduct than did peers in mother-care and other-care groups. Quality of after-school care has yet to be investigated systematically.

Unfortunately, researchers have also paid inadequate attention to developmental differences and have failed to study the psychosocial adjustment of the youngest children left unsupervised. In light of demographic data suggesting that some kindergartners are left alone regularly, it is noteworthy that the research literature has focused on children in Grade 3 or higher, with most studies concerned with young adolescents. Third graders seem to do better academically and behaviorally when they are in formal after-school programs, although this may not be true of children from more affluent families. Continuing from Grade 5, children who are regularly at home behave and perform similarly whether or not an adult is present, but the distance from adult supervision explains differences in the outcomes of unsupervised children who do not go home after school. Parental disciplinary practices appear to modulate these differences in predictable ways. Unfortunately, all of these findings are compromised by the absence of longitudinal data and the strong possibility that differences among children (in their preferences to be and act with peers, for example) may precede rather than be consequences of the differing types of supervision.

CONCLUSION

Researchers have now demonstrated quite convincingly that nonparental care need not have harmful effects on children's development and on their family relationships, although it can do so. The relationships enjoyed with parents by the majority of infants and children receiving out-of-home care do not differ systematically from those experienced by the majority of children cared for exclusively at home. Most children in out-of-home facilities remain attached to their parents and still prefer their parents over teachers and care providers. Meaningful relationships are often established with peers and care providers, however, and these can affect children's later social behavior, personality maturity, and cognitive development for good and for ill, depending on the quality and stability of these relationships. In addition, early exposure to nonparental care fosters excessive assertiveness, aggression, and noncompliance in some children for reasons that are not yet well understood, although poor relationships with care providers may mediate these effects. Children in high-quality facilities who enjoy good relationships with stable providers are not more aggressive than peers who have experienced care only from their parents. High-quality care appears to have positive effects on most children, and increasing awareness that the quality of care may play a crucial role in determining how children are affected by nonparental care has fostered efforts to understand how care providers behave and how they should be trained to provide growth-promoting care for children (Bredekamp, 1987a, 1987b).

Unfortunately, high-quality alternative care is a construct that is much more difficult to define than one might think (Lamb, 1998). Some simple and concrete measures can be used to assess structural aspects of the quality of care, including adult–child ratios, levels of care provider training and experience, staff stability, and the adequacy of the physical facilities. These dimensions are most likely to be emphasized by state standards, which set the minimal acceptable standards of care (Phillips & Zigler, 1987). Structural characteristics affect the likelihood of high-quality care but they do not guarantee it: Centers that are characterized by good adult to child ratios and are staffed by well-trained providers may still provide care of poor quality. Extensive training, education, and experience, like generous adult-to-child ratios, have to be translated into sensitive patterns of interaction, displays of appropriate emotion, and the intuitive understanding of children that make the experiences richly rewarding for children. The ease with which and the extent to which structural factors are translated into quality clearly vary depending upon the culture, the context, and the alternative opportunities available to children, care providers, and parents although there is reliable evidence that scores on structural and "process" measures of quality tend to be correlated (Lamb, 1998). Even the benefits of high-quality care may be compromised when the demands of the parents' work roles result in excessively long periods of nonparental care, however, thus making it impossible to write a recipe for high-quality care that is universally applicable. High-quality care needs to be defined with respect to the characteristics and needs of children and families in specific societies and subcultures rather than in terms of universal dimensions.

During the 1990s, fortunately, researchers have come to recognize the diversity and complexity of child-care arrangements and their effects on children. Children differ at birth, grow up in a heterogeneous array of cultural and family circumstances, and experience multiple types of nonparental care. As a result, day care per se is unlikely to have clear, unambiguous, and universal effects, either positive or negative, when other important factors are taken into account (Lamb, 1998; Lamb, Sternberg, Hwang, & Broberg, 1992). Instead, researchers must focus on the nature, extent, quality, and age-at-onset of care, as well as the way in which these factors together affect children with different characteristics, from different family backgrounds, and with different educational, developmental, and individual needs. In this endeavor, researchers will need to focus on the crucial intersection between familial and nonfamilial child-care settings. Similarity in the practices and values manifest in the two contexts may play an important role in facilitating healthy development.

Over time, the focus has clearly shifted from between-group to within-group (correlational) strategies, as exemplified by the focus on quality of care. The magnitude of the effect of quality is considerably less clear than its reliability, however, and the fact that researchers must estimate the importance of quality in the context of complex correlational models that also include a range of other potential predictors makes it doubtful that we will ever really know how important quality is in an absolute sense. Furthermore, the recent and widespread focus on the quality of care often leads to an unwarranted neglect of the many other factors that affect children's development. Developmentalists now know that all aspects of behavioral development are determined multiply and redundantly, and as a result, the absolute magnitude of each individual influence is likely to be quite small when all important factors are taken into account simultaneously.

Although the evidence seldom receives the amount of attention it deserves, it is clear that the quality of children's interactions and relationships with their parents and family members and the quality of care children receive at home continue to be the most important sources of influence on the development of young children, even when they receive substantial amounts of care outside the home. It remains an article of faith that nonparental care is likely to be most beneficial when it complements the quality of family care most successfully and most likely to be harmful when there are differences in ideology, belief, and behavior.

In all, we have learned a great deal about the effects of out-of-home care and we have, in so doing, learned that these effects are a good deal more complex than was once thought. The challenge for the next decade is to determine how different experiences inside and outside the home are associated with specific outcomes for children in defined contexts and cultures.

REFERENCES

Ainslie, R. C., & Anderson, C. W. (1984). Daycare children's relationships to their mothers and caregivers: An inquiry into the conditions for the development of attachment. In R. C. Ainslie (Ed.),

The child and the day care setting: Qualitative variations and development (pp. 98–132). New York: Praeger.

Ainsworth, M. D. S. (1969). Object relations, dependency, and attachment: A theoretical review of the infant-mother relationship. *Child Development, 40,* 969–1025.

Anderson, C. W., Nagle, R. J., Roberts, W. A., & Smith, J. W. (1981). Attachment to substitute caregivers as a function of center quality and caregiver involvement. *Child Development, 52,* 53–61.

Andersson, B.-E. (1992). Effects of day care on cognitive and socioemotional competence of thirteen-year-old Swedish school children. *Child Development, 63,* 20–36.

Barnas, M. V., & Cummings, E. M. (1994). Caregiver stability and toddlers' attachment-related behavior towards caregivers in day care. *Infant Behavior and Development, 17,* 141–147.

Barton, M., & Schwarz, J. C. (1981, August). *Daycare in the middle class: Effects in elementary schools.* Paper presented at the meeting of the American Psychological Association, Los Angeles, CA.

Bates, J. E., Marvinney, D., Kelly, T., Dodge, K. A., Bennett, D. S., & Pettit, G. S. (1994). Child-care history and kindergarten adjustment. *Developmental Psychology, 30,* 690–700.

Belsky, J. (1986). Infant day care: A cause for concern? *Zero to Three, VI,* 1–9.

Belsky, J. (1988). The "effects" of infant day care reconsidered. *Early Childhood Research Quarterly, 3,* 235–272.

Belsky, J. (1989). Infant-parent attachment and day care: In defense of the Strange Situation. In J. Lande, S. Scarr, & N. Gunzenhauser (Eds.), *Caring for children: Challenge to America* (pp. 23–48). Hillsdale, NJ: Lawrence Erlbaum Associates.

Belsky, J., & Eggebeen, D. (1991). Early and extensive maternal employment and young children's socioemotional development: Children of the National Longitudinal Survey of Youth. *Journal of Marriage and the Family, 53,* 1083–1098.

Belsky, J., & Steinberg, L. D. (1978). The effects of day care: A critical review. *Child Development, 49,* 929–949.

Blanchard, M., & Main, M. (1979). Avoidance of the attachment figure and social-emotional adjustment in day-care infants. *Developmental Psychology, 15,* 445–446.

Blehar, M. C. (1974). Anxious attachment and defensive reactions associated with day care. *Child Development, 46,* 801–817.

Bowlby, J. (1951). *Maternal care and mental health.* Geneva, Switzerland: World Health Organization.

Bowlby, J. (1958). The nature of the child's tie to his mother. *International Journal of Psychoanalysis, 39,* 350–373.

Bowlby, J. (1969). *Attachment and loss: Vol. 1. Attachment.* New York: Basic Books.

Bredekamp, S. (Ed.) (1987a). *Accreditation criteria and procedures of the National Academy of Early Childhood Programs.* Washington, DC: National Association for the Education of Young Children.

Bredekamp, S. (1987b). *Developmentally appropriate practice in early childhood programs serving children from birth through age 8.* Washington, DC: National Association for the Education of Young Children.

Broberg, A. G., Hwang, C. P., Lamb, M. E., & Ketterlinus, R. D. (1989). Child care effects on socioemotional and intellectual competence in Swedish preschoolers. In J. S. Lande, S. Scarr, & N. Gunzenhauser (Eds.), *Caring for children: Challenge to America* (pp. 49–75). Hillsdale, NJ: Lawrence Erlbaum Associates.

Broberg, A. G., Wessels, H., Lamb, M. E., & Hwang, C. P. (1997). The effects of day care on the development of cognitive abilities in eight-year-olds: A longitudinal study. *Developmental Psychology, 33,* 62–69.

Bronfenbrenner, U. (1976). Who cares for America's children. In V. C. Vaughn & T. B. Brazelton (Eds.), *The family: Can it be saved?* (pp. 3–32). Cambridge, MA: Harvard University Press.

Brooks-Gunn, J., McCarton, G. M., Casey, P. H., McCormick, M. C., Bauer, C. R., Bernbaum, J. L., Tyson, J., Swanson, M., Bennett, F. C., Scott, D. T., Tonascia, J., & Meinert, C. L. (1994). Early intervention in low-birth-weight premature infants: Results through age 5 years from the Infant Health and Development Program. *Journal of the American Medical Association, 272*, 1257–1262.

Burchinal, M. R., Lee, M., & Ramey, C. T. (1989). Type of day care and preschool intellectual development in disadvantaged children. *Child Development, 60*, 182–187.

Burchinal, M. R., Ramey, S. L., Reid, M. K., & Jaccard, J. (1995). Early child care experiences and their association with family and child characteristics during middle childhood. *Early Childhood Research Quarterly, 10*, 33–61.

Caldwell, B., Wright, C., Honig, A., & Tannenbaum, J. (1970). Infant day care and attachment. *American Journal of Orthopsychiatry, 69*, 690–697.

Campbell, F. A., Burchinal, M., Wasik, B. H., Bryant, D. M., Sparling, J., & Ramey, C. T. (1995). *Early intervention and long term predictors of school concerns in African American children from low-income families.* Unpublished manuscript, University of North Carolina, Chapel Hill.

Campbell, F. A., & Ramey, C. T. (1994). Effects of early intervention on intellectual and academic achievement: A follow-up study of children from low-income families. *Child Development, 65*, 684–698.

Campbell, F. A., & Ramey, C. T. (1995). Cognitive and school outcomes for high risk African-American students at middle adolescence: Positive effects of early intervention. *American Education Research Journal, 32*, 743–772.

Clarke-Stewart, K. A. (1984). Day care: A new context for research and development. In M. Perlmutter (Ed.), *The Minnesota symposium on child psychology* (Vol. 17, pp. 61–100). Hillsdale, NJ: Lawrence Erlbaum Associates.

Clarke-Stewart, K. A. (1987). Predicting child development from child care forms and features: The Chicago Study. In D. A. Phillips (Ed.), *Quality in child care: What does research tell us?* (pp. 21–42). Washington, DC: National Association for the Education of Young Children.

Clarke-Stewart, K. A., Gruber, C. P., & Fitzgerald, L. M. (1994). *Children at home and in day care.* Hillsdale, NJ: Lawrence Erlbaum Associates.

Clarke-Stewart, K. A., Umeh, B. J., Snow, M. E., & Pederson, J. A. (1980). Development and prediction of children's sociability from 1 to 2½ years. *Developmental Psychology, 16*, 290–302.

Cost, Quality, and Child Outcome in Child Care Centers (1995). Denver: Economics Department, University of Colorado at Denver.

Cummings, E. M. (1980). Caregiver stability and day care. *Developmental Psychology, 16*, 290–302.

Dunn, L. (1993). Proximal and distal features of day care quality and children's development. *Early Childhood Research Quarterly, 8*, 167–192.

Farber, E. A., & Egeland, B. (1982). Developmental consequences of out-of-home care for infants in a low-income population. In E. F. Zigler & E. Gordon (Eds.), *Day care* (pp. 102–125). Boston: Auburn.

Farran, D. C., & Ramey, C. T. (1977). Infant day care and attachment behaviors toward mothers and teachers. *Child Development, 48*, 1112–1116.

Field, T. (1991). Quality infant day care and grade school behavior and performance. *Child Development, 62*, 863–870.

Field, T., Masi, W., Goldstein, D., Perry, S., & Parl, S. (1988). Infant day care facilitates preschool behavior. *Early Childhood Research Quarterly, 3*, 341–359.

Finkelstein, N. (1982). Aggression: Is it stimulated by day care? *Young Children, 37*, 3–9.

Galambos, N. L., & Garbarino, J. (1983). Identifying the missing links in the study of latchkey children. *Children Today, July/August*, 2–4, 40–41.

Galambos, N. L., & Maggs, J. L. (1991). Out-of-school care of young adolescents and self-reported behavior. *Developmental Psychology, 27*, 644–655.

Galinsky, E., Howes, C., & Kontos, S. (1995). *The family child care training study.* New York: Families and Work Institute.

Galinsky, E., Howes, C., Kontos, S., & Shinn, M. (1994). *The study of children in family child care and relative care.* New York: Families and Work Institute.

Genser, A., & Baden, C. (Eds.) (1980). *School-aged child care: Programs and issues.* Urbana, IL: ERIC Clearinghouse, University of Illinois.

Golden, M., Rosenbluth, L., Grossi, M., Policare, H., Freeman, H., & Brownlee, E. (1978). *The New York City Infant Day Care Study.* New York: Medical and Health Resource Association of New York City.

Goosens, F. A., & van IJzendoorn, M. H. (1990). Quality of infants' attachments to professional caregivers: Relation to infant-parent attachment and day-care characteristics. *Child Development, 61*, 832–837.

Harper, L. B., & Huie, K. S. (1985). The effects of prior group experience, age, and familiarity on the quality and organization of preschoolers' social relationships. *Child Development, 56*, 704–717.

Haskins, R. (1985). Public school aggression among children with varying day-care experience. *Child Development, 56*, 689–703.

Hegland, S. M., & Rix, M. K. (1990). Aggression and assertiveness in kindergarten children differing in day care experiences. *Early Childhood Research Quarterly, 5*, 105–116.

Howes, C. (1988). The peer interactions of young children. *Monographs of the Society for Research in Child Development, 53* (1, Serial no. 217).

Howes, C. (1990). Can the age of entry into child care and the quality of child care predict adjustment in kindergarten? *Developmental Psychology, 26*, 292–303.

Howes, C., & Hamilton, C. E. (1992a). Children's relationships with caregivers: Mothers and child care teachers. *Child Development, 63*, 859–866.

Howes, C., & Hamilton, C. E. (1992b). Children's relationships with child care teachers: Stability and concordance with parental attachments. *Child Development, 63*, 867–878.

Howes, C., & Hamilton, C. E. (1993). The changing experience of child care: Changes in teachers and in teacher–child relationships and children's social competence with peers. *Early Childhood Research Quarterly, 8*, 15–32.

Howes, C., Hamilton, C. E., & Matheson, C. C. (1994). Children's relationships with peers: Differential associations with aspects of the teacher–child relationship. *Child Development, 65*, 253–263.

Howes, C., Matheson, C. C., & Hamilton, C. E. (1994). Maternal, teacher, and child care history correlates of children's relationships with peers. *Child Development, 65*, 264–273.

Howes, C., & Olenick, M. (1986). Family and child care influences on toddler compliance. *Child Development, 57*, 202–216.

Howes, C., Phillips, D. A., & Whitebook, M. (1992). Thresholds of quality: Implications for the social development of children in center-based child care. *Child Development, 63*, 447–460.

Howes, C., Smith, E., & Galinsky, E. (1995). *The Florida Child Care Quality Improvement Study.* New York: Families and Work Institute.

Infant Health and Development Program. (1990). Enhancing the outcomes of low-birth-weight, premature infants: A multisite, randomized trial. *Journal of the American Medical Association, 263*, 3035–3042.

Kagan, J., Kearsley, R., & Zelazo, P. (1978). *Infancy: Its place in human development.* Cambridge, MA: Harvard University Press.

Ketterlinus, R. D., Bookstein, F. L., Sampson, P. D., & Lamb, M. E. (1989). Partial least squares analysis in developmental psychopathology. *Development and Psychopathology, 1*, 351- 371.

Lamb, M. E. (1998). Nonparental child care: Context, quality, correlates, and consequences. In W. Damon (General Ed.) & I. E. Sigel & A. Renninger (Vol. Eds.), *Handbook of child psychology: Child psychology in practice* (5th ed., Vol. 4, pp. 73–133). New York: Wiley.

Lamb, M. E., Hwang, C. P., Bookstein, F. L., Broberg, A., Hult, G., & Frodi, M. (1988). Determinants of social competence in Swedish preschoolers. *Developmental Psychology, 24*, 58–70.

Lamb, M. E., Hwang, C. P., Broberg, A., & Bookstein, F. L. (1988). The effects of out-of-home care on the development of social competence in Sweden: A longitudinal study. *Early Childhood Research Quarterly, 3,* 379–402.

Lamb, M. E,, Sternberg, K. J., Hwang, C. P., & Broberg, A. (Eds.) (1992). *Child care in context: Cross-cultural perspectives.* Hillsdale, NJ: Lawrence Erlbaum Associates.

Melhuish, E. C., Hennessy, E., Martin, S., & Moss, P. (1990, September). *Social development at six years as a function of type and amount of early child care.* Paper presented at the International Symposium on Child Care in the Early Years, Lausanne, Switzerland.

Moskovitz, D. S., Schwarz, J. C., & Corsini, D. A. (1977). Initiating day care at three years of age: Effects on attachment. *Child Development, 48,* 1271–1276.

National Institute of Child Health and Human Development Early Child Care Research Network (1996, April). *Infant child care and attachment security: Results of the NICHD study of early child care.* Symposium presented at the International Conference on Infant Studies, Providence, RI.

National Institute of Child Health and Human Development Early Child Care Research Network (1997, April). *Mother-child interaction and cognitive outcomes associated with early child care: Results of the NICHD study.* Symposium presented at the Society for Research in Child Development Convention, Washington, DC.

Oppenheim, D., Sagi, A., & Lamb, M. E. (1988). Infant-adult attachments on the kibbutz and their relation to socioemotional development four years later. *Developmental Psychology, 24,* 427–433.

Phillips, D. A., & Zigler, E. F. (1987). The checkered history of federal child care regulation. In E. Z. Rothkopf (Ed.), *Review of research in education* (Vol. 14, pp. 3–41). Washington, DC: American Educational Research Association.

Pianta, P. C., & Nimetz, S. L. (1991). Relationship between children and teachers: Associations with classroom and home behavior. *Journal of Applied Developmental Psychology, 12,* 379–393.

Portnoy, F. C., & Simmons, C. (1978). Day care and attachment. *Child Development, 49,* 239–242.

Posner, J. K., & Vandell, D. L. (1994). Low-income children's after-school care: Are there beneficial effects of after-school programs? *Child Development, 63,* 440–456.

Presser, H. B. (1986). Shift work among American women and child care. *Journal of Marriage and the Family, 48,* 551–563.

Presser, H. B. (1988). Shift work and child care among young dual-earner American parents. *Journal of Marriage and the Family, 50,* 133–148.

Prodromidis, M., Lamb, M. E., Sternberg, K. J., Hwang, C. P., & Broberg, A. G. (1995). Aggression and noncompliance among Swedish children in center-based care, family day care, and home care. *International Journal of Behavioral Development, 18,* 43–62.

Ragozin, A. S. (1980). Attachment behavior of day care children: Naturalistic and laboratory observations. *Child Development, 51,* 409–415.

Ramey, C. T., Ramey, S. L., Hardin, M., & Blair, C. (1995, May). *Family types and developmental risk: Functional differentiations among poverty families.* Paper presented at the meeting of the Fifth Annual Conference of the Center for Human Development and Developmental Disabilities, New Brunswick, NJ.

Reynolds, A. J. (1994). Effects of a preschool plus follow-on intervention for children at risk. *Developmental Psychology, 30,* 787–804.

Richardson, J. L., Dwyer, K., McGuigan, K., Hansen, W. B., Dent, C., Johnson, C. A., Sussman, S. Y., Brannon, B., & Flay, B. (1989). Substance use among eighth grade students who take care of themselves after school. *Pediatrics, 84,* 556–566.

Rodman, H., Pratto, D., & Nelson, R. (1985). Child care arrangements and children's functioning: A comparison of self-care and adult-care children. *Developmental Psychology, 21,* 413–418.

Roopnarine, J. L., & Lamb, M. E. (1978). The effects of day care on attachment and exploratory behavior in a strange situation. *Merrill-Palmer Quarterly, 24,* 85–95.

Roopnarine, J. L., & Lamb, M. E. (1980). Peer and parent–child interaction before and after enrollment in nursery school. *Journal of Applied Developmental Psychology, 1,* 77–81.

Rubenstein, J., Howes, C., & Boyle, P. (1981). A two-year follow-up of infants in community-based day care. *Journal of Child Psychology and Psychiatry, 8,* 1–11.

Sagi, A., Lamb, M. E., Lewkowicz, K. S., Shoham, R., Dvir, R., & Estes, D. (1985). Security of infant-mother, -father, and -metapelet attachments among kibbutz-reared Israeli children. In I. Bretherton & E. Waters (Eds.), *Growing points of attachment theory and research* (pp. 257–275). *Monographs of the Society for Research in Child Development, 50* (1–2, Serial No. 209).

Schwarz, J. C., Strickland, R., & Krolick, G. (1974). Infant day care: Behavioral effects at preschool age. *Developmental Psychology, 10,* 502–506.

Seltenheim, K., Ahnert, L., Rickert, H., & Lamb, M. E. (1997, May). *The formation of attachments between infants and care providers in German day care centers.* Paper presented at the meeting of the American Psychological Society Convention, Washington, DC.

Sroufe, L. A., Fox, N., & Pancake, V. (1983). Attachment and dependency in developmental perspective. *Child Development, 54,* 1615–1627.

Steinberg, L. (1986). Latchkey children and susceptibility to peer pressure: An ecological analysis. *Developmental Psychology, 22,* 433–439.

Steinberg, L. (1988). Simple solutions to a complex problem: A response to Rodman, Pratto, and Nelson (1988). *Developmental Psychology, 24,* 295–296.

Sternberg, K. J., Lamb, M. E., Hwang, C. P., Broberg, A., Ketterlinus, R. D., & Bookstein, F. L. (1991). Does out-of-home care affect compliance in preschoolers? *International Journal of Behavioral Development, 14,* 45–65.

Thornburg, K. R., Pearl, P., Crompton, D., & Ispa, J. M. (1990). Development of kindergarten children based on child care arrangements. *Early Childhood Research Quarterly, 5,* 27–42.

Vandell, D. L., & Corasaniti, M. A. (1988). *Variations in early child care: Do they predict subsequent social and emotional and cognitive differences?* Unpublished manuscript, University of Texas at Dallas, Richardson, TX.

Vandell, D. L., & Corasaniti, M. A. (1990a). Child care and the family: Complex contributors to child development. *New Directions in Child Development, 49,* 23–38.

Vandell, D. L., & Corasaniti, M. A. (1990b). Variations in early child care: Do they predict subsequent social, emotional, and cognitive differences? *Early Childhood Research Quarterly, 5,* 555–572.

Vandell, D. L., & Posner, J. (in press). Conceptualization and measurement of children's after-school environments. In S. L. Friedman & T. D. Works (Eds.), *Assessment of the environment across the lifespan.*

Vandell, D. L., & Ramanan, J. (1992). Effects of early and recent maternal employment on children from low-income families. *Child Development, 63,* 938–949.

Volling, B. L., & Feagans, L. V. (1995). Infant day care and children's social competence. *Infant Behavior and Development, 18,* 177–188.

Weisner, T. S., & Gallimore, R. (1977). My brother's keeper: Child and sibling caretaking. *Current Anthropology, 18,* 971–975.

Wessels, H., Lamb, M. E., Hwang, C. P., & Broberg, A. G. (1997). Personality development between 1 and 8 years of age in Swedish children with varying child care experiences. *International Journal of Behavioral Development, 21,* 771–794.

Woods, M. B. (1972). The unsupervised child of the working mother. *Developmental Psychology, 6,* 14–25.

Chapter 4

Primary Caregiving Fathers

GRAEME RUSSELL
Macquarie University, Sydney, Australia

Fathers as significant day-to-day caregivers of children—an aberration in the 1960s, a curiosity in the 1970s, a subject of serious research in the 1980s, widespread, understood and accepted in the 1990s? Well, not quite. Although most analyses and social commentaries indicate that there are a substantial number of families in which fathers are the primary caregivers, our understanding of this type of family pattern is still limited by a lack of research. Pleck (1997), for example, reported a U.S. study which indicates that ". . . 23% of employed married mothers with a child under five years reported the father was the primary childcare source during the mother's working hours" (p. 74). Yet, a review of the literature conducted for this chapter indicates that the curiosity and serious research have not been sustained and may even have subsided since the heightened interest in the early 1980s. This is also evident in the comprehensive analysis of fatherhood literature (Lamb, 1997), where the issue of fathers as primary caregivers receives little serious analysis. There are still very few research studies and those studies that do exist have continued to be on restricted and small samples (e.g., Geiger, 1996, studied a sample of 14 families; Grbich, 1992, a sample of 25; and Russell, 1989, a sample of 20). This outcome, however, is consistent with other analyses that indicate that research into fathers is still underrepresented in both the academic literature (Russell & Radojevic, 1992) and in dissertation studies (Silverstein & Phares, 1996).

This outcome is somewhat unexpected given the potential significance of the study of this type of caregiving arrangement both for the theoretical understanding of family processes and for strategies to promote social changes aimed at ensuring gender equity through an emphasis on the *responsibilities* men have to care for and nurture their children (cf. Levine & Pitt, 1995; Russell & Radojevic, 1992; Silverstein, 1996). It is also unexpected when the research and social contexts since the mid-1980s are considered, that is, a continuing social and academic interest in understanding gender differences and the different influences mothers and fathers have, changes in patterns of employment (e.g., increased levels of unemployment for men, more opportunities for parental leave, increased levels of maternal employment), the emphasis on gender equity and equal employment opportunity in the paid workforce, the child-care debate, continued popular interest in the role of fathers, as well as the increasing men's movement and the questioning of traditional masculinity.

This chapter (like all other analyses of this topic), therefore, is based on a partial picture of fathers as caregivers. Gaps remain: in descriptive analyses of the defining family characteristics and in our understanding both of the factors that lead to the adoption and maintenance of this family pattern and of the consequences for children and parents. This chapter has four main aims: First, to describe the characteristics of this family pattern and examine the extent to which it differs from traditional patterns. Second, to examine the reasons why people adopt this pattern, emphasizing both the possible antecedents and the social and personal factors that tend to facilitate it. Third, to review findings about the impact that such arrangements have on children, fathers, and mothers. And, finally, to address the more fundamental question about how to conceptualize and measure father participation in family life. This framework is then used to organize and analyze research findings. It is this issue that is considered first.

DIMENSIONS OF PARTICIPATION IN FAMILY LIFE

Who performs a task—who actually does the caregiving or spends the time on it—is the usual way that we think about involvement in family life when there are dependent children. Obviously, there is more to family life than this. Pleck (1997) provided a review of approaches to the conceptualization of paternal involvement and distinguished between quantitative and qualitative measures of involvement. His analysis relied heavily on the quantitative approach of Lamb, Pleck, Charnov, and Levine (1985, 1987). This involves three components: (a) Paternal engagement—direct interaction with the child in terms of caretaking, play or leisure; (b) accessibility or availability to the child; and (c) responsibility for the care of the child, as distinct from the performance of care. Other analyses (e.g., Russell, James & Watson, 1988; Russell, 1995) of paternal involvement in family life, however, indicate that a broader range of components need to be considered. Six domains can be identified, and for each, there are two levels: involvement and responsibility.

1. *Employment and family financial support.* (a) Involvement: Who is employed and how many hours are spent in paid work; (b) Responsibility: Continuing and longer term responsibility for family financial support and for the development of job or career skills (e.g., time spent on study).

2. *Day-to-day care of and interaction with children.* (a) Involvement: Physical and psychological time available to children. (b) Responsibility: Time spent caring for children, that is, having the sole responsibility (but, there is a need

to consider the context, for example, at home alone versus other parent being present, having responsibility on an outing).

3. *Child management and socialization.* (a) Involvement: This includes time spent and frequency of looking after basic child-care needs (e.g., bathing, dressing); child health (e.g., taking to doctor); social needs (e.g., play), emotional needs (e.g., comfort child when upset, praise and discipline); school needs (e.g., supervising homework, attend school functions); general cognitive development (e.g., answering child's why questions); and taking child to and attending their activities (e.g., sport, music). (b) Responsibility: Making decisions and setting standards, for example, for child behavior; monitoring the child's moods and needs for support; monitoring the child's standards in school work.

4. *Household work.* (a) Involvement: Time spent and frequency of doing household tasks, for example, fixing things, house improvements, garden and car maintenance, shopping and preparing meals, paying the bills, cleaning, washing, and ironing. (b) Responsibility: Organizing and planning household needs and family activities, organizing and monitoring family financial matters.

5. *Maintaining relationships between caregivers.* (a) Involvement: Time spent together as a couple, types of activities shared. (b) Responsibility: Initiating change or discussions about family problems, ensuring that good communication occurs between caregivers (e.g., exchange of information about a child), and support (e.g., cooperation and teamwork, resolving conflicts).

6. *Parental commitment/investment.* (a) Involvement: Relative time spent with children in relation to paid work and personal leisure, time spent seeking information and new skills about parenting. (b) Responsibility: The extent to which a person adjusts his or her life and routines to take account of family needs, involvement in job, and career.

EMPLOYMENT AND CHILD CARE CHARACTERISTICS

Families in which fathers participate highly in child care have been studied in Australia (Grbich, 1990, 1992, 1995; Harper, 1980; Russell, 1983; Russell, 1989); Israel (Sagi, 1982); Norway (Gronseth, 1978), Sweden (Hwang, 1986; Lamb, Frodi, Hwang, Frodi & Steinberg, 1982; Lamb, Frodi, Hwang & Frodi, 1983); and the United States (De Frain, 1979; Field, 1978; Geiger, 1996; Kimball, 1984; Levine, 1976; Pruett, 1985, 1987; Radin, 1981, 1982, 1985, 1994; Radin & Goldsmith, 1985; Williams, Radin & Allegro, 1992). However, little emphasis in this research has been placed on providing basic descriptive details about paternal participation in family life, and therefore it is difficult to be certain about the specific nature of the families studied. Nevertheless, findings are reasonably clear for two of the participation domains—employment and day-to-day child care.

Employment

Studies have included families that can be defined by two types of parental employment patterns: (a) those in which only the mother is employed and the father is at home full-time as the primary day-time caregiver (e.g., Grbich, 1992; Pruett, 1987), and (b) those in which both parents are employed, and they share child care, but where fathers usually have more responsibility for caregiving during the day (e.g., Geiger, 1996; parts of the samples included in Russell, 1983, 1989). Nevertheless, studies have not been consistent in providing specific details of either maternal or paternal employment characteristics (e.g., the nature of jobs, hours of employment, work schedules). Radin (1982) and Sagi (1982), for example, provided minimal data only for maternal employment status. A notable exception to this approach is the study of Geiger (1996), where comprehensive details of employment characteristics were provided.

Day-to-Day Child Care and Interaction

In comparison to modal patterns of involvement (see Pleck, 1997, for a comprehensive review), the caregiving fathers described in these studies were indeed highly participant, although many studies are lacking in specific details. In her U.S. study, Radin (1982) defined as father-prime a group that had primary responsibility for the children for 57% of the time. In the Swedish studies (Hwang, 1986; Lamb et al., 1982), fathers were included who had spent more than one month at home alone as the primary caregiver. The average number of months spent as primary caregivers reported were 3.0 (Hwang, 1986) and 2.82 (Lamb et al., 1982). In a U.S. study (Geiger, 1996), 36% of the fathers had been the primary caregivers since birth (mean age of the children at the time of the study was 13 months) and 64% had been in this situation since the baby had been age 4 to 8 months. Other studies have used time spent each week by fathers as primary caregiver as the key indicator. In Russell's (1983, 1989; later figures are shown in brackets) studies, caregiving fathers spent an average of 26 [26.2] hours per week taking sole responsibility for their children during the day when they were awake (compared to 16 [14.8] hours per week for their partners and one [5.8] hour for traditional fathers). Further, they were available to their children for an average of 54 [68.9] hours per week, in contrast to 33 [36.7] hours for the traditional-father comparison group. Grbich (1992), in another Australian study, included only fathers who took sole responsibility for the care of their preschool age children for a minimum of 25 hours during the traditional working week (8 a.m. to 6 p.m.).

Child Management and Socialization

Both Radin (1982) and Sagi (1982) used scores on a Paternal Child Care Involvement Index to classify families. In the original index there were five dimensions:

(a) overall amount of father involvement in child care; (b) amount of father involvement in socializing the child; (c) amount of father involvement in physically caring for the child; (d) involvement in decision making about the child; and (e) father's availability to the child. Families in the top one third on this index were classified as father-primary caregiving. DeFrain (1979), in his U.S. study, reported that fathers performed 46% of child-care tasks. Geiger (1996) reported that mothers and fathers primarily shared a range of child-care tasks (bathing, feeding, diapering, comforting, putting to sleep) when they were both at home. Compared to the mothers, however, fathers were more likely to bath and feed their babies when they were both at home. Fathers in Russell's (1983) study performed 43% of child-care tasks (compared to 11% for traditional fathers), spending a average of 8 hours per week doing them. These fathers also reported they spent approximately an equal length of time as their partners in play activities (23.4 hours per week; much higher than the figure of 10.2 for traditional fathers). Differences in gender of parent were consistently found in research studies for play type (e.g., fathers engaging in more outdoor play), and although considerably reduced in these families, were still statistically significant (Russell, 1983, 1989).

Household Work

Most studies concentrated on divisions of labor for child care. In contrast, Russell (1989) investigated divisions of labor for domestic household tasks, home handyman tasks, and responsibility for family finances. Compared with traditional fathers, caregiving fathers were found to perform more domestic tasks but fewer handyman tasks. Mothers who were secondary caregivers also performed fewer domestic tasks than their traditional counterparts. Primary caregiving fathers, like traditional fathers, however, maintained the major responsibility for handyman tasks.

Conclusion

Comprehensive details are yet to be provided for the specific nature of paternal participation or of the characteristics of these families. As is clear from the earlier analysis, researchers tend to state simply that fathers were highly participant (e.g., that they were the primary caretakers), to report that fathers were the primary caretakers for a specified time period, or to report fathers' participation relative to the mothers' participation or relative to other fathers' participation. This approach to the definition of high father participation is consistent with the general tendency of researchers to define families in terms of only one dimension (e.g., whether a mother is employed or not). Definitions have also been more likely to emphasize measures of general involvement, and the frequency of, or amount of time spent on, performing basic child-care tasks.

Research findings show that high father involvement in day-to-day child care combined with maternal employment does not always lead to sharing other aspects of parenting or family life (e.g., household work). In some families, the mother still retains the greater responsibility for child management and socialization (Russell, 1983) and performs more child-care tasks than the father. She could also have more responsibility for planning, monitoring, and anticipating the needs of the children. This suggestion is consistent with Radin's (1982) finding of a relatively low correlation between decision making about child care and other dimensions of father involvement. In contrast, Russell (1989) did not report a parental difference for taking responsibility for child needs. It needs to be remembered, however, that these families had chosen to adopt their caregiving patterns and fathers were active participants in the process of family change.

A complete analysis of nontraditional child-care patterns, therefore, needs to include considerations of divisions of labor for employment, the provision of day-to-day child care, the performance of child care as well as household tasks, and the acceptance and implementation of shared responsibilities and commitment for family management and child socialization.

POSSIBLE ANTECEDENTS
OF FATHER-CAREGIVING FAMILIES

Understanding the sources that result in fathers being significant day-to-day child carers is critical both for interpreting possible effects and for developing policies to support families who either choose or are forced to adopt this type of family lifestyle. Few research studies have systematically examined this issue, although there has been a noticeable shift in emphasis toward the study of explanations of more general patterns of father involvement (cf. Feldman, Nash & Aschenbrenner, 1983; Levy-Shiff & Israelashvili, 1988; McHale & Huston, 1984; see also Pleck, 1997). A major limitation in being definitive about the father-primary caregiving pattern is the fact that there has not been a comprehensive study that has sampled on a random basis. Most studies have involved some form of purposeful sampling.

Pleck (1997) provided a comprehensive analysis of studies that have examined the sources of paternal involvement. Mainly based on Lamb, Pleck, Charnov, and Levine (1987), five dimensions were differentiated: (a) Child characteristics and paternal sociodemographic characteristics; (b) motivation; (c) skills and confidence; (d) social support and stresses; (e) institutional factors and practices. Pleck, however, did not systematically differentiate nontraditional from traditional family patterns. The antecedents of a father-caregiving pattern would be expected to differ from those associated with whether a father will interact with or take responsibility for his children during the evenings or on the weekends when he is home from paid work. Given this, the following analysis includes additional perspectives to those proposed by Pleck (1997). The most significant of these is the consideration of parents' own explanations.

Parental Explanations

The family pattern described earlier, both in terms of parental employment patterns (e.g., father not employed and mother employed) and involvement in family life (e.g., father as primary caregiver), is still a radical departure from accepted cultural beliefs and norms for family lifestyles—despite the apparently increasing acceptance of diversity in family patterns. That this type of family pattern is either adopted in the first place or continued in the face of implicit or explicit social criticism (see later) suggests that the motivators must be very strong indeed.

Four categories of parental explanations, which have remained constant across twenty years of research and different cultures, were delineated (e.g., Geiger, 1996; Grbich, 1992; Kimball, 1984; Radin, 1985; Russell, 1983, 1989):

1. Inability of the father to gain employment.
2. Family income increased, either by having both parents employed or by having the mother employed when she had a greater earning capacity.
3. Career factors, mainly associated with the strong desire of mothers to pursue a career, but also associated with the father having less interest in his job or career (Geiger, 1996; Grbich, 1992; Russell, 1989). In Grbich's (1992) sample, for example, 13 fathers said they were not committed to a career path; 4 needed a change from a long term job; 3 had flexible careers; 3 had been retrenched; 1 was ill; and 1 had been fired.
4. Egalitarian beliefs about child-care responsibilities and sex roles (see later).

The first two types of explanations are usually associated with changes linked to economic necessity, whereas the others are usually more a matter of choice. It was noted in Russell (1983) that all but 10 families in his sample were better off financially after they had changed caregiving patterns. Families who see the change in their employment and child-care patterns as a matter of choice are also more likely to be identified with the professional middle class (Geiger, 1996; Russell, 1983, 1989).

Although family financial or employment situations are prominent in parental explanations, it is also clear that these factors cannot explain everything. There are several possibilities for family change given economic and career demands. If a family is in financial difficulty, the most common alternatives are that father takes a second job or that both parents work and children are cared for by someone else. Why is it then that in some families the alternative chosen is to have fathers become a significant caregiver? And, why is it that some of the families who have egalitarian beliefs choose this pattern and others do not? Are there any personal characteristics that make it more likely that this group of families makes this choice? Research indicates that there are.

Child and Family Characteristics

Analyses conducted in earlier studies indicated that, although child gender was not a defining characteristic, having fewer and older children was. In the sample of 71 studied by Russell (1983), 52% had only one child, and only 10 had a child under 6 months of age (although all had a preschool-age child). Other studies, however, included fathers who were caring for infants (e.g., Grbich, 1992; Geiger, 1996; Pruett, 1987). These latter findings appear to contradict arguments (Radin, 1985; Russell, 1983) that fathers will only either take on or continue in this pattern if child-care demands are low or if there is less conflict with cultural beliefs about child care, for example, the desirability of breastfeeding, the importance of mother–infant bonding, or the belief that mothers are more important to infants (cf. Lamb, Frodi, Hwang & Frodi, 1983). Without having a broadly based representative random sample of families, however, it is impossible to determine what contributions child and family characteristics make to the adoption of this type of family pattern.

Beliefs About Child Care and Parental Responsibilities

A critical additional motivating factor that has been identified (Geiger, 1996; Russell, 1983) is the belief that the family should retain the major responsibility for child care and, therefore, the major influence over their children's development. Geiger (1996) explored these issues in more depth and found that parents had a strong belief that child care could not satisfy their infant's psychological and physical needs. She also noted that secondary caregiving mothers spoke about these issues using the plural pronoun *we*, whereas primary caregiving mothers expressed themselves more using the first person singular *I*. They also felt that fathers could be competent caregivers and that child care was not the exclusive domain of mothers. They had been influenced in their views by information they had acquired about research findings on the importance of fathers to a child's development.

A More Active Role for Fathers?   In Russell's (1983) sample, mothers were perceived as being more influential in the decision to change lifestyles. In only 30% of the families was the father's desire to be more actively involved a major driving force. In what might be seen as an emerging trend, Grbich (1992) reported that the main explanation given in her sample was that fathers wanted to be involved in childrearing and household tasks. This trend is also evident in Russell's (1989) and Geiger's (1996) studies. Russell (1989) recruited families on the basis that they had chosen this lifestyle and that fathers were active participants in this. In

Geiger's (1996) sample, fathers had rejected stereotypical beliefs about the role of fathers in child care and accepted that sharing child care with their partner was the only fair arrangement. The mothers also adopted an ethic of sharing and believed in equity both inside and outside the home.

Developmental History

Two equally plausible, but differing, hypotheses about the contribution of a father's developmental history have been put forward (cf. Pleck, 1997; Radin, 1981; Sagi, 1982). Both hypotheses received support from studies that obtained fathers' retrospective accounts of their own fathers' involvement. Support for the hypothesis that fathers will become highly participant as a reaction to their own father's lack of involvement comes from DeFrain (1979), Eiduson and Alexander (1978), and Kimball (1984). Support for the hypothesis that fathers will model their own highly involved fathers comes from the study of Sagi (1982), who found high correlations between the two generations on six specific measures of involvement, and from Radin (1994), who found a link with stability of high paternal involvement over 11 years.

Grbich (1990) adopted a slightly different perspective and conducted a broader analysis of the contribution of socialization to social change. Findings indicate that the early socialization of the couples was consistent with the norms and values of a patriarchal society: "males were directed toward instrumental roles and females towards expressive roles" (p. 521), and that the strength of these was evident in their earlier adoption of traditional parenting and career roles. Two factors were identified as being key for men: later socialization and the development of equality in parenting ideologies influenced by changes in the social and political ethos of the 1970s, and the experience of occupational crises.

It could also be that mothers' developmental history plays an important role as this pattern involves a radical departure from cultural norms for them as well (being employed and not being the primary caregiver). As was reported earlier, mothers were perceived to be more influential in the decision to change. Mothers having a nurturant relationship with their own father have been found to be associated with the adoption of and continuation of a high paternal involvement pattern (Radin, 1982, 1985). High father involvement has also been associated with mothers whose own mothers had been employed (Radin, 1982, 1985) or had shared work on farms or in family businesses (Grbich, 1990).

Personal Characteristics

Self-Esteem and Values. Given both that there is an absence of role models for caregiving fathers and that this contradicts accepted cultural beliefs, it may only be people who are high on self-esteem and independence who will either contemplate, adopt, or feel comfortable in going against the tide in this way. Little research has been conducted to investigate this hypothesis; however, two findings give some support to it. Coysh (1983), in a study of traditional families, found that fathers with higher self-esteem prenatally were more likely to become involved in child care (see also Blair, Wenk & Hardesty, 1994). Russell (1983) reported that nontraditional parents are more likely than traditional parents to value their children being independent in thought and action, and less likely to value them conforming to social norms, values that are consistent with their behavior and perhaps with their own personalities.

Gender Role Orientation.   One of the earliest hypotheses investigated was that fathers who are highly involved in child care would be less stereotyped as masculine. It might be expected that primary caregiving fathers will be more likely to be androgynous—that is, they will endorse both traditional masculine characteristics (e.g., independence, self-confidence, assertiveness) as well as traditional feminine characteristics (e.g., interpersonal sensitivity, expressiveness), or alternatively, that they will be higher on traditional femininity. Findings, however, do not give consistent support to this hypothesis. Studies by Russell (1983) and Kimball (1984) provided positive evidence, whereas those of DeFrain (1979), Lamb et al. (1982), and Radin (1982) provided contrary evidence. In her follow up study, however, Radin (1994) reported a relationship between the masculinity dimension and low involvement in physical care.

As most commentators and researchers point out (Pleck 1997; Russell, 1983), finding a relationship between gender role orientation and paternal involvement does not establish cause and effect. There is no certainty about what is causing what—whether the lifestyle is a consequence of personality or whether personality factors are a consequence of the lifestyle (cf. Abrahams, Feldman, and Nash, 1978). Further, it may yet be that even though gender role orientation is not critical for the adoption of the lifestyle, it may be critical both for the process of adjustment, especially if fathers perceive themselves as having been forced to change, and for the longer term continuation in the lifestyle. Longitudinal studies are needed to answer these questions.

Beliefs About Gender Roles.   Pleck (1997), after reviewing findings across a range of family types, concluded that there were about equal numbers of studies that support and do not support a relationship between egalitarian beliefs about women or gender roles and paternal involvement. But sex-role ideology may be more critical in the adoption of a primary caregiving pattern (e.g., for fathers, not having a strong belief that breadwinning is the overriding responsibility of men). Evidence presented earlier from the studies of Geiger (1996) and Grbich (1992) tend to support this hypothesis, as do the findings of DeFrain (1979) and Kimball (1984). Primary caregiving fathers are less career oriented, and therefore are less likely to be constrained by cultural views about breadwinning responsibilities. Again, however, it is not clear whether this belief is an antecedent to or a consequence of adopting an alternative lifestyle. However, the findings of Radin (1985) suggest that it might be critical for the maintenance of this family pattern.

Skills and Knowledge

Beliefs and feelings about the competence of fathers and mothers to provide for the needs of children might also contribute to the adoption of this family pattern. A common objection to proposals that fathers could share more in the responsibility for child care is that fathers are not competent. Earlier research showed that parents in families where fathers were primary caregivers were more likely than those in traditional families to agree that fathers could be competent caregivers (Russell, 1983) and that they were more likely to have attended childbirth classes, the actual birth, and to have read books on childrearing (Russell, 1983). In another study, Russell (1989) found that caregiving fathers rated themselves more highly than traditional fathers on feelings of competence as a parent; self-confidence in handling their children and their problems; and the frequency with which they felt they understood their children and their needs. These studies, however, do not allow us to determine whether the experience of this family pattern has changed these parents' beliefs about their role as a parent or their perceived competence. Nevertheless, it is still a reasonable hypothesis that these aspects of parenting will operate in a very powerful way to influence the type of child care arrangement that they adopt, especially if they perceive consequences for their children's development.

Potential for and Type of Employment

Probably the most consistent finding to date is that this type of family pattern is associated with mothers having higher status and potentially more rewarding jobs than their spouses (Geiger, 1996; Grbich, 1992; Kimball, 1984; Radin, 1985; Russell, 1983, 1989). Associations with paternal employment characteristics have not been consistently reported, except (as has already been reported) that there is a trend toward fathers being less career oriented. Fathers being caregivers has also been found to be associated with flexibility in or reduced hours of employment (DeFrain, 1979; Geiger, 1996; Kimball, 1984; Radin, 1985; Russell, 1983). Nevertheless, Russell (1983) reported that in 29% of his sample, parents had either changed their jobs, had selected work hours to enable them to change caregiving patterns, or had reduced their commitments to their jobs. Accommodation of work to family commitments was also more common for fathers than for mothers.

The fact that fathers becoming primary caregivers depends on an interaction between job flexibility and other factors is supported by findings about participation patterns in the parental leave scheme in Sweden. Commenting on the consistent findings that having flexibility in work hours and leave provisions does not result in a marked increase in fathers' family involvement, Lamb, Pleck,

Charnov, and Levine (1985) argued that changes in institutional practices might only be critical for fathers who are highly motivated and feel they have the necessary skills.

Couple Relationships: Antecedent or Consequence?

A final possible antecedent of high paternal participation is the nature of the couple relationship, both in terms of the level of support they give to each other to adopt a nontraditional family pattern and the quality of the couple relationship. The process of support could work in two ways. First, mothers could support fathers in their caregiving role. As was noted earlier, mothers are major contributors to the decision for families to adopt a pattern in which fathers are significant caregivers and are supportive of fathers being competent caregivers (Geiger, 1996; Russell, 1983). Second, fathers could support mothers in their employment role. Radin (1985) found that the maintenence of this lifestyle is associated with fathers being supportive of the career involvement of their spouses (Radin, 1985).

Pleck (1997) argued that the quality of the marital relationship might also contribute to high levels of paternal involvement. After reviewing the full range of research, he concluded that: ". . . high paternal involvement is more grounded in good marital relationships than poor ones" (p. 90). The majority of the studies reviewed by Pleck, however, did not include families in which fathers were actively involved in day-to-day child care. The two studies that have conducted systematic analyses of marital relationships using a standard measure (Spanier's Dyadic Adjustment Scale) provide contradictory findings. It needs to be noted yet again, however, that both suffer from the same methodological limitations as those described earlier and therefore must be treated with caution when considering cause and effect.

Russell (1983) reported that families in which fathers were significant caregivers were lower on marital adjustment than parents in a comparison group of traditional families and suggested that this outcome was a consequence of the lifestyle. This difference, however, was primarily attributable to differences in responses which occurred on one subscale, dyadic satisfaction, which included items such as whether they had considered ending their relationship and items associated with recent quarrelling and getting on one another's nerves. Russell (1983) suggested that these findings have two possible interpretations. First, it could be that a nontraditional lifestyle has the effect of increasing tension in couple relationships, especially given the problems that might be associated with negotiating new family patterns and new divisions of labor. Second, it could be that these couples are more sensitive to these issues and are more open about reporting intimate aspects of their relationships in a research study. An additional finding, reported by Russell (1983), indicates that when fathers were more influential in the decision to change, they also rated their marital relationship more highly. This suggests (in agreement with Pleck, 1997) that for some fathers, high-quality couple relationships might be an antecedent.

In a second study (Russell, 1989), shared caregiving and traditional samples were matched on family characteristics and choice of lifestyle; all had chosen their particular lifestyle. Significant family differences were not found either on the original Spanier subscales or on the additional scales formed (relationship satisfaction, commitment, and negative interactions). There were, however, family-type differences in relationships between marital and family context variables (e.g., involvement in paid and family work), indicating that aspects of the lifestyle do impact on couple relationships. These issues are considered in the section on consequences for couple relationships.

Longer Term Considerations

The analysis thus far has focused on possible sources of the initial adoption of this type of family. Equally important, however, are the factors that may contribute to maintaining this pattern or to decisions to revert to a more traditional pattern. It could be that the actual experience of a nontraditional lifestyle will result in changes in people's views and that the reasons why they continue are different from the reasons why they adopted the lifestyle in the first place. Four research studies followed primary caretaking and role-sharing fathers over a period of time, and all point to the relative instability of this pattern. Only two studies provided data on possible reasons for the changes.

Lamb et al. (1982) conducted a study of Swedish families in which fathers had taken paternity leave and found difficulty in retaining a sample of families in which fathers were at home, despite their having planned to do so before the birth. Longer term instability is a characteristic of Grbich's (1992) sample. She studied a group of 25 primary caregiving fathers over a 6-year period (from 1983 to 1989). In 1989, there were 12 fathers still in the primary caregiving role (and 6 of these had preschool-age children at home); 7 had returned to paid work (and in 4 of these families both parents were in paid work and shared child tasks); and 6 couples had separated. Unfortunately, neither of these studies reports data on the reasons why these families reverted to more traditional patterns. Pruett (1985) followed up his 17 families two years after the initial recruitment and found that 8 fathers were still primary caregivers, and in 4 of these families, there were now second children.

Russell (1983) reinterviewed 27 of his sample of 71 families two years later. Only 10 out of these were in exactly the same family pattern, whereas 11 had reverted to traditional family roles with the mother at home and the father employed. In 4 of the other 6 families, the children were of school age and both parents were employed, but it was the mother who took more responsibility for child care. Finally, in two families the parents had separated, with one family opting for a shared custody arrangement. Two factors were identified as being critical for a reversion to traditional child-care patterns.

The first factor was how far caregiving and employment patterns differed from cultural norms and expectations. Reversion was more likely when there were very young children and when the father was not in paid employment. Fathers not being employed and caring for a 6-month-old would be expected to generate more social disapproval than one in which a father is employed part-time and cares for a four-year-old child. Fathers also indicated that, with time, the absence of genuine social support from peers made it more difficult to cope with the day-to-day family demands and the social isolation.

The second factor was economic in nature. Nine out of the 11 families were better off financially after reversion. Further, two of these families were among the most strongly committed to egalitarian values in the initial interview—for them, this was the most significant reason why they adopted their nontraditional lifestyle. There were two major drivers for the continuation: for mothers, it was the satisfaction they derived from their jobs; and for fathers, it was the positive impact of having improved relationships with their children (see later).

Radin and Goldsmith (1985) followed up the families from Radin's original study 4 years later (see also Radin, 1985, and Williams, Radin, and Allegro, 1992). Only 25% were found to have remained as primary caregiving fathers with their 7-to-9-year-old children. Unlike Russell's (1983) finding, lack of peer or family support was not a critical factor. Reasons given covered a number of areas: career factors, child needs, and financial factors (a result that is similar to Russell's, 1983, study). Factors reported by Radin (1985) to be critical for the longer term stability of this family pattern were residing in a community which is supportive of a nontraditional pattern; mothers having a strong investment in their careers, being supported in this by their families and earning a high salary; fathers having flexibility in work hours; fathers finding caring for the children gratifying; and the demands of child care (in terms of number of children and characteristics of children) remaining low. In a subsequent, more detailed analysis (Radin & Goldsmith, 1985), the longer term antecedents were found to differ by sex of child. In families with daughters, high father involvement 4 years later was linked with mothers' negative views of her own father's involvement, whereas in families with sons, the link was with paternal variables (e.g., negative views about the involvement of his own father). Radin and Goldsmith (1985) argued that this relationship for sons can be explained by fathers "becoming more invested in his son and in a mentorship role" during the middle childhood period of development (p. 382).

Conclusions

It is clear that high father involvement in day-to-day child care is associated with a multitude of factors and it is not possible to present a list of necessary or sufficient conditions (cf. Pleck, 1997). What is needed is a more broadly based longitudinal study of a random, and therefore, representative sample of these families. All studies to date involved some type of purposeful or convenience sampling.

What we do know, however, is that, for some families, financial factors override all others; for others, financial considerations represent necessary preconditions for change, but the change is likely to be mediated by gender role orientation and egalitarian beliefs. We also know that beliefs about parental roles and the perceived competence of men as caregivers appear to provide the necessary and sufficient conditions for change, as do their own experiences of being parented (either positive or negative). Kimball (1984), after reviewing the available literature, argued that apart from financial factors (e.g., father losing a job), the most important sustaining factors are egalitarian gender role beliefs and an acceptance that men can be competent caregivers.

The contribution of fathers themselves to the adoption or maintenance of this lifestyle is not well understood. This topic clearly deserves much more attention especially given the trend in recent studies to emphasize more the active role of fathers in caregiving decisions. Research might usefully follow up on the factors already noted as possible contributors: early socialization experiences, for example, compensating for their own father's lack of involvement, especially with sons; more recent socialization experiences, for example, the influence of the changed social and political ethos supporting the equality of parenting; and the desire of men to make a significant contribution to their children's development.

CONSEQUENCES OF FATHERS BEING CAREGIVERS

There has been surprisingly little research into the influence that high father involvement in daily caregiving has on family relationships or individual outcomes. Yet, one of the first questions asked by both researchers and policy makers about different family patterns is "What influence do they have on children?" and a question being increasingly asked is "What influence does it have on the lifespan development of parents, and especially on fathers?" Given the interactive nature of the family system, an emphasis on all family members seems especially important.

Consequences for Children

Probably the most consistent research finding is that high paternal involvement in daily caregiving seems to have less influence on children than might be expected. A summary of findings is presented here in terms of father–child relationships; sex-role development; cognitive development; and social competence.

Father–Child Relationships. As was noted earlier, fathers who are caregivers interact differently from those in traditional families in terms of time spent together, frequency of interactions, and content of interactions (e.g., style of play). It might be expected therefore, that these differences will result in differences in the quality of father–child relationships and that children will have closer relationships with caregiving fathers. Self-report data (reviewed later) from fathers certainly support such an hypothesis; however, findings from observation studies appear less consistent.

In Lamb et al.'s (1982) study of Swedish families, support was not found for the hypothesis that high father involvement will result in changes in the quality of father–child relationships or in the quality of attachment between the father and child. It is likely, however, that these fathers had not been primary caregivers for a sufficient time to enable an adequate test of this hypothesis. Further, Lamb et al. (1983) argued that the most critical variable for the quality of father–child relationships might be that associated with play rather than simple involvement, and in comparison with findings from relatively uninvolved U.S. fathers, Swedish fathers were not renowned for their playfulness.

Geiger (1996) conducted two videotaped 25-minute home observations (when the child was awake). There were three semistructured parts to each session: (a) one parent observed interacting alone with the infant; (b) other parent observed interacting alone with the infant; and (c) the infant was observed interacting with a friendly stranger. Although traditional gender differences were maintained for some dimensions (e.g., fathers engaged in more rough and tumble play), in contrast to the findings of the Lamb studies, several significant caregiver effects were observed.

Primary caregivers (both fathers and mothers) displayed more affection toward infants than secondary caregivers, and overall, primary caregiving fathers were the most affectionate of all. Primary caregiving fathers and their infants were also found to be more attuned to each other's play behavior. In terms of infant behaviors directed at parents, it was found that under nonstressful conditions: (a) Infants displayed more affection toward their primary caregiver; and (b) Infants in father-primary families displayed less anxious attachments than those in mother-primary families. Under conditions of stress, it was found that: "...infants invariably preferred the parent who had provided them with care and affection for the greatest part of the day, with total disregard for their gender" (Geiger, 1996, p. 94). Geiger argued that the differences in findings from her study and those conducted in Sweden can be accounted for by the differences in the level of involvement of the fathers in day-to-day caregiving. It should also be noted that Pruett (1987) observed (although quantitative data are not provided) that all of his primary caregiving fathers developed "deep reciprocal nurturing attachments" with their infants (p. 76).

Gender Role Orientation and Beliefs.   Radin (1982) in the United States and Sagi (1982) in Israel, using essentially the same methodology, both reported that high father involvement did not have an impact on the sex-role development of boys (as measured by the IT scale). In contrast, Sagi (1982) found that girls with highly involved fathers scored higher on the masculinity component. Difference in types of sample used (e.g., in Sagi's sample, 55% of the mothers were not employed) and the fact that the studies were conducted in two different countries are likely to explain these differences in findings.

Studies are needed to examine possible longer term effects on sex-role development, gender role orientation, and sex-role attitudes and interests in adolescence and adulthood, and on the types of parental roles adopted. The 11-year follow-up of Radin's original sample addresses some of these issues (Williams, Radin, & Allegro, 1992). Findings indicate that high paternal involvement in the preschool years predicted adolescent approval of nontraditional employment patterns, and high paternal involvement in the middle childhood period predicted approval of nontraditional childrearing patterns. Nevertheless, these researchers failed to find support for the hypothesis that children raised in these nontraditonal families would have less traditional sex role attitudes in general.

Cognitive Development.   Radin (1982) reported positive correlations between the degree of father involvement and verbal intelligence scores for both boys and girls. Highly involved fathers also spent more time in efforts to stimulate their children's cognitive growth, and this pattern was more pronounced for sons than for daughters. Although this latter finding suggests that the "effect" on cognitive test performance is associated with increased stimulation from two involved parents (compared to most families where there is usually only one—the mother), it may be that these fathers have different childrearing values (see earlier) and are more achievement oriented.

Social Competence.   Radin (1982) and Sagi (1982) used the same methodology to investigate relationships between father participation and children's empathy and locus of control. Sagi reported that higher levels of empathy were associated with higher father involvement, suggesting that this outcome is linked in these families with fathers being more supportive, nurturant, sensitive, and warm (see also the findings of Geiger reported earlier). Both studies supported the hypothesis that high father participation would be associated with higher levels of internality. Parents in these families would be expected to be higher on internality themselves in order to engage in a nontraditional lifestyle. Additional research, based on hypotheses generated from a modeling perspective, needs to examine links between parental and child locus of control.

Although lacking in detail, Pruett (1985) also reported a positive influence of fathers adopting a primary caregiving role. Using the Yale Developmental Schedule, he found that many of these infants were well above the expected norms on these standardized developmental tests, for example, infants age two to twelve months "performed problem-solving tasks on a level of four to twelve months older, while social skills were two to ten months in advance of the norm" (p. 376).

Conclusions.   Given the small number of studies, differences in methods used, and the restricted samples studied, definitive conclusions about the impact of high father involvement in daily caregiving are premature. Further, apart from Gei-ger's (1996) study, reported studies have not provided specific details about the nature of father involvement, and therefore, certainty is not yet possible about whether there has been an adequate test of the effects of different caregiving pat-terns. Nevertheless, some tentative conclusions can be drawn.

To start, high father participation appears to have neither a significant negative nor a significant positive effect. Rather, the more noteworthy finding is the lack of apparent effects. This is consistent with the self-reported assessments of parents (Russell, 1983). Seventy-six percent of fathers and 64% of mothers reported their children had not experienced any difficulties at all, and 44% of fathers and 40% of mothers felt that their children had gained considerably from the change in life-styles. The majority linked positive effects to the improved relationship with the father. In contrast to reports of limited consequences for children, parents have been found to be much more likely to report consequences for themselves. These are the issues discussed next.

Effects on Fathers

Although fathers report increased day-to-day hassles in handling child needs and negotiating a new family lifestyle with their partner, friends, and relatives, research findings generally indicate positive outcomes for fathers. Studies have covered two major outcomes for fathers: relationships with children and personal development.

Father–Child Relationship.   Several studies have reported that fathers (and their partners) feel that the changed lifestyle has resulted in greater closeness, increased sensitivity, and increased tension and conflict in the father–child relationship (for reviews, see Russell, 1983; Russell & Radin, 1983). Indeed, in one study (Russell, 1983), two thirds of both mothers and fathers indicated that the major advantage of their shared caregiving lifestyle for fathers was the improved (and closer) rela-tionship the father had with the child. Russell (1989) also found that caregiving fathers were significantly higher than traditional fathers on self-ratings of close-ness to their children. Further, Pruett (1987) described the process of change in fathers' feelings toward their infants as they experienced the intense daily inter-actions in their role as primary caregiver. For many, the "depth and rapidity" of the development of the attachment relationship was a surprise (p. 76).

Three studies (Russell, 1983, 1989; Gronseth, 1978) found that caregiving fa-thers, compared to traditional fathers, feel they have a greater understanding of their children and are more sensitive to them. Russell's (1983) and Pruett's (1987) studies also indicate that it is not simply the increased time fathers spend with their children that affects their understanding, but the way in which the time is spent. Specifically, it is spending time alone with their children, taking sole re-sponsibility for them on a continuing day-to-day basis. It has also been found that this increased understanding and sensitivity produces a change in views about their roles as parents. Fathers felt more self-confident and effective as parents (Pruett, 1987; Russell, 1983, 1989). Increased tension and conflict in father–child relationships has also been noted (Russell, 1983; see also Russell and Radin, 1983), but not in all studies (cf. Russell, 1989).

Personal Development. Several studies have found that fathers who are more highly participant in child care report enhanced self-esteem, self-confidence, or satisfaction personally and in their parental role (Geiger, 1996; Gronseth, 1978; Lamb et al., 1982; Lein, 1979; Pruett, 1987; Russell, 1983, 1989; Sagi, 1982). Pruett, for example, described how the fathers had actively incorporated their infants into their lives: "There appeared to have been a very literal 'taking in' of these babies by their fathers as a profound emotional event" (1987, p. 77).

Other research has highlighted the difficulties fathers experience in the initial stages in adjusting to the caregiving role (e.g., Pruett, 1987; Russell, 1983). Some also found initial adjustment more difficult because of the lack of support from friends (especially male friends), family, and neighbors (e.g., Geiger, 1996; Grbich, 1992; Russell, 1983). Although Russell (1983) found that this lack of support was a significant motivator for some fathers to revert to a traditional pattern, neither Geiger (1996) nor Grbich (1992) support this finding.

Effects on Mothers

Few studies have examined the possible impact of fathers as caregivers on mothers and most studies ignore this issue altogether, focusing instead on fathers and children. Possible effects on mothers have been noted in two areas: mother–child relationships and the impact of paid employment. As has already been argued, effects would be expected to be mediated by the reasons why families adopted this pattern in the first place, and especially by whether the pattern had been chosen or had been forced on a family.

Mother–Child Relationships. Four research studies are relevant in this context: observational studies conducted in Sweden (Lamb et al., 1982), in the United States (Geiger, 1996), and the Australian interview studies of Russell (1983, 1989). Lamb et al. (1982) found that the quality of mother–child relationships in nontraditional families was not significantly different in major ways from those in traditional families. In contrast, although Geiger (1996) did not find differences between primary and secondary caregiving mothers under nonstressful conditions, infants were less likely to display attachment behaviors to secondary caregiving mothers when stress was introduced.

In agreement with these general findings, Russell (1989) did not report significant differences between primary and secondary caregiving mothers on self-reported ratings of closeness to their children, satisfaction with their relationships, or on understanding of children. Further, Russell (1983), using interview data, found that 67% of mothers and 59% of fathers felt that the mother–child relationship had not changed in any significant way. Nevertheless, some mothers reported feelings of guilt from leaving their children and 33% reported that they disliked the reduced contact that they had with their children. In the follow-up study of these families (Russell, 1983), this reduced contact with the children was given as a major disadvantage of the caregiving pattern. This was especially the case for mothers who saw themselves as having been forced to change because of financial factors.

Employment: Mixed Reactions.   Russell (1983) found that mothers enjoyed increased satisfaction, self-esteem, and independence from their involvement in employment and the opportunity they had to pursue their career. Similar to findings from studies of employed mothers, however, these mothers also reported that because of their dual roles, they constantly felt physically and emotionally exhausted. This was also an influential factor for mothers in the reversion to traditional caregiving patterns (Russell, 1983). Studies tend to show that fathers are as highly participant in housework as they are in child care, and that indeed, mothers in father caregiving families are much more highly participant in housework than their "traditional father counterparts" (Russell, 1983, 1989). Additional systematic data are needed on the degree to which fathers at home share in all aspects of family work and on the influence this division of labor has on mothers, fathers, and on the couple relationship.

Consequences for Couple Relationships

Arguments about whether the quality of the couple relationship is an antecedent to or consequence of the changed caregiving patterns were considered earlier. In the absence of longitudinal studies, insights about possible consequences can be obtained by examining parents' own perceptions of changes (Russell, 1983) as well as the links between key family variables and the quality of the couple relationship (Russell, 1989).

Perceptions of Changes.   Russell (1983) found that 45% of parents reported positive consequences for their marital relationship (e.g., increased sensitivity and understanding). In contrast, 40% reported negative consequences associated with greater couple conflict and lifestyle pressures (e.g., tiredness, irritability, and spending less time together). The majority, however, found that difficulties occurred more in the first few months, when there was uncertainty about housework and child-care responsibilities (cf. Geiger, 1996) and when both parents were adjusting to new physical and emotional demands. Having increased conflict in the first few months of making such a radical change in lifestyles is to be expected. This is probably all the more likely if people are genuinely trying to share the responsibilities for child care and housework.

Dominant sources of tension for fathers were (a) feelings of resentment because their partners considered them to be secondary parents (e.g., not allowing fathers to make decisions about the children or about how and when housework should be done); and (b) the apparent lack of genuine support given by mothers to their partners. Although the majority of spouses accepted that fathers were competent child carers and expressed pride in them being caregivers, many also found it difficult to accept fathers in the domestic role and to acknowledge that fathers might have problems.

The dominant sources of tension for mothers were (a) resentment associated with the children becoming closer to fathers; (b) irritation because their partners had lower standards of housework and child care (a common criticism was that fathers were too soft with the children); (c) the status and credit that other people (and especially other women) often gave their spouses because of their involvement in child care.

Links Between Family Variables and Couple Relationships. In a more extensive study of couple relationships, Russell (1989) reported findings that are somewhat different from those in his earlier study (keeping in mind, however, that families in this sample chose their lifestyle). In particular (as was reported earlier), these couples were not less satisfied with their relationships than traditional couples, and they did not report more negative interactions or less commitment. In agreement with the hypotheses of the earlier study, processes associated with the changed lifestyle did influence couple relationships. Mothers who were more dissatisfied with their couple relationship had partners who had taken over more of the childrearing responsibilities, were less supportive of mothers' approaches to childrearing, and reported having greater understanding of their children. Fathers were more dissatisfied when their partner was less approving and supportive of their approach to childrearing and when mothers participated less in traditional home handyman tasks. Russell (1989) concluded that these findings provide further support for the argument that some mothers are reluctant to give up their power and status within the domestic domain and find it difficult to be supportive of their partner in the child-care role. It is also clear that this perceived lack of support has a negative impact on fathers.

Community Reactions and Tensions in Male and Female Relationships

Although women have been found to be more supportive of fathers being caregivers than men are (Russell, 1983), fathers who are highly committed to being caregivers commonly question whether the support they receive from women in the community is genuine. Fathers who shared in child care sometimes found themselves being described by women as just good babysitters; not being trusted by other mothers to care for their children (because of the fear of child abuse); not being accepted by women as one of the group in the neighborhood or at school functions; and not being given genuine support during some of the tough times that recur during times of caring for children. Some fathers also discussed the problems of developing close supportive networks with women in the neighborhood because many see this as a threat to the marital relationship. What this might mean in the longer term, however, is that fathers at home become even more socially isolated than women at home. This is obviously an issue that requires more attention by researchers and practitioners. We need to understand better the difficulties that both men and women experience in adjusting to changes in men and their increased involvement in family life.

CONCLUSIONS

As has been concluded by others who have reviewed this research area (Radin, 1994), our ability to reach firm conclusions on the nature of this family pattern, its antecedents, or its consequences are restricted. Most studies have included small and highly selective samples and most have significant methodological limitations. Studies have relied either on comparisons between father-caregiving and traditional families or on correlations between measures of paternal involvement and child development, parental, and relationship outcomes. Nevertheless, some consistent patterns have emerged.

First, there appears to be a multitude of factors that antecede the adoption of this family pattern and interact in complex ways in different families. Two major groups of families have been identified: those who have adopted this pattern essentially out of economic necessity, and those who have chosen this lifestyle based on considerations of career aspirations for mothers, commitments to egalitarian male and female roles, or the desire of fathers to be active participants in caregiving. Other factors that have been found to be either antecedents or mediators include mothers who are more highly educated and have higher status jobs; flexibility in career structure and work times; earlier and later socialization experiences of fathers and mothers; gender role orientation; beliefs that men are competent caregivers and that they are important in their child's development; and support and encouragement from the mother for the father to be the caregiver. Other studies (e.g., Geiger, 1996; Grbich, 1992) have highlighted a more active role for fathers in the process of becoming caregivers. Social changes emphasizing gender equity and research findings on the role of fathers in children's development appear particularly influential in supporting such decisions. Further studies should also investigate the possible role of changing views about the roles and responsibilities of men (e.g., those associated with the men's movement).

It has also been found that the reasons why people adopt this lifestyle are not necessarily the factors that maintain the lifestyle over a longer period of time. People who initially espoused strong beliefs about equality reverted to a traditional pattern when they encountered adjustment difficulties. Equally, some families were motivated by positive experiences to continue despite the fact that the initiating economic difficulties had since been overcome.

The clear pattern in findings to date is that there are not dramatic negative effects on either individual or family outcomes. In the case of the children, positive outcomes have been highlighted in several studies; however, the findings are perhaps more noteworthy for the lack of influence on outcomes. Findings (both self-report and observation) indicate that a significant consequence is the improved father–child relationship and the increased understanding fathers have of their children. Initial adjustment difficulties, however, were reported for both individuals and couples. Findings especially highlighted difficulties fathers had in adjusting to the demands of child care and domestic life and the lack of support that they received from male peers and women at the community level.

Difficulties in marital relationships during the early period of change were also noted by parents (especially in families where the change was seen as being necessary) and continuing tensions between mothers and fathers about power and influence in child care and domestic responsibilities were linked with poorer quality couple relationships. It is still not certain, however, whether the quality of couple relationships is an antecedent to or a consequence of fathers being caregivers.

Future studies need to include large samples of randomly selected families using both longitudinal and matched sample designs. Also needed are extensive descriptive details of the nature of the family pattern, especially details of the level and type of involvement of fathers in every aspect of family life. Systematic research is especially needed of the full range of possible antecedents, including early and recent socialization experiences, personality, beliefs, social support, and couple relationships. Studies also need to consider the possibility that consequences for individuals and families could be mediated by variables other than those associated with the quality and quantity of father involvement. Parental differences might occur on a range of variables (e.g., child rearing values) and effects may be associated with these rather than specific differences in father involvement.

Continuing social changes will probably mean that the father as caregiver option will be chosen by an increasing number of families in the future. Uncertainty about employment security will also mean that a range of families will continue to be forced into the lifestyle through economic necessity. It seems important, therefore, that more attention be given to these two different types of families both by researchers, family practitioners and family educators. The serious study of these families can also help to answer important questions about the influences of family processes on outcomes for children and parents (e.g., the impact of gender as opposed to caregiving responsibilities).

REFERENCES

Abrahams, B., Feldman, S. S., & Nash, S. C. (1978). Sex-role self-concept and sex-role attitudes: Enduring personality characteristics, or adaptations to changing life situations. *Developmental Psychology, 14,* 393–400.

Blair, S. L., Wenk, D., & Hardesty, C. (1994). Marital quality and paternal involvement: Interconnections of men's spousal and parental roles. *Journal of Men's Studies, 2,* 221–237.

Coysh, W. S. (1983, August). Predictive and concurrent factors related to fathers' involvement in childrearing. Paper presented at the meeting of the American Psychological Association, Anaheim, CA.

DeFrain, J. (1979). Androgynous parents tell who they are and what they need. *The Family Coordinator, 28,* 237–243.

Eiduson, B. T., & Alexander, J. W. (1978). The role of children in alternative family styles. *Social Issues, 34,* 149–167.

Feldman, S. S., Nash, S. C., & Aschenbrenner, B. G. (1983). Antecedents of fathering. *Child Development, 54,* 1628–1636.

Field, T. (1978). Interaction behaviors of primary versus secondary caretaker fathers. *Developmental Psychology, 49,* 183–184.

Geiger, B. (1996). *Fathers as primary caregivers.* Westport, CT: Greenwood.

Grbich, C. (1990). Socialisation and social change: A critique of three positions. *British Journal of Sociology, 41,* 517–530.

Grbich, C. (1992). Societal response to familial role change in Australia: Marginalisation or social change? *Journal of Comparative Family Studies, 23*(1), 79–94.

Grbich, C. (1995). Male primary caregivers and domestic labour: Involvement or avoidance? *Journal of Family Studies, 1,* 114–129.

Gronseth, E. (1978). Work sharing: A Norwegian example. In R. Rapoport & R. N. Rapoport (Eds.), *Working couples* (pp. 108–121). St. Lucia, Queensland: University of Queensland Press.

Harper, J. (1980). *Fathers at home.* Melbourne, Australia: Penguin.

Hwang, C.-P. (1986). Behavior of Swedish primary and secondary caretaking fathers in relation to mother's presence. *Developmental Psychology, 22,* 749–751.

Kimball, G. (1984). Why do couples role share? Unpublished manuscript, University of California, Chico.

Lamb, M. E. (Ed.). (1997). *The role of the father in child development* (3rd ed.). New York: Wiley.

Lamb, M. E., Frodi, A. M., Hwang, C.-P., Frodi, M., & Steinberg, J. (1982). Mother– and father–infant interaction involving play and holding in traditional and nontraditional Swedish families. *Developmental Psychology, 18,* 215–221.

Lamb, M. E., Frodi, M., Hwang, C-P., & Frodi, A. M. (1983). Effects of paternal involvement on infant preferences for mothers and fathers. *Child Development, 54,* 450–458.

Lamb, M. E., Pleck, J. H., Charnov, E. L., & Levine, J. A. (1985). Paternal behavior in humans. *American Zoologist, 25,* 883–894.

Lamb, M. E., Pleck, J. H., Charnov, E. L., & Levine, J. A. (1987). A biosocial perspective on paternal behavior and involvement. In J. B. Lancaster, J. Altman, A. Rossi, & L. R. Sherrod (Eds.), *Parenting across the lifespan: Biosocial perspectives* (pp. 11–42). New York: Academic.

Lein, L. (1979). Male participation in home life: Impact of social supports and breadwinner responsibility on the allocation of tasks. *The Family Co-ordinator, 29,* 489–496.

Levine, J. (1976). *Who will raise the children? New options for fathers (and mothers).* New York: Bantam.

Levine, J. A., & Pitt, E. W. (1995). *New Expectations: Community strategies for responsible fatherhood.* New York: Families and Work Institute.

Levy-Shiff, R., & Israelashvili, R. (1988). Antecedents of fathering: Some further exploration. *Developmental Psychology, 24,* 434–440.

McHale, S. M., & Huston, T. L. (1984). Men and women as parents: Sex role orientations, employment, and parental roles with infants. *Child Development, 55,* 1349–1361.

Pleck, J. H. (1997). Paternal involvement: Levels, sources and consequences. In M. E. Lamb (Ed.), *The role of the father in child development* (3rd ed., pp. 66–103). New York: Wiley.

Pruett, K. (1985). Children of the fathermothers: Infants of primary nurturing fathers. In J. Hall,

E. Galenson, & R. Tyson (Eds.), *Frontiers of Infant Psychiatry* (pp. 375–380). New York: Basic Books.

Pruett, K. (1987). *The nurturing father.* New York: Warner.

Radin, N. (1981). Childrearing fathers in intact families: An exploration of some antecedents and consequences. *Merrill-Palmer Quarterly, 27,* 489–514.

Radin, N. (1982). Primary caregiving and role-sharing fathers of pre-schoolers. In M. E. Lamb (Ed.), *Nontraditional families: Parenting and child development* (pp. 173–204). Hillsdale, NJ: Lawrence Erlbaum Associates.

Radin, N. (1985, February). *Antecedents of stability in high father involvement.* Paper presented at the meeting of the Conference on Equal Parenting: Families of the Future. University of California, Chico.

Radin, N. (1994). Primary-caregiving fathers in intact families. In A. E. Gottfried & A. W. Gottfried (Eds.), *Redefining families: Implications for children's development* (pp. 55–97). New York: Plenum.

Radin, N. & Goldsmith, R. (1985). Caregiving fathers of preschoolers: Four years later. Merrill-Palmer Quarterly, 31, 375–383.

Russell, G. (1983). *The changing role of fathers?* St. Lucia, Queensland: University of Queensland Press.

Russell, G. (1989). Work/family patterns and couple relationships in shared caregiving families. *Social Behaviour,* 4(4), 265–284.

Russell, G. (1995). Sharing the pleasures and pains of family life. *Family Matters, 37,* 13–19.

Russell, G., James, D., & Watson, J. (1988). Work/family policies, the changing role of fathers and presumption of shared responsibility for parenting. *Australian Journal of Social Issues, 23,* 249–267.

Russell, G., & Radin, N. (1983). Increased paternal participation: Fathers' perspectives. In M. E. Lamb & A. Sagi (Eds.), *Fatherhood and family policy* (pp. 139–166). Hillsdale, NJ: Lawrence Erlbaum Associates.

Russell, G., & Radojevic, M. (1992). The changing role of fathers? Current understandings and future directions for research and practice. *Infant Mental Health Journal, 13,* 296–311.

Sagi, A. (1982). Antecedents and consequences of various degrees of parental involvement in childrearing: The Israeli project. In M. E. Lamb (Ed.), *Nontraditional families: Parenting and child development* (pp. 205–232). Hillsdale, NJ: Lawrence Erlbaum Associates.

Silverstein, L. B. (1996). Fathering is a feminist issue. *Psychology of Women Quarterly, 20,* 3–37.

Silverstein, L. B., & Phares, V. (1996). Expanding the mother-child paradigm. *Psychology of Women Quarterly, 20,* 39–53.

Williams, E., Radin, N., & Allegro, T. (1992). Sex role attitudes of adolescents reared primarily by their fathers: An 11-year follow-up. *Merrill-Palmer Quarterly, 38,* 457–476.

Chapter 5

The Consequences of Father Absence

SARA MCLANAHAN
JULIEN TEITLER
Princeton University

Increases in divorce and nonmarital childbearing have dramatically altered the family lives of children in the United States. Whereas in the early 1960s, nearly 90% of all children lived with both of their biological parents until age 18; today less than half of children grow up with both parents. Nearly one third are born to unmarried parents, the vast majority of whom never live together, and another one third are born to married parents who divorce before the child reaches adulthood. Many children who live apart from their biological fathers spend time in a stepparent family, and a substantial proportion of these children experience multiple disruptions.

These changes in children's family arrangements have created considerable concern among policy makers and have stimulated heated debate about the causes and consequences of father absence. Some analysts argue that growing up with a single mother is the primary cause of many of the United States' most serious social problems, including poverty, high school dropout, teen pregnancy, and delinquency (Blankenhorn, 1995; Popenoe, 1988; Whitehead 1993). Others argue that poverty and economic insecurity are the real culprits. Still others claim that the problems associated with family disruption are rooted in marital discord that begins long before the parents separate or divorce (Skolnick, 1991; Stacy, 1993).

In this chapter, we seek to shed some light on this debate by reviewing the findings of several major studies of the effects of father absence on adolescent behavior and transitions to young adulthood. We draw heavily from the research of McLanahan and Sandefur, as reported in their book, *Growing Up With a Single Parent: What Hurts, What Helps*, and we supplement their findings with studies by several other authors. Most of the studies discussed in this chapter use nationally representative, longitudinal data, and most contain large enough samples to allow us to distinguish among different types of single-parent families and to assess effects separately by gender, race, and social class. The primary data sets used in the review are the Panel Study of Income Dynamics (PSID), the National Lon-

TABLE 5.1
Description of Major Data Sets

The Panel Study of Income Dynamics (PSID) is a study of 5,000 families followed since 1968. The primary objective of the study was to measure income dynamics. These data are very useful for addressing questions about the relationships between father absence and family income. Because the PSID follows the children of panel families after they leave home and set up their own households, these data can be used to examine child outcomes such as graduating from high school and college and early childbearing.

The National Longitudinal Survey-Youth Cohort (NLSY) is a sample of approximately 13,000 young adults who were first interviewed in 1979 when they were between the ages of 14 and 21 and who have been interviewed each year since then. Like the PSID, these data contain information on family income during adolescence and on outcomes in young adulthood. They also measure children's test scores and attitudes toward school.

The High School and Beyond Study (HSB) is a study of more than 10,000 high school sophomores who were first interviewed in 1980 and were followed up in 1982, 1994, and 1996. It contains fairly detailed information on children's perceptions of parental practices—involvement, supervision, and support—which can be used to study the relationship between father absence and parental resources. The HSB data also provide information on educational attainment and early family formation.

The National Survey of Children (NSC) followed a randomly sampled cohort of children who were 7 to 11 years old in 1976. Initially, 2,279 children from 1,747 households were interviewed, as well as a parent. Follow-up interviews were conducted 5 years later and 11 years later (when the youth were 18 to 23 years old) for a subset of 1,146 youths. Detailed data on parent marital and relationship histories were collected as well as on child outcomes, including educational outcomes and fertility behaviors. Because the study is longitudinal and many of the families that eventually separated were intact in earlier waves, it is possible to control for family and youth characteristics prior to divorces.

The National Survey of Families and Households (NSFH) contains approximately 13,000 households interviewed in 1987 (NSFH-I) and again in 1993 (NSFH-II). These NSFH data provide retrospective information on children's family histories as well as extensive information on current parenting practices and family relationships.

The National Child Development Survey (NCDS) consists of a cohort of children born in Great Britain during the first week of March, 1958. The children were followed through age 33. The original sample consisted of 17,414 births (98% of those born during the 1-week period) but attrition reduced that number to 11,407 by the 33-year later follow-up.

---

gitudinal Survey of Youth (NLSY), the High School and Beyond Study (HSB), the National Survey of Children (NSC), the National Survey of Families and Households (NSFH), and the British National Child Development Study (NCDS). See Table 5.1 for more details on each of these data sets.

Our review focuses on three major outcomes in young adulthood: educational achievement and attainment, teenage childbearing and nonmarital childbearing, and early labor force attachment and earnings. Each of these outcomes or events represents a marker of how well prepared young adults are for productive and stable lives, and each is a pretty good predictor of future economic and social well-being. The review is organized around several questions: First, are children raised apart from their fathers worse off than children raised by both biological parents?

Next, are there variations in outcomes depending on personal characteristics and family structure characteristics? And finally, to what extent are differences in outcomes caused by father absence?

DIFFERENCES IN YOUNG ADULT OUTCOMES

Educational Attainment

Dropping out of high school is a relatively rare occurrence in the United States. About 73% of young people graduate from high school with a diploma. An additional 12% eventually receive a General Equivalency Diploma (GED). Although the incidence of dropping out of high school is relatively rare, the consequences are dramatic. Without a diploma and the skills associated with a high school education, most youth have a difficult time finding and keeping a steady job. The jobs that remain open to them tend to be poorly remunerated and to offer minimal prospects for advancement.

In their research on the consequences of single parenthood, McLanahan and Sandefur (1994) found that growing up with just one biological parent approximately doubles the risk of dropping out of high school, from approximately 15% in two-parent households (defined as households with two biological parents) to about 30% in one-parent households (defined as households in which one biological parent is absent). These differences hold up after controlling for parental race and educational level, family size, and place of residence. Effects of similar magnitude were obtained by Kiernan (1992), Furstenberg and Teitler (1994), and Wojtkiewicz (1993).

Family structure also appears to be important when we consider less extreme indicators of educational achievement and attainment, such as grade point average, school attendance, test scores, and college expectations. In the High School and Beyond Study, youth in two-parent families had slightly higher grade point averages than youth in one-parent families (4.13 vs. 3.92 on a one to seven scale; Astone & McLanahan, 1991). Youth in two-parent families also had somewhat higher standardized test scores (2.62 vs. 2.51) and were more likely to report that they expected to attend college (37.5% vs. 32.2%). Finally, youth raised by both biological parents had better school attendance records. The differences in educational achievement and absenteeism persist even when controlling for test scores. In contrast, both groups had similar, favorable, attitudes toward school and desires to go to college (80%).

College enrollment and graduation, too, are affected by father absence. In the NLSY, when controlling for family background characteristics, youth in disrupted families were less likely to attend college (54% vs. 59%) and less likely to graduate from college (20% vs. 27%; McLanahan & Sandefur, 1994). These results are consistent with those found in the other large nationally representative data sets.

Family Formation

Next we focus on a set of indicators that relate to early family formation, which is a strong predictor of future earnings potential and economic stability. Girls who become mothers while still in their teens are less likely than girls who delay child-bearing to finish high school and to gain on-the-job training. They are also more likely to become single mothers. Similarly, young women who are unmarried at the time they give birth have substantially higher poverty rates than young women who cohabit with a partner or husband.

All the studies we looked at found that adolescent girls in father absent families were more likely than girls in two-parent families to become teen mothers. About 20% of the young women in the studies we looked at had a child before age 20. The proportion was much higher in father-absent families, however. About 27% of the young women in the NLSY who did not live with their biological fathers became mothers by age 20 compared to 11% of those in two-parent families. Across the different data sets, the increase in teen childbearing associated with family disruption ranges from 50% in the HSB and NSFH to 145% in the NLSY (McLanahan & Sandefur, 1994).

Family structure is also associated with a higher incidence of premarital child-bearing. All of the studies we examined reported large differences in rates of non-marital childbearing between girls raised in father-absent homes as compared with girls raised in two-parent homes. The differences were particularly large for White and Hispanic women (Cherlin, Kiernan, & Chase-Lansdale, 1995; Fursten-berg & Kiernan, 1997; Wu, 1996; Wu & Martinson, 1993).

One way in which family structure may influence youth pregnancy and births is by affecting the timing of sexual initiation. Adolescents may respond to the breakup of their parents' marriage or to a new stepparent by *acting out*, which may include having sexual relationships earlier than they would otherwise have done. The earlier that youth initiate intercourse, the longer they are exposed to the risk of teenage pregnancy, and the less likely they are to use contraceptives, which also increases their chances of becoming pregnant. Data from several na-tional studies provide support for the contention that changes in family structure affect the timing of sexual initiation. In the NSC data set, 50% more youth from disrupted families had initiated sex before age 17 (Furstenberg & Teitler, 1994) and the age-specific rate of first sexual intercourse was found to be substantially higher in both the NLSY and NSFG studies (Wu, Cherlin, & Bumpass, 1997). These effects, however, do not appear to explain much of the effect of father ab-sence on early pregnancy (Kiernan & Hobcraft, 1997).

Labor Force Attachment and Earnings

A final indicator of future socioeconomic attainment is whether young men and women become attached to the labor force after leaving school. This transition is especially problematic for youth who do not finish high school or who do not receive postsecondary schooling. Youth who are neither in school nor at work are considered idle insofar as they are not building up their human capital, and here too, family structure appears to be relevant. Youth in two-parent families are more likely than are youth in one-parent families to make a successful transition from school into the labor market.

By their early 20s, a majority of young men are either in college or working, but a substantial minority are not. There is some discrepancy in how large this minority is—from 12% in the HSB to about 25% in the NLSY—due in large part to different ways of measuring idleness. However, the surveys are consistent in showing similar effects of father absence. Young men in one-parent families are about 1.5 times more likely to be idle than are those in two-parent families (Haveman & Wolfe, 1994; McLanahan, 1997; McLanahan & Sandefur, 1994). These effects subside only partly when differences in ability are taken into account. Four fifths of the effect of family structure on successful transitions remain, even after controlling for earlier test scores (McLanahan & Sandefur, 1994).

Studies of the effect of family structure on employment and earnings are scarce and report somewhat mixed findings, depending on the type of family structure. One study by Peters and Mullis (1997) showed that growing up with a single parent reduces earnings but living with a stepparent does not. Another study by Hauser and Sweeney (1997) found poorer labor market outcomes among children of divorced and remarried parents but not among children of widowed parents. The fact that these studies do not find consistent effects for all measures of employment and earnings suggest that, on balance, the effects are weak.

VARIATIONS IN FAMILY STRUCTURE EFFECTS

Thus far we have discussed the consequences of family structure for the average child who lives apart from his or her biological father. Not all youth are affected in the same way, however. In the next section, we discuss how different factors exacerbate or attenuate the effects of father absence. We focus first on differences in personal characteristics, such as race, gender, and socioeconomic status, to see if some groups are more affected than others by father absence. Then we focus on differences in the context in which father absence occurs, such as the type of family structure and the duration of exposure to different forms of family structure.

Variability By Personal Characteristics

There are several reasons for expecting the effects of father absence on youth to differ by gender, race, and parents' educational and occupational attainment. For instance, one might expect that boys are more dependent than girls on male adult role models, which might cause them to be more severely affected by the loss of a father. There is also some speculation that girls are more threatened and more likely to reject a new man in the household (Thornton & Camburn, 1987). Because their financial situation is more precarious and family disruption is more likely to deprive them of some of their most basic needs, children of parents with low education levels may be more vulnerable than children of middle-class families to father absence. Alternatively, children from middle-class families have more to lose as a consequence of divorce, and the absolute drop in income is probably greater for this group (see Newman, 1988, for example).

If low socioeconomic background exacerbates the impact of divorce, then Black youth may be more affected than White youth by father absence, because the former are poorer, on average, than the latter. Again, however, there may be compensatory factors that push in the opposite direction. The greater prevalence of divorce and single parenthood among Blacks may translate into more social supports in the community (Stack, 1974), softening the impact of father absence on youth.

Responses to changes in family structure may also depend on the type of neighborhood a youth lives in or the quality of the school he or she attends. Associating with peers involved in deviant behaviors may be a more likely consequence of divorce if youth reside in neighborhoods with a greater prevalence of delinquency. Both neighborhood and school quality are closely associated with socioeconomic status and race.

Gender roles may also affect how young men and women respond to the departure of a parent or the entrance of a stepparent. For instance, teenage girls may react to a change in family structure by engaging in early sexual activity or becoming pregnant, whereas boys may skip school or involve themselves in delinquent activities.

In most of the studies we looked at, father absence affects girls' educational achievement as much as it does boys'. A notable exception is early school leaving in the British NCDS survey. There, the stepfamily effect was significant and of similar magnitude for boys and girls, but the lone-mother effect was twice as large for boys as for girls. Because the NCDS includes every child born during one week of March, 1958, it is unlikely that the gender difference is the result of sampling variability. More likely, it reflects country level differences in education systems between Great Britain and the United States.

The effect of family structure on educational outcomes does not vary by race, either. Father absence approximately doubles the risk of dropping out of school regardless of a young person's race or ethnicity. In contrast, father absence has a much greater effect on the risk of having a child outside marriage among White and Hispanic teens than among Blacks. It doubles the risk for White and Hispanics, and increases the risk by about 25% for Blacks. Because Blacks have a higher underlying risk to begin with, the actual percentage point differences associated with father absence are much smaller across the different groups—2.5 points for Whites, 5 points for Hispanics, and 4 points for Blacks (Wu & Martinson, 1993).

Parental education appears to be linked to the influence of family structure changes, but only among Whites. The effects of family structure on dropout rates are highest for White youth with highly educated parents. The dropout for these youth is three times higher if their parents separated. Among Blacks and Hispanics, the family structure effect is similar across class levels.

Variability By Event Characteristics

As was true for personal characteristics, a number of theories suggest that the impact of father absence should depend on the circumstances surrounding the change in family structure or the type of family structure. For example, if growing up without a father figure is what matters, then we might expect youth who grow up in single mother households to do worse than youth who grow up in stepfamilies. We might also expect children who never lived with their biological fathers and whose mothers never married to do even worse than children who spend some of their childhood living with a father or adult male figure. Alternatively, if changes in family structure per se are consequential, then remarriage may not help and in fact may aggravate the circumstances because remarriage represents an additional change in family structure. Similarly, if loss is the underlying mechanism, children who never live with their fathers may suffer less than children who start off in two-parent families and subsequently experience family disruption. Finally, youth who live with single parents as a result of the death of the other parent may respond differently to father absence for several reasons. First, death is an involuntary event and children are less likely to feel abandoned by their fathers. Second, they are not exposed to postdivorce conflict between the parents. And third, widowed mothers are eligible for more economic support (i.e., survivors' insurance) than other single mothers. So, although children who experience the death of a father may be greatly affected emotionally, the long term consequences in terms of their family formation and achievement may be smaller for these other reasons.

Children's age at the time of their parents' separation may also be consequential. Research in developmental psychology has underscored the importance of early childhood in shaping cognition and psychological development (Baydar & Brooks-Gunn, 1991; Vaughn, Block, & Block, 1988). Parental separations that occur when the child is very young may therefore be more consequential than disruptions in later childhood. Here, too, a counterargument exists, however. If changes in family structure affect youth by leading them to engage in behaviors that compromise their future, then we might expect older youth to suffer greater long term consequences than very young children because the ways in which they "act out" (e.g. dropping out of school, engaging in unprotected sex) are more consequential in the long run. Very young children may be emotionally affected by the separation of their parents, but the behavioral responses are less likely to have long-term consequences.

The data from the national studies are consistent in showing that the effects of father absence on educational attainment, teen birth risk, and idleness vary little by type of family structure. The notable exception is the attainment of children living in households headed by widowed mothers. In the latter, children do nearly as well as children who live with both parents growing up. Otherwise, for children living in never-married mother families, divorced-single mother families, and stepfamilies, the high school completion rates, GPA, levels of school attendance, and rates of teen parenthood are considerably lower than for two-parent families. There is some evidence that children from never-married families do worse than those from disrupted families early on, but these differences in educational outcomes subside when youth reach their teens (Astone & McLanahan, 1991; McLanahan, 1997; McLanahan & Sandefur, 1994; Wojtkiewicz, 1993).

A few researchers have attempted to determine whether duration in a single-parent household or remarriage matter. The results are mixed. Using the NLSY study, Wojtkiewicz (1993) found that the negative effect on high school graduation of being born in a mother-only family did not increase with additional years but that a greater amount of time spent in stepfamilies had a negative effect, offsetting the initial positive effect of the mother remarrying. Wu and Martinson (1993) found some evidence of duration effects in mother-only family structures, though these varied by race. The difficulty in measuring the effect of duration spent in different family structures is that the effects are confounded with the type of family structure, the age of the child at the time of separation, and the number of family structure changes. Youth who have spend the longest periods of time in single-mother families are also likely to be those who were born outside of marriage, whose parents separated when they were very young, or whose custodial parent never remarried.

Findings on the influence of additional changes in family structure (subsequent separations and remarriages) are also somewhat mixed depending on the behaviors examined. Additional changes appear to be positively associated with out-of-wedlock childbearing (Wu & Martinson, 1993) but not with teen pregnancies or dropout rates (McLanahan & Sandefur, 1994).

The hypothesis that children whose parents separated during early childhood do worse than others does not bear out in the actual data. In fact, disruptions during adolescence appear to be more harmful than disruptions that occur at very young ages. This may be because adolescents act out in ways that are more consequential in the long run than the reactions of young children. It may also be because the greatest consequences of family disruptions are ephemeral and we are measuring outcomes closer to the age of the teens, or that the children whose parents separate when they are very young achieve as well as those whose parents remained intact throughout their childhood, but they have more severe emotional problems that our outcomes do not capture. This could explain why some of the clinical studies that are better at measuring the emotional well-being of youth and young adults find very large long-term effects of early separations.

The presence of other adults in the household, particularly grandmothers, has been shown to mitigate the negative effects of family disruption (Kellam, Ensminger, & Turner, 1977). However, this finding is not borne out in the large scale studies we looked at. In fact, grandmother presence is associated with much higher dropout rates than for single-mother-only families (60% vs. 31%). This may be because the youth in the studies we looked at are older than those in some of the other studies, as are their mothers and grandmothers. During later periods in the child's life, grandparents may provide less assistance and in fact may compete for some of the household resources rather than augmenting them. Conversely, they may move into the household in order to help the mother with a difficult child. But regardless of the effect of residential grandmothers, positive or negative, they cannot affect many households. Fewer than 5% of households in the United States with 16-year-old children include grandmothers (McLanahan & Sandefur, 1994).

WHY FATHER ABSENCE MATTERS

Having discussed the size and direction of family structure effects on different youth outcomes, we now turn our attention to why father absence matters. Here we focus on three possible explanations: economic deprivation and instability, lower levels of parental resources (the quantity and quality of parental time), and lower community resources. We also discuss the possibility that the correlation between father absence and child outcomes is due to some other factor (unobserved by the researchers) that leads certain parents to live apart and also reduces youth achievement and social adjustment.

Loss of Economic Resources

The argument that children who live apart from their fathers do less well than children who live with both parents because they have lower financial resources appears sound (Duncan & Brooks-Gunn 1997; see Mayer, 1997, for a conflicting view). With fewer resources, single parents may not be able to afford certain goods and services, which may affect the children's health and development. Poor parents may be constrained to live in neighborhoods with poor quality schools whereas families with higher incomes can afford to live in neighborhoods with better public schools or send their children to private schools if they wish. Single parents may also be forced to work more to make ends meet, thus having less time available to care for and help their children. Poverty may affect the emotional well-being of the parents, which in turn may translate into poorer family environments.

One-parent families headed by divorced or never-married mothers clearly do have significantly fewer financial resources than two-parent families and have reduced access to the advantages money can buy. According to the U.S. Census Bureau, in 1995 the median income of two-parent families with children under age 18 was slightly more than $50,000, as compared with somewhat less than $18,000 for female-headed families (U.S. Bureau of the Census, 1996). Half (50.3%) of families headed by single mothers were below the poverty line compared to 10% of two-parent families (Baugher & Lamison-White, 1996). Even in well-off families, income loss exerts a powerful negative force on children's well-being. Non-poor families lose, on average, 50% of their income when parents separate.

Although it is possible that economic disadvantage is a cause as well as a consequence of marital disruption, analyses looking at changes in earnings following separation confirm that a disruption during adolescence leads to a substantial loss of household income, regardless of the racial and educational backgrounds of the families. The PSID data show that, over 5 years, the median family income of stable families rose by roughly 8% while that of unstable families declined by 40%.

The PSID data also indicate that financial differences between one-parent and intact two-parent families account for a large portion—roughly one half—of the differences in outcomes between the two groups. The six percentage point difference in high school dropout between children in intact families and those in single mother families drops to a three percentage point difference after accounting for differences in income. Similarly, the differential in teen birth risk for women drops from 9% to 4%, and the idleness risk differential drops from 11% to 7% when income differences are taken into account (McLanahan & Sandefur, 1994).

Income differences explain none of the stepfamily effect, however. This is not so surprising because the income of stepfamilies is similar to that of intact two-parent families. We should also recall that remarriage appears to decrease dropout rates, at least initially, while it did not decrease the risks of teen births. This is consistent with our discussion about earnings differentials. Income variability should affect outcomes associated with achievement more than it affects family formation, which is likely to be more sensitive to emotional stability and family relationships.

The fact that children in stepfamilies do as poorly as do children in single-mother families on educational outcomes suggests that the effect of income loss or income instability is not easily redressed. The initial decline in income appears to have consequences that outlive future gains brought about by remarriage.

The evidence on the effect of mothers' employment on youth is not clear because, although mothers' employment may be associated with diminished maternal care, the benefits in terms of increased income appear to make up for that (Haveman, Wolfe, & Spaulding, 1991).

Loss of Parental Resources

Income is not the only type of family resource that promotes youth achievement. Parental resources may be equally important and may decline when families separate. Children clearly need their parents to read to them, discuss problems, help with homework, and supervise and discipline them. In a single-parent family, there is usually much less parenting to go around.

Interacting with the child's mother and building a new relationship with the child can be a difficult and painful experience, and many fathers respond by disengaging from their children (Wallerstein & Kelly, 1980). Children also have strong feelings about the separation, which may further damage the already weakened father–child relationship. Most children are angry when their parents separate; many feel betrayed and abandoned by their fathers, even in families where the parents' decision was mutual or where the father did not want the separation (Wallerstein & Kelly, 1980). Because the mother usually retains custody of the children, the father is often perceived as leaving the family, and the child's anger is often directed at him. If the parents are angry with each other, as is frequently the case, they may communicate this anger to the children, who may feel pulled in two directions. Even in families where the separation is amicable, nearly all children feel uncertain about how family members should relate to one another after a divorce. No matter what happens, children's trust has been seriously shaken.

Some fathers argue that they would like to see their children more often but are prevented from doing so by mothers. Just as social norms governing the economic obligations of nonresident fathers are weak, norms governing fathers' rights are also weak. Most states do not actively enforce a father's right to spend time with his child, nor do they prevent mothers from moving out of state. Even social service professionals may discourage fathers from maintaining contact with the child if they believe that contact will lead to conflict between the parents or endanger the mother.

Separation may also affect children's relationship with custodial mothers or the quality of the mothering that they receive. Forced to play two roles—that of both father and mother—single mothers may experience higher levels of stress, which, in turn, undermine parenting ability. In a lengthy review of research on Black families and children, Vonnie McLoyd (1990) argued that economic hardship and insecurity lead to poorer parenting practices among low-income, single mothers primarily through increases in depression and psychological distress. Similarly, in their study of middle-class families, Hetherington and her colleagues (1978) reported that the departure of the father from the household is associated with disruptions in household routines, such as meals and bed times, and inconsistent rules and discipline. Clearly, with their time, energy, and spirit stretched, some single mothers become too lenient and others become too rigid or strict.

The absence of the father also affects the system of checks and balances that help keep a two-parent household running effectively. Without a co-parent in the household to consult and to ensure that she "does the right thing," a single mother may exhibit uneven or inconsistent parenting behavior. Hetherington and her colleagues (1992) called this parental "buffering"—when one parent shields the children from erratic or dysfunctional behavior on the part of the other parent.

The quality of the parenting may continue to be lower even when the mother remarries. For a child who has already suffered through the parents' divorce, the appearance of a new stepparent can amount to yet another disruption (Hethering-ton & Clingempeel, 1992). With another change in personnel can come new rules, new roles, and new confusion. Where a child's welfare is concerned, a stepparent is no substitute for the departed real parent. Moreover, with less commitment to the child, the stepparent is not likely to be as effective a check on the mother's behavior as the biological father. Nor does the presence of a stepfather ensure that the mother will have more time and energy for parenting. Rather, a stepfather often competes with the children for the mother's time and attention, leaving the mother more stretched than ever (Furstenberg & Cherlin, 1991).

The argument that parental resources are beneficial and that they are greater in two-parent families than one-parent families presupposes that the quality of parenting is good. That may not always be the case, particularly in families that subsequently disrupt. In high conflict families or families with an abusive parent, the departure of a parent may result in an improvement in parenting. Parents who devoted much of their time and energy to arguing with one another may pay greater attention to their children after they are separated, and the child's exposure to conflict and to abuse may diminish, resulting in a net benefit to the child. So we might expect children in high-conflict families to do better and children in low-conflict families to do worse after their parents' separation.

Some of the empirical evidence bears out theories about the smaller amounts of parental time and contact available to children whose parents have separated or divorced. We know, for example, that a substantial proportion of children spend very little time with their biological fathers and that contact diminishes over time (Furstenberg, Morgan, & Allison, 1987). (It is interesting that most of the research based on large nationally representative data sets does not find a positive association between father's involvement and children's well-being [King, 1994; Furstenberg & Harris, 1992]).

We also know that single mothers are less likely than married mothers to eat regular meals with their children. On the other hand, single women compensate for missed dinners by reading to their children more often than their married peers (Astone & McLanahan, 1991; Thomson, McLanahan, & Braun-Curtin, 1992). The parents who are least involved appear to be remarried mothers, who both read less and eat fewer meals with their children. Although these findings appear to support the theory that stepparents diminish, rather than enhance, parental resources, the picture is more complex. When McLanahan and her colleagues combined the time spent with mothers and stepfathers, the total amount of time available to children in stepparent families surpassed that of time available to children with single mothers. In a small number of stepfamilies, children may enjoy access to more rather than diminished parental resources. They may even end up with more parent time than their counterparts from intact two-parent homes if they maintain significant contact with the departed parent and, perhaps, a stepparent.

Parents' authority may be measured by whether they know their children's whereabouts, whether they leave them home alone, whether they establish a curfew, and whether they set rules for television watching, bedtime, and household chores. The survey results demonstrate that single mothers exercise less control over their children than married mothers. The difference is particularly large when we compare married mothers, on the one hand, with never-married mothers and mothers cohabiting with partners, on the other. More than 30% of intact families report never leaving a child home alone, compared to 20% of mothers with partners and 19% of never-married mothers. Remarried mothers report about the same level of supervision as mothers in intact families.

Lower levels of parental involvement and control might predate the family disruption. Is it possible that parental conflict causes both the family disruption and the shortage of parental authority? McLanahan and Sandefur (1994) compared two sets of students from the HSB sample. Both groups had intact families in their sophomore years; the families in the first group were still intact by the senior year, whereas those in the second group had experienced divorce or separation. We would expect some decrease in involvement in either case, due simply to the children's maturation, but the decline was substantially greater in disrupted families. Moreover, parental aspirations for their children—an important determinant of their success in achieving a college education and career—increased between the sophomore and senior years in intact families, whereas it decreased in nonintact families. These results suggest that the disruption itself does indeed result in a decline in parental involvement.

We can establish how much the changes in parenting that accompany divorce and separation are a factor in the children's wellbeing by repeating the procedure we used to determine the effect of income. We observe how much the effect of family structure decreases after controlling for measures of postdisruption parental involvement, supervision, and aspirations. In the HSB, children from single-parent families had dropout rates that were six percentage points above those in two-parent families, they had teen birth risks that were five percentage points higher, and an idleness risk that was three percentage points higher. In an analysis that controlled for parental resources factors, these differences reduce to three, four and zero percentage points, respectively. In other words, on average, about half of the effect of family structure is due to differential allocations of parenting resources. This varies by outcome, however. Parenting factors explain all of the increase in the risk of idleness associated with family disruption, half of the effect on dropout, and very little of the effect on teen births. It also varies by type of family structure. Much less of the differences in outcomes between intact and stepparent families is accounted for by measures of parenting. This may be why other research that combined single and stepfamilies into one disrupted family type found that little of the effect of marital breakup was accounted for by parenting (Astone & McLanahan, 1991).

Conflict between the two divorced or separated parents is another important factor in the difficulties experienced by their offspring. Children in high-conflict families have more problems than children in low-conflict homes (Cummings & Davies, 1994; Emery, 1982). As we did with income, it is important to separate cause from effect. As many before us have pointed out, the conflict between the mother and father is often not the *result* of family instability so much as it is the *cause*. If alcoholism, addiction, or abuse is at the heart of the conflict, parental resources are lost regardless of a separation or divorce. In that instance, the departure of the addicted or violent parent may be in the best interest of the children.

We should note, however, that the degree and nature of the conflict bears consideration; not all divorces are caused by something as dramatic as addiction or violence. What if one parent abandons the marriage because he or she feels unfulfilled or falls in love with someone else? Even if the parents' relationship is less than perfect, the presence of both parents in the household may well be better for the children than a divorce or separation.

The empirical evidence also lends support to the contention that some of the effect of separation on youth outcomes is the result of parental conflict during and after the separation (Amato, 1993). In the NSFH, conflict accounts for a small part of the family disruption effect on a wide range of behavioral and achievement outcomes (from a just a few percentage points to approximately 20% depending on the outcome). And youth who were not exposed to high levels of conflict prior to their parents' separations were more likely to suffer adverse consequences of divorce (Hanson, 1995). This confirms the hypothesis discussed earlier that quantity of parenting interacts with quality of parenting to produce net benefits or losses for children. Children can gain from greater amounts of positive parenting and from lesser amounts of negative parenting.

These findings suggest that the loss of income and parental resources together account for much, if not most, of the difference in the measurable outcomes between children in single-parent and two-parent homes.

Loss of Community Resources

Community resources and social capital are another type of resource that may benefit youth and that may be affected by changes in family structure. Access to community resources—the web of facilities, programs, people, and care providers that can supplement and support parents' efforts—may be decreased when families are forced to move. The longer a family resides in the same community, the more likely the parents are to know about and take advantage of opportunities for their children. The loss of community resources can have deleterious effects on a child's education. An intact family that has been in the same community for a number of years learns about the best educational resources. The parents are more likely to know the after-school programs and the names of the best teachers, and they are more likely to have the connections and influence to access resources for which demand is high and supply limited. Additionally, the loss of income that typically accompanies divorce and separation constrains families to move to poorer communities. These communities may have fewer institutions and networks to begin with.

Children who do not move may also lose access to people and other resources. For example, they may be cut off from the custodial mother's network if the mother is stressed and depressed and does not have the time or energy to maintain those old relationships.

Social capital can also be an important factor in a child's success in landing a first job. Children in one-parent homes are more likely to live in poorer communities with fewer employment opportunities. In addition, a father might have valuable information about jobs and connections with the people who can give them; a child living apart from his father may be at a considerable disadvantage.

The evidence confirms that one-parent families do indeed move more frequently than intact families, and stepfamilies move even more often. The PSID data indicate that single-parent families move nearly twice as often as intact families, and stepfamilies move nearly three times as often. These data also provide some idea of the reasons behind relocations. Involuntary moves are much more common among single-mother households than two-parent families and stepfamilies. According to the PSID data, 34% of single mothers' moves are involuntary, more than double the proportion for intact families and stepfamilies. Just 6% of single mothers' moves were for "productive" reasons—a better job—in contrast with 21% of intact families' moves (Astone & McLanahan, 1994).

Although race is by far the most potent factor in determining the type of community in which a child resides, family structure also matters. Census tract data show that the average neighborhood quality of a White child in a single-parent family is poorer (greater prevalence of welfare use, higher dropout rates, higher poverty rates) than the average neighborhood quality of a White child in a two-parent family. Similarly, the High School and Beyond study indicates that children in stepfamilies and single-parent families, as compared with children from intact families, attend schools of lower quality, that is, schools with higher dropout rates and more student behavior problems.

Having shown that children in disrupted families tend to live in communities with inferior resources, we now ask: How significant a factor is this disadvantage in determining young adult outcomes? The community resource effect is particularly important with respect to stepfamilies, accounting for about 40% of the higher school failure rates. The HSB data show a five percentage point difference between the graduation rates of children in stepfamilies and children in intact families. However, when school quality and residential mobility are accounted for, the difference falls to three percentage points. For single parents who have not remarried, school quality and mobility do not explain the family structure differences in high school graduation.

Selection into One-Parent Families

Up until now, we have assumed that the correlation between father absence and poorer outcomes in young adulthood is causal, and we have tried to explain why father absence might lead to lower attainment. Many researchers, however, question this assumption and argue that some other variable may be responsible for the fact that children in one-parent families do less well than children in two-parent families. Some have argued that low income or high conflict might be the culprits because both these variables are associated with divorce as well as with negative youth outcomes. However, as discussed earlier, research has indicated that although low income and conflict can explain some of the disadvantages associated with divorce, differences between children in one-parent and two-parent families persist even after predivorce income and conflict are taken into account. Nevertheless, the issue of whether father absence causes children to do poorly or whether the correlation is due to the selection of problem families into divorce continues to plague this line of research. And the debate is likely to continue. Because we cannot randomly assign families to one-parent and two-parent statuses, we can never rule out the possibility that some other variable is responsible for both father absence and poorer outcomes in children.

Aside from controlling for variables, such as low income and conflict, which have been identified as alternative explanations for the effect of father absence, researchers have attempted to deal with the problem of "self-selection" into family type in a number of ways. Some have attempted to control for child well-being prior to divorce or separation. This approach allows the researcher to examine the effects of family disruption on changes in child outcomes, which is a more conservative test of the hypothesis that divorce causes reductions in child well-being. Cherlin and his colleagues (1991) used this strategy in an well-known *Science* paper, which showed that predivorce characteristics account for about half of the lower math scores among British boys. Others have used similar approaches with similar results (Hanson, McLanahan, & Thomson, 1997). Controlling for predivorce differences, however, has its limits. Many of the young-adult outcomes that we are most interested in—dropping out of high school, becoming a teen parent—are one-time events and do not lend themselves to the types of change models described earlier. More important, even if we could measure and control for all the predivorce characteristics we can identify, skeptics would still argue that some variable unmeasured by the researcher might be causing both father absence and lower achievement in children.

To get around this problem, some researchers have used statistical techniques to adjust for the possible correlation between family instability and unmeasured variables. To date, researchers who have applied these techniques have found that the negative effects of father absence persist, even using the more complicated models. However, these techniques themselves are based on very strong assumptions that may not be valid and that makes them less reliable measure of the true effect of father absence (Haveman & Wolfe, 1994; Manski, Sandefur, McLanahan, & Povers, 1992; McLanahan & Sandefur, 1994).

One of the most creative approaches to this problem is a study by Furstenberg and Kiernan (1997) who compared children whose parents divorced before they reached age 17 with children whose parents divorced when the child was older. Using the NCDS data, these researchers found that children whose parents stayed together until the child was an adult were less likely than children whose parents separated earlier to become teen mothers or have a child outside marriage. However, the data also show that delaying separation had no benefits on offsprings' chances of divorce or unemployment. These results indicate the growing up with a father is more important for early family formation than for other outcomes.

CONCLUSION

The evidence indicates that, on average, children who grow up with both biological parents do better in terms of human capital development and early family formation behavior than children who grow up with only one of their parents. It also indicates that a stepfather cannot fully compensate for the loss of a biological father. These results are surprisingly consistent across multiple outcomes and multiple data sets, and they do not appear to vary much by race/ethnicity, sex of the child, or parents' social class. The fact that there is such consistency across different surveys and different subgroups increases our confidence in the body of research on this topic.

We also find a good deal of consistency with respect to the mechanisms that underlie the negative association with father absence and attainment in young adulthood. Low income and income loss appear to account for about half of the disadvantage that comes from living apart from a father, and loss of social capital —defined as relationships between children and parents and children and other adults in the community—accounts for the rest.

In spite of the consistency in the evidence, we end our chapter with two important caveats. First, and most important, none of the findings discussed here are based on experimental data. Thus, we cannot say for sure that the correlation between father absence and child well-being is due to father absence per se as opposed to some other variable unobserved by the research, such as parents' psychological functioning or altruism. Either of these two variables might be causing both father absence and lower attainment among children. Because we cannot randomly assign couples to divorce and nondivorce, and because the best "natural" experiment we have thus far—the death of the father—is not really comparable, researchers will have to live with this unresolved question awhile. Because of the uncertainty, however, researchers should be cautious in their interpretation of the evidence and continue to explore ways of finding a suitable control group with which to compare children in father-absent families.

The second caveat has to do with the size of the effects and their probabilistic nature. Clearly, not all children raised in father-absent households do worse than children in two-parent families. The effects described in this chapter are differences in the risk of experiencing a negative event, such as stopping school prematurely or becoming a teen mother. Father absence is not a determining factor insofar as all children who experience such an event do worse than all children who do not. Moreover, the effect sizes that we observe in the various studies are not large enough to account for many of the problems facing adolescents and young adults today, as some people outside the academic community have suggested. In their book, *Growing Up With a Single Parent,* McLanahan and Sandefur (1994) note that eliminating divorce and single parenthood would reduce the high school dropout rate by only 33%. And this number is likely to overstate the benefits of a two-parent family because it is based on the assumption that the correlation between father absence and schooling is causal.

Finally, we would urge our colleagues not to let their personal biases or concerns about stigmatizing single mothers prevent them from seeking the truth about the strengths and weaknesses of mother-only families. Despite the scientific difficulties and the politicization of the topic, the subject is too important to be left to ideologues. In cases where children's and parents' interests may diverge, social science research is critically important both for clarifying the issues for parents and for informing the policy debate over how to best protect children in families where the biological parents choose to live apart.

REFERENCES

Amato, P. R. (1993). Children's adjustment to divorce: Theories, hypotheses, and empirical support. *Journal of Marriage and the Family, 55*(1), 23–54.

Astone, N., & McLanahan, S. (1991). Family structure, parental practices, and high school completion. *American Sociological Review, 56,* 309–320.

Astone, N., & McLanahan, S. (1994). Family structure, residential mobility, and school dropout: A research note. *Demography, 31*(4), 575–584.

Baugher, E., & Lamison-White, L. (1996). *Poverty in the United States: 1995* (U.S. Bureau of the Census, Current Population Reports, Series P60-194). Washington, DC: U.S. Government Printing Office.

Baydar, N., & Brooks-Gunn, J. (1991). Effects of maternal employment and child-care arrangements on preschoolers' cognitive and behavioral outcomes: Evidence from the children of the National Longitudinal Survey of Youth. *Developmental Psychology, 27*(6), 932–945.

Blankenhorn, D. (1995). *Fatherless America: Confronting our most urgent social problem.* New York: Basic Books.

Cherlin, A. J., Furstenberg, F. F., Chase-Landsdale, P. L., Kiernan, K., Robins, P., Morrison, D., & Teitler, J. (1991). Longitudinal studies of effects of divorce on children in Great Britain and the United States. *Science, 252,* 1386–1389.

Cherlin, A. J., Kiernan, K., & Chase-Lansdale, P. L. (1995). Parental divorce in childhood and demographic outcomes in young adulthood. *Demography, 32*(3), 299–318.

Cummings, E. M., & Davies, P. (1994). *Children and marital conflict: The impact of dispute and resolution.* New York: Guilford.

Duncan, G., & Brooks-Gunn, J. (Eds.). (1997). *Consequences of growing up poor.* New York: Russell Sage Foundation.

Emery, R. (1982). Interpersonal conflict and the children of discord and divorce. *Psychological Bulletin, 92,* 310–330.

Furstenberg, F. F., & Cherlin, A. J. (1991). *Divided families: What happens to children when parents part.* Cambridge, MA: Harvard University Press.

Furstenberg, F. F., & Harris, K. (1992). The disappearing American father? Divorce and the waning significance of biological parenthood. In S. J. South & S. Tolnay (Eds.), *The changing American family: Sociological and demographic perspectives* (pp. 197–223). Boulder, CO: Westview Press.

Furstenberg, F. F., & Kiernan, K. (1997). Delayed parental divorce: How much do children benefit? Unpublished manuscript.

Furstenberg, F. F., Morgan, S. P., & Allison, P. D. (1987). Paternal participation and children's well-being after marital dissolution. *American Sociological Review, 52,* 695–701.

Furstenberg, F. F., & Teitler, J. (1994). Reconsidering the effects of marital disruption: What happens to children of divorce in early adulthood? *Journal of Family Issues, 15*(2), 173–190.

Hanson, T. (1995). Does parental conflict explain why divorce is negatively associated with child welfare? Unpublished manuscript.

Hanson, T., McLanahan, S., & Thomson, E. (1997, March). Divorce, family resources, and children's welfare. Paper presented at the annual meeting of the Population Association of American, Washington, DC.

Hauser, R., & Sweeney, M. (1997). Does poverty in adolescence affect the life chances of high school graduates? In G. Duncan & J. Brooks-Gunn (Eds.), *Consequences of growing up poor* (pp. 541–595). New York: Russell Sage Foundation.

Haveman, R., & Wolfe, B. (1994). *Succeeding generations on the effects of investments in children.* New York: Russell Sage Foundation.

Haveman, R., Wolfe, B., & Spaulding, J. (1991). Childhood events and circumstances influencing high school completion. *Demography, 28*(1), 133–157.

Hetherington, M., Cox, M., & Cox, R. (1978). The aftermath of divorce. In J. H. Stevens, Jr. & M. Matthews (Eds.), *Mother–Child, Father–Child Relations* (pp. 110–155). Washington DC: National Association for the Education of Young Children.

Hetherington, M., & Clingempeel, W. G. (1992). *Coping with marital transitions: A family systems perspective.* Chicago: University of Chicago Press.

Kellam, S. G., Ensminger, M. E., & Turner, R. J. (1977). Family structure and the mental health of children. *Archives of General Psychiatry, 34,* 1012–1022.

Kiernan, K. (1992). The impact of family disruption in childhood on transitions made in young adult life. *Population Studies, 46,* 213–234.

Kiernan, K., & Hobcraft, J. (1997). Parental divorce during childhood: Age at first intercourse, partnership, and parenthood. *Population Studies, 51,* 41–55.

King, V. (1994). Nonresident father involvement and child well-being: Can dads make a difference? *Journal of Family Issues, 15*(1), 78–96.

Manski, C. F., Sandefur, G. D., McLanahan, S. S., & Povers, D. (1992). Alternative estimates of the effect of family structure during adolescence on high school graduation. *Journal of the American Statistical Association, 87,* 12–37.

Mayer, S. (1997). *What money can't buy: Family income and children's life chances.* Cambridge, MA: Harvard University Press.

McLanahan, S. (1997). Parent absence or poverty: Which matters more? In G. Duncan & J. Brooks-Gunn (Eds.), *Consequences of growing up poor* (pp. 35–48). New York: Russell Sage Foundation.

McLanahan, S., & Sandefur, G. (1994). *Growing up with a single parent: What hurts, what helps?* Cambridge, MA: Harvard University Press.

McLoyd, V. (1990). The impact of economic hardship on Black families and children: Psychological distress, parenting, and socioemotional development. *Child Development, 61,* 311–346.

Newman, K. (1988). *Falling from grace: The experience of downward mobility in the American middle class.* New York: Free Press.

Peters, H. E., & Mullis, N. C. (1997). The role of family income and source of income in adolescent achievement. In G. Duncan & J. Brooks-Gunn (Eds.), *Consequences of growing up poor* (pp. 340–381). New York: Russell Sage Foundation.

Popenoe, D. (1988). *Disturbing the nest: Family change and decline in modern societies.* New York: A. de Gruyter.

Skolnick, A. S. (1991). *Embattled paradise: The American family in an age of uncertainty.* New York: Basic Books.

Stack, C. (1974). *All our kin.* New York: Harper & Row.

Stacy, J. (1993). Good riddance to "The family": A response to David Popenoe. *Journal of Marriage and the Family, 55*(3), 545–547.

Thomson, E., McLanahan, S., & Braun-Curtin, R. (1992). Family structure, gender, and parental socialization. *Journal of Marriage and the Family, 54,* 25–37.

Thornton, A., & Camburn, D. (1987). The influence of the family on premarital sexual attitudes and behavior. *Demography, 24*(3), 323–340.

U.S. Bureau of the Census. (1996). Money Income in the United States: 1995 (Current Population Reports, Series P60-193). Washington, DC: U.S. Government Printing Office.

Vaughn, B. E., Block, J. H., & Block, J. (1988). Parental agreement on child rearing during early childhood and the psychological characteristics of adolescents. *Child-Development, 59*(4), 1020–1033.

Wallerstein, J., & Kelly, J. (1980). *Surviving the breakup: How parents and children cope with divorce.* New York: Basic Books.

Whitehead, B. D. (1993, April). Dan Quayle was right. *Atlantic Monthly, 47,* 84.

Wojtkiewicz, R. (1993). Simplicity and complexity in the effects of parental structure on high school graduation. *Demography, 30*(4), 701–717.

Wu, L. (1996). Effects of family instability, income, and income instability on the risk of a premarital birth. *Demography, 61,* 386–406.

Wu, L., Cherlin, A., & Bumpass, L. (1997). *Family structure, early sexual behavior and premarital births* (Institute for Research on Poverty Discussion paper, DP#1125-97), University of Wisconsin, Madison.

Wu, L., & Martinson, B. (1993). Family structure and the risk of a premarital birth. *American Sociological Review, 58,* 210–232.

Chapter 6

Noncustodial Parents

Ross A. Thompson
Deborah J. Laible
University of Nebraska

What does it mean to be a parent? What are the core responsibilities and privileges of parenting that help to define this role to oneself and in the eyes of others? To most individuals, parenting involves essential responsibilities: providing for economic and maternal needs, offering guidance and instruction, and exercising authority in the lives of offspring. It also involves the satisfaction of sharing everyday experiences with children that provide a foundation for affection, mutual understanding, and developing relationships. When one or more of these facets of parenting are denied them, adults are likely to feel that their parenting role has been significantly abridged.

A noncustodial parent must recreate a parenting role in which many of these responsibilities and privileges are limited. Although the adult is legally recognized as a parent and usually provides some financial support, the informal obligations and prerogatives of parenting must be adapted to a visiting relationship that is often experienced as constrained and artificial. As a consequence, although many noncustodial parents maintain satisfying lifelong relationships with their offspring, many others eventually become peripheral figures. Not only parents but also children perceive the limitations of a noncustodial parenting relationship. In one study, only half the school-age children from divorced homes included their noncustodial fathers when asked to list their family members, although virtually all included the biological parent with whom they lived and most also listed stepfathers, if their residential parent had remarried (Furstenberg & Nord, 1985). In a sense, noncustodial parenting challenges not only the integrity of contemporary concepts of *parenting,* but also understandings of *family.*

There are, as a result, few socially supported, constructive roles that help to establish noncustodial parenting. In most respects, the noncustodial parent is an ill-defined figure, identified in public perception more by the responsibilities that are abdicated (e.g., the "deadbeat dad," the absentee father, the abandoning mother) than by positive attributes. This is surprising in light of the prevalence of this role in contemporary society. Due to the current plateau of divorce rates at historically high levels, since the 1970s more than one million couples have divorced annually (Shiono & Quinn, 1994). About 60% of these divorces involve children, with an increasing proportion of these involving young children (Cherlin, 1992; Norton & Miller, 1992). Remarriages tend to be more unstable than first marriages, which means that adults may have caregiving responsibilities to offspring from more than one marriage, while simultaneously being stepparents to children to whom they are not biologically related (Cherlin, 1992; Hetherington & Clingempeel, 1992). Furthermore, single-parent families (constituting 3 out of 10 family groups) are also changing significantly, with father-only families the most rapidly growing family type in the United States, and noncustodial mothers an increasingly common parenting role (Meyer & Garasky, 1993; Norton & Miller, 1992).

Noncustodial parents strongly influence their offspring whether they are involved or disinterested parents because of the impact of their commitment on children. A child's socioemotional, economic, and relational well-being are meaningfully affected by the nature and depth of a noncustodial parent's involvement with them, and thus understanding the reasons that parents become devoted or distant after divorce is crucial to advancing children's best interests. This chapter surveys the factors that either enhance or undermine effective noncustodial parenting and their relevance to public policies that can strengthen the quality of the parent–child relationship. This review draws primarily on research concerning noncustodial fathers that is supplemented, whenever possible, by comparative studies of noncustodial mothers. The chapter opens with consideration of the various influences affecting the adaptation to postdivorce life of mothers and fathers who are noncustodial parents. Issues concerning the maintenance of a visiting relationship with offspring and fidelity to child support orders are considered next because they constitute two of the most important contributions of noncustodial parents to a child's well-being. In a final concluding section, the implications of this research for divorce policy are considered.

ADAPTING TO POSTDIVORCE LIFE

Understanding noncustodial parenting requires an appreciation of divorce itself: how it is initially experienced, how adults negotiate and adapt, and why parents undergo the process of divorce in gendered ways. This is because the quality of postdivorce parenting is directly tied to the success with which custodial and noncustodial parents accommodate to the demands of single parenting, negotiate a new relationship with the ex-spouse, and meet the other challenges of postdivorce life.

Men and women experience different joys and challenges in marriage, and they remain in difficult marriages for different reasons (Bernard, 1972). For women, fears concerning inadequate financial resources sometimes keep them in unhappy relationships, whereas for men, worries over losing contact with off-spring can have the same effect (Hetherington & Stanley-Hagan, 1986, 1997). Consequently, divorce is experienced differently by each partner (Emery, 1994; Hetherington & Tryon, 1989). Women report having anticipated the end of their marriage long before discussing divorce with the partner and, after doing so, they are prepared to move ahead into a new life. Men, by contrast, often do not accept the end of marriage and resist the negotiations over divorce and custody that signal its demise.

Men and women thus enter into divorce negotiations differently because of the different readiness, expectations, and emotions that accompany marital dissolution. They enter into negotiations differently also because of the different marital roles and responsibilities they assumed for economic provision, domestic labor, and childrearing. For most couples, the mother's assumption of the physical custody of offspring after divorce and the father's noncustodial parenting role are the natural consequences of the childrearing responsibilities assumed by each during their marriage (Maccoby, 1995; Thompson, 1994). Although men are usually financially advantaged after divorce because of the career assets they developed during marriage, women (whether or not they also worked outside the home) have a stronger claim to child custody because of their predominant marital role in child care. Men and women also enter divorce negotiations differently because of their need to "bargain in the shadow of the law" (Mnookin & Kornhauser, 1979). There is some evidence, for example, that fathers do not assert a claim to as much physical custody of offspring as they want, perhaps on the advice of legal counsel who believe that a claim for sole or joint physical custody is likely to fail in court (Maccoby, 1995; Maccoby & Mnookin, 1992). Divorce negotiations concerning child custody and visitation are thus shaped by a variety of formal and informal influences on each parent.

The outcome of these negotiations is highly predictable, however, and has been consistent over the past several decades. Although joint custody is an option in most states, and although an increasing number of couples share legal custody of their offspring after divorce, between 85% and 90% of children from divorced families live primarily with their mothers, with around 10% living primarily with their fathers (Fox & Kelly, 1995; Kelly, 1994; Meyer & Garasky, 1993; Seltzer, 1990). To be sure, these formal custody awards often mask considerable flexibility and change over time in the childrearing responsibilities assumed by each parent after divorce in response to changing life circumstances, temporary needs, and the changing preferences of offspring (Maccoby & Mnookin, 1992). Yet the consensual decision by the overwhelming majority of divorcing couples that children (especially young children) should be primarily in the care of their mothers is one of the most striking, and enduring, characteristics of postdivorce life. This decision radically changes the nature of each parent's relationship with offspring.

The challenges of creating new relationships with offspring are not the only postdivorce relational challenges facing noncustodial parents. They must also negotiate a new relationship with the ex-spouse. This is often surprising to former partners who enter divorce with the expectation of making a clean break from a marital partner, only to discover that because children are involved, ex-spouses must continue to confront each other in the context of visitation negotiations, support arrangements, and other child-oriented concerns. Moreover, continuing encounters between ex-spouses are even more necessary when they share legal custody of offspring and must consult concerning educational decisions, health and medical care, insurance, and other matters. Some former spouses abdicate these responsibilities to offspring by avoiding interaction (and potential conflict) as the noncustodial parent gradually becomes an absent figure. When they remain in contact, however, parents vary considerably in the extent to which they can negotiate amicably about child-related issues. Their success in doing so is a significant predictor of children's adjustment (Cummings & Davies, 1994; Emery, 1988), as well as of the ease with which the noncustodial parent remains involved in the child's life through regular and reliable visitation and child support.

Noncustodial Fathers

In the typical situation in which mothers assume physical custody and fathers become noncustodial parents of offspring, mothers and fathers adapt to life after divorce in very different ways (Emery, 1994; Furstenberg & Cherlin, 1991). Mothers must begin to juggle full-time jobs, childrearing, and domestic and other responsibilities that were formerly shared with a spouse. These challenges can be overwhelming and are especially difficult when they are accompanied by having to search for a job (or a second job), find (or substantially revise) child-care arrangements, move to a new residence, engage in protracted and acrimonious negotiations with the ex-spouse over visitation or child support, or cope with a markedly reduced standard of living (see McLanahan & Teitler, chap. 5, this volume). Not surprisingly, during the period immediately following divorce, mothers often experience exhaustion and depression, difficulties in their relationships with offspring owing to the adjustment difficulties that children experience, and the emotional impact of these personal challenges.

Anger and bitterness, diminished self-esteem, and feelings of loss and regret are sometimes felt more significantly by fathers during the period after divorce because of their experience of simultaneously losing spouse, children, and residence (Hetherington & Stanley-Hagan, 1986, 1997). Noncustodial fathers must also cope with legal child-support obligations, altered social support networks, and new domestic responsibilities as a consequence of divorce. Whereas financial worries are among the preeminent concerns for divorcing mothers, relational concerns are preeminent for fathers. Creating a new, workable visiting relationship with offspring is among the greatest challenges and stresses for noncustodial fathers, who often experience feelings of being cut off or detached from their children shortly after divorce. Initially, the challenges to visitation consist of establishing consensual arrangements with the former spouse for seeing offspring, creating a home environment suitable for children to visit, overcoming inexperience with everyday caretaking routines, and coping with children's emotional problems in adjusting to divorce (Fox & Blanton, 1995). Subsequent challenges to the maintenance of visitation include keeping current with children's ongoing life experiences and developmental achievements and remaining emotionally connected with them when they are away. Other challenges include integrating visitation with changes in the parent's life (such as new intimate relationships) and the custodial parent's circumstances (such as a residential move or remarriage). It is perhaps unsurprising that difficulties associated with visitation are among the most significant postdivorce stressors for noncustodial fathers, contributing to feelings of guilt, sadness, loneliness, and anxiety (Kitson, 1992).

Noncustodial Mothers

Whereas noncustodial fathers are a social commonplace, mothers who become noncustodial parents after divorce assume a strikingly unconventional role (Arditti, 1995; Depner, 1993; Herrerias, 1995). Because motherhood is commonly identified as entailing a primary, fundamental commitment to childrearing, mothers who do not assume physical custody of offspring after divorce may elicit suspicion that they are selfish or unfit parents. Consequently, many noncustodial mothers report feeling guilty and uncomfortable in this role (Greif, 1987; Greif & Pabst, 1988; Herrerias, 1995). Moreover, children may experience considerably greater disruption in the transition from a typical intact family to a postdivorce family in which the mother is a noncustodial parent (Depner, 1993). Confusion, distress, and feelings of rejection are among the reported reactions of children who must adapt to a visiting relationship with their mothers (Herrerias, 1995; Warshak & Santrock, 1983).

Although fathers enter into noncustodial parenting as a natural and expected consequence of their predivorce involvement with offspring, the transition to noncustodial mothering is more complicated. The causes of noncustodial mothering are also more complex. The large majority of the mothers interviewed report relinquishing their claim to custody willingly, but also describe circumstances that may have made an alternative decision difficult, such as significant financial difficulties, a destructive relationship with the ex-spouse, and personal problems. For other mothers, the decision to become a noncustodial parent was a result of the father's strong commitment to parenting, their own competing interests, or children's preferences (Depner, 1993; Greif, 1987; Greif & Pabst, 1988; Herrerias, 1995).

Although there are differences in how mothers and fathers typically assume a noncustodial parenting role, their views of the challenges and difficulties of this role are very similar. Mothers without custody report, just as noncustodial fathers do, missing daily contact with offspring, not having enough time with their children, conflict with the custodial parent over visitation arrangements, and experiencing loneliness and guilt over their parental role (Arditti, 1995; Greif, 1987; Greif & Pabst, 1988). They also often experience difficulty integrating a noncustodial parenting role into the other changes occurring in their postdivorce lives.

Taken together, the personal, economic, social, and relational adjustments experienced by mothers and fathers during the first year after divorce are potentially overwhelming. These adaptations make the task of negotiating new parental roles with offspring, whether as a custodial or a noncustodial parent, or as a mother or a father, especially challenging. Consequently, it is not surprising that the first two years after marital dissolution are a particularly crucial period for the reconstitution of domestic life, the renegotiation of family relationships, and the establishment of enduring themes of postdivorce life for all family members. For noncustodial parents, the initial two postdivorce years are a period when fidelity to visitation and child support obligations either becomes established or begins to decline. Given the significant changes that occur in the lives of all family members during this period, it is not surprising that patterns of predivorce involvement with offspring are only moderately predictive of the amount of postdivorce commitment shown by noncustodial fathers to their children (Hetherington, Stanley-Hagan, & Anderson, 1989; Kruk, 1991; Wallerstein & Kelly, 1980). In other words, the quality of the relationship between the noncustodial parent and his or her offspring is shaped primarily by influences of postdivorce life, not by what preceded it.

VISITATION

To offspring as well as parents, regular and reliable visitation is one of the most important obligations of the noncustodial parent. Children intensely desire continuing contact with both parents and are dismayed when the visiting parent sees them inconsistently or not at all (Hetherington, 1989; Hetherington et al., 1989; Wallerstein & Kelly, 1980; Warshak & Santrock, 1983). To both ex-spouses, moreover, the noncustodial parent's fidelity in visiting regularly is a significant marker of a broader commitment to the child. Consequently, research reviewed in this section explores why most noncustodial parents gradually disengage from their offspring during the initial years following divorce and whether this can be altered by changing the conditions of visitation or the broader circumstances of postdivorce life or both.

Although visitation may initially be high during the first year after the divorce, during each successive year noncustodial fathers tend to visit less and less frequently (Furstenberg & Nord, 1985; Furstenberg, Nord, Peterson, & Zill, 1983; Hetherington & Stanley-Hagan, 1986; Maccoby & Mnookin, 1992; Seltzer, 1991b). However, there is recent evidence that by comparison with widely cited earlier estimates (i.e., Furstenberg & Nord, 1985; Furstenberg et al., 1983), paternal visitation rates have increased meaningfully in recent years (Kelly, 1994; Maccoby, Buchanan, Mnookin, & Dornbusch, 1993; Maccoby & Mnookin, 1992; Seltzer, 1991b; Seltzer & Brandreth, 1994; Zill & Nord, 1996). Noncustodial fathers themselves report higher rates of visitation than do custodial mothers, on whose reports all other studies rely (Braver, Wolchik, Sandler, Fogas, & Avetina, 1991; Seltzer & Brandreth, 1994). Moreover, contrary to popular portrayals of noncustodial fathers, the large majority of fathers who have little or no contact with their offspring regret this loss (Greif, 1997). Noncustodial mothers show greater fidelity and reliability in visitation than fathers do, although their visits also decline significantly with time (Furstenberg & Nord, 1985; Furstenberg et al., 1983; Greif & Pabst, 1988; Maccoby & Mnookin, 1992; Zill & Nord, 1996). Although popular portrayals of the absent father in postdivorce life require some revision, many noncustodial parents gradually lose contact with their offspring, and thus it remains important to understand the contributors to noncustodial parents' fidelity to, or abandonment of, their visitation obligations.

The Visiting Parent–Child Relationship

One of the challenges to visitation that is commonly cited by fathers and mothers is the unnatural and uncomfortable circumstances in which visitation commonly occurs (Fox & Blanton, 1995; Kruk, 1991). Indeed, the term *visitation* seems inconsistent with the parenting role (which connotes an intimate, ongoing, involved relationship), and the psychological and physical conditions of visitation often pose obstacles to the maintenance of satisfying relationships with offspring. These conditions are described in this way by researchers who have studied noncustodial fathers:

> At its core, the visiting relationship is ambiguous and therefore stressful. A visiting father is a parent without portfolio. He lacks a clear definition of his responsibility or authority. He often feels unneeded, cut off from the day-to-day issues in the child's life that provide the continuing agenda of the parent-child relationship. The narrow constraints of the visit are often reflected in the need to schedule a special time and place to be with one's child, the repeated leave-taking, and the need to adapt flexibly to the complex changing needs of the child. The forced interface with new adult figures within what sometimes is the father's former home, and the continued crossing and recrossing of new family boundaries in the child's life, are murky and burdensome aspects of the visiting parent's role because they are largely undefined and therefore unsupported by social convention. They generate a changing mix of frustration, anxiety and gratification. The conflicting psychological strains on the visiting father usually pull him between the need to remain close to his children out of his love, dependence, sense of commitment, and legal obligation, and the countervailing desire to take flight in order to escape the painful feelings associated with the failed marriage. For a significant number of fathers, the urge to take flight can be irresistible. (Wallerstein & Corbin, 1986, p. 114)

Because parent–child relationships are nurtured and renewed in the ordinary variety of daily, shared activities—whether they consist of domestic tasks, bedtime routines, shopping trips, or supervising homework assignments—the visiting relationship must capture these features of everyday life for postdivorce relationships with offspring to remain vital and relevant (Lamb, in press). Unfortunately, the scheduling of visits during weekends or vacations, usually in settings divorced from the child's neighborhood, school, and peer networks, and requiring an interruption of the typical patterns of daily life for the child (as well as the noncustodial parent) means that the visiting relationship is often experienced as constrained and artificial. A noncustodial parent's well-meaning efforts to organize visits around recreational or social activities, to be indulgent or permissive during their brief times together, or to coordinate visits with trips to see extended family members further contributes to the sense that the noncustodial parent has ceased to function as a typical or genuine parent in the child's life.

Consistent with this view, several studies have found that visiting relationships with fathers are more likely to be satisfactorily maintained over time when a visitation schedule is created early after the divorce and when overnights are included on the schedule to provide children with a place to stay and a sense of predictable family routine (Maccoby et al., 1993; Maccoby & Mnookin, 1992; Wallerstein & Kelly, 1980; Zill & Nord, 1996). One study that compared noncustodial mothers with noncustodial fathers found that the former group were more likely to have overnight visits with the child and to spend a week or more with the child, and offspring reported that the noncustodial mother's home was more like their own and they had a place to keep their things there (Furstenberg & Nord, 1985). It is possible that the greater reliability of visitation by noncustodial mothers compared to fathers derives from the mother's greater capacity to use these ways to reestablish a sense of familiar daily routine during her visits.

Predictors of Visitation Success or Failure

The extent to which the noncustodial parent can recapture or recreate the varieties of everyday experiences that support parent–child relationships is thus an important predictor of the reliability and satisfaction of visitation (Fox & Blanton, 1995; Hetherington & Stanley-Hagan, 1986, 1997). As earlier noted, the duration of time since the divorce is also a predictor of the reliability of visitation, with less consistency in noncustodial parent–offspring contact as years pass because noncustodial parents and children each develop new interests, relationships, and experiences that are not shared with the other. There are other factors that influence the ongoing quality or quantity of contact between noncustodial parents and their children (see Furstenberg et al., 1983; Hetherington & Stanley-Hagan, 1986, 1997; Maccoby & Mnookin, 1992; Seltzer, 1991b; Seltzer & Bianchi, 1988; Seltzer, Schaeffer, & Charng, 1989; Wallerstein & Kelly, 1980; Zill & Nord, 1996). The residential relocation of either parent can pose a significant obstacle to visitation, especially if a parent moves a considerable distance away. Visitation frequency is positively related to the reliability of child support payments, although in complicated ways, as discussed later. The remarriage of either parent diminishes the frequency of visitation, especially if it entails the assumption of responsibility for stepchildren by the noncustodial parent, or that parent's belief that remarriage of a former spouse diminishes the need for child support (see Hetherington & Stanley-Hagan, this volume). Visitation frequency is also related to socioeconomic status because the enhanced resources that high income and education provide support the maintenance of a visiting relationship.

In addition to these influences, the quality of the postdivorce relationship between former spouses is a significant influence on the reliability of noncustodial parent visitation. The importance of the interparental relationship begins at the time of divorce, because how the divorce was negotiated (involving litigation, mediation, or private agreement) foreshadows the reliability of visitation years later (Zill & Nord, 1996). The extent of cooperation or acrimony between parents after divorce also strongly predicts the reliability of visitation. This is to be expected. Negotiating visitation arrangements forces ex-partners to try to agree with each other and, when they remain angry and hostile, parents can avoid painful encounters simply by reducing or obstructing visits with offspring. Fathers may simply neglect to remain in contact with their children. Mothers may be unavailable when visits are scheduled to occur, or may reschedule visits for inconvenient times or raise objections to alternative visitation arrangements. The extent to which visitation can remain a forum for ongoing animosity between former spouses is reflected in the frequency with which conflict over visitation continues to characterize their postdivorce relations: according to some researchers, one fourth to one half of fathers report serious visitation conflicts with their ex-spouses (Braver et al., 1991; Fulton, 1979; Furstenberg, 1988; Furstenberg et al., 1983; Haskins, 1988; Pearson & Thoennes, 1988). Unfortunately, when conflict between parents is extreme—entailing physical and verbal aggression—the potential benefits of noncustodial parent visitation may be undermined by the risks to the child of becoming enmeshed in interparental conflict, although it is not known how extreme interparental conflict must be for the benefits of visiting to be destroyed (Johnston, 1994).

Many of the predictors of visitation success or failure reflect the dynamics of postdivorce family life: residential relocation, remarriage, and even the changing interests and needs that accompany the passage of time can each undermine visitation as family members create new lives after marital dissolution. For this reason, the initial years after divorce are crucial for establishing patterns and contexts of visitation that will enable the parent–child relationship to be more easily maintained into future years. Creating a visitation plan that enables regular and everyday kinds of interaction between parent and child, developing a means of negotiation between former spouses that avoids acrimony in the interests of cooperating for the sake of offspring, and embarking on a reliable plan of child support payments can each contribute to the psychological context that fosters the maintenance of a visiting relationship. The very limited research concerning noncustodial mothers suggests that similar factors predict the reliability of this visiting relationship also (e.g., Greif & Pabst, 1988; Herrerias, 1995).

Visitation and Children's Best Interests

How important is visitation to a child's well-being after divorce? There are some suggestive studies of children living with their fathers to indicate that children benefit from reliable contact with their noncustodial mothers, although the findings are insufficiently strong to be definitive (Camera & Resnick, 1988; Maccoby et al., 1993). By contrast, there is more research concerning the effects of continuing contact with noncustodial fathers, but conclusions are equally uncertain. Comprehensive reviews of this research indicate that, although some studies indicate that children consistently benefit from frequent visitation with their noncustodial fathers, other studies yield negligible effects—and a few studies indicate detrimental results from paternal visits (Amato, 1993, 1994). Taken together, this research literature may indicate that the question being posed is too simple. Rather than considering whether children uniformly benefit from paternal visitation, it may be more important to consider the mediators of these benefits. For example, children may not benefit from visits with their fathers when interparental conflict is high because of the problems that occur when they become embroiled in parental squabbling and the loyalty conflicts that accompany visitation (Amato & Rezac, 1994; Healey, Malley, & Stewart, 1990). Conversely, children may benefit from visitation when the overall quality of the father–child relationship is positive (Hetherington et al., 1989; Wallerstein & Kelly, 1980) and when they can experience a genuinely parental relationship rather than an entertaining or recreational one (Amato, 1997). Contrary to initial expectations, therefore, the benefits to children of noncustodial father visitation may be contingent rather than certain. Because the quality and quantity of paternal visitation is tied to a variety of other influences that shape children's postdivorce life, the benefits of visitation depend on the psychological contexts in which it occurs.

This conclusion is affirmed by the results of a recent meta-analysis by Amato and Gilbreth (1997), who surveyed the literature on the effects of noncustodial fathers on their children's well-being. In addition to examining the importance of visitation frequency and the payment of child support, Amato and Gilbreth also identified two other features of postdivorce fathering that had previously been neglected: active parenting (reflected in activities such as helping with homework, participating in projects with the child, using noncoercive discipline to deal with misbehavior, listening to children's problems and giving advice, and related behaviors), and emotional bonding (indexing the strength of the emotional ties between father and child, including affection, mutual respect, and identification). They found that the strength of the emotional bond between fathers and children, and the extent to which fathers engage in active parenting, are each strongly predictive of children's well-being (in the case of active parenting, its influence is even stronger than the influence of economic child support). In other words, it is important that fathers are capable of functioning like real parents during their encounters with offspring, and the quality of their parenting during visitation may be even more important to children than the sheer frequency of visits. Both active parenting and emotional bonding may—or may not—occur in the context of conventional visitation arrangements, but they are important to postdivorce parenting.

A renewed focus on the quality of parenting as well as the frequency of visits is also consistent with the desires of offspring following divorce. Because children themselves strongly desire to maintain relationships with both parents after divorce, continuing visitation is likely to contribute to their happiness and well-being. To the extent that children may also benefit, as they grow up, from ongoing access to their fathers and mothers for guidance and support and a link to their family heritage, efforts to ensure that noncustodial parents do not disappear from the child's life after divorce are worthwhile. In some respects, the reliability of parental visitation is not just a predictor of the family's postdivorce adjustment but also one of its outcomes. When parents experience or anticipate a meaningful role in the lives of offspring, they are likely to confirm their identities as parents in a reliable visiting relationship despite the obstacles they encounter (Braver, Wolchik, Sandler, & Sheets, 1993; Braver, Wolchik, Sandler, Sheets, Fogas, & Bay, 1993). The fidelity of a significant and growing proportion of noncustodial parents in maintaining regular contact with offspring several years after divorce attests to the fact that diminished visitation is neither a necessary nor a long-term accompaniment of noncustodial parenting.

A visiting relationship with a child is challenging to establish and maintain because of its inherent contradictions: it is difficult for a parent to remain intimately involved in a child's experience in contexts that are divorced from the relational routines of everyday life. Yet the factors contributing to a successful visiting relationship (e.g., regularly scheduled visits with overnights, interparental cooperation, geographic proximity, financial support) enable noncustodial parents and children to recover elements of satisfactory family experience in their postdivorce lives. Although the research evidence remains unclear, there are many reasons to believe that the creation of such visiting arrangements will advance children's well-being.

CHILD SUPPORT

Child support is, like visitation, one of the central obligations to their offspring of noncustodial parents after divorce. This is especially true in light of the economic hardship commonly experienced by custodial parents, especially mothers. Although researchers disagree concerning the extent of their financial decline, virtually all agree that custodial mothers and their offspring suffer considerable economic distress after divorce, primarily owing to the loss of the father's economic contribution (Teachman & Paasch, 1994). The research reviewed in this section explores why this is so, what accounts for the failure of many fathers to provide financially for their offspring, and what avenues exist for improving children's postdivorce economic well-being. The discussion focuses on noncustodial fathers' child support obligations because little is known about the economic support provided by noncustodial mothers. Custodial fathers are more likely to be economically advantaged after divorce, of course, and consequently noncustodial mothers are less likely than their paternal counterparts to pay child support, although they may be more reliable in their payments (Greif & DeMaris, 1991; Meyer & Garasky, 1993; Scoon-Rogers & Lester, 1995).

Compliance with Child Support Awards

The economic difficulties of single mothers and their children exist, in part, because of the nature of child support awards and compliance to those awards by noncustodial fathers. By the early 1990s, 73% of custodial mothers who were divorced received child support awards (this rate is markedly lower for never-married custodial mothers; Scoon-Rogers & Lester, 1995). For the minority without a child support award, the reasons varied: some mothers doubted the father's ability or willingness to pay, others were unable to locate the former partner, and a high proportion did not want or were unwilling to pursue a child support award, perhaps owing to interparental conflict or the mother's wish to avoid any obligations to the father deriving from his support (see also Maccoby & Mnookin, 1992). For mothers with child support awards, approximately half received the full amount that was due, roughly one fourth received partial payment, and the rest received no child support at all from the father (Scoon-Rogers & Lester, 1995). There is some evidence that fidelity to child support obligations declines over the years following divorce (Seltzer, 1991b; Seltzer et al., 1989; Teachman & Paasch, 1994; Zill & Nord, 1996), although the evidence is inconsistent (Meyer & Bartfeld, 1997). Furthermore, at least one study indicates that long-term patterns of compliance with child support obligations are set during the first year after divorce: noncustodial fathers who will consistently fulfill their support obligations tend to begin doing so early (Meyer & Bartfeld, 1997).

The average child support payment received by divorced or separated women with some child support payment was $3,442 in 1991, which is substantially higher than the amount received by never-married women but remains inadequate to the true costs of raising children. These estimates, derived from reports obtained from custodial mothers, do not typically include health insurance coverage (43% of ever-married custodial mothers had health insurance benefits included in their child support awards) and informal economic support provided by noncustodial fathers (such as expenses during visits, payments to third parties such as physicians and dentists, and purchases of clothing, gifts, and other material items; Scoon-Rogers & Lester, 1995; Teachman, 1991b). Moreover, fathers typically report providing higher payments and being more reliable in their child support obligations than mothers report (Braver, Fitzpatrick, & Bay, 1991; Seltzer & Brandreth, 1994). Nevertheless, these estimates suggest that child support payments currently provide inadequate assistance to custodial parents seeking to raise offspring by themselves (Teachman & Paasch, 1994).

This is significant, because there is evidence that a father's reliable child support provides meaningful benefits for his children, with positive outcomes in educational attainment, reduced behavior problems, and other indicators of well-being (Furstenberg, Morgan, & Allison, 1987; McLanahan, Seltzer, Hanson, & Thomson, 1994; Zill & Nord, 1996; see Amato, 1997, for a review). These benefits derive not only from the direct gains to children of the enhanced economic security afforded by reliable child support, but also from the indirect benefits to children through the custodial parent's enhanced financial security. Welfare dependency is reduced when fathers provide regular support payments, for example, and an important source of personal stress to single mothers is reduced when they can rely on reliable child support payments.

Reasons Fathers Fail to Provide

These patterns of child support and compliance have changed little since the late 1970s and raise important questions concerning the reasons for noncustodial fathers' variable fidelity to their support obligations (Bartfeld & Meyer, 1994; Meyer, in press; Meyer & Bartfeld, 1996). As with visitation, various influences apply, suggesting (again, contrary to popular perceptions) that the causes of failure to provide child support are heterogeneous, not simply related to a divorced father's unwillingness to support his children. The father's financial capacity to provide reliable support, for example, is an important impediment for a substantial proportion of nonpayers. This is especially so when capacity is defined not just in terms of low income but also in terms of the proportion of income required to satisfy the child support award (Bartfeld & Meyer, 1994; Chambers, 1979; Haskins, 1988; Meyer & Bartfeld, 1996; Seltzer et al., 1989; Teachman, 1991b). In other words, lower income is associated with lower support compliance, but compliance is lower also if the child support award constitutes approximately one third or more of the father's income (Bartfeld & Meyer, 1994; Meyer & Bartfeld, 1996). Noncustodial parents with lower incomes also have fewer ancillary resources on which to depend if they fall behind in their child support obligations (Haskins, 1988). For such fathers, stronger child support enforcement procedures should be secondary to programs designed to enhance the parent's earning capacity in order to increase his child support payments.

Nevertheless, current research also indicates that a substantial proportion of fathers have sufficient income to provide full child support, but fail to do so (Meyer, in press). What other influences can account for their behavior? Seltzer and her colleagues argued that child support must be viewed in the context of the other responsibilities and privileges of noncustodial parenting: fathers are more likely to provide reliable child support when they have assumed other meaningful roles in the child's life (Seltzer, 1991b; Seltzer et al., 1989). A noncustodial father who provides full, regular child support in the absence of any other involvement with offspring is likely to be a rarity. Noncustodial fathers are more likely to maintain regular child support obligations, for example, when they live in geographical proximity to offspring, which facilitates regular contact (Teachman, 1991a, 1991b; Zill & Nord, 1996). They are also more likely to provide reliable support in the context of an amiable relationship with the custodial parent that permits greater access to offspring (Teachman, 1991a, 1991b). A higher proportion of fathers in joint custody maintain child support obligations, compared with fathers in other custody arrangements, and they are more likely to provide their children with other benefits besides support payments because of their enhanced involvement with offspring (Pearson & Thoennes, 1985; Seltzer, 1991a; Teachman, 1991a).

Consistent with this view, moreover, visitation and child support are related, although their association is complex (Furstenberg, 1988; Furstenberg et al., 1983; Pearson & Thoennes, 1988; Scoon-Rogers & Lester, 1995; Seltzer, 1991b; Seltzer et al., 1989; Teachman, 1991b; Zill & Nord, 1996; but see Arditti & Keith, 1993). Fathers who visit frequently are more likely to maintain regular child support payments due, in part, to common demographic causes. In other words, fathers with higher incomes and who live nearby are more likely to visit offspring and to support them financially. The remarriage of either parent may simultaneously alter both noncustodial parent visitation and child support payments because of changing (perceived) needs and alternative obligations. Visitation and child support not only are associated by common demographic correlates, but also are motivationally associated as well. Fathers who do not visit with their children may be less prone to pay child support because they lack a commitment to offspring or because they feel less obligated to maintain child support when they perceive significant obstacles to their efforts to visit. It is also true that sometimes fathers who are unable to maintain child support payments drop out of their children's lives because they wish to avoid detection, or because they are denied access by the custodial parent, or because they cannot justify visiting offspring whom they cannot assist financially. To be sure, identifying cause-and-effect relationships in the association between visitation and child support is difficult because each of these obligations fluctuates over time, especially during the initial years following divorce (see, however, Seltzer et al., 1989; Zill & Nord, 1996). The association between visitation and child support underscores the view, however, that when financial incapacity does not limit the father's ability to comply with child support obligations, reliable financial support is tied to the extent to which fathers can assume other meaningful roles in the lives of offspring.

Stricter Enforcement and Other Reforms

Finally, there is evidence that mandatory withholding of child support payments increases compliance with child support awards (Meyer & Bartfeld, 1996). This is important in light of the movement to more systematic, supervised, and stricter child support enforcement procedures resulting from the Family Support Act of 1988, which provided strong incentives for states to establish consistent guidelines for child support awards and to significantly strengthen enforcement efforts through salary withholding, interstate cooperation in locating delinquent fathers, and other means (Garfinkel, Melli, & Robertson, 1994). As an illustration, Wisconsin has procedures for calculating and enforcing child support in which support awards are determined straightforwardly as a percentage of the noncustodial father's income and, in most counties, are automatically withheld from that parent's paycheck. Other proposals for reform include enlisting the Internal Revenue Service in enforcing child support awards, establishing a national child support guideline that would apply to all states, and supplementing rigorous child support enforcement with an assured benefit plan as a minimum federal guarantee of child support, to be provided by the government if noncustodial parents are unable to do so (Garfinkel et al., 1994; Roberts, 1994).

Although public policymakers have typically resisted formally linking child support enforcement with visitation guarantees, current research on the links between child support and visitation suggests that as child support awards become more systematically calculated and rigorously enforced, noncustodial fathers will not only be more reliable in their financial obligations but also may become more consistent in visiting offspring (Zill & Nord, 1996). After all, as fathers are required to be financially enfranchised into the child's life, they may choose to become so relationally also. However, the greater rigor of child support enforcement might also reduce the flexibility of many families to adapt to changing patterns of parental care over time. If noncustodial parents visit more regularly and extensively, for example, they are likely to assume a greater share of the costs of child care that may not be adequately reflected in child support awards determined years earlier. Moreover, greater sharing of child care by noncustodial parents potentially also offers greater freedom and flexibility for custodial mothers, which may further alter child support requirements. These considerations suggest that greater formal linkages between visitation and child support might be warranted in the future, by which the amounts of child support awards are systematically calibrated and recalibrated to the proportion of time each parent cares for their offspring (such a scheme has recently been developed in California). Although doing so provides added but perhaps inappropriate incentives for noncustodial parents to see their offspring more regularly (i.e., due to the financial incentives provided by reduced child support requirements), it remains to be seen whether this is necessarily a bad thing. Children may enjoy seeing their noncustodial parents more often, even if the initial motivation for the adult to do so was to reduce their financial support obligations. In the end, in a society that remains deeply concerned about the abandonment of children by their fathers after divorce, connecting child support to visitation may help to keep fathers more involved with their children in multifaceted ways.

In the end, efforts to improve the economic well-being of single mothers and their children must consider child support obligations within the broader context of postdivorce family life. Just as it would be unrealistic to expect an adult in a nondivorced family to regard writing a monthly check as a meaningful or rewarding parenting role, it may be unrealistic to fashion child support enforcement procedures around the goal of enhancing fathers' financial contributions, but little else. More thoughtful approaches to improving fidelity to child support obligations should emphasize improving fathers' capacity to pay—when failure derives from financial incapacity—and improving fathers' meaningful involvement in the postdivorce lives of offspring.

CONCLUSION

Parenting is an enduring status but a dynamic experience. After becoming a parent, a man or woman remains so for as long as family members live. But parenthood is altered significantly over time by the changing developmental needs of offspring, the varied life experiences of adults, and the changing condition of the family. Just as being a parent is not more or less ensured by whether children are infants or adolescents, or whether the adult is young or middle-aged, parenthood is also an enduring condition whether parents live near offspring or far away, whether they relate amiably to the other parent or not at all, and whether they are married, divorced, or remarried.

One of the challenges of divorce policy is to ensure that adults remember that although they may dissolve an unhappy marriage, they cannot divorce offspring. Divorce and remarriage may create competing obligations (especially when remarriage entails the assumption of responsibility for stepchildren), but parental responsibilities continue beyond the end of a marriage. Moreover, when children are involved, divorce policy should disabuse parents of the belief that they can make a clean break of a former spouse while moving on to create a new life. Enduring obligations to offspring mean that parents should assume that divorce provides a forum for creating a new relationship with a former spouse that advances the interests of children.

One way of accomplishing these goals is to alter conventional thinking about the "winners" and "losers" of custody disputes. A report from the U.S. Commission on Child and Family Welfare (1996) proposed abandoning the distinction between custodial and noncustodial (visiting) parents with new terms that affirm the shared parenting responsibilities that endure after divorce (see also Bartlett, in press). By defining postdivorce parenting roles in terms of relative amounts of "residential responsibility," for example, each parent should be offered a meaningful opportunity to develop and maintain a natural, everyday postdivorce relationship with offspring rather than perceiving one parent as the winner of such custodial care and the other parent as losing such an opportunity. When each parent is accorded both the responsibility and the opportunity to assume meaningful residential care of children, the incentives toward enduring parenting involvement are enhanced.

Consistent with this goal, divorce policy must create incentives for parents to cooperate amiably on behalf of their children. Current professional interest in mediation during the process of divorce reflects the view that if parents can negotiate noncontentiously over divorce-related issues, it will establish a framework for more constructive postdivorce interaction over child-related concerns (Emery, 1994). Parenting plans that incorporate procedures for negotiating changes in caregiving responsibilities that inevitably accompany changes in family life offer another avenue to strengthening the harmony of the interaction between ex-spouses over children (see Kelly, 1993). When parents have established a framework of mutual understanding that not only outlines the enduring responsibilities of each to the well-being of offspring but also provides avenues for the nonadversarial renegotiation of these obligations as needs and circumstances arise, each parent is ensured a meaningful future role in a child's life. Moreover, because each divorcing couple must obtain the state's ratification of marital dissolution, the courts have profound opportunities to ensure that parents are made aware of their enduring responsibilities to children through parent education and other avenues. In these ways, the process of divorce should be regarded as the inauguration of the postdivorce family, not merely as the end of a former life.

More systematic and rigorous child support enforcement will help to improve the quality of interparental exchanges as these financial obligations become a matter of administrative regularity. But more rigorous enforcement may solve only some of the problems of inadequate child support. For many fathers who fall significantly short of their financial obligations to offspring, an incapacity rather than unwillingness to pay suggests that public efforts to strengthen the parent's earning capacity are well advised. Coupled with this, a public responsibility to children whose nonresidential parents are unable to contribute to their economic well-being seems an important step to ensuring that children are not unduly victimized by their parents' divorce. Although proposals concerning a minimum, public assured child support benefit have some problematic aspects, they reflect a public commitment to the children whose well-being is at the center of other divorce-related policies.

One of the conclusions of the research reviewed in this chapter is that the initial years after divorce provide an enduring framework for postdivorce family life. Noncustodial parents who visit their offspring regularly tend to establish this pattern in the year or two after divorce. Similarly, enduring fidelity to child support obligations are inaugurated in the initial year after marital dissolution, but fathers who will fail to support offspring financially begin neglecting their support obligations early on. These findings suggest that policies that offer incentives to noncustodial parents to remain involved in the lives of their children during the initial postdivorce years are likely to have enduring benefits for offspring. Court-ordered parent education, mediation services, negotiated parenting plans, carefully structured visitation arrangements that include overnight visits, and other approaches that help all family members to weather the cataclysmic changes of the initial postdivorce years and to create adaptive new patterns for daily life may help to keep both parents securely committed to their children's well-being for the long term. Especially important are contexts and arrangements for the maintenance of a visiting relationship that will enable the noncustodial parent to have a true parenting role in the child's postdivorce life.

Divorce poses formidable and painful challenges to all family members. But in the end, the children whose lives are most significantly affected by their parents' divorce often remain the most hopeful. In the sample of children from divorced families described in the opening paragraphs of this chapter, in which close to half had not seen their noncustodial parents during the preceding year, more than 75% regarded that parent as continuing to love them (Furstenberg & Nord, 1985). Other researchers have reported similar results (Maccoby et al., 1993). It is possible that their continuing optimism concerning the commitment of a rarely seen parent reflects the enduring symbolic value of this parent–child relationship for children of divorce, even when the parent is rarely seen. On the other hand, their fidelity to this parent may reflect children's hope that the past does not necessarily foreshadow the future. In either case, it is incumbent on the adults who divorce, and who fashion divorce policy, to respect the importance of *both* parents to the well-being of children.

REFERENCES

Amato, P. R. (1993). Children's adjustment to divorce: Theories, hypotheses, and empirical support. *Journal of Marriage and the Family, 55*, 23–38.

Amato, P. R. (1994). Life-span adjustment of children to their parents' divorce. *The Future of Children, 4*, 143–164.

Amato, P. R. (1997). *More than money? Men's contributions to their children's lives.* Unpublished manuscript, University of Nebraska-Lincoln.

Amato, P. R., & Gilbreth, J. (1997). *Nonresident fathers and children's well-being: A meta-analysis.* Unpublished manuscript, Department of Sociology, University of Nebraska, Lincoln.

Amato, P. R., & Rezac, S. J. (1994). Contact with nonresident parents, interparental conflict, and children's behavior. *Journal of Family Issues, 15*, 191–207.

Arditti, J. A. (1995). Noncustodial parents: Emergent issues of diversity and process. *Marriage & Family Review, 20*, 283–304.

Arditti, J. A., & Keith, T. Z. (1993). Visitation frequency, child support payment, and the father–child relationship postdivorce. *Journal of Marriage and the Family, 55*, 699–712.

Bartfeld, J., & Meyer, D. R. (1994). Are there really deadbeat dads? The relationship between ability to pay, enforcement, and compliance in nonmarital child support cases. *Social Service Review,* *68,* 219–235.

Bartlett, K. T. (in press). Improving the law relating to postdivorce arrangements for children. In R. A. Thompson & P. Amato (Eds.), *The postdivorce family: Research and policy issues.* Newbury Park, CA: Sage.

Bernard, J. (1972). *The future of marriage.* New York: World Books.

Braver, S. L., Fitzpatrick, P. J., & Bay, R. C. (1991). Noncustodial parent's report of child support payments. *Family Relations, 40,* 180–185.

Braver, S. L., Wolchik, S. A., Sandler, I. N., Fogas, B. S., & Avetina, D. (1991). Frequency of visitation by divorced fathers: Differences in reports by fathers and mothers. *American Journal of Orthopsychiatry, 61,* 448–454.

Braver, S. L., Wolchik, S. A., Sandler, I. N., & Sheets, V. I. (1993). A social exchange model of nonresidential parent involvement. In C. Depner & J. Bray (Eds.), *Nonresidential parenting* (pp. 87–108). Newbury Park, CA: Sage.

Braver, S. L., Wolchik, S. A., Sandler, I. N., Sheets, V. I., Fogas, B., & Bay, R. C. (1993). A longitudinal study of noncustodial parents: Parents without children. *Journal of Family Psychology, 7,* 9–23.

Camera, K., & Resnick, G. (1988). Interparental conflict and cooperation: Factors moderating children's post-divorce adjustment. In E. M. Hetherington & J. Arasteh (Eds.), *Impact of divorce, single parenting, and stepparenting on children* (pp. 169–195). Hillsdale, NJ: Lawrence Erlbaum Associates.

Chambers, D. L. (1979). *Making fathers pay: The enforcement of child support.* Chicago: University of Chicago Press.

Cherlin, A. (1992). *Marriage, divorce, remarriage* (Rev. ed.). Cambridge, MA: Harvard University Press.

Cummings, E. M., & Davies, P. (1994). *Children and marital conflict: The impact of family dispute and resolution.* New York: Guilford.

Depner, C. E. (1993). Parental role reversal: Mothers as nonresidential parents. In C. E. Depner & J. H. Bray (Eds.), *Nonresidential parenting* (pp. 37–57). Newbury Park, CA: Sage.

Emery, R. E. (1988). *Marriage, divorce, and children's adjustment.* Newbury Park, CA: Sage.

Emery, R. E. (1994). *Renegotiating family relationships: Divorce, child custody, and mediation.* New York: Guilford.

Fox, G. L., & Blanton, P. W. (1995). Noncustodial fathers following divorce. *Marriage & Family Review, 20,* 257–282.

Fox, G. L., & Kelly, R. F. (1995). Determinants of child custody arrangements at divorce. *Journal of Marriage and the Family, 57,* 693–708.

Fulton, J. A. (1979). Parental reports of children's post-divorce adjustment. *Journal of Social issues, 35,* 126–139.

Furstenberg, F. F., Jr. (1988). Marital disruptions, child custody, and visitation. In A. J. Kahn & S. B. Kamerman (Eds.), *Child support: From debt collection to social policy* (pp. 277–305). Newbury Park, CA: Sage.

Furstenberg, F. F., Jr., & Cherlin, A. J. (1991). *Divided families: What happens to children when parents part.* Cambridge, MA: Harvard University Press.

Furstenberg, F. F., Jr., Morgan, S. P., & Allison, P. D. (1987). Paternal participation and children's wellbeing after marital dissolution. *American Sociological Review, 52,* 695–701.

Furstenberg, F. F., Jr., & Nord, C. W. (1985). Parenting apart: Patterns of childrearing after marital disruption. *Journal of Marriage and the Family, 47,* 893–904.

Furstenberg, F. F., Jr., Nord, C. W., Peterson, J. L., & Zill, N. (1983). The life course of children of divorce: Marital disruption and parental contact. *American Sociological Review, 48,* 656–668.

Garfinkel, I., Melli, M. S., & Robertson, J. G. (1994). Child support orders: A perspective on reform. *The Future of Children, 4,* 84–100.

Greif, G. L. (1987). Mothers without custody. *Social Work, 32,* 11–17.

Greif, G. L. (1997). *Out of touch: When parents and children lose contact after divorce.* New York: Oxford University Press.

Greif, G. L., & DeMaris, A. (1991). When a single custodial father receives child support. *American Journal of Family Therapy, 19,* 167–175.

Greif, G. L., & Pabst, M. S. (1988). *Mothers without custody.* New York: Lexington.

Haskins, R. (1988). Child support: A father's view. In A. J. Kahn & S. B. Kamerman (Eds.), *Child support: From debt collection to social policy* (pp. 306–327). Newbury Park, CA: Sage.

Healey, J. M., Malley, J. E., & Stewart, A. J. (1990). Children and their fathers after parental separation. *American Journal of Orthopsychiatry, 60,* 531–543.

Herrerias, C. (1995). Noncustodial mothers following divorce. *Marriage & Family Review, 20,* 233–255.

Hetherington, E. M. (1989). Coping with family transitions: Winners, losers, and survivors. *Child Development, 60,* 1–14.

Hetherington, E. M., & Clingempeel, W. G. (1992). *Coping with marital transitions: A family systems perspective. Monographs of the Society for Research in Child Development, 57* (2–3, Serial no. 227).

Hetherington, E. M., & Stanley-Hagan, M. M. (1986). Divorced fathers: Stress, coping, and adjustment. In M. E. Lamb (Ed.), *The father's role: Applied perspectives* (pp. 103–134). New York: Wiley.

Hetherington, E. M., & Stanley-Hagan, M. M. (1997). The effects of divorce on fathers and their children. In M. E. Lamb (Ed.), *The role of the father in child development* (3rd ed., pp. 191–211). New York: Wiley.

Hetherington, E. M., Stanley-Hagan, M. M., & Anderson, E. R. (1989). Marital transitions: A child's perspective. *American Psychologist, 44,* 303–312.

Hetherington, E. M., & Tryon, A. S. (1989, November/December). His and her divorces. *The Family Therapy Networker, 15,* 1–16.

Johnston, J. R. (1994). High-conflict divorce. *The Future of Children, 4,* 165–182.

Kelly, J. B. (1993). Developing and implementing post-divorce parenting plans. In C. Depner & J. Bray (Eds.), *Nonresidential parenting* (pp. 136–155). Newbury Park, CA: Sage.

Kelly, J. B. (1994). The determination of child custody. *The Future of Children, 4,* 121–142.

Kitson, G. C. (1992). *Portrait of divorce: Adjustment to marital breakdown.* New York: Guilford.

Kruk, E. (1991). Discontinuity between pre- and post-divorce father–child relationships: New evidence regarding paternal disengagement. *Journal of Divorce and Remarriage, 16,* 195–227.

Lamb, M. E. (in press). Non-custodial fathers and their impact on the children of divorce. In R. A. Thompson & P. Amato (Eds.), *The postdivorce family: Research and policy issues.* Newbury Park, CA: Sage.

Maccoby, E. E. (1995). Divorce and custody: The rights, needs, and obligations of mothers, fathers, and children. In G. B. Melton (Ed.), *The individual, the family, and social good: Personal fulfillment in times of change. Nebraska Symposium on Motivation* (Vol. 42, pp. 135–172). Lincoln: University of Nebraska Press.

Maccoby, E. E., Buchanan, C. M., Mnookin, R. H., & Dornbusch, S. M. (1993). Postdivorce roles of mothers and fathers in the lives of their children. *Journal of Family Psychology, 7,* 24–38.

Maccoby, E. E., & Mnookin, R. H. (1992). *Dividing the child: Social and legal dilemmas of custody.* Cambridge, MA: Harvard University Press.

McLanahan, S. S., Seltzer, J. A., Hanson, T. L., & Thomson, E. (1994). Child support enforcement and child well-being: Greater security or greater conflict? In I. Garfinkel, S. S. McLanahan, & P. K. Robins (Eds.), *Child support and child well-being* (pp. 239–256). Washington, DC: The Urban Institute.

Meyer, D. R. (in press). Compliance with child support orders in paternity and divorce cases. In R. A. Thompson & P. Amato (Eds.), *The postdivorce family: Research and policy issues.* Newbury Park, CA: Sage.

Meyer, D. R., & Bartfeld, J. (1996). Compliance with child support orders in divorce cases. *Journal of Marriage and the Family, 58,* 201–212.

Meyer, D. R., & Bartfeld, J. (1997). *Patterns of child support compliance in Wisconsin.* Unpublished manuscript, Institute for Research on Poverty, University of Wisconsin, Madison.

Meyer, D. R., & Garasky, S. (1993). Custodial fathers: Myths, realities, and child support policy. *Journal of Marriage and the Family, 55,* 73–89.

Mnookin, R. H., & Kornhauser, L. (1979). Bargaining in the shadow of the law: The case of divorce. *Yale Law Journal, 88,* 950–997.

Norton, A. J., & Miller, L. F. (1992). *Marriage, divorce, and remarriage in the 1990's* (Current Population Reports, Series P23-180). Washington, DC: U.S. Government Printing Office.

Pearson, J., & Thoennes, N. (1985). Child custody, child support arrangements, and child support payment patterns. *Juvenile and Family Court Journal, 36,* 49–56.

Pearson, J., & Thoennes, N. (1988). The denial of visitation rights: A preliminary look at its incidence, correlates, antecedents, and consequences. *Law and Policy, 10,* 363–380.

Roberts, P. G. (1994). Child support orders: Problems with enforcement. *The Future of Children, 4,* 101–120.

Scoon-Rogers, L., & Lester, G. H. (1995). *Child support for custodial mothers and fathers: 1991* (Current Population Reports, Series P60-187). Washington, DC: U.S. Government Printing Office.

Seltzer, J. A. (1990). Legal and physical custody arrangements in recent divorces. *Social Science Quarterly, 71,* 250–266.

Seltzer, J. A. (1991a). Legal custody arrangements and children's economic welfare. *American Journal of Sociology, 96,* 895–929.

Seltzer, J. A. (1991b). Relationships between fathers and children who live apart: The father's role after separation. *Journal of Marriage and the Family, 53,* 79–101.

Seltzer, J. A., & Bianchi, S. M. (1988). Children's contact with absent parents. *Journal of Marriage and the Family, 50,* 663–677.

Seltzer, J. A., & Brandreth, Y. (1994). What fathers say about involvement with children after separation. *Journal of Family Issues, 15,* 49–77.

Seltzer, J. A., Schaeffer, N. C., & Charng, H. (1989). Family ties after divorce: The relationship between visiting and paying child support. *Journal of Marriage and the Family, 51,* 1013–1032.

Shiono, P. H., & Quinn, L. S. (1994). Epidemiology of divorce. *The Future of Children, 4,* 15–28.

Teachman, J. D. (1991a). Contributions to children by divorced fathers. *Social Problems, 38,* 358–371.

Teachman, J. D. (1991b). Who pays? Receipt of child support in the United States. *Journal of Marriage and the Family, 53,* 759–772.

Teachman, J. D., & Paasch, K. M. (1994). Financial impact of divorce on children and their families. *The Future of Children, 4,* 63–83.

Thompson, R. A. (1994). The role of the father after divorce. *The Future of Children, 4,* 210–235.

U.S. Commission on Child and Family Welfare. (1996). *Parenting our children: In the best interest of the nation.* Washington, DC: U.S. Government Printing Office.

Wallerstein, J. S., & Corbin, S. B. (1986). Father–child relationships after divorce: Child support and educational opportunity. *Family Law Quarterly, 20,* 109–128.

Wallerstein, J. S., & Kelly, J. B. (1980). *Surviving the breakup.* New York: Basic Books.

Warshak, R. A., & Santrock, J. W. (1983). The impact of divorce in father-custody and mother-custody homes: The child's perspective. In L. A. Kurdek (Ed.), *Children and divorce* (pp. 29–47). San Francisco: Jossey-Bass.

Zill, N., & Nord, C. W. (1996). *Causes and consequences of involvement by non-custodial parents in their children's lives: Evidence from a national longitudinal study.* Unpublished manuscript.

Chapter 7

The Effects of Divorce and Custody Arrangements on Children's Behavior, Development, and Adjustment

Michael E. Lamb
Kathleen J. Sternberg
National Institute of Child Health and Human Development

Ross A. Thompson
University of Nebraska

A group of experts from developmental and clinical psychology, sociology, social welfare, and law met at a conference center in Middleburg, Virginia on December 1–4, 1994, under the sponsorship of the U.S. National Institute of Child Health and Human Development.[1] The group's mandate was to evaluate existing knowledge regarding the ways in which children are affected by divorce and the varying custody arrangements that follow it. Many of the discussions also addressed the ways in which the adverse effects of divorce might be ameliorated by changes in policy or practice. This document represents a statement cosigned by most of the participants summarizing areas of agreement regarding the current status of knowledge in this area and outlining topics in need of further research. The report is designed to guide various legislatures, the judiciary, the bar, and the various mental health professionals who are involved in counseling or educating families

---

[1] The members of the expert group, on whose behalf this report was prepared, were, in alphabetical order, Paul Amato, University of Nebraska; David L. Chambers, University of Michigan Law School; Gary Crippen, Minnesota Court of Appeals; E. Mark Cummings, Notre Dame University; Robert Emery, University of Virginia; Phillip W. Esplin, private practice, Phoenix, AZ; Irwin Garfinkel, Columbia University; Kathleen Gilbride, University of California, Los Angeles; E. Mavis Hetherington, University of Virginia; Guillermina Jasso, New York University; Janet Johnston, Center for the Family in Transition, Corte Madera, CA; Joan B. Kelly, Northern California Mediation Center, Corte Madera, CA; Michael E. Lamb, National Institute of Child Health and Human Development; Sara McLanahan, Princeton University; Kathleen J. Sternberg, National Institute of Child Health and Human Development; Joyce Thomas, People of Color Institute, Washington, DC; Ross A. Thompson, University of Nebraska; and Nicholas Zill, Westat, Inc. This report is in the public domain.

125

experiencing separation or divorce, as well as those who mediate or adjudicate the disputes regarding the custody of minor children. The preliminary draft of this consensus document was prepared by Michael E. Lamb and Kathleen J. Sternberg following the 3-day conference, with additional redrafting by Ross A. Thompson. The draft was reviewed and revised by the other participants over the ensuing months. This report, revised in accordance with the participants' comments, is a product of this process.

A primary purpose of this document is to summarize the relevant empirical data and clear away much of the contention that obscures substantial areas of agreement concerning the effects of divorce, custody, and visitation. Because it represents the consensus of a number of scholars and practitioners from a variety of backgrounds, this document focuses on broad areas of agreement rather than on areas of continuing uncertainty or disagreement, although the latter are also identified. In order to facilitate our presentation and avoid debate over which aspects of individual reports should be emphasized, we have avoided explicit references to the scholarly literature in this document.

THE PROBLEM

Concerns about the risks associated with divorce and single parenthood have been enhanced by the high rate of divorce in many industrialized countries. In the United States, about 45% of all first marriages are now dissolved and in the United Kingdom, 41% divorce within 14 years. This statement is focused on the development and well-being of children who began life in two-parent unions and who, as a result of divorce, experience significant disruptions in their relationships with their parents during childhood. We can only speculate about the relevance of this document to the experience of children born to single mothers, who are also a rapidly expanding proportion of children in the United States and other countries.

Insight into the consequences of divorce for children can be gleaned from consideration of its immediate effects on all the individuals involved. Most family members experience substantial psychological and emotional disturbance around the time of divorce, although this is sometimes mixed with more positive feelings, especially when there is relief regarding resolution of the problems leading to divorce. Whatever the antecedents, family dissolution is clearly disruptive for mothers, fathers, and children, most of whom experience varying degrees of distress, depression, loneliness, regret, lack of control, helplessness, and anger. These psychological symptoms are not simply acute responses to immediate stress. For many families, symptoms are still at peak levels a year or two after the separation, and there is wide variability in the length of time most individuals take to achieve a new equilibrium. Preoccupation with their own emotional turmoil clearly limits parents' abilities to support their children emotionally and enforce consistent expectations and demands. This is true of both nonresidential (noncustodial) and residential parents and, not surprisingly, the overall psychological and economic well-being of residential parents often ranks as one of the most powerful predictors of children's adjustment following divorce.

Divorce is also associated with relocation of at least one and often all family members. This may exacerbate stress and increase the risk of social isolation for all concerned by limiting the ability of friends and relatives to provide the social and emotional support needed during these stressful times, although it may sometimes involve increased support for those who move closer to their families of origin. The establishment and maintenance of two separate residences also imposes economic burdens that are unequally experienced by the separating parents. These burdens are typically greatest for women because of their poorer wage-earning opportunities and because they are usually responsible for most postdivorce childcare responsibilities: the vast majority of the children affected by divorce reside primarily in their mothers' households. At least initially, furthermore, the economic circumstances of most, though not all, divorced fathers tend to improve whereas those of divorced mothers and their children decline before stabilizing below predivorce levels. Economic factors thus add significantly to the forces that make divorce and separation harmful to the development and psychological well-being of the children involved. Remarriage often has economic benefits for single parents and their children, but it also entails further adjustment to stepparents and stepsiblings. Although children's adjustment to blended families has been studied relatively little, we know that readjustment can be stressful. On the other hand, remarriages often restore mothers' economic circumstances to their predivorce status because of the supplementary income provided by stepfathers, and relationships with stepparents can provide emotional support to children as well as to the remarrying parents.

Overall, most children of divorce experience dramatic declines in their economic circumstances; abandonment (or the fear of abandonment) by one or both of their parents; the diminished capacity of both parents to attend meaningfully and constructively to their children's needs (because they are preoccupied with their own psychological, social, and economic distress as well as stresses related to the legal divorce); and diminished contact with many familiar or potential sources of psychosocial support (friends, neighbors, teachers, schoolmates, etc.) as well as familiar living settings. As a consequence, the experience of divorce is a psychosocial stressor as well as a significant life transition for most children, with long-term repercussions for many. Some children from divorced homes show long-term behavior problems, depression, poor school performance, acting out, low self-esteem and (in adolescence and young adulthood) difficulties with intimate heterosexual relationships.

Although divorce is a painful experience that increases children's psychosocial vulnerability, the long-term effects of divorce should not be exaggerated. Despite the significant and troubling risks of maladjustment among children whose parents divorce, the majority of children in these circumstances appear, in the long run, to be developing within the normal range—without identifiable psycho-social scars or other adverse consequences—even when the process of marital dis-solution was painful for them. In addition, divorce may offer members of dys-functional families the opportunity to escape from family stress and conflict.

When ex-spouses are able to work through their anger, disappointment, and loss in a timely manner and can establish healthy interpersonal relationships with other adults, divorces can be considered successful. Fortunately, the majority of divorcing adults are able to achieve this status, although one fourth to one third have considerable difficulty and 5% to 10% clearly fail to attain this goal. The latter remain embittered and actively hostile for many years, and this places their children at a considerably higher risk of psychosocial problems. These high-conflict parents and couples are identified with multiple characteristics: high rates of litigation and relitigation; high degrees of anger and distrust; intermittent ver-bal or physical aggression or both; difficulty focusing on their children's needs as distinct from their own; and chronic difficulty coparenting and communicating about their children after divorce. Their interparental struggle assumes center stage and, as a consequence, children's personal circumstances and developmental needs are often given inadequate attention.

Because of the persistence of high divorce rates since the 1970s, this accumulat-ing subgroup of high-conflict divorced couples has come to pose serious problems for society. These families clog the family courts, taking more than their share of available resources. Their children are substantially more likely to be clinically disturbed, and they thus consume a disproportionate share of the community's mental health resources as well. When one considers the extent of the stress expe-rienced by most children in these circumstances, it is perhaps remarkable that even more children from high-conflict families do not show severe psychopathol-ogy. Nevertheless, their enhanced risk of maladjustment is sobering, given the numbers of children involved, and highlights the importance of identifying why some children in comparable circumstances are spared these effects. Although many researchers have studied biological differences in children's vulnerability and resilience, it has not yet been possible to identify characteristics that make some individual children intrinsically more resilient in the face of divorce whereas others are more susceptible to adverse impact. It is also important to note that some children, particularly those who were living in high-conflict or abusive en-vironments, may even manifest improvements in their behavior and mental health following their parents' divorce. Clearly, more research is needed on this topic.

The extent to which children receive economic support from their nonresiden-tial parents is consistently associated with more positive adaptation. Simply put, children whose nonresidential parents continue to support them financially are at lower risk of extended educational disadvantage than those whose nonresidential parents do not pay any child support. There is also a clear association between pay-ment of child support and the amount of contact between nonresidential parents and their children. The benefits to children's adjustment may thus arise from the economic benefits of child support, a reduction in the level of stress experienced by residential parents, the psychological benefits of maintaining relationships with nonresidential parents, or some combination of these interrelated factors.

Unfortunately, the majority of nonresidential fathers fail to maintain or are prevented from maintaining significant contact with their children during the years following divorce. Declines in the amount of contact between nonresidential parents and their children appear to be, at least in part, attributable to difficulties in visitation arrangements that reduce or eliminate the opportunities for nonresidential parents to be involved in broad areas of their children's lives, making their relationships seem peripheral or artificial. Rather than experiencing the everyday encounters associated with schooling, homework, play, and sports that most parents share with their offspring, nonresidential parents and their children must often create a new visiting relationship that is quite distant from the ordinary experiences of both the children and the adults. This is difficult and, combined with the mutual desires of former spouses to lead independent lives (sometimes in the context of remarriage), may help explain why many nonresidential fathers gradually reduce and eventually abandon visitation altogether.

Most children of divorce want to maintain contact with both parents, and some researchers have shown that the maintenance of an ongoing relationship between nonresidential parents and their children is associated with better adjustment by children. The effects of maintaining contact with both parents are less profound and less consistent than might be expected, however. In part, this seems to reflect the fact that increased contact between nonresidential parents and their children often involves increased and continued contact between the two former spouses. When the relationship between the two parents is civil, the benefits of continued contact with each parent are more apparent than when there is substantial conflict between the two. In some circumstances, the level of hostility between the two parents is so high and so recalcitrant that children are harmed rather than helped by frequent contact with each of their parents. Researchers have thus far failed to measure the threshold level of interparental hostility necessary to undermine the benefits to children of continuing contact with both parents and, quite likely, this depends on many factors that are specific to the lives of the parents and children in question. In addition, nonresidential parents who maintain parental roles (providing guidance, discipline, supervision, and educational assistance) may affect their children more profoundly than those who are limited to functioning as occasional visiting companions.

Disagreements are part of any relationship and exposure to conflict is not necessarily harmful to children. Indeed, exposure to parental conflict can have salutary effects on children when they are able to observe and learn from the constructive resolution of manageable conflict. By contrast, exposure to destructive and unresolved conflict (especially when it is focused on the children) places children at increased risk of behavioral and psychological maladjustment. Although all divorcing families are not characterized by high levels of conflict before the decision to separate, some degree of conflict commonly occurs during the divorcing process as individuals decide to disengage from each other. Perhaps for this reason, longitudinal studies have shown that the behavior problems of children whose parents have divorced often predated parental separation. It thus becomes important for professionals working with divorcing families to guide disagreements and conflicts toward constructive and explicit resolutions. Such resolutions benefit both the parents themselves, as well as their children.

POLICY CONSIDERATIONS

Under U.S. family law, married parents are their children's joint legal custodians, with joint and separate authority to make major decisions regarding the fate of their minor children. When marriage ends, shared responsibility for offspring should remain, even though the realities of divorce significantly alter how (and whether) these obligations are exercised or maintained.

In the large majority of postdivorce families, however, mothers assume de jure or de facto primary physical custody of offspring whereas fathers usually become increasingly distant figures in their children's lives. This means that the immediate and long-term adjustment of children is closely related to the residential parents' overall well-being and to the quality of the relationship between residential parents and their children. The extent to which residential parents are able to create and maintain a satisfactory economic standard of living, function effectively as single parents, and re-establish a sense of psychosocial well-being after divorce directly and indirectly benefits the children in their care. As a result, policies that enhance the psychological, social, and financial well-being of residential parents —such as child-support enforcement, public income support, and counseling— can be of great importance.

Central to these achievements are the economic conditions of residential parents and their children during the period immediately following the divorce, and in the years thereafter. The (sometimes steep) decline in the standard of living of divorced mothers and their children after separation clearly has important implications for the living conditions, educational options, emotional stresses, and other factors associated with the well-being of parents and offspring. In the United States, although most children of legally divorced parents receive child support from their nonresidential parents, the awards have historically covered less than half of the actual costs of raising children, and only half of the nonresidential parents pay the full amount awarded. Recent attempts to increase compliance with child-support orders, such as by mandatory wage garnishment, should be associated with improvements in children's adjustment that result from the residential parents' greater economic security, consistent with the research earlier described. It is possible that enhanced child-support enforcement might also result in more extensive visitation by nonresidential parents. But because we cannot assume that mandatory compliance with child-support orders has the same benefits for child adjustment as does voluntary child support compliance, further research on the correlates and effects of child-support enforcement in our rapidly changing social circumstances is clearly necessary.

Even in the context of full compliance, child-support awards account for only a fraction of the total incomes of residential parents. For many divorced mothers, obtaining or updating vocational skills, completing educational goals, and finding satisfying and economically rewarding work are among the most significant stresses of immediate and long-term postdivorce life. For some women, a period of reliance on public welfare is an almost inevitable accompaniment of this transition. The importance of an adequate income for residential parents and their offspring thus includes not only satisfactory child-support enforcement but also programs that ensure decent minimum incomes (as well as food and medical care, when necessary), the possibility of transitional support from former spouses, and other forms of assistance.

Noneconomic factors, such as the parents' psychological adjustment and the emotional support derived from developing new adult relationships, also affect the well-being of residential parents and the quality of the relationships they have with their children. In some cases, furthermore, enhancing the residential parents' well-being and the quality of care they provide involves a complex mixture of economic and noneconomic considerations, such as those involved in residential moves to assume new employment. In our discussions, circumstances like these presented the most difficult and complex challenges for public policy because of their conflicting implications for children's well-being. On the one hand, residential moves are often followed by enhanced standards of living, together with other changes that can benefit residential parents and children alike. On the other hand, such moves also entail the interruption of relationships with peers, extrafamilial care providers, and others on whom children come to rely, and the disruption of familiar routines and experiences. Most significantly, they imperil the maintenance of ongoing relationships with nonresidential parents.

Most children in two-parent families form psychologically important and distinctive relationships with both of their parents, even though one may be a primary caretaker. These relationships are not redundant, because mothers and fathers each make unique contributions to their children's development and individuality. The majority of children experiencing parental divorce express the desire to maintain relationships with both of their parents after separation. Therefore, in addition to enhancing the psychosocial and economic well-being of residential parents and supporting their relationships with offspring, postdivorce arrangements should also aim to promote the maintenance of relationships between nonresidential parents and their children. The manner in which this occurs can take many forms, depending on individual circumstances, such as the relative location of the parents' residences, their work schedules, the ages of the children, the parents' capacities, and the nature of the parents' involvement with the children prior to divorce.

In order to maintain high-quality relationships with their children, parents need to have sufficiently extensive and regular interaction with them, but the amount of time involved is usually less important than the quality of the interaction that it fosters. Time distribution arrangements that ensure the involvement of both parents in important aspects of their children's everyday lives and routines—including bedtime and waking rituals, transitions to and from school, extracurricular and recreational activities—are likely to keep nonresidential parents playing psychologically important and central roles in the lives of their children. How this is accomplished must be flexibly tailored to the developmental needs, temperament, and changing individual circumstances of the children concerned. Children benefit from regularity, consistency, and continuity, both psychological and geographical. Both before and after divorce, therefore, young children are helped when both of their parents have similar daily routines with respect to the children's bedtime, sleeping arrangements, and meal times, and when there is substantial agreement between parents regarding discipline and basic childrearing philosophy. Children also benefit when they are able to maintain relationships within the same peer groups, when they experience care from the same extrafamilial care providers, and when they attend the same schools. When children have meaningful predivorce relationships with both parents, the psychological continuity achieved by helping them maintain harmonious relationships with both parents after divorce generally, though not always, outweighs the disadvantages arising from transitions between parental homes, provided that attempts are made to reduce other areas of instability and inconsistency. When children do not have meaningful relationships with both parents, by contrast, the relative costs and benefits may be quite different.

Decisions regarding the distribution of time between the two parents are complicated; they involve weighing the potential benefits of maintaining meaningful relationships with both parents against the costs associated with continuation of those contacts. In light of these considerations, the specific arrangements chosen to promote children's relationships with each of the parents should be clearly articulated in detail to reduce the need for further negotiation, argument, and possible relitigation. Such specification should be sensitive to the inevitable adjustments required as children's needs and circumstances change with age, and as their parents' circumstances change also. For example, relocation by either parent might preclude arrangements involving relatively frequent transitions between homes (particularly on school nights), but specification in advance of what processes will be used to modify visitation schedules when and if this becomes necessary for either predictable (e.g., age of child) or unexpected reasons can help to make such transitions manageable and less conflictful.

In both intact and divorced households, some parents are clearly unfit to supervise and care for their children because of mental illness or incapacity, serious substance abuse, or because past acts of violent child maltreatment place children at physical or psychological risk. These considerations may outweigh the potential benefits to children of maintaining continuing relationships with such parents. Adults who have a history of chronic spouse abuse or battery also represent threats both to former partners and children. When such histories exist, the potential costs of terminating the children's relationships with their violent parents need to be evaluated thoroughly by trained and impartial professionals whose recommendations concerning the termination of parent–child contact should be made and implemented expeditiously.

In and of itself, violence toward a spouse or partner does not necessarily indicate that a parent represents a threat to the child's well-being, although it frequently does. Professionals should be especially cautious in their recommendations concerning children whose parents have engaged in mutual or unidirectional acts of violence around the time of divorce, but otherwise have a history of nonviolent conflict resolution. Custody and timesharing plans for children from violent homes need to recognize the merits and characteristics of each case and the quality of the children's relationships with each of their parents.

PUBLIC EDUCATION

Greater efforts must clearly be made to inform the public, mental health professionals, the bar, and the judiciary regarding the effects of divorce and parental separation on children's well-being and development. More children would surely experience healthy psychosocial growth if fewer children were exposed to divorce in their formative years because their parents better understood the costs to both children and parents relative to the expected benefits of marital dissolution. Certainly there exist cases in which the mental health, financial security, and even the physical survival of one or more family members depends on marital dissolution, but there are others in which a failure to recognize the prolonged and profound psychological and economic costs leads individuals to seek divorce precipitously and perhaps inappropriately. To date, however, changes in the legally acceptable grounds for divorce are not indicated by the evidence.

Some of the adverse effects of divorce on children might be ameliorated by seeking to minimize the conflict that surrounds the establishment of custody and visitation arrangements, particularly those involving legal procedures. Children are best served by arrangements that are reached by genuinely mutual consent and in a timely fashion. They may also benefit from arrangements that allow both parents to view themselves as winners in the conflict. Such resolutions can occur when parents are guided toward consensual agreements regarding their children's custody without adversarial legal action.

On balance, the economic and psychological well-being of children would be enhanced if information about divorce and its effects were widely disseminated and skilled mediation services were available to those parents who might be able to reach agreement when offered the opportunity and information to guide such discussions. Such mediation would be especially valuable when it is voluntarily sought by divorcing parents, and when efforts are made to prohibit either partner from gaining unfair advantage over the other. Various case management and arbitration services, as well as litigation, would, of course, remain available for the minority of couples in which intractable disagreements precluded such decision-making procedures. Educational programs focused on assisting parents and children to negotiate the process of divorce might also reduce some of the adverse effects of divorce.

FURTHER RESEARCH

Despite many years of careful research, there is much that remains to be learned about the effects of divorce and custody arrangements on children. Some of the most prominent lacunae are identified in this section.

Because most children are placed primarily in the physical custody of their mothers following divorce, most of the extant research has focused on children living with custodial mothers. As a result, we know relatively little about the psychosocial and economic circumstances of children living primarily with custodial fathers, or in the joint physical custody of their two parents. Indeed, most of the existing research on joint physical custody involves families who voluntarily seek such a postdivorce arrangement, raising doubt concerning whether judicially imposed joint physical custody arrangements would offer similar benefits for the children involved. The lack of information about custodial fathers and joint custody arrangements significantly delimits the conclusions that can be offered about them.

The participants also agreed that we know very little about the postdivorce adjustment patterns of children and parents who are not White and reasonably affluent. To an embarrassing extent, the research reviewed in this document describes the status of more affluent White children. The generalizability of those findings to children and parents from other backgrounds is unknown.

Finally, considerably greater information is needed about the factors predicting successful as well as unsuccessful postdivorce adjustment. As indicated earlier, for instance, we require much greater insight from studies of postdivorce custody and visitation to understand what typically occurs during visits between nonresidential parents and their offspring, what obstacles impede the success of their continuing relationships, and how continuing conflict between former spouses affects the success of visiting relationships. Moreover, researchers know much less about the processes contributing to psychosocial well-being in residential and nonresidential parents and their offspring than they do about the factors contributing to dysfunction and decline. As indicated earlier in this statement, for example, we must learn more about how children facing similarly difficult circumstances associated with their parents' divorces respond differently, with some succumbing to psychosocial dysfunction and poorer mental health while others seem unperturbed, and even improve emotionally, as a consequence. Quite likely, factors both within the family environment but also outside it (e.g., in sources of social support to children outside the home) are involved. It is likely that a better understanding of what constitutes successful divorce may contribute to more informed policy recommendations in the future.

Chapter 8

Stepfamilies

E. Mavis Hetherington
University of Virginia

Margaret M. Stanley-Hagan
University of North Carolina at Charlotte

The stepfamily is the fastest growing family type in the United States (U.S Bureau of the Census, 1992). Approximately 17% of all families headed by a married couple with children under age 18 are stepfamilies (Glick, 1989). However, stepfamilies are diverse in their structures, histories, and circumstances. Biological parents may or may not have been married. Previous adult relationships may have ended with the death of a spouse or partner, a breakdown in a former cohabitation, or a divorce. The custodial parent, noncustodial parent, or both may remarry. Parents or stepparents may have residential or nonresidential children from previous relationships adding stepsiblings to the family. Slightly more than half of remarried custodial parents have children with their new spouses adding half-siblings to the family (General Household Survey, 1993). Finally, divorces occur more frequently and rapidly in remarriages than in first marriages, with one fourth of remarriages being disrupted within five years (Martin & Bumpass, 1989). Couples with remarried wives are almost twice as likely to divorce as those with remarried husbands, in part because of the 50% higher rates of dissolution in marriages in which children are present (Tzeng & Mare, 1995). One out of every ten children will experience at least two divorces of their residential parents before turning 16 (Furstenberg, 1988). Thus, for many children remarriage is just one link in a chain of marital transitions and household reorganizations involving alterations in family roles and relationships.

Interest in the impact of both divorce and remarriage on children and family relationships has grown as the number of families affected has grown. However, most of the early research on family transitions focused on the impact of divorce. It is only since the 1980s that a systematic body of research on stepfamilies has begun to build. Many of the early studies were based on clinical populations and a deficit model in which circumstances, relationships, and outcomes within stepfamilies were compared to those within first-marriage families (Ganong & Coleman, 1994; Orleans, Palisi, & Caddell, 1989). Differences were viewed as evidence of poor functioning and adjustment in stepfamilies. The growing recognition in recent years of the wide variations evident in parents', stepparents', and children's responses to family transitions has led investigators to focus on the diverse experiences and family processes that contribute to individual differences in adjustment (Hetherington, 1989, 1991, 1993; Hetherington et al., 1992; Hetherington & Jodl, 1994). The deficit model has been all but abandoned in favor of risk and resiliency models that incorporate family systems, ecological, and developmental theories (Amato & Keith, 1991b; Garmezy, 1993; Hetherington, in press-b; Wolin & Wolin, 1993). Such models provide the frameworks to examine individual, family, and extrafamilial factors and processes that put individuals at risk or that protect them from adverse outcomes during and after family transitions (Hetherington, 1993). The picture emerging from this research is not only one of risks confronted during the period of transition but also one of resiliency as the family restabilizes.

Each family transition requires the reorganization of family roles and relationships with accompanying alterations in stresses, risks, and resources (Hetherington, 1993). Thus, there is an initial period of disequilibrium associated with divorce and remarriage followed by the eventual restabilization of the new family system (Hetherington et al., 1992). Restabilization following divorce typically takes two to three years (Hetherington, 1989), and it has been estimated that the rate of restabilization in stepfamilies may take as long as five to seven years (Cherlin & Furstenberg, 1994). Because of the early timing and higher rates of divorce in remarriages, a new family homeostasis may not have occurred before the relationships are disrupted.

There are diverse pathways to family restabilization and adaptation of family members following marital transitions. To some extent, response to a transition depends on what has preceded it and on the family history. Children from families with highly conflictual marital relationships show a decrease in behavior problems following divorce, whereas those from families with little overt acrimony experience increased problems following divorce (Amato, Loomis, & Booth, 1995). The move from a single-parent family to a stepfamily may improve financial resources, and another adult can provide emotional support and childrearing support for the parent and involvement, care, supervision and an additional role model for the children (Zill, 1994; Zill, Morrison, & Coiro, 1993). However, a new stepparent may be viewed as an intruder and his or her entry may be resisted by children who have had a close relationship with a parent in a single-parent household or an involved noncustodial parent (Hetherington, 1989, 1991; Hetherington & Jodl, 1994).

The course of adaptation to a family transition involves the dynamic interaction among risks and protective factors that will differ for different transitions, at different points in the transition, and for different families and family members. These adaptive trajectories are modified by multiple interacting factors, including the need to integrate new and previous family relationships and experiences; the quality and stability of family relationships; practical circumstances such as changes in financial resources, residence, employment, and school; and the individual characteristics of both parents and children. The risk to individual adjustment tends to increase as the stability of family relationships is challenged by the loss of a family member through separation or divorce or the addition of new members through remarriage. Individuals may be more vulnerable to the challenges associated with a family transition at some normative developmental periods such as puberty than in others, and certain changes associated with developmental transitions may trigger latent, delayed effects. Moreover, although most parents and children are remarkably resilient in the face of change, as the number of concurrent changes or sequential changes in a brief period of time increases, so does the risk of adverse outcomes. As well as increasing challenges and risk, marital transitions may introduce positive life changes, new resources, and the opportunity for new fulfilling family relations, which contribute to the well-being of parents and children.

Remarriage and stepfamily formation offer unique challenges to family members. Stepfamilies not only involve the addition of nonbiologically related family members to the household, but also, especially if both parents remarry, to much more complex kin networks within and outside of the family in a linked family system (Jacobson, 1982). Coping with relationships in a linked family system while trying to build a family is usually a difficult task. Adults must establish a strong and positive marital relationship while simultaneously adjusting existing parent–child relations and building stepparent–stepchild relations. These processes are made more complex by the need to integrate sometimes disparate family histories and traditions and negotiate a new workable model of the family. All of these processes take place with limited guiding social norms (Keshet, 1990). How successful families are in meeting challenges depends in part on their beliefs and expectations at the outset. Research suggests that expecting or forcing the stepfamily to fit the model of a traditional biological family can lead to new problems or exacerbate existing problems (Bray & Burger, 1993). Stepfamilies that weather the initial challenges of family formation tend to be those that recognize that building a sense of family takes time, family boundaries must be flexible to accommodate existing ties to noncustodial parents and extended family, and stepparents cannot replace biological parents and may need to develop a separate, nontraditional parenting role.

Despite the diversity in stepfamily structures, most stepfamily households occur when a single custodial mother remarries. It is therefore not surprising that the focus of most studies has been on stepfather families. A few studies have examined stepmother families and a very few have examined blended or complex households in which both partners bring custodial children to the family. Across studies, the primary targets have been the children and the relationships and factors that play on children's vulnerability and support their resiliency. The discussion that follows reflects this research balance. We begin by reviewing the adjustment of children in stepfamilies with a focus on how individual characteristics such as developmental status and gender influence children's responses to remarriage transition. There is a general consensus among researchers that family processes and relationships are more important than family structure in explanations of individual differences in child adjustment; thus, we continue with a discussion of the family environment. Examined are the processes characteristic in the marital, parent–child, stepparent–stepchild, and sibling relationships in newly forming and restabilized remarried families. Finally, we end with a short review of social policy issues and recommendations.

CHILD ADJUSTMENT

Generally, both cross-sectional and longitudinal studies that have compared the adjustment of children in stepfamilies to those in first-marriage families have found children in stepfamilies to be less well adjusted; to exhibit more behavioral or emotional problems, poorer academic achievement, lower social competence and social responsibility (Amato, 1994; Hetherington et al., 1992; Hetherington & Jodl, 1994; Zill, 1994), and to manifest more health problems. In addition, they have more problems in relationships with parents and siblings and, in adulthood, with spouses (Amato & Keith, 1991a, 1991b; Hetherington, in press-b). However, the problems experienced can vary depending on the child's developmental status, race, and gender.

Child Developmental Status

Children who experience parental divorce before they turn 5 have a 59% chance of becoming part of a stepfamily before they turn 18 (Bumpass & Sweet, 1989). If they are between the ages of 5 and 9 at the time of divorce, the children have a 35% change of experiencing life in a stepfamily and if they are adolescents, the probability drops to 14%. Thus, compared to their older siblings, young children in divorcing families are more likely to experience the remarriage of a parent. Research suggests that the younger the child at the time of remarriage, the more easily the child establishes an attachment to a new stepparent (Hetherington, 1993; Perry, 1995). However, although young children are more likely to develop and benefit from a positive stepparent–stepchild relationship, they also are more likely to experience the risks associated with multiple family transitions (Thomson, 1994).

The remarriage transition can be more difficult for early adolescents than for their younger siblings, especially younger siblings who have not experienced multiple family transitions (Perry, 1995). Adolescents are more likely to demonstrate sustained internalizing and externalizing problems and deficits in social responsibility and academic competence (Hetherington et al., 1992). Adolescents may resent the intrusion of the stepparent into their established relationships with their residential parent—relationships often characterized by greater responsibilities and freedoms. Their resentment is evident in the quality of their relations with stepparents. Even in restabilized stepfamilies, adolescents, especially girls, remain less warm and responsive and more coercive toward their stepfathers (Hetherington et al., 1992; Hetherington & Jodl, 1994). Adolescent girls often assume a contemptuous attitude towards their stepfathers and are less communicative, speaking one third less to their stepfathers than do daughters with fathers in first-marriage families (Vuchinich, Hetherington, Vuchinich, & Clingempeel, 1991). Eventually, about one third of adolescent boys and one fourth of adolescent girls disengage from their families, spending little time in family activities or at home. Disengagement and early home leaving is higher in girls in stepfamilies than in any other group, and stepdaughters attribute this to family conflict (Cherlin & Furstenberg, 1994; Hetherington, in press-a). It is not uncommon for these teens to seek support elsewhere, and a close relationship with another adult, such as the parent of a friend, who provides guidance and support can be an adaptive solution to a distressing family situation. However, there is a risk that the disengaged adolescent will become involved with antisocial peers or will receive no alternative adult supervision. In such cases, there is an increased probability that the adolescent will engage in antisocial and self-destructive behaviors.

Problems may not end when stepchildren enter adulthood. Youth from divorced and remarried families in comparison to first-marriage families are less satisfied with their lives, have more adjustment problems, greater marital instability, lower socioeconomic attainment, and are more likely to be on welfare (Amato & Keith, 1991b; Hetherington, in press-a; McLanahan & Sandefur, 1994). Girls from these families are at special risk for the sequence of teenage childbearing and school dropout (McLanahan & Sandefur, 1994) and, for girls in stepfamilies, to the consequences of leaving home at an earlier age (Cherlin & Furstenberg, 1994; Hetherington, In press-a).

Child Gender

Amato and Keith (1991a), in a meta-analysis of the effects of marital transitions on children's adjustment, concluded that the presence of a stepfather improves well-being in boys but has no effect or exacerbates problems in girls. Although large gender differences in response to parental remarriage tend to be found in older rather than newer studies, research indicates that gender differences in children's relationships with parents and stepparents do occur but usually when the children are preadolescents. Boys, especially preadolescent boys, are more likely to accept and adapt more quickly to the entry of a stepparent (Brand, Clingempeel, & Bowen-Woodward, 1988). A close relationship with a supportive stepfather is more likely to facilitate the well-being and achievement of stepsons than stepdaughters (Amato & Keith, 1991a; Hetherington, 1993; Hetherington et al., 1992;

Lindner-Gunnoe, 1993; Zill et al., 1993). Preadolescent girls who have more trouble adjusting to the entry of a stepparent (Brand et al., 1988; Hetherington et al., 1992) are at greater increased risk for poor adjustment and low achievement when they are in either a stepfather or stepmother family than in a first-marriage family (Lee, Burkham, Zimiles, & Ladewski, 1994). In general, parents and stepparents respond negatively to children's externalizing and positively to children's social competence (Hetherington et al., 1992). Preadolescent and early adolescent stepdaughters tend to be more negative and resistant toward stepparents (Bray & Burger, 1993; Clingempeel, Brand, & Ievoli, 1984; Hetherington et al., 1992). Thus, these gender differences may result more from the children's responses to their stepparents than to the stepparents' parenting overtures.

Child Race

Some research has suggested that living in a stepfamily may be more beneficial to Black than to White adolescents, although the aspects of adolescent adjustment affected differs for males and females. In contrast to the finding with White youths, young Black women in stepfamilies have the same rates of teenage parenthood as those in two-parent, first-marriage families, and young Black men in stepfamilies are at no greater risk to drop out of high school than those in two-parent families (McLanahan & Sandefur, 1994). McLanahan and Sandefur (1994) proposed that the income, supervision, and role model provided by a stepfather may be more advantageous for Black children because they are more likely than White children to live in poverty in neighborhoods with many risks and few resources and social controls. However, it should be remembered that rates of remarriage are low in Black families and not many Black children from divorced or single parent families are likely to encounter the potential benefits of a stepfather.

Extent and Duration of Adjustment Problems Associated With Remarriage

Regardless of age or gender, the frequency of behavioral, emotional, and academic problems experienced by children growing up in stepfamilies appears more similar to those observed in children growing up in single-parent families than to those in first-marriage families (Amato, 1994; Cherlin & Furstenberg, 1994; Dawson, 1991; Hetherington & Jodl, 1994). Some investigators have suggested that many of the adjustment problems in stepchildren are attributable to experiences they had earlier in a conflict ridden first marriage or in a home with a divorced single parent (Furstenberg, 1988). Although this may be the case, problems tend to escalate following remarriage (Bray & Burger, 1993; Hetherington et al., 1992; Hetherington & Jodl, 1994) and then restabilize at about the same level or a slightly higher level (Amato & Keith, 1991a) than that found in divorced single-parent families. The new stresses and adaptive challenges confronting children in stepfamilies seem to counter the economic benefits and other resources accompanying their parent's remarriage.

Despite the general pattern of problems for children in stepfamilies compared to children in first-marriage families, there has been considerable controversy about the extent, seriousness, and persistence of the adjustment problems in children in divorced families and stepfamilies. Some investigators point out that the average differences in adjustment between children in divorced and remarried families and those in first-marriage families are statistically significant but modest (Amato, 1994; Amato & Keith, 1991a). Other investigators point out that there is about a twofold increase in such things as school dropout rates, academic difficulties, unemployment and idleness, conduct disorders, teenage pregnancy and total behavior problems (Hetherington, 1989, 1991; Hetherington & Jodl, 1994; McLanahan & Sandefur, 1994; Zill et al., 1993). About 10% of children in first-marriage families compared to about 20% to 25% of children in divorced and remarried families have these problems. However, because these problems tend to co-occur (Mekos, Hetherington, & Reiss, 1996), it means the vast majority of children who have undergone their parents' marital transitions are not experiencing these problems and are able to adapt to their new family system.

The life changes and challenges associated with divorce and remarriage do place children at risk for poor behavioral, emotional, and academic outcomes. Many children experience these transitions as painful and some exhibit behavioral and emotional disruptions in the immediate aftermath of their parents' marital transitions (Hetherington et al., 1992; Hetherington & Jodl, 1994). Although most children adapt over time, there are those who experience sustained and severe problems (Amato & Keith, 1991b; Hetherington, in press-a). Thus, attention has turned to the search for factors to explain the individual differences in child outcomes. Primary targets have been processes within family relationships.

FAMILY RELATIONSHIPS

Most investigators conclude that family process is more important than family type or structure in influencing children's adjustment (Amato, 1994; Demo & Acock, 1996; Zill, 1994). Children are at greater risk when they reside in highly conflictual, dysfunctional first marriages than in well functioning, supportive single-parent or remarried families (Amato, 1993; Amato & Keith, 1991a; Furstenberg & Cherlin, 1991; Hetherington, 1989). Supportive, harmonious family relations that encourage individuation and personal responsibility promote the well-being of all family members. However, although most families do gradually restabilize with new roles and relationships, support and harmony may seem elusive to family members facing the challenges of adjusting and establishing relationships during the months and years following stepfamily formation.

Marital Relationships

Critical to the stability of any family is the strength of the marital relationship. However, research indicates that strong, well-functioning marital relationships in stepfamilies may differ from those observed in first-marriage families. Spouses in second marriages view their relationships as less romantic but more pragmatic, more egalitarian with respect to both household and childrearing responsibilities (Furstenberg, 1987), and more open, especially when confronting areas of conflict (Bray & Burger, 1993; Furstenberg, 1987). In addition, observational studies find that more negativity is exhibited in marital interactions in stepfamilies (Bray & Burger, 1993; Hetherington, 1993; Hetherington et al., 1992; Hetherington & Jodl, 1994). Despite these differences, remarried couples report levels of marital satisfaction that parallel those reported by first-marriage couples (Hetherington et al., 1992; Hetherington & Jodl, 1994), although there may be differences in patterns of changes in marital satisfaction over time. Couples in both first and later marriages report declines in marital satisfaction, particularly as children enter adolescence, but there is evidence that the reported decline may be greater for remarried couples (Booth & Edwards, 1992). The higher risk of divorce among remarried couples may be attributed to a number of factors, including the greater negativity that may characterize a couple's interactions, the challenge of integrating spouses' different attitudes and marital histories, and the unique complexity of family relationships. Furthermore, marital dissatisfaction and instability may be exacerbated by the difficulties for stepparents in assuming an active parenting role. Perhaps because the adoption of a disciplinarian role frequently meets with conflict and resistance from stepchildren, stepfathers in contrast to biological fathers tend to report higher marital satisfaction when they do not try to adopt such a role.

Associations Between the Marital Relationship and the Parent–Child Relationship

The results of system-based research on first marriages illustrate the strong associations between marital quality and the warmth, negativity, and discipline styles within the parent–child relationship (Kerig, Cowan, & Cowan, 1993). Generally, a comparable pattern of positive associations has been found in remarried families (Bray & Burger, 1993; Fine & Kurdek, 1995; Hetherington et al., 1992; Visher & Visher, 1988). However, exceptions to this pattern have been found, especially in stepfamilies with preadolescent children. For preadolescent sons who had troubled, coercive relationships with their mothers, the entry of a stepfather may be seen as a potential resource and as protection against a difficult parent–child relationship (Hetherington, 1993; Hetherington et al., 1992; Hetherington & Jodl, 1994) especially if the remarriage is satisfying and harmonious. In contrast, the resistance and negativity exhibited toward stepfathers by preadolescent girls may be greater, particularly early in the remarriage, if the parents are in a happy marriage (Hetherington, 1993).

When a remarriage occurs when children are adolescents, both stepsons and stepdaughters are more likely to accept a stepfather if there is a close marital relationship. Why should the response of preadolescent and adolescent girls to the quality of their parents' remarriage differ? It has been proposed that with the emergence of biological changes and sexual concerns that occurs in early adolescence, a satisfying marriage may be perceived by both the adolescent and parents as a protective buffer against inappropriate intimacy between stepfathers and stepdaughters (Hetherington, 1991, 1993; Hetherington & Jodl, 1994). Biologically related fathers and daughters have difficulty dealing with affection, especially physical affection, as the daughter becomes increasingly sexually mature. These tensions and concerns about appropriate expression of affection and support may be even more intense with nonbiologically related stepdaughters and stepfathers.

Recognition that the associations between marital and parent–child subsystems are bidirectional focuses attention on the permeability of the marital relationship in stepfamilies. There is a general consensus that marital relationships in remarried families are more permeable to the influences of problems in children's adjustment and difficulties in parent and stepfamily relations than are first marriages (Bray & Burger, 1993; Hetherington et al., 1992). The greater permeability is reflected in greater complaints about childrearing conflict and stress in stepfamilies (Hetherington & Jodl, 1994) and the significantly higher rates of divorce in stepfamilies in which children are present (Tzeng & Mare, 1995). However, how adaptive or detrimental permeability in the boundaries of family subsystems may be in stepfamilies is yet to be resolved. It may be that the permeability is one part of the greater adaptive flexibility needed in stepfamilies. On the other hand, the greater permeability may mean that new marriages are less likely to insulate themselves from problems elsewhere in the family system and less likely to maintain strong positive couple relations. Regardless of how this is resolved, however, it is important to note that differences between first-married couples and remarried couples are typically low in magnitude (Booth & Edwards, 1992), and, although the risk of divorce is notably greater for remarried couples, many eventually establish strong, positive marital relationships and an adaptive, well-functioning parenting environment.

Parent–Child Relationships

An authoritative parenting style characterized by high warmth and support, high monitoring of children's activities, and firm, consistent discipline is positively related to children's adjustment in first-marriage, divorced, and remarried families. However, the ability of the custodial parent to achieve or maintain an authoritative style is challenged during the relationship disequilibrium and stresses characteristic of the early years of remarriage. For stepparents, the challenge may be to establish a positive relationship with the stepchild, one that may differ qualitatively from that of either the custodial or noncustodial biological parent.

Residential Parent–Child Relationships. For mothers, conflict and low monitoring and control typically characterize relations with their children during the early months of the remarriage transition (Bray & Burger, 1993; Hetherington et al., 1992; Hetherington & Jodl, 1994) and the negative mother–child interactions are related to more disengagement, dysfunctional family roles, poorer communication, and less cohesion in stepfamilies (Bray, 1990). The mother–child relationship does restabilize over time but the qualities of the restabilized relationship vary depending on the child's age at the time the remarriage takes place. If the remarriage occurs before the child enters adolescence, maternal monitoring and control problems improve and come to resemble that of mothers in first-marriage families (Bray & Burger, 1993; Hetherington et al., 1992; Hetherington & Jodl, 1994). On the other hand, if the remarriage occurs while the child is an early adolescent, the risks of long term problems in the mother–child relationship increase. Parents and children across all family types must realign their relations as they negotiate the children's transition into adolescence and these realignments typically include decreases in parental warmth, monitoring, and control and increases in conflict (Hetherington, 1993; Steinberg, 1988). However, if a remarriage occurs when children are early adolescents and parent–child relations are in flux, problems can be magnified. Maternal monitoring and control do eventually stabilize in these families but at levels lower than that in first-marriage families.

During their time as single parents, custodial fathers tend to develop a parenting style that differs from that observed in custodial mothers. Mothers and fathers appear to be equally warm and nurturing but custodial fathers have fewer problems with control and more problems in communication and monitoring (Chase-Lansdale & Hetherington, 1990; Furstenberg, 1988). The difficulties fathers have in monitoring their children's whereabouts, companions, and behavior is notable in adolescence especially with daughters (Buchanan, Maccoby, & Dornbusch, 1992; Maccoby, Buchanan, Mnookin, & Dornbusch, 1993). However, after their families have restabilized after the divorce, custodial fathers report less child-rearing stress, better parent–child relations, and fewer behavior problems in their children than do custodial mothers (Amato & Keith, 1991a; Clarke-Stewart & Hayward, 1996; Furstenberg, 1988).

When custodial fathers remarry, they experience disruptions in parent–child relations, especially with daughters, that parallel those observed when custodial mothers remarry (Clingempeel et al., 1984). However, fathers may alter their caretaking relationships more radically than mothers do because they are more likely to expect a stepmother to play a major role in household tasks and parenting (Hetherington & Stanley-Hagan, 1995, 1997). Regardless of this difference, relations between remarried, custodial fathers and their children restabilize over time and eventually look similar to those father–child relations in first-married families. Thus, both new remarried mothers and fathers often experience an initial decline in their parenting but, except in families with early adolescent children, the parenting of residential remarried and never-divorced parents eventually become more similar than different.

Nonresidential Parent–Child Relationships. Despite evidence that a positive co-parenting relationship between former spouses and the continued involvement of both parents can be pivotal factors in children's postdivorce adjustment (Hetherington, 1991), many nonresidential fathers eventually withdraw and have limited or no contact with their children (Furstenberg, 1988; Hetherington & Jodl, 1994; Seltzer, 1991). Only about 25% of these fathers maintain weekly contact with their children (Seltzer, 1991). Those who do maintain or increase contact are more likely to adopt a recreational-companionate role than a disciplinary or teaching role (Furstenberg & Cherlin, 1991; Hetherington, 1993; Lindner-Gunnoe, 1993). Perhaps because of his companionable role, the continued involvement of the nonresidential father does not conflict with the stepfather's efforts to establish authoritative relations with the stepchild and the dual relationships may benefit the children, particularly boys (Lindner-Gunnoe, 1993; Hetherington, 1993; Hetherington & Jodl, 1994; White, 1994).

In contrast to fathers, nonresidential mothers are almost twice as likely to remain in contact with their children following divorce (Lindner-Gunnoe, 1993; Hetherington, 1993; Hetherington & Jodl, 1994). Mothers who were involved and competent prior to divorce stay involved even after the remarriage of the custodial father (Hetherington, 1993). Although nonresidential mothers tend to exhibit lower control and monitoring than custodial mothers, they are higher on these parenting dimensions than are noncustodial fathers (Hetherington & Jodl, 1994). Moreover, noncustodial mothers are more likely than noncustodial fathers to take an active parenting role, to rearrange their living quarters to accommodate their children, and to be interested in their children's concerns and activities. It is therefore not surprising that children report feeling closer to noncustodial mothers than to noncustodial fathers (Lindner-Gunnoe, 1993). Unfortunately, in contrast to the apparent lack of conflict between the roles of nonresidential fathers and residential stepfathers, the continued involvement of the mother may bring mother and stepmother into conflict, at least from the perspective of the children involved. Children in stepmother families often report feeling caught between their mother and stepmothers and the perceived loyalty conflicts can lead to difficulties in the stepmother–stepchild relationship (Furstenberg, 1987; Lindner-Gunnoe, 1993; Salwen, 1990).

Stepfather–Stepchild Relationships

The limited contact between most fathers and their noncustodial children serves to increase the significance of stepfathers' roles in the lives of their stepchildren

(Ganong & Coleman, 1994; Marsiglio, 1992). However, there is little clarity or agreement about what a stepparent's role should be and this lack of clarity is related to low stepfather parenting satisfaction (Kurdek & Fine, 1991; Peck, Bell, Waldren, & Sorrell, 1988) and to low maternal, family, marital, and life satisfaction (Kurdek & Fine, 1991). Over half of parents and stepparents think stepparents should share equally with parents in childrearing responsibilities and play an active parenting role (Marsiglio, 1992) whereas many stepchildren may believe that stepparents should not be parents (Visher & Visher, 1988). The absence of social norms is exacerbated by the absence of legal parental status. With the exception of a few states that require stepfathers to contribute to the financial support of their stepchildren, stepfathers have no legal rights or responsibilities. Thus, a significant number of stepfathers report that they feel unprepared to integrate themselves into the existing family (Marsilglio, 1992). Even when they can develop a rapport with their stepchildren, many feel more like friends than parents, a feeling supported by observations of stepfather–stepchild interactions wherein stepfathers have been found to act more like polite strangers than parents (Vuchinich et al., 1991).

Compared to biological parents, most stepfathers are less involved and communicative (Thomson, McLanahan, & Curtin, 1992), provide less warmth and nurturance (Amato, 1987; Hetherington et al., 1992; Thomson et al., 1992), and view their relationships with stepchildren in less positive ways (Fine, Voydanoff, & Donnelly, 1993; Hetherington et al., 1992). Results of studies of stepfather control have been more mixed. In some studies, stepfathers have been found to exert less control than biological fathers (Amato, 1987; Hetherington et al., 1992). Other studies have found no family type differences in paternal control (Thomson et al., 1992). Still other studies have found violent control attempts reflected in homicides perpetrated on stepchildren by stepfathers being 100 times greater than those of biological fathers and children. These rates are most marked for infants and preschool children (Daly & Wilson, 1996). Inconsistencies such as those in the studies of paternal control reflect the great diversity in stepfathers' parenting. To some extent, the differences among stepfathers' parenting styles are influenced by the parenting role expectations that mothers' communicate to them, stepchildren's responses to their relationship overtures, and whether stepfathers have custodial or noncustodial children of their own.

Positive, authoritative mother–child relations may encourage a close, supportive association between stepfathers and their stepchildren (Marsiglio, 1992). However, mothers have been referred to as the gatekeepers to relationships of other people with their children. This is especially noticeable in children's relations with both noncustodial fathers and stepfathers. Thus, a mother's expectations and encouragement of the stepfather's role help shape his parenting efforts. When remarried mothers welcome and support stepfathers' involvement in discipline and stepfathers are able to establish authoritative relationships with their stepchildren, the children experience fewer adjustment problems. However, mothers themselves may be unsure of the roles their new partners should take. When stepfathers receive the resultant ambiguous messages, they may respond by disengaging or never engaging in the first place.

The ease with which stepfathers adopt a disciplinary role also may vary as a function of the child's developmental status. As indicated in the discussion of children's adjustment, children who are early adolescents at the time of the remarriage are more likely to be resistant and negative in response to stepfathers' parenting overtures (Hetherington, 1989; Hetherington & Anderson, 1989; Hetherington et al., 1992; Santrock, Sitterle, & Warshak, 1988). However, comparisons of well-functioning and dysfunctional stepfamilies have found evidence that regardless of children's ages, stepchildren in dysfunctional families tend to respond with negativity to stepfathers efforts at both warmth and authority (Anderson & White, 1986; Brown, Green, & Druckman, 1990; Hetherington et al., 1992). Early in a remarriage, especially with adolescent children, the adolescent may play a more salient role in shaping the stepfather's behavior than the reverse. Resistance, behavior problems, and low social competence in adolescent stepchildren leads to subsequent increased negativity and lowered positivity and support by stepfathers (Hetherington et al., 1992). Children's repeated rejections of stepfathers may lead to the development of strong maladaptive biological parent–child alliances, which can put the marriage at risk (Anderson & White, 1986; Messinger, Walker, & Freeman, 1978).

When stepchildren share their residence with the children of their new stepfathers in a blended or mixed stepfamily, they are likely to be engaged in more stepfather–stepchild conflicts and to receive less warmth, support, control, and monitoring from stepfathers than do his own biologically related children (Henderson, Hetherington, Mekos, & Reiss, 1996; Hetherington & Jodl, 1994). Although there is some evidence that stepfathers residing with both their own children and stepchildren may be more likely to engage in activities with both and through these shared activities assume a parenting role with all children in the house, differential treatment of own and stepchildren is found in most studies (Henderson et al., 1996; Marsiglio, 1991, 1992).

In contrast, the results of studies that have examined the impact of the noncustodial father's remarriage on parent–child relations have been mixed. In a process labeled by Furstenberg (1988) as the "transient father syndrome" or "child swapping," some researchers have found that noncustodial fathers who remarry tend to transfer their parenting to their stepchildren (Furstenberg, 1988; Popenoe, 1994; Seltzer & Bianchi, 1988; White, 1994). When this occurs, the affective and time commitments made by stepfathers to stepchildren may occur at the expense of their involvement with their own children. However, other researchers have found that fathers with nonresidential children experience cognitive dissonance as they try to balance the needs of children in two families. The result is that responsibilities to their own children win out at the expense of any parenting role they may have assumed with their stepchildren (Clingempeel, Colyar, & Hetherington, 1994). These conflicting results may reflect differences in the degree to which the men sustain contact with their noncustodial children. Those who have minimal contact may be the men Furstenberg (1988) described as "transient fathers" whereas those who do remain involved in the lives of their children may find it difficult to justify support of new stepchildren.

Despite confused role definitions and family expectations, a small but significant number of stepfathers, particularly those with younger stepchildren, become active and involved authoritative parents. Boys especially may benefit from such relationships (Hetherington et al., 1992; Hetherington & Jodl, 1994; Lindner-Gunnoe, 1993). However, perhaps in response to role ambiguity, resistance of children, and problems encountered in their early relations with their stepchildren, most stepfathers remain or become disengaged. A few disengage completely. Others manage to develop close relationships with their stepchildren but do not assume an active disciplinarian role. Research suggests that this last model may be adaptive, at least in the early stages of stepfamily formation. Stepfathers initially do best when they establish a warm, supportive relationship with their stepchildren but refrain from direct, active control and instead support the mother's efforts to discipline (Bray & Burger, 1993; Fine et al., 1993; Hetherington et al., 1992; Hetherington & Jodl, 1994). More authoritative parenting can be attained only gradually and, in many stepfamilies, may not be attained at all (Bray & Burger, 1993).

Stepmother–Stepchild Relationships

Few child adjustment differences have been found between stepfather and stepmother families (Fine, Kurdek, & Hennigen, 1992; Ganong & Coleman, 1994). However, research suggests that parenting stepchildren is more difficult for stepmothers than for stepfathers (Clingempeel et al., 1984; Furstenberg, 1987; MacDonald & DeMaris, 1996; Santrock et al., 1988). One explanation for this difference has been that societal gender role expectations are played out in stepmother families. Stepmothers expect and are expected to assume the primary nurturer and caretaker roles (Salwen, 1990; Whitsett & Land, 1992). Thus, despite any conflict they experience between these parenting roles and their feelings toward their stepchildren (Fine et al., 1993; Thomson et al., 1992; Whitsett & Land, 1992), stepmothers are usually more involved with their stepchildren than are stepfathers and take a more active role in discipline (Fine et al., 1993; Thomson et al., 1992). In turn, more involvement provides more opportunities in which to encounter childrearing difficulties and conflict. It is interesting that a study that compared the parenting difficulties and satisfaction of stepmothers and stepfathers found evidence that, even when differences in degree of involvement are controlled for, stepmothers experience more problems in their relationships with stepchildren (MacDonald & DeMaris, 1996). These results suggest that qualities other than simple involvement are critical to the stepmother–stepchild relationship.

Compared to biological mothers, stepmothers are less positive, controlling, and involved in monitoring their stepchildren's behavior. They are, however, less likely to criticize or to use coercive techniques to control stepchildren than they are to control their own biological children's behavior (Henderson et al., 1996; Hetherington & Jodl, 1994). Stepchildren concur in viewing their stepmothers as unsupportive and uninvolved (Santrock et al., 1988). In addition, children consider their relations with stepmothers as more stressful than those with stepfathers (Furstenberg, 1987) and a threat to their relationships with their biological mothers (Salwen, 1990; Santrock et al., 1988). It appears that children have more difficulty balancing biological parent and stepparent relationships when the stepparent is a stepmother (Furstenberg, 1987).

Despite expectations that the stepmother will take an active childrearing role, there is evidence that the pattern observed in stepfather families may be adaptive in stepmother families. The quality of the stepmother–stepchild relationship has been found to be positively related to the degree to which the biological father supervises and controls his children's activities (Fine & Kurdek, 1992). In other words, if the father is the control figure, the stepmother feels less pressure to assume a disciplinary role that can exacerbate conflict in her relations with her stepchild.

In summary, compared to parent–child relations in first-marriage families, parent–child relations during the early stages of remarriage are more disrupted and conflictual and parenting tends to be less authoritative. However, over time the parenting of biological residential parents in stepfamilies tends to stabilize at levels comparable to that observed in first-marriage families. Regardless of time since family formation, stepparents are less authoritative and more disengaged with stepchildren than they are with their own biological children in blended stepfamilies or than biological parents in first marriages are with their children. However, it may be adaptive for stepparents to establish relationships with stepchildren that are qualitatively unique, particularly if noncustodial parents remain actively involved (Bray & Burger, 1993; Ganong & Coleman 1994; Fine et al., 1993).

Sibling Relationships

Although most studies of stepfamilies have focused on parent–child relationships, some findings are emerging on sibling relationships. Two hypotheses might be proposed about what marital transitions could do to sibling relationships. The first is that siblings might become more rivalrous and conflicted in their relationships as they compete for the scarce resources of mothers' attention and affection as she becomes more preoccupied and engaged in other relationships in the remarriage. The second is that they might draw closer together and become mutually supportive to protect themselves against unstable, unreliable adult relationships.

The first hypothesis is the one most clearly supported by the little research on siblings in stepfamilies. Biologically related siblings, whether full siblings from a mother's previous marriage or half-siblings with one from a previous marriage and one born to the new union in the remarriage, are less positive and involved and more contentious and rivalrous than those in first-marriages (Hetherington, 1993; Hetherington & Jodl, 1994). However, biologically related adolescents, whether in first-marriage families or stepfamilies are more likely to have competitive conflictual relationships than are unrelated stepsiblings living in the same household. At least with adolescent siblings in stabilized stepfamilies, there is less aggression and rivalry (Ganong & Coleman, 1994; Hetherington & Jodl, 1994) but also less teaching and helping between nonbiologically related stepchildren in blended families than between biologically related siblings (Ganong & Coleman, 1994). However, full stepsiblings are more likely to be friendly, and although there is a risk that they will become detached or disengaged, many residential stepsiblings seem to form successful satellite relationships (Ihinger-Tallman, 1988) and often provide mutual support and companionship. Warm relationships are more likely to occur with female siblings in stepfamilies. Males in stepfamilies are less likely to receive support from either male or female siblings (Hetherington et al., 1992; Hetherington & Jodl, 1994).

Although, on the average, relations among stepsiblings are less contentious than those among biologically related siblings, to some extent this may be due to ambiguity in the stepsibling role and lack of involvement of many stepsiblings. In reply to the question, "Who is your immediate family?" Furstenberg (1987) found that 41% of children did not include stepsiblings. Furthermore, Furstenberg found that these exclusions were not related to the length of time spent living together in a stepfamily.

It may be that disengagement and diminished rivalry among residential stepsiblings occurs because both children have access to a residential parent for support and affection. Furthermore, it is likely that children may more readily justify and accept differential parental treatment of siblings on the basis of biological relatedness of parent and child. Finally, it may be that unrelated stepsiblings may be less reactive to each other than full biological siblings because of having been spared a shared history of exposure to the stressful experiences of their parents' divorces. There is some evidence in the animal literature that young litter mates who experienced stress together were later more aggressive toward each other than toward unfamiliar animals (Berkowitz, 1983).

Sibling relationships in stepfamilies are important. Warm, supportive relationships are associated with greater social competence and responsibility in children and sibling rivalry and aggression with antisocial behavior (Hetherington et al., 1992; Hetherington & Jodl, 1994). To some extent, positive supportive sibling relations among girls can help to protect children from some of the deleterious effects of divorce and remarriage (Hetherington, 1989, 1991, 1993; Hetherington & Jodl, 1994).

SOCIAL POLICY

Despite the wide variations in stepfamily types and histories, much of what is known about relationships and outcomes in stepfamilies is based on studies of stepfather families. This is not surprising given that this structure comprises the majority of stepfamilies headed by a married couple (U.S. Bureau of the Census, 1992). More longitudinal research is needed to investigate individual adjustment and family relationship dynamics in stepfamilies with less typical structures, which include stepmother families, mixed stepfamilies, families headed by single parents who marry for the first time, and families headed by cohabiting adults. In addition, a greater understanding of the impact of multiple marital transitions on children and parents is needed because the adverse effects of multiple transitions are more severe and enduring than those of a single transition (Amato & Booth, 1991). In these studies, care must be taken to examine diverse adaptive trajectories associated with marital transitions and timing and patterns of risks and vulnerability and protective factors that contribute to adverse outcomes or resiliency following marital transitions.

There also is a need for new and expanded family policies that address issues unique to stepfamilies (Brooks-Gunn, 1994; Fine, 1994; Mahoney, 1994,1995). Expansions of existing family policies and any new policies designed to address the special needs of stepfamilies must consider the diversity of stepfamilies (Fine, 1994). Laws helpful to some may be ineffective or even harmful to others. Moreover, new or expanded policies should take into account that in some families a continued relationship can be positive for both stepparents and stepchildren and can survive the dissolution of the stepfamily (Fine, 1994). Thus, guidelines that support the continued stepparent–stepchild relationship might be an included topic in divorce mediation policies and procedures.

Perhaps most beneficial to stepfamilies would be policies designed to help stepparents and stepchildren establish legal relationships and responsibilities with each other (Fine, 1994; Jaff, 1988; Mahoney, 1994). In contrast to adoption, which terminates the rights of the noncustodial parent, new stepparent policies must preserve the rights and responsibilities of both custodial and noncustodial parents (Fine, 1994; Brooks-Gunn, 1994). There may be a need to prioritize or delineate child-care decision rights. For example, a stepparent might be given the right to have access to a stepchild's academic records and to participate in parent–teacher conferences but not be given the right to take the child out of the state without the consent of both biological parents. Such policies should also be sensitive to the fact that some stepparents may not chose to assume a parenting role or that to do so might not be in the best interests of a particular child. Thus, stepparents might be required to petition for parental rights with the agreement of both biological parents and for a specific period of time (e.g., until the child's eighteenth birthday).

A model for such a policy, the England's Children's Act of 1989, was implemented in 1991 (Masson, 1992). Careful monitoring of the impact of this act could provide valuable information for the framing of a similar policy in the United States. The provision of legal status to stepparents would help legitimate step relationships. It could result in increased stepparent commitment to the stepchild, reassure the stepchild that their step relationship are not transitory, and help both adults and children to achieve a clearer family identity.

SUMMARY AND CONCLUSION

Remarriage requires changes in and additions to family roles and relationships, which challenge all family members. The stresses associated with these challenges are reflected in problems in stepchildren's adjustment. Children entering a stepfamily tend to experience difficulties in emotional and behavioral adjustment, social relations, and school achievement. However, although problems may reemerge or develop in late adolescence and adulthood, the percentage of children who experience severe, lasting problems is relatively small. Research based on risk and resiliency models rather than deficit models has led to a growing recognition and acceptance of the fact that most children in stepfamilies adapt and develop into competent individuals (Bray & Burger, 1993; Hetherington, 1993, in press-a; Hetherington et al., 1992; Hetherington & Jodl, 1994).

In addition, there is a growing recognition and acceptance that stepfamilies differ from other family types in their patterns of functioning, organization, and relationships. Compared to first-married couples, most couples in stabilized remarriages report similar levels of marital satisfaction but also note that their relationships are more egalitarian and may be more permeable to the influences of other family subsystems, particularly the stepparent–stepchild relationship. The challenges associated with stepfamily formation are evident in the diminished parenting exhibited by both mothers and fathers in the early months and years following the remarriage transition. However, with the possible exception of mothers who remarry when their daughters are preadolescents, the parenting of remarried mothers and fathers in stabilized stepfamilies is more similar than different from the parenting of their counterparts in first marriage families. The ideal situation for stepchildren might be one in which both biological parent and stepparent establish and maintain an authoritative parenting environment. Unfortunately, authoritative stepparenting may be a difficult if not impossible goal for stepparents confronted with the challenges of simultaneously developing relationships with both spouse and stepchildren and finding ways to balance relations with stepchildren and biological children in the absence of guiding norms and in the face of possible opposition from their stepchildren. In stabilized remarried families, stepparents are more likely to be disengaged than authoritative. However, the characteristics of the disengaged parent may differ for biological parents and stepparents. In contrast to the disengaged biological parents who are characteristically neglecting, indifferent, and uninvolved, the disengaged stepparent may be warm and supportive of stepchildren but involve themselves in control and discipline indirectly through their support of the biological parent's efforts. Evidence suggests that this approach may be adaptive especially during the early stages of stepfamily formation and when stepparents are unwilling or unable to establish authoritative relations with their stepchildren. Thus, relationship characteristics and family processes that are adaptive for stepfamilies may differ from those that are adaptive for first-marriage or single-parent families. These differences have important implications for those who work with stepfamilies, including clinicians and policymakers.

REFERENCES

Amato, P. R. (1987). Family processes in one-parent, stepparent, and intact families: The child's point of view. *Journal of Marriage and the Family, 49*, 327–337.

Amato, P. R. (1993). Children's adjustment to divorce: Theories, hypothesis, and empirical support. *Journal of Marriage and the Family, 55*, 23–38.

Amato, P. R. (1994). The implications of research findings on children in stepfamilies. In A. Booth & J. Dunn (Eds.), *Stepfamilies: Who benefits? Who does not?* (pp. 81–87). Hillsdale, NJ: Lawrence Erlbaum Associates.

Amato, P. R., & Booth, A. (1991). Consequences of parental divorce and marital unhappiness for adult well-being. *Social Forces, 69*, 895–914.

Amato, P. R., & Keith, N. (1991a). Parental divorce and adult well-being: A meta-analysis. *Journal of Marriage and the Family, 53*, 43–58.

Amato, P. R., & Keith, N. (1991b). Parental divorce and the well-being of children: A meta-analysis. *Psychology Bulletin, 110*, 26–46.

Amato, P. R., Loomis, L. S., & Booth, A. (1995). Parental divorce, marital conflict, and offspring well-being during early adulthood. *Social Forces, 73*(3), 895–915.

Anderson, J., & White, G. (1986). Dysfunctional intact families and stepfamilies. *Family Process, 25*, 407–422.

Berkowitz, L. (1983). Aversively stimulated aggression: Some parallels and differences in research with animals and humans. *American Psychologist, 38*, 1135–1144.

Booth, A., & Edwards, J. N. (1992). Starting over: Why remarriages are more unstable. *Journal of Family Issues, 13*(2), 179–194.

Brand, E., Clingempeel, W. G., & Bowen-Woodward, K. (1988). Family relationships and children's adjustment in stepmother and stepfather families. In E. M. Hetherington & J. D. Arasteh (Eds.), *Impact of divorce, single-parenting, and stepparenting on children* (pp. 299–324). Hillsdale, NJ: Lawrence Erlbaum Associates.

Bray, J. H. (1990, August). The developing family II: Overview and previous findings. Paper presented at the annual meeting of the American Psychological Association, Boston, MA.

Bray, J. H., & Burger, S. H. (1993). Developmental issues in stepfamilies research project: Family relationships and parent-child interactions. *Journal of Family Psychology, 7*, 76–80.

Brooks-Gunn, J. (1994). Research on stepparenting families: Integrating disciplinary approaches and informing policy. In A. Booth & J. Dunn (Eds.), *Stepfamilies: Who benefits? Who does not?* (pp. 167–189). Hillsdale, NJ: Lawrence Erlbaum Associates.

Brown, A. C., Green, R. J., & Druckman, J. (1990). A comparison of stepfamilies with and without child-focused problems. *American Journal of Orthopsychiatry, 60*(4), 556–566.

Bumpass, L., & Sweet, J. A. (1989). *Children's experience in single-parent families: Implications of cohabitation and marital transitions* (NSFH Working Paper No. 3). Madison: University of Wisconsin, Center for Demography and Ecology.

Chase-Lansdale, P. L., & Hetherington, E. M. (1990). The impact of divorce on life-span development: Short and long-term effects. In P. B. Baltes, D. L. Featherman, & R. L. Lerner (Eds.), *Life-span development and behavior* (Vol. 10, pp. 105–150). Hillsdale, NJ: Lawrence Erlbaum Associates.

Cherlin, A., & Furstenberg, F. F. (1994). Stepfamilies in the United States: A reconsideration. In J. Blake & J. Hagen (Eds.), *Annual review of sociology* (pp. 359–381). Palo Alto, CA: Annual Reviews.

Clarke-Stewart, K. A., & Hayward, C. (1996). Advantages of father custody and contact for the psychological well-being of school-age children. *Journal of Applied Developmental Psychology, 17,* 239–270.

Clingempeel, W. G., Brand, E., & Ievoli, R. (1984). Stepparent–stepchild relationships in stepmother and stepfather families. *Child Development, 57,* 474–484.

Clingempeel, W. G., Colyar, J. J., & Hetherington, E. M. (1994). Toward a cognitive dissonance conceptualization of stepchildren and biological children loyalty conflicts: A construct validity study. In K. Pasley & M. Ihinger-Tallman (Eds.), *Stepparenting: Issues in theory, research, and practice* (pp. 151–173). Westport, CT: Greenwood.

Daly, M., & Wilson, M. I. (1996). Violence against stepchildren. *Current Directions in Psychological Science, 5*(3), 77–81.

Dawson, D. A. (1991). Family structure and children's health and wellbeing: Data from the 1988 National Health Interview Survey on Child Health. *Journal of Marriage and the Family, 53,* 573–584.

Demo, D. H., & Acock, A. C. (1996). Family structure, family process, and adolescent well-being. *Journal of Research on Adolescence, 6*(4), 457–488.

Fine, M. A. (1994). Social policy pertaining to stepfamilies: Should stepparents and stepchildren have the option of establishing a legal relationship? In A. Booth & J. Dunn (Eds.), *Stepfamilies: Who benefits? Who does not?* (pp. 197–204). Hillsdale, NJ: Lawrence Erlbaum Associates.

Fine, M. A., & Kurdek, L. A. (1992). The adjustment of adolescents in stepfather and stepmother families. *Journal of Marriage and the Family, 54,* 725–736.

Fine, M. A., & Kurdek, L. A. (1995). Relation between marital quality and (step)parent–child relationship quality for parents and stepparents in stepfamilies. *Journal of Family Psychology, 9*(2), 216–223.

Fine, M. A., Kurdek, L. A., & Hennigen, L. (1992). Family structure, perceived clarity of (step)parent roles, and perceived self-competence in young adolescents. *Family Perspective, 25,* 261–282.

Fine, M. A., Voydanoff, P., & Donnelly, B. W. (1993). The relations between parental control and warmth and child well-being in stepfamilies. *Journal of Family Psychology, 7,* 222–232.

Furstenberg, F. F., Jr. (1987). The new extended family: The experience of parents and children after remarriage. In K. Pasley & M. Ihinger-Tallman (Eds.), *Remarriage and stepparenting: Current research and theory* (pp. 42–61). New York: Guilford.

Furstenberg, F. F., Jr. (1988). Child care after divorce and remarriage. In E. M. Hetherington & J. D. Arasteh (Eds.), *Impact of divorce, single parenting, and stepparenting on children* (pp. 245–261). Hillsdale, NJ: Lawrence Erlbaum Associates.

Furstenberg, F. F., Jr., & Cherlin, A. (1991). *Divided families: What happens to children when parents part*. Cambridge, MA: Harvard University Press.

Ganong, L. H., & Coleman, M. (1994). *Remarried family relationships*. Thousand Oaks: Sage.

Garmezy, N. (1993). Stressors of childhood. In N. Garmezy & M. Rutter (Eds.), *Stress, coping, and development in children* (pp. 43–84). New York: McGraw-Hill.

General Household Survey. (1993). A. Bridgwood & D. Savage, (Eds.). HMSO.

Glick, P. C. (1989). Remarried families, stepfamilies, and stepchildren: A brief demographic profile. *Family Relations, 38,* 24–27.

Henderson, S. H., Hetherington, E. M., Mekos, D., & Reiss, D. (1996). Stress, parenting, and adolescent psychopathology in nondivorced and stepfamilies: A within-family perspective. In E. M. Hetherington & E. H. Blechman (Eds.), *Stress, coping, and resiliency in children and families* (pp. 39–66). Mahwah, NJ: Lawrence Erlbaum Associates.

Hetherington, E. M. (1989). Coping with family transitions: Winners, losers, and survivors. *Child Development, 60*, 1–14.

Hetherington, E. M. (1991). Families, lies, and videotapes. *Journal of Research on Adolescence, 1*, 323–348.

Hetherington, E. M. (1993). An overview of the Virginia longitudinal study of divorce and remarriage with a focus on early adolescence. *Journal of Family Psychology, 7*, 1–18.

Hetherington, E. M. (in press-a). Social capital and the development of youth from nondivorced, divorced, and remarried families. In A. Collins (Ed.), *Relationships as developmental contexts: The 29th Minnesota Symposium on Child Psychology.* Mahwah, NJ: Lawrence Erlbaum Associates.

Hetherington, E. M. (in press-b). Teenaged childrearing and divorce. In S. Luthar, J. A. Burack, D. Cicchetti, & J. Weisz (Eds.), Developmental psychopathology: Perspective on risk and disorders (pp. 350–373).

Hetherington, E. M., & Anderson, E. R. (1989). The effects of divorce and remarriage on early adolescents and their families. In M. D. Levine & E. R. McAnarney (Eds.), *Early adolescent transitions* (pp. 49–67). Lexington, MA: Heath.

Hetherington, E. M., Clingempeel, W. G., Anderson, E. R., Deal, J., Stanley-Hagan, M., Hollier, E. A., & Lindner, M. (1992). Coping with marital transitions: A family systems perspective. *Monographs of the Society for Research in Child Development, 57*(2–3, Serial No. 227).

Hetherington, E. M., & Jodl, K. M. (1994). Stepfamilies as settings for child development. In A. Booth & J. Dunn (Eds.), *Stepfamilies: Who benefits? Who does not?* (pp. 55–79). Hillsdale, NJ: Lawrence Erlbaum Associates.

Hetherington, E. M., & Stanley-Hagan, M. (1995). Parenting in divorced and remarried families. In M. Bornstein (Ed.), *Handbook of parenting* (pp. 233–255). Hillsdale, NJ: Lawrence Erlbaum Associates.

Hetherington, E. M., & Stanley-Hagan, M. (1997). The effects of divorce on fathers and their children. In M. Lamb (Ed.), *The role of the father in child development* (pp. 191–211). New York: Wiley.

Ihinger-Tallman, M. (1988). Research on stepfamilies. *Annual Review of Sociology, 14*, 25–48.

Jacobson, D. S. (1982, August). Family structure in the age of divorce. Paper presented at the annual convention of the American Psychological Association, Washington, DC.

Jaff, J. (1988). Wedding bell blues: The position of unmarried people in American law. *Arizona Law Review, 30*, 207–242.

Kerig, P. K., Cowan, P. A., & Cowan, C. P. (1993). Marital quality and gender differences in parent–child interaction. *Developmental Psychology, 29*, 931–939.

Keshet, J. K. (1990). Cognitive remodeling of the family: How remarried people view stepfamilies. *American Journal of Orthopsychiatry, 60*(2), 196–203.

Kurdek, L. A., & Fine, M. A. (1991). Cognitive correlates of adjustment for mothers and stepfathers in stepfather families. *Journal of Marriage and the Family, 53*, 565–572.

Lee, V. E., Burkham, D. T., Zimiles, H., & Ladewski, B. (1994). Family structure and its effect on behavioral and emotional problems in young adolescents. *Journal of Research on Adolescence, 4*(3), 405–437.

Lindner-Gunnoe, M. L. (1993). *Noncustodial mothers' and fathers' contributions to the adjustment of adolescent stepchildren.* Unpublished doctoral dissertation, University of Virginia.

Maccoby, E. E., Buchanan, C. M., Mnookin, R. H., & Dornbusch, S. M. (1993). Postdivorce roles of mothers and fathers in the lives of their children. *Journal of Family Psychology, 7*, 24–38.

MacDonald, W. L., & DeMaris, A. (1996). Parenting stepchildren and biological children: The effects of stepparents' gender and new biological children. *Journal of Family Issues, 17*, 5–25.

Mahoney, M. M. (1994). Reformulating the legal definition of the stepparent–stepchild relationship. In A. Booth and J. Dunn (Eds.), *Stepfamilies: Who benefits? Who does not?* (pp. 191–196). Hillsdale, NJ: Lawrence Erlbaum Associates.

Mahoney, M. M. (1995). *Stepfamilies and the law.* Ann Arbor: University of Michigan Press.

Marsiglio, W. (1991). Paternal engagement activities with minor children. *Journal of Marriage and the Family, 53,* 973–986.

Marsiglio, W. (1992). Stepfathers with minor children living at home: Parent perceptions and relationship quality. *Journal of Family Issues, 13*(2), 195–214.

Martin, T., & Bumpass, L. (1989). Recent trends in marital disruption. *Demography, 26,* 37–51.

Masson, J. (1992). Stepping into the nineties: A summary of the legal implications of the Children Act 1989 for stepfamilies. In B. Dimmock (Ed.), *A step in both directions* (pp. 4–14). London: National Stepfamily Association.

McLanahan, S., & Sandefur, G. (1994). *Growing up with a single parent: What hurts, what helps.* Cambridge, MA: Harvard University Press.

Mekos, D., Hetherington, E. M., & Reiss, D. (1996). Sibling differences in problem behavior and parental treatment in nondivorced and remarried families. *Child Development, 67*(5), 2148–2165.

Messinger, L., Walker, K., & Freeman, S. (1978). Preparation for remarriage following divorce: The use of group techniques. *American Journal of Orthopsychiatry, 48,* 263–272.

Orleans, M., Palisi, B. J., & Caddell, D. (1989). Marriage adjustment and satisfaction of stepfathers: Their feelings and perceptions of decision making and stepchildren relations. *Family Relations, 38,* 371–377.

Peck, C., Bell, N., Waldren, T., & Sorrell, G. (1988). Patterns of functioning in families of remarried and first-married couples. *Journal of Marriage and the Family, 50,* 699–708.

Perry, B. (1995). Step-parenting: How vulnerable are stepchildren? *Educational and Child Psychology, 12*(2), 58–70.

Popenoe, D. (1994). The evolution of marriage and the problem of stepfamilies: A biosocial perspective. In A. Booth & J. Dunn (Eds.), *Stepfamilies: Who benefits? Who does not?* (pp. 2–27). Hillsdale, NJ: Lawrence Erlbaum Associates.

Salwen, L. V. (1990). The myth of the wicked stepmother. *Women and Therapy, 10,* 117–125.

Santrock, J. W., Sitterle, K. A., & Warshak, R. A (1988). Parent–child relationships in stepfather families. In P. Bronson & C. P. Cowan (Eds.), *Contemporary fathers.* New York: Wiley.

Seltzer, J. A. (1991). Relationships between fathers and children who live apart: The father's role after separation. *Journal of Marriage and the Family, 53,* 79–101.

Seltzer, J. A., & Bianchi, S. M. (1988). Children's contact with absent parents. *Journal of Marriage and the Family, 50,* 663–677.

Steinberg, L. (1988). Pubertal maturation and family relations: Evidence for the distancing hypothesis. In G. R. Adams, R. Montemayor, & T. P. Gullotta (Eds.), *Advances in adolescent development* (pp. 71–97). Beverly Hills, CA: Sage.

Thomson, E. (1994). "Settings" and "development" from a demographic point of view. In A. Booth & J. Dunn (Eds.), *Stepfamilies: Who benefits? Who does not?* (pp. 89–96). Hillsdale, NJ: Lawrence Erlbaum Associates.

Thomson, E., McLanahan, S. S., & Curtin, R. B. (1992). Family structure, gender, and parental socialization. *Journal of Marriage and the Family, 54,* 368–378.

Tzeng, J. M., & Mare, R. D. (1995). Labor market and socioeconomic effects on marital stability. *Social Science Research, 24,* 329–351.

U.S. Bureau of the Census. (1992). *Marriage, divorce, and remarriage in the 1990s* (Current Population Reports, pp. 23–180). Washington, DC: U.S. Government Printing Office.

Visher, E., & Visher, J. S. (1988). *Old loyalties, new ties.* New York: Brunner/Mazel.

Vuchinich, S., Hetherington, E. M., Vuchinich, R. A., & Clingempeel, W. G. (1991). Parent and child interaction and gender differences in early adolescents' adaptation to stepfamilies. *Developmental Psychology, 27,* 618–626.

White, L. (1994). Stepfamilies over the life course: Social support. In A. Booth & J. Dunn (Eds.), *Stepfamilies: Who benefits? Who does not?* (pp. 109–138). Hillsdale, NJ: Lawrence Erlbaum Associates.

Whitsett, D., & Land, H. (1992). The development of a role strain index for stepparents. *The Journal of Contemporary Human Services, 73*(1), 14–22.

Wolin, S., & Wolin, S. (1993). *The resilient self: How survivors of troubled families rise above adversity.* New York: Villard.

Zill, N. (1994). Understanding why children in stepfamilies have more learning and behavior problems than children in nuclear families. In A. Booth & J. Dunn (Eds.), *Stepfamilies: Who benefits? Who does not?* (pp. 97–106). Hillsdale, NJ: Lawrence Erlbaum Associates.

Zill, N., Morrison, D. R., & Coiro, M. J. (1993). Long-term effects of parental divorce and parent–child relationships, adjustment, and achievement in young adulthood. *Journal of Family Psychology, 7*(1), 91–103.

Chapter 9

Adoptive Families

HAROLD D. GROTEVANT
JULIE K. KOHLER
University of Minnesota

Just as *nontraditional* and *family,* the words in the title of this book, mean different things to different people, so does the word *adoption.* Although it refers to the
legal transfer of responsibility for parenting a specific child from one adult or couple to another adult or couple, the term is used to refer to a number of different
family situations.

The purpose of this chapter is to provide the reader with an overview of research about adoptive families. The chapter begins by detailing data on rates of
various types of adoption. Second, we review the research that has been conducted
on these different adoptive family forms. The third section provides a view of the
processes that link the various parties involved in adoption and reviews the effects
of adoption on each of these parties. Finally, the chapter concludes by highlighting
some of the emerging adoption-related issues that the authors predict will help refine our current understanding of adoption and adoptive family processes.

FREQUENCY OF ADOPTION

There are more than 5 million adults and children living in the United States who
have been adopted, and more than 1 million children presently live in adoptive
families (Center for Adoption Research and Policy, 1997). Some adoptions occur
within the context of a biological relationship. For example, following remarriage,
a stepparent might legally adopt the child of his or her new spouse, or a nonparent
relative might adopt a child. Adoptions of children unrelated to their adopting parents are also quite varied. At placement, adopted children vary in age from new-
born infants to adolescents. They also vary in terms of racial, ethnic, and national
origin, and of the correspondence between their origin and that of their adopting
parents. Some adopted children are physically and mentally healthy at placement;
others have identified disabilities or are at risk for developing disabilities because

of genetic, prenatal, or preplacement factors. Some children are adopted alone; others are adopted along with one or more siblings. Some move from birth family to foster family (possibly multiple times) before parental rights are terminated and a permanent adoptive placement is made.

In part because of the definitional complexities mentioned, it is quite difficult to document the frequency with which adoption occurs in the United States. Accurate and current adoption statistics are difficult to locate. The challenge is further complicated because there is no comprehensive system in place to collect reliable adoption data in the United States. The federal government stopped collecting uniform adoption data in 1975, when the National Center for Social Statistics was dissolved (National Committee for Adoption, 1989). After becoming aware of the problems associated with the lack of data, the U.S. Congress passed legislation in 1986 that required national adoption and foster care data to be collected by 1991. However, this goal was not met. The announced target date for implementation of the Adoption and Foster Care Analysis and Reporting System (AFCARS) is December, 1998 (Vick, 1995). In the meantime, nongovernmental organizations such as the National Council for Adoption (NCFA), the American Public Welfare Association (APWA), and the Child Welfare League of America (CWLA) have attempted to compile adoption statistics. Their efforts, however, are limited by the inconsistent ways in which states and other entities keep adoption records.

The most comprehensive available data were published in the Adoption Factbook (National Committee for Adoption, 1989), which is based on 1986 data that were collected in 1988 (see Table 9.1). The number of domestic adoptions across

TABLE 9.1
Adoptions in the United States, 1986

Adoption Type	Adopter/Agency	Number	
Domestic	Relatives	52,931	
	Unrelated/Public	20,064	
	Unrelated/Private	15,063	
	Unrelated/Individually arranged	16,040	
	Total		104,098
International			10,019[a]
All adoptions			114,117
Special needs			13,568
Infants			24,589
	Ratio infant adoption per 1000 live births		6.5
	Ratio infant adoption per 1000 nonmarital live births		28.0

Note: Source is Stolley, Kathy S. Statistics on adoption in the United States. *The Future of Children* (Spring 1993) 3(1), 26–42. Reprinted with permission of the Center for the Future of Children of the David and Lucile Packard Foundation.
[a]In 1995, the number was 9,679.

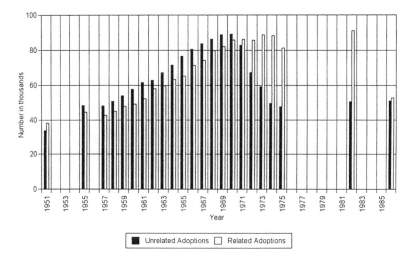

FIG 9.1.   Related and unrelated domestic adoptions, 1951–1986. *Source:* Stolley, Kathy S. Statistics on Adoption in the United States. *The Future of Children* (Spring 1993) 3,1:26– 42. Reprinted with permission of the Center for the Future of Children of the David and Lucile Packard Foundation.

unrelated families rose steadily from the early 1950s to 1970 and then declined steeply to 1975, at which point it leveled off around the rate experienced in the mid-1950s (see Fig. 9.1). NCFA is in the process of collecting and analyzing more recent data. Preliminary results suggest that the aggregate annual number of domestic adoptions of children unrelated to their adopting parents in the United States is approximately the same as that reported in 1989, or 51,167 (P. Purtill, personal communication, August 22, 1996).

Among these non-relative adoptions, the mixture of public agency, private agency, and independent adoptions has also changed across this time interval (see Fig. 9.2). The percentage of non-relative adoptions arranged by public agencies rose from just under 20% in the 1950s to just under 40% in 1986. Independent adoptions accounted for more than 50% of placements in the 1950s and declined to a little more than 20% in the mid-1970s. By 1986, independent placements occurred more frequently (31.4%) than those through private agencies (29.4%); public agency placements accounted for the remaining 39.2% (Stolley, 1993). The current number of independent adoptions in the United States is probably underreported and has probably risen since the mid-1980s (McDermott, 1993).

Much better data are available about international adoptions, because the U.S. State Department keeps information on children's visas. Overall, the total number of international adoptions per year appears to be roughly the same in 1996 as it was in 1986 (10,019), although the number declined somewhat following 1988 but

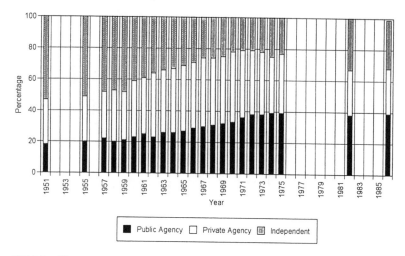

FIG 9.2.   Placement arrangements of unrelated adoptions, 1951–1986, by percentage. *Source:* Stolley, Kathy S. Statistics on Adoption in the United States. *The Future of Children* (Spring 1993) 3,1:26–42. Reprinted with permission of the Center for the Future of Children of the David and Lucile Packard Foundation.

then rose again (P. Purtill, personal communication, August 22, 1996). Although the total numbers are roughly the same, the proportion of adoptions from specific countries has changed dramatically within this 8-year period.

DIMENSIONS ALONG WHICH ADOPTIONS DIFFER

The dimensions along which adoptions differ include characteristics of the adoptive family system, adoptive parents, and adopted children. In this section, we discuss seven types of adoptions that highlight the plurality of the 1990s' adoptive families. The first, stepparent adoption, represents characteristics of the adoptive family system; the others either represent characteristics of adoptive parents (single-parent adoptions and adoptions by gay and lesbian couples); adopted children (children with handicapping conditions and children who have spent time in foster care); or both parents and children, as in the cases of transracial and international adoptions. The diversity of adoptive families is largely a result of the changes in family structure that have occurred since the 1970s. Stepparent adoptions are a prominent byproduct of increased rates of divorce, remarriage, and nonmarital childbearing and will consequently be covered first. However, although the primary focus of this chapter is on non-relative adoptions, they will not be reviewed in depth. For a more detailed review of the stepfamily literature, see Hetherington and Stanley-Hagan (chap. 8, this volume.)

Adoptions by Stepparents

Exact figures on the rates of adoptions by stepparents are not available. In the *Adoption Factbook*, rates of stepparent adoption are subsumed in the category of adoption by relatives, which totaled 52,931 in 1986 (National Committee for Adoption, 1989). Although precise data are not available, adoptions by stepparents are typically cited as being the most prevalent type of adoption in the United States (Cole & Donley, 1990; Reitz & Watson, 1992), with stepfathers being the most frequent adopting parent. Despite their prevalence, however, stepparent adoptions have not been a primary focus of the adoption literature.

Some researchers (e.g. Reitz & Watson, 1992) have begun to document the family dynamics that are often associated with stepparent adoption. They report that in cases of stepfather adoption, the child's father has typically died, disappeared, or stopped contact and financial support. Stepparent adoption is less likely to occur in situations in which a child is highly involved and in regular contact with both parents (Reitz & Watson, 1992). Stepparent adoption may be desired as a way to give the stepfather legal authority over the children he is raising and formalize his role in the family. However, it has also been suggested that children may simultaneously feel a sense of loss, attachment, and loyalty, and clinicians generally recommend that parents discuss the possibility of adoption with their child or stepchild before making a final decision (Reitz & Watson, 1992).

Single-Parent Adoption

The increased societal acceptance of a plurality of family structures has created an environment in which adoption has become a viable option for single adults. Although precise demographic data on the numbers of single-parent adoptions in the United States are lacking, the rates have increased in recent years. Many researchers have noted, however, the disproportionate numbers of single adults adopting children with special needs. Recent estimates indicate that single-parent adoption currently constitutes about 25% of all special needs adoptions (Shireman, 1995).

The term *special needs* is used to describe children who are likely to be in need of special services or those for whom permanent placement has traditionally been more difficult. Included in the special needs category are children who are older than 4 years at the time of placement, physically handicapped children, children belonging to a sibling group, children with emotional or behavioral problems, or children who belong to a minority ethnic or racial group. The likelihood that a single adult will adopt a special needs child is increased when the adoption is handled through an agency (Shireman, 1995). Because married couples are still often preferred by agency staff or birth parents or both, single parents tend to adopt children for whom placement has been more difficult. In contrast, others have argued that parent–child compatibility is the reason for the disproportionately high rates of special needs children that are placed in single-parent homes. They argue that single adults may be well suited to adopt special needs children, because their single status may enable them to devote more one-on-one time with children for whom such time would be the most beneficial. Regardless of the cause of this discrepancy, single adoptive parents differ on a number of dimensions from married couples who adopt. They may also face different challenges as adoptive parents.

Researchers have noted that single adoptive parents differ from married adoptive parents on a number of demographic characteristics. Shireman (1988, as cited in Rosenthal & Groze, 1992) noted that single adoptive parents tend to have lower incomes than their married counterparts. This finding is largely attributed to the lower number of potential wage earners in the single-parent family structure as well as the lower earning power of women, who constitute the majority of single adoptive parents. From data gathered from single-parent adoption organizations, researchers (e.g. Shireman, 1995) reported that many single parents are in their middle to late 30s, have graduate degrees, and hold stable jobs, often in helping professions. This distinguishes single adoptive parents from single parents in general.

Single adoptive parents are more likely than married adoptive parents to adopt older children and less likely than married adoptive parents to adopt sibling groups or children for whom they have served as foster parents (Rosenthal & Groze, 1992). Research by Groze and Rosenthal (1991) reported that a greater proportion of singles who adopt special needs children are African American than are couples, who tend to be White. Single adoptive mothers tend to be older than their married female counterparts. The research is mixed on whether boys or girls are more likely to be adopted by single parents. Barth, Berry, Yoshikami, Goodfield, and Carson (1988) and Barth and Berry (1988) reported that single parents are more likely than married couples to adopt boys, whereas other research has found that the majority of single adoptive parents adopt children of the same gender (Shireman, 1995).

Economic stress, rate of disruption, and social isolation are three variables commonly investigated in conjunction with single-parent adoptive families (Barth & Berry, 1988; Groze, 1991; Kagan & Reid, 1986; Shireman, 1995). Lower incomes, combined with fewer family members participating in the paid labor force and the additional financial costs associated with special needs children, can easily lead to increased economic stress for single adoptive parents. Adoption subsidies for adoptive parents with special needs children, authorized under Title IV-E of the 1980 Adoption Assistance and Child Welfare Act, can be used by single adoptive parents to help to alleviate the financial burden.

Adoption disruption is said to occur when a child is removed from an adoptive placement before the adoption has been legally finalized. Disruption is differentiatied from *dissolution*, which occurs when a legalized adoption is annulled (Festinger, 1990). Rates of disruption in single-parent families have been investigated in a number of studies (Barth & Berry, 1988; Kagan & Reid, 1986; Partridge, Hornby, & McDonald, 1986), with mixed findings. Noting certain methodological problems, such as small sample sizes, in all of these studies, Groze (1991) concluded that the overall pattern suggests that "marital status has little, if any, effect on adoption outcome as it relates to disrupted or intact adoptions" (p.326).

Similarly, Shireman (1995) reported mixed findings on rates of social isolation among single adoptive parents. In her Chicago Child Care Study, she found that few children had the opportunity to interact with an adult of the opposite gender of their parent. However, in her discussion, Shireman (1995) stated she was unclear if this finding was related to the adoptive parents' marital status or another confounding factor, such as the area where her sample resided. Overall, this research attempted to counter negative societal perceptions of single adoptive parents by examining their strengths as well as their strains. After providing a more thorough look at the factors involved in single-parent adoptions, she concluded that "adoption has been a good plan for these children" (p. 324).

Adoption by Lesbian and Gay Couples

Another indication of the way that changing social norms have affected adoption has been the growing numbers of gay and lesbian couples who have become adoptive parents in recent years. However, despite the increasing numbers, gay and lesbian couples are still often viewed as the second-best option for children eligible for adoption. In addition, gay and lesbian couples have been hindered by the fact that agency policies regarding gay and lesbian adoptions are still largely in the development stage. The Child Welfare League of America (CWLA) first published standards regarding the sexual orientation of applicants as a component of their Standards for Adoption Service (1988), but only in 1994 published their official policy regarding adoption by gay or lesbian individuals. Their 1994 policy stipulates that "gay/lesbian adoptive parents should be assessed the same as any other adoptive applicant" because "[i]t should be recognized that the sexual orientation and the capacity to nurture a child are separate issues" (CWLA, 1995, p. 41). However, the CWLA's guidelines also state that "Some biological parents may choose not to consider gay or lesbian families, and agencies usually follow the expressed wishes of the parent" (CWLA, 1995, p. 42).

Despite the CWLA's standards, controversy over gay and lesbian adoption remains. Although the CWLA dismisses many criticisms of gay and lesbian adoption as being based largely on misinformation, stereotypes, and myths (Sullivan, 1995), these stereotypes remain a pervasive force in public perception and the development of agency guidelines and state policy. Agencies may have policies precluding gay and lesbian adoption, and states such as New Hampshire and Florida have established policies banning adoption by gays and lesbians (Stacey, 1996). Such policies may become more widespread as part of the backlash against legalization of same-sex marriages. Consequently, many gay and lesbian couples arrange their adoptions through private attorneys or adopt as single parents.

Sexual orientation, rather than adoptive status, has tended to be the salient variable in research that has focused on children being raised by gay and lesbian parents. Little is known about the influence of adoption in these families. In general, research has reported few or no differences between children raised by gay and lesbian parents and children raised by heterosexual parents (Golombok & Tasker, 1996; Gottman, 1989; Patterson, 1992; Tasker & Golombok, 1995). For further information about gay or lesbian families, please refer to the chapter by Patterson and Chan, chap. 10 in this volume.

Children With a Handicapping Condition

Children with handicapping conditions are categorized as having special needs. Although the concept of special needs adoption has been previously introduced, it will be discussed here in greater detail, with specific attention paid to characteristics of adopted children and the effects and outcomes of such adoptions. Like the term *special needs*, a *handicapping condition* can encompass a wide variety of situations, such as a vision, hearing, or physical impairment; mental retardation; and serious medical conditions, including HIV or AIDS, leukemia, or cancer (Rosenthal & Groze, 1992). Children with these handicapping conditions frequently require more specialized or intensive care, often the extent of which is unknown at the time of placement. HIV infection or prenatal drug exposure, for example, can have profound effects on children's later development.

Much of the research on adoptive families with children who have developmental disabilities or physical handicaps has focused on rates of disruption. Barth and Berry (1988) reported that adoptions of children with developmental disabilities had higher rates of disruption than did adoptions of children without such a disability. In contrast, Rosenthal and Groze (1992) concluded that, "most parents who have adopted children with handicaps derive considerable satisfaction from these adoptions, and [most of these] adoptions can be characterized as successful" (p.151). Other research (e.g. Glidden, 1991) supported this position, finding that the level of adopted children's functioning did not relate to parental stress or satisfaction and suggesting that even children with severe disabilities can be placed successfully in adoptive homes.

Families who have adopted children with handicapping conditions often need financial assistance because they typically incur exceptionally high medical expenses. Title IV-E, created by the 1980 Adoption Assistance and Child Welfare Act, provides subsidies for medical, maintenance, and special services to families adopting children with special needs. Originally, Title IV-E assistance was provided only to families who applied for adoption assistance before the adoption was finalized. This rule was eventually challenged in court, for many children's medical or emotional problems did not surface until years after their adoption, leaving their parents financially exhausted. In 1992, the Administration of Children, Youth, and Families (ACF) at the U.S. Department of Health and Human Services (HHS) issued Policy Interpretation Question (PIQ) 92-02. Although PIQ 92-02 did not change federal regulations pertaining to Title IV-E, this statement did authorize the use of case-by-case exemptions for cases where extenuating circumstances prevented adoptive parents from applying for Title IV-E assistance prior to the finalization of their adoption (O'Hanlon, 1995). In the early 1990s, adoption researchers (e.g. Marcenko & Smith, 1991; Rosenthal & Groze, 1992) began to investigate the postadoption needs of families adopting children with disabilities and give postadoption service recommendations. In addition to financial subsidies, it has been recommended that parents adopting children with handicapping conditions be provided with thorough background information about the child as well as access to respite care services and support groups.

Children Who Have Spent Time in a Foster-Care Placement

An additional category of adopted children designated as having special needs is children who have spent time in foster care prior to their adoption. In 1995, it was estimated that 494,000 children were receiving some form of out-of-home care, approximately 15% of whom had the permanency goal of adoption (Spar, 1997). Some of these children have been or will be adopted by foster parents or other nonbiologically related adoptive parents, but increasing numbers have been or will be adopted by extended biological family members such as grandparents, aunts, uncles, and siblings.

The increasing number of children in out-of-home care adopted by adults who share kinship ties has largely been a result of two movements within the child welfare field: (a) the move toward permanency planning, and (b) the recognition of the importance of children's emotional relationships with biological kin. The 1980 Adoption Assistance and Child Welfare Act sought to reduce the population of children living in out-of-home care by providing goal-directed and time-limited social work and legal services, avoiding foster-care placement when possible, and shortening the time children spend in foster care. Although reunification with biological parents is typically the preferred permanency goal, the 1980 Act also encouraged adoption as a permanency goal when reunification was not a possibility (Rosenthal & Groze, 1992). This practice is further supported by statutes in states such as California, Colorado, Kansas, and Minnesota, in which a preference for adoptive placements with biological relatives is explicitly stated (Oppenheim & Bussiere, 1996). However, no state uses biological ties as the sole criterion over the adoption placement decision for children in out-of-home care. In states where preference is given to biological relatives, the preference is considered within the context of the best interest of the child.

Transracial Adoption

Whereas many of the types of adoptions previously described have been subject to considerable controversy, perhaps no type has sustained controversy as publicly and as long as has transracial adoption. For purposes of this chapter, we consider transracial adoptions as occurring within the United States but across racial lines. We discuss international adoptions in a separate section, because transracial and international adoptions have been associated with vastly different issues and areas of scholarship and debate.

Transracial adoptions have been particularly controversial. Once banned in the United States by segregationist policies, transracial placements began to occur with regularity in the 1960s and 1970s, initiated largely by the decline in the number of White infants available for adoption and the Civil Rights movement's call for integration. In nearly all cases, transracial adoptions involve children of color being placed with White adoptive parents (Hayes, 1992). In the 1970s, transracial adoptions received criticism by organizations such as the National Association of Black Social Workers (NABSW), who argued that agencies used unreasonable criteria to favor prospective White adoptive parents over prospective African American adoptive parents. The NABSW further argued that "black children in white homes are cut off from the healthy development of themselves as black people" (National Association of Black Social Workers, 1972, pp. 2–3). The NABSW's statement led to a policy reversal by the Child Welfare League of America. In 1968, the CWLA's policy stated that couples should be encouraged to consider adopting a child from a different racial background; the 1973 standards stated that within-race placement was preferable because they allowed adopted children to be better integrated into their family and community (McRoy, 1988).

Opposition to the adoption of African American children by White couples was strengthened when the Indian Child Welfare Act (ICWA; P.L. 95-608) was enacted in 1978. The ICWA was enacted based on concerns raised by Native-American groups over the high rates (over 80%) of placement of Native-American children in White homes (McRoy, 1988). The act provides the strongest legal preference for adoption by relatives (Oppenheim & Bussiere, 1996) and has dramatically decreased rates of transracial adoptions of Native-American children. The ICWA states the following preferences for placement of Native-American children eligible for adoption: (a) a member of the child's extended family; (b) other members of the child's tribe; (c) other Native-American families, in the absence of good cause to the contrary. The ICWA also ensures that extended family and tribal members can be involved in adoption proceedings and allows adoptions to be invalidated if the act's provisions are violated (Indian Child Welfare Act, 1978).

Since the 1970s, research has sought to determine the effects of transracial adoptions. Some researchers (e.g. Simon & Alstein, 1987) concluded that transracial adoption has positive effects and that children placed with families outside of their racial group were well adjusted. Other research (McRoy & Zurcher, 1983) concluded that transracially adopted children may experience problems developing an "unambiguous, positive racial identity" (McRoy, 1988, p.153). Based on their findings, McRoy and Zurcher (1983) concluded that same-race placement is preferable and recommended that transracial adoption be considered only when same-race placement is not possible.

Agency practice followed the trends in research and policy. During the 1970s and 1980s, adoption agencies shifted their practice away from transracial adoptions. However, noting the low numbers of prospective adoptive parents of color, proponents of transracial adoptions (e.g., the National Committee for Adoption, NCFA) raised concerns about the length of time children would linger in foster care if transracial adoptions were eliminated. In 1994, the Multiethnic Placement Act (MEPA) was passed by the U.S. Congress. The purposes of MEPA were to (a) decrease the length of time children waited for adoption; (b) prevent discrimination in the placement of children in adoptive homes on the basis of race, color, or national origin; and (c) increase the pool of prospective same-race adoptive and foster parents. The Act prohibited adoption agencies that receive federal financial assistance and are involved in adoption or foster care from "categorically denying to any person the opportunity to become an adoptive or foster parent solely on the basis of the race, color, or national origin of the adoptive or foster parent or the child" and "from delaying or denying the placement of a child solely on the basis of race, color, or national origin of the adoptive or foster parent or parents involved" (U.S. Department of Health and Human Services, 1995). The Act further specified that agencies must be involved in the active recruitment of foster or adoptive parents of color and consider "the child's cultural, ethnic, and racial background and the capacity of prospective foster or adoptive parents to meet the needs of a child of this background" when making a placement decision (U.S. Department of Health and Human Services, 1995).

More recently, the Adoption Promotion and Stability Act of 1996 (APSA) overturned MEPA and completely eliminated race of the child, adoptive parent, or foster parent as a determining factor in adoptive and foster placements. Although it appears that the ICWA will supersede this legislation and Native-American children will be exempted from APSA's guidelines, other agency practices may be subject to major overhaul or revision. In 1998, several states were in the midst of transitioning to the new policy guidelines. Because the law contradicts many agencies' previous practices, it may be subject to court challenges.

International Adoption

Although they also typically involve couples adopting children of different ethnic origins than their own, international adoptions have generally not been met with the same degree of controversy as have domestic transracial adoptions. Also unlike domestic transracial adoptions, rates of international adoptions have not decreased in recent years. However, although the number of international adoptions has remained relatively stable over the past decade, the countries that U.S. families have adopted from have fluctuated widely. In 1957, European children comprised 70% of all international adoptions (McNamara, 1975). This was largely a result of

World War II, when many European children orphaned or abandoned after the war were later brought to the United States for adoption. In 1995, 9,679 children were adopted internationally. These children were adopted from nearly every continent in the world, with the largest proportion coming from such Asian countries as China and Korea, followed by Russia (U.S. Department of State, 1996). The international adoption of Korean children began after the Korean War and increased steadily until the late 1980s (Wilkenson, 1995). Other major international events, such as the Vietnam War, the fall of the Communist regime in Romania, and the collapse of the former Soviet Union brought attention to these respective countries and initiated new waves of international adoption.

Children who enter the United States for the purposes of adoption must be orphans, which the Immigration and Naturalization Service (INS) defines in the following ways: when a child has no parents or those parents placed the child for adoption through a child welfare agency; when the child was abandoned; or when parental rights were terminated (Wilkenson, 1995). After children have arrived in their adoptive homes, internationally adopted children may face a series of psychological challenges. For example, they typically have little proficiency in English and have limited means of communication with their adoptive parents. Additionally, internationally adopted children may be malnourished and accustomed to sleeping arrangements that are different from those they experience in their new homes. Consequently, behaviors such as hoarding food and sleep terrors are not uncommon among internationally adopted children and may, in fact, be a part of children's adjustment process (Wilkenson, 1995).

Prior research (e.g., Jenista & Chapman, 1987) examined the medical conditions that have frequently been found to affect internationally adopted children. Children's health is an area of concern in international adoptions. Due to inadequate prenatal and postnatal medical care, internationally adopted children may be suffering from or at risk of developing a number of illnesses and medical conditions. Due to poor record keeping in the children's countries of origin, adoptive parents may be unaware of their child's special medical needs. Additionally, because other genetically mediated diseases may not be observable at the time of placement, adoptive parents may be unprepared for their onset (Daly & Sobol, 1993).

For many potential adoptive parents, the cost of international adoption may be prohibitive. Although various countries and states in the United States have different requirements governing international adoption, it is not uncommon for one or both parents to be required to travel to the child's country of origin for a period of time before the adoption can be finalized. As a result, when arranged independently or through a private agency, total adoption costs of $10,000–$18,000 or higher are not uncommon for international adoptions (AdoptioNetwork, 1996).

Unethical practices in international adoption have been spotlighted in the past few years, initiated largely by the onslaught of adoptions from Romania in the early 1990s. Following the fall of Nicolae Ceauşescu's communist regime, the deplorable conditions in Romanian orphanages received considerable media attention and generated worldwide interest in the adoption of Romanian children (Wilkenson, 1995). However, because Romania had no system or procedures in place for international adoption, the situation was ripe for abuse, including practices of illegal baby selling. In response to the chaos that erupted, Romania halted international adoption in June, 1991, so that the Romanian Adoption Committee could formulate controlled procedures governing international adoptions (Daly & Sobol, 1993). In 1991, 2,552 Romanian children were adopted in the United States. The following year, this number declined to 145 (U.S. Department of State, 1993, cited in Wilkenson, 1995).

FAMILY PROCESSES

Adoptive families must be understood within the context of their larger family system, which includes the child, his or her adoptive parents (and their extended family members), and his or her birth parents (and extended family members). Traditionally, the child, adoptive parents, and birth parents have been referred to as the *adoption triad*. The phrase, however, seems inadequate to capture the complexity of relationships in the child's life. One may also consider adoptive families as a form of *yoked family* (e.g., Reiss, 1992), in which the child joins a family of birth and a family of adoption, thus forming an *adoptive kinship network*.

In this section, we highlight six processes that are especially salient in adoptive kinship networks. The first three concern the dynamics of adoptive families: acknowledgment of difference, compatibility, and control. The second three concern individual processes: identity, entitlement, and coping with loss. Each of these issues must be considered within the context of the dynamics of secrecy or openness occurring in the adoptive kinship network. Because of the major changes with regard to openness occurring in adoption practice since the 1970s, this issue is considered first.

Openness: The Dynamics of Secrecy and Communication

Prior to the 1970s, most adoptions in North America were arranged so that no contact was permitted between birth mothers and adoptive parents. Birth fathers and other birth family members were left outside the adoption process. Such practices were consistent with attitudes of that era: stigma was associated with pregnancy outside marriage, and parenting children outside marriage was largely considered unacceptable. However, with the advent of various human rights movements and greater acceptance of diversity in family structures, birth parents found themselves in a more accepting environment that allowed them to be more vocal about their feelings of grief and loss, which did not go away postplacement, as had been claimed by advocates of confidential adoption. Adopted persons became vocal about their need to understand their past in order to have a clear sense of identity (e.g., Fisher, 1973). And, in an effort to parent their children more effectively, adoptive parents sought to fill gaps created by secrecy and missing information (Reitz & Watson, 1992).

Since the 1970s, professionals involved in adoption and members of the adoption community have responded to these dissatisfactions by questioning adoption practices and changing them. Their belief was that options permitting contact and communication would help birth parents feel less pain and guilt, promote consideration of adoption as an alternative to abortion or parenting, ease adoptive parents' fear and questions, provide adopted persons with biological continuity, and humanize the adoption process (Sorich & Siebert, 1982).

However, these innovative practices continue to be controversial, primarily because openness is relatively new and its impact on the adoption triad has only recently been addressed in empirical research (Berry, 1993; Bevan & Pierce, 1994; L. Caplan, 1990; Chapman, Dorner, Silber & Winterberg, 1986, 1987a, 1987b; Curtis, 1986; Demick & Wapner, 1988; Kraft, Palombo, Mitchell, Woods, & Schmidt, 1985; Kraft, Palombo, Mitchell, Woods, Schmidt, & Tucker, 1985; Kraft, Palombo, Woods, Mitchell, & Schmidt, 1985; National Committee for Adoption, 1989). A few studies with reasonably sized samples have been conducted (see Table 9.2), but most studies are methodologically problematic for various reasons, especially because of small and unrepresentative samples.

Because the research on this topic has been inadequate to answer basic questions about the dynamics of adoptive families involving contact between the families of birth and rearing or to guide adoption policy, Grotevant and McRoy (1997, 1998) designed a research project that focused on the consequences of variations in openness in adoption for birth mothers, adoptive parents, and adopted children, and for the relationships within these family systems. Three levels of openness were investigated: confidential adoption, in which no identifying information was shared between birth parent(s) and the adoptive family and no contact occurred after six months postplacement; mediated adoption, in which a third party (typi-

TABLE 9.2
Representative Sample Sizes in Adoption Kinship Network Research

Study[a]	Sample Size and Type
Berry, 1993	1,268 California adoptive families
Grotevant et al., 1994	190 adoptive families
	169 birth mothers
Belbas, 1987	12 adoptive couples
Demick, 1993	30 families
Blanton & Deschner, 1990	59 birth mothers
Etter, 1993	56 families
Siegel, 1993	21 families

[a]Studies are listed in References.

cally the adoption agency) serves to relay nonidentifying communications between the birth parent(s) and adoptive family; and fully disclosed adoption, in which identifying information has been shared among the parties and ongoing contact (usually in the form of face-to-face meetings) occurs. A few key highlights are presented below; details of the study's results may be found in several reports (Christian, McRoy, Grotevant, & Bryant, 1997; Grotevant & McRoy, 1997, 1998; Grotevant, McRoy, Elde, & Fravel, 1994; McRoy, Grotevant, & Ayers-Lopez, 1994; Wrobel, Ayers-Lopez, Grotevant, McRoy, & Friedrick, 1996).

The findings of the study are consistent with the view that adoption is an ongoing process rather than a discrete event; not only do initial choices differ, but also arrangements with regard to contact or communication change over time. With regard to effects on children, results of the study are not compatible with speculations (e.g., Kraft et al., 1985) that such arrangements would damage children's self-esteem and cause them confusion over who their real parents are. On the other hand, results do not support the contrasting position that more openness would enhance children's self-esteem. The children in this study, however, were interviewed during middle childhood; the ongoing longitudinal follow-up at adolescence (in progress) will yield important information about longer term openness effects, especially with regard to identity development.

Relationships between birth mothers and adoptive parents appear to involve an ongoing process of negotiation, in which all parties work across time to forge relationships that function within a mutually acceptable "comfort zone" of communication and contact. Persons entering such relationships should be aware of the issues entailed in regulating the boundaries in such complex family systems. The data also suggest, however, that opting for confidentiality does not avoid these complexities, as the unknown counterparts in their adoption triad are psychologically even if not physically present to them (Fravel, 1995).

When looking across the spectrum of openness (from confidential to fully disclosed), some similarities stand out: most adoptive parents feel relatively secure in their roles, nor are they extremely afraid that the birth mother might try to reclaim the child as her own. Most are satisfied with their control over the birth mother's involvement in their family life. In the ongoing mediated and fully disclosed adoptions, the satisfaction appeared to be based on the adoptive parents' experience with the birth parent(s) and on their sense that the amount and type of contact was negotiated mutually. In confidential adoptions, satisfaction was based on the assumption that legal or procedural safeguards were in place to control unwanted involvement.

However, other clear differences were evident across levels of openness. The strong general pattern is that parents in fully disclosed adoptions demonstrate higher degrees of empathy about adoption, talk about it more openly with their children, and are less fearful that birth mothers might try to reclaim their children than are parents in confidential adoptions. The sense of permanence in the relationship with their adopted child also followed this pattern, but less strongly from a statistical vantage point. The ratings of parents with ongoing mediated adoptions tend to fall in between those of parents with confidential and fully disclosed adoptions. Despite the concerns raised by critics of openness, the results of this study are not compatible with the hypothesis that openness necessarily produces undesirable outcomes for adoptive families.

Four to twelve years after placing a child for adoption, birth mothers who have ongoing contact with the adoptive family through either ongoing mediated or fully disclosed adoptions show better resolution of grief than do birth mothers who have had mediated contact that subsequently ended (Christian et al., 1997). This finding provides some empirical support for Silber and Dorner's (1990) belief that relationships with adoptive parents formed in open arrangements may ameliorate birth mother grief experienced over child placement. It contradicts claims (e.g., Kraft, Palombo, Woods, et al., 1985) that open adoption arrangements would prolong the grief process and prevent birth mothers from coming to terms with the placement. However, it is important to note that having a fully disclosed adoption does not guarantee successful grief resolution, as is evidenced by the broad range of grief resolution ratings among birth mothers in fully disclosed adoptions in this study. Other factors, such as subsequent infertility and guilt, may also influence this process. Developing a trusting, secure relationship with the adoptive family through direct or indirect contact seems to lead some birth mothers to the gradual acceptance of the adoptive family's entitlement to the child, while allowing the birth mother to develop positive self-feelings about her role with her child.

Although it may be tempting to conclude that fully disclosed open adoptions are best, because adoptive parents in those families show higher levels of acknowledgment and empathy about adoption, have less fear than in the other types of adoption, and have strong senses of control and permanence, we do not draw such a conclusion, because what may be best for one party in the adoption triad at one point in time may not be best for other parties (Grotevant, van Dulmen, & McRoy, 1997). Furthermore, parties' needs for greater or lesser openness may change over time, and not always in synchrony with other triad members.

Acknowledgment of Difference

One of the few social science theories specifically addressing the dynamics of adoptive families was developed in the 1950s and early 1960s by H. David Kirk, a sociologist and adoptive father. According to this theory (e.g., Kirk, 1964, 1981, 1995), couples who adopt because of infertility suffer from a role handicap because they become parents by a route that is not normative. There are at least two ways to cope with this challenge. In the days when children were placed with adoptive parents whom they might physically resemble, some parents coped by rejecting any difference between biological and adoptive parenthood, even pretending that their child was biologically related to them. On the other hand, Kirk's shared fate theory and accompanying research suggested that the health of the parent–child relationship and its grounding in mutual trust hinge on honest acknowledgment that adoptive parenthood is different from biological parenthood in some respects. A major contribution of Kirk's work has been to remove any sense of shame from adoptive parenthood and to help professionals and the public view adoption as a different route to parenting, but not a deviant one.

Drawing on his clinical experience, Brodzinsky (1987) suggested that acknowledgment can be taken too far, and that too much acknowledgment ("insistence of difference") can be harmful to the family. For example, parents who always introduce their child as "our adopted daughter" create distance in the parent–child relationship by always indicating that their kinship is due to adoption rather than to birth. Thus, Brodzinsky viewed the relation between acknowledgment of difference and healthy functioning as curvilinear, with adaptive functioning relating to a moderate degree of acknowledgment and problematic functioning relating to very low (denial) or very high (insistence) emphasis on difference.

The empirical research on acknowledgment of difference is quite limited, although Kaye and colleagues (Kaye, 1990; Kaye & Warren, 1988) conducted microanalytic discourse analyses of discussions between adoptive parents and their children. Their work generally supported the curvilinear model proposed by Brodzinsky but also suggested that viewing acknowledgment versus rejection of difference as a unidimensional tension between coping strategies was oversimplified.

One of the current challenges with the acknowledgment of difference construct and associated measures involves bringing them up-to-date with adoption practice. When the concept was developed in the 1950s and 1960s, adoptive parents did not always tell their children that they were adopted. Now, the practice norm is to tell children in a developmentally appropriate way from a very early age. Current issues of confronting difference may involve whether the child or family would search for birth parents or whether identified meetings would occur rather than whether the child should be told he or she is adopted.

In our research on variations in openness, interviews of adoptive mothers and fathers were rated for the degree to which they showed interest in the adopted child's history or background beyond medical information and the degree to which birth parents were considered to be part of the child's background and history. Parents in fully disclosed open adoptions were rated higher on acknowledgment of difference (although not shading into "insistence") than were parents in confidential and time-limited mediated adoptions, and parents in ongoing mediated adoptions were rated as higher in acknowledgment than those in confidential adoptions (Grotevant et al., 1994). Overall, the results of this study were fully consistent with Kirk's statements that were formulated during the era of confidential adoption: ". . . empathy and communication are key requirements for dynamic stability of families not regulated by tradition. By 'dynamic stability' I meant social relationships which are both reliable and flexible, which provide a secure base for the small child's growth and development while making allowance for changes, for maturation, and the child's need to become an independent adult" (1981, p. 40).

Compatibility

Lamb and Gilbride (1985) defined a compatible parent–child relationship as one in which the behaviors of the partners are meshed well, with communication between them being efficient and accurate. Thus, compatibility involves family members' ability to attain this state and to retain it through interaction over time. The research of Grotevant, McRoy, and colleagues investigates the relations between compatibility of the adopted child and adoptive family and developmental outcomes and pathways.

In prior work, perceived incompatibility between the child and his or her adoptive family emerged as an important predictor or correlate of child outcomes. In the authors' study of adopted and nonadopted adolescents in residential treatment, results from interview analyses suggest that several clusters of factors contribute to the problems experienced by adopted adolescents, including incompatibility between parent and child (Grotevant, McRoy, & Jenkins, 1988; McRoy, Grotevant, & Zurcher, 1988). From a complementary perspective, perceived similarity has been found to be one of the best predictors of positive outcomes for children in research on nonclinical families (S. Ramey, personal communication, 1991).

In the first wave of data collection in the openness in adoption project (Grotevant & McRoy, 1997, 1998), Ross (1995) focused on familial predictors of externalizing problems, internalizing problems, and self-esteem for the sample of nonclinical adopted children assessed during middle childhood. Parent–child compatibility was assessed by a scale constructed from four subscales of the Parenting Stress Index (Abidin, 1986). Higher scores indicate more stress resulting from perceived incompatibility of the child with the family. Incompatibility of the child with the family (as perceived by parents) emerged as the strongest predictor of both perceived externalizing and internalizing difficulties.

Because the residential treatment study involved a clinical sample and all confidential adoptions, the longitudinal follow-up of the adopted children in varying openness arrangements (in progress) extends this line of research by examining adjustment outcomes in a nonclinical sample of adopted children, adoptive families, and birth mothers in confidential, mediated, and fully disclosed adoptions. Thus, prospective data with a nonclinical sample are being used to examine issues such as compatibility, which had been identified retrospectively by adolescents in treatment.

Control

Control is a complex issue for adoptive families. Couples typically adopt after they have been unsuccessful in having biological children; thus, they come to adoption after losing control of their fertility. Birth parents often place children for adoption because they were born at a time when parenting would have been difficult or impossible; often when circumstances were out of control. Adoption plans are made for some children because birth parents' parental rights have been terminated by the courts; that is, the control vested in parenting was taken away. It is ironic that adopted children, the beneficiaries of this process, had no control whatsoever over the fact that they were adopted. Thus, all parties come to adoption feeling a loss of control. The roles that the medical, legal, and social welfare systems play often exacerbates feelings of loss of control.

Parties to adoption often take various actions to gain some semblance of control: adoptive parents might choose the type of agency they work with, or whether to adopt a child internationally, or whether to accept a child with certain disabilities. Birth parents might choose the couple who ultimately adopts the child or choose an agency whose philosophy is compatible with theirs.

However, the issue of control can play itself out in complex ways over time. When adoptions involving contact or communication are negotiated, how do the parties decide when, where, and how frequently to meet? When one party desires more (or less) contact than another, how is this difference negotiated?

Identity

Identity involves one's definition of self within a particular historical and social context, one's subjective sense of coherence of personality, and one's sense of continuity over time (Grotevant, 1997). Development of identity is a life-long process, proceeding through phases of openness, when one is exploring, reviewing, or reconsidering life choices, as well as phases of consolidating or integrating commitments. Most of the unique identity challenges facing adopted persons are about "givens" in their lives rather than about choices they are to make. However, although adopted persons did not choose their adoption situations, they do have choices about how they come to terms with them and about how these identity components become woven into their personal narrative.

Changes in adoption practice and policy have had significant bearing on the development of identity among all parties involved in adoption. As societal views of adoption have moved away from secrecy toward openness, adopted persons and their parents by birth and adoption have been challenged to reconsider what it means to be involved in adoption.

For adopted persons, identity development becomes increasingly complex as additional dimensions of "differentness" from other family members are added, such as differences in physical appearance, ethnic or cultural origin, disabilities, or talents. The identity process also involves integrating other aspects of one's pre-adoption history, including experiences such as multiple foster placements or abuse.

The question, "Who am I?" becomes extended to "How am I similar to and different from my birth parents? Where do I fit in their world? How does their world fit into mine?" If a person is adopted from another culture, additional issues are raised. The person may ask, "How do I deal with issues of cultural difference and with the disparity between how I look and how my adoptive family members look—or perhaps between how I look (for example, Chinese) and how I feel inside (perhaps just a typical U.S. citizen)." If the child is adopted across racial lines found in the United States, particularly from a community of color into a White family, the child must also consider, "Who am I? Can I fit in? Where do I want to fit in? To which group do I have responsibility or allegiance? Must I choose, or can I live in both worlds? Will society let this be my free choice?"

Ultimately, the identity quest can lead to an integrated sense of identity constructed into a narrative that includes one's adoption circumstances as well as all the other aspects of identity important to adult functioning. This is not always attained, however, as indicated by the following vignette:

> Mark, a musician in his thirties, remembers the exact moment he tuned out. At the age of four, he asked if he could meet the mother he had been told about when he was two and a half. "It was the first time I wanted and needed something they [his adoptive parents] wouldn't consider. They said I had to wait until I was eighteen, which is like ninety to a young child. I didn't ask any more questions after that. The fact of my adoption burst like a bubble in my mind, then sealed over. It became important for my sense of coherence as a self to imagine myself as not adopted." (Lifton, 1994, p. 51)

The limited literature on identity development in adopted persons comes from three sources: first-person accounts, clinical reports, and research studies. The few empirical research studies that have examined links between identity and adoption have typically found no differences between adopted and nonadopted adolescents on global scales of identity development (e.g., Goebel & Lott, 1986; Stein & Hoopes, 1985). However, the issue of integration of adoption into one's sense of identity was not addressed in these studies. A survey study of 881 adolescents who were adopted as infants documented the connection between adoption and identity. Benson, Sharma, and Roehlkepartain (1994) found that 27% of adopted adolescents endorsed the statement that *adoption is a big part of how I think about myself,* and 41% said they thought about adoption at least 2 to 3 times per month or as frequently as daily. Girls were more likely than boys to report that adoption informed their identity, and they reported thinking about adoption more frequently than did boys. On average, the adopted adolescents in the study demonstrated levels of self-esteem comparable to that of nonadopted age-mates, and the results did not support clinically based assertions that adopted children in general are poorly adjusted. However, a substantial number of those adolescents reported that adoption is on their mind frequently and that it plays an important role in how they think about themselves.

Virtually all of the relevant literature, however, involved confidential adoptions. It is possible that greater openness in adoption could make the process of constructing one's sense of identity less complicated, because secrecy and uncertainty regarding the adopted person's origins would be reduced. For example, in a sample of adolescents from confidential adoptions, issues of attachment and entitlement were the best parental predictors of child disturbance (Cohen, Duvall, & Coyne, 1994). It is not known whether these processes would occur the same way with more open adoptions.

The construction of identity is a normal human process; one that may be more challenging for some people than for others and one that is life long (Erikson, 1968). Because identity involves the ongoing negotiation between the person's psychological interior and his or her social context, challenges to identity are more likely to occur when major contextual shifts take place. Thus, adoption professionals concerned with educational and preventive efforts and clinical interventions could benefit by anticipating such contextual changes and developing appropriately timed approaches for working with their clients.

There is already a need for adoption-related services to be available for persons who were adopted in an era when records were sealed and identity of birth parents was kept secret. Such individuals are living in a time when these practices and the assumptions underlying them are being questioned and changed. Thus, it is likely that a number of these people are experiencing challenges to their own sense of identity and place in the world. Discussion and support groups could be very appropriate services.

Among the major normative contextual changes facing adults are the leaving home transition, the transition to marriage or a committed relationship, and the transition to parenthood. Each of these challenges the individual's understanding of self in fundamental ways because they involve shifts in the person's primary relationships—with parents, with a life partner, with a child. Thus, these transitions afford the opportunity for renegotiating the balance between self and other that is such a key element of identity development (e.g., Kroger, 1996). Because adoption itself is so rooted in primary relationships, it should not be surprising that identity issues relating to adoption might be revisited during such life transitions.

Entitlement

An important issue facing adoptive parents is developing a sense of entitlement to act as the child's full parent, which indicates that the adoptive parents have the "legal and emotional right to parent their child" (Reitz & Watson, 1992, p. 125). Although the legal right is conferred by the courts, claiming the emotional right is something that parents must do psychologically (Reitz & Watson, 1992). The concept of entitlement has been used widely in literature written by adoption educators and is a popular topic of discussion at conferences designed for adoptive parents. However, almost no empirical work has been conducted on the concept.

Cohen, Coyne, and Duvall (1996) suggested that adoptive parents' failure to develop an adequate sense of entitlement could result in their inability or unwillingness to provide adequate discipline and structure for their adopted child, ultimately leading to externalizing problems. They further expanded the concept by hypothesizing that entitlement problems are not unique to adoptive families.

For their research with families seeking mental health services and nonclinical families, Cohen et al. (1996) developed a self-report questionnaire to assess entitlement. Factors that emerged included parents' feelings of distance from their child, doubts about their parenting ability, beliefs that the child saw them as their real parent, feelings of success in disciplining the child, and comfort with providing discipline. The feelings of unworthiness, powerlessness, and fear of rejection by the child were common in both adoptive and nonadoptive families, contrary to expectations. The authors drew an important conclusion: "We must be mindful of assuming that adoptive families are unique on variables that have been examined only in adoptive populations" (p. 451). Thus, the concept of entitlement may be important in understanding families with clinical issues; however, it does not appear to be uniquely connected to adoptive families.

The concept has also been raised in connection with the movement toward greater openness in adoption. Adoption professionals concerned with this trend asserted that in open adoptions, parents would not feel that they had full parenting rights and responsibilities because the birth parent(s) would continue to be involved with their family (Kraft, Palombo, Mitchell, et al., 1985). However, no empirical evidence was provided for this assertion.

In the authors' study of openness in adoption (Grotevant et al., 1994), perception of entitlement was coded from lengthy interviews conducted individually with 190 adoptive mothers and 190 adoptive fathers. The level of entitlement did not differ statistically across levels of openness for adoptive fathers or adoptive mothers. Thus, although the concept of entitlement is an appealing one and would appear to make sense clinically, further research is needed to clarify its special role in adoptive families and whether it does differentiate among groups in predicted ways.

Coping With Loss

It has been asserted that adoption is an institution that is built on loss. Birth mothers relinquish the right to parent their child, adopted children experience the loss of their birth families and genetic continuity, and adoptive parents typically opt for adoption after experiencing the loss of their ability to have children by birth.

Much of the literature relevant to this topic equates successful coping with acknowledgment and resolution of the grief associated with such losses. In the process of preparing couples for adoption, many social workers note the importance of prospective adoptive parents' having resolved their grief by mourning the loss of their fantasized biological child and mourning the loss of their fantasies of being parents by birth (Brinich, 1990). In some agencies, this topic is assessed in the preparation process, and couples who have not adequately dealt with the loss of their fertility are considered unfit to become adoptive parents.

There is also literature relevant to birth mothers' grief resolution over the placement of their child for adoption (see Christian et al., 1997, for review). For adopted persons, coping with loss of one's biological kin is often dealt with in the literature on identity, with the assumption that effective coping would permit individuals to form an adaptive sense of identity that integrates their biological and adoptive heritages.

EMERGING ISSUES

Research Issues

The topic of adoptive families provides varied opportunities for research from sociological, anthropological, psychological, and biological approaches. Many current research issues have already been highlighted above.

In our view, the adoption area is in need of more process-oriented research. Many studies have focused on differences in outcomes (typically related to intellectual abilities or mental health) between adoptive and nonadoptive families. Recent studies concerning the process of family adaptation to adoption over time (e.g., Pinderhughes, 1996) will provide important windows for understanding what happens in families as children and their family members interact. Studies involving how changes in openness are negotiated over time (e.g., Grotevant & McRoy, 1998) and how individuals reconcile the discrepancies between physical and psychological presence or absence of members of the adoptive kinship network (e.g., Fravel, 1995) will provide more detailed understanding of adoptive family processes.

Policy Issues

A number of policy issues concerning adoption have already been raised in this chapter. In this section, we briefly discuss three areas that are subjects of considerable debate: termination of parental rights, the use of assisted reproductive technologies, and the role of the Internet.

Termination of Parental Rights. A growing number of children are candidates for adoption because they have been removed from their birth parents' home by protective services, typically because of abuse or neglect. Although many service providers work hard to reunite these children with their parent(s) following appropriate interventions, some children will never be able to return home. Frequently, they are placed in foster care until a clear determination regarding the feasibility of family reunification can be made. If reunification does not appear to be possible, the social service system may have to petition the court for involuntary termination of parental rights so that it will be possible to place the child in a permanent adoptive home.

At present, social service providers are experiencing the tension between working toward reunification and minimizing the child's time in foster care. Because children in the recent past have been in foster homes for years pending possible reunification, children's rights advocates are now pressing for the ability to resolve the child's placement sooner. In other words, service providers and the courts will need to make decisions about the potential involuntary termination of parental rights within a relatively short time. Exactly how long this time span should be in the best interest of the child is a subject of active debate.

Because of several highly publicized cases (e.g., Baby Jessica, Baby Richard), there is also much policy attention being given to birth fathers' rights. Theoretically, adoption requires that both the birth mother and birth father consent to having their parental rights terminated. However, in some states, birth mothers can declare the birth father unknown or can declare their intent to terminate his rights through the official notices column of a newspaper, and the birth father may not have consented actively to his rights termination. In some contested cases, birth fathers have claimed that the birth mother lied to them about being pregnant and that they had no opportunity to step forward as the child's parent. States are now struggling to determine how to give birth fathers the right to exercise their parenting responsibilities while also facilitating timely closure if the birth mother seeks to make an adoption plan and the birth father is unknown or unavailable. One policy being discussed is the establishment of a putative birth father registry, in which any male who might have caused a pregnancy could, within a defined time interval, register the possible pregnancy with the state. If, after delivery of the child, the birth mother agreed to have her parental rights terminated in order to facilitate an adoption and the birth father did not actively consent, the registry must be reviewed to see if such a man had indicated his paternity around the time of conception. If he had not made such a claim, his parental rights could automatically be terminated after thirty days following the delivery. If he had made such a claim, his rights would not be terminated without his active consent. Although not without its difficulties, this policy would ensure birth fathers the opportunity to exercise their parental rights while not preventing adoption plans from going forward after a reasonable time interval.

Reproductive Technologies.   With the advent of assisted reproductive technologies (ARTs), additional options have become available to infertile couples. ARTs encompass a range of procedures, including but not limited to donor insemination (DI), in vitro fertilization (IVF), gamete intrafallopian transfer (GIFT), ovum donation, and surrogacy. ARTs differ from non-relative adoptions in that offspring usually share a genetic link to one or both of their social parents. However, Daly and Sobol (1993) also noted some striking parallels between prior adoption and current ART practices. As previously mentioned, adoption practices used to be clouded in secrecy. Many parents did not tell their children they were adopted as a way to avoid the social stigma associated with infertility or their different method of family formation. Today, parents of ART offspring are similarly counseled not to tell others about the way their child was conceived (Daly & Sobol, 1993), and many clinics have developed policies to ensure the anonymity of sperm or ovum donors. This may, in part, be due to the ethical, legal, and medical controversies that surround the use of ARTs (e.g., A. Caplan, 1994; Corea, 1985; Klein, 1989; Roland, 1992). Nonetheless, many predict that the issues associated with adoption, including identity, acknowledgment of differences, and openness, will also emerge as central issues among families who have used ARTs. We predict that over the coming years, medical practitioners, clinic staff, and families using ARTs will all be forced to grapple with these issues and re-evaluate many of their current practices.

Finally, it is extremely likely that ARTs, like adoption, will be subject to changing state and national policies. The legal system has already handled a number of custody disputes among families using ARTs, including the highly publicized Baby M surrogacy case. However, by 1998, only a few states had set policies regarding surrogacy, and virtually no states had enacted policies surrounding the use of IVF or donor insemination. It is anticipated that these issues will generate considerable attention in the policy arena throughout the coming years.

Adoption and the Internet.   As with many areas of family life, the Internet has taken on a strong role in the adoption field. Discussion groups and chat rooms for birth parents, adopted persons, adoptive parents, and other interested parties have multiplied quickly. Many web sites have emerged, some reflecting advocacy positions, some offering services, and others providing information. The Internet has also become a useful tool for bringing together prospective adoptive families and hard-to-place children. However, several areas of controversy have emerged: confidentiality issues (e.g., publishing children's photos and biographies on the Internet), financial exploitation of couples seeking children, and the accurate and unbiased nature of information presented. It is likely that the role of the Internet in the adoption area will expand in the future, significantly enhancing the accessibility of information about adoption and facilitating adoptive placements. On the other hand, it will be important for Internet users to be critical evaluators of the information they do find.

CLOSING COMMENT

In this chapter, we have discussed the varying forms that adoptive families take in contemporary Western society. We have discussed factors in the historical and current social and political contexts that have shaped the nature of adoption. We have also discussed several of the psychological and interpersonal processes that play themselves out in adoptive families.

Upon reflection, it seems that the existing social science literature on adoption is more problem focused than the daily lives of many adoptive families. Much of the literature begins by assuming that adoption presents a problem to be solved (unwed parenthood, infertility), focuses on the clinical risks for adopted persons, or explores psychological variables that can put members of the adoptive kinship network at risk for dysfunction. Little of the social science literature is oriented toward the strengths of adoptive family members or birth mothers.

Fortunately, advocacy groups and organizations with an educational focus support and encourage the development of strengths in members of the adoption kinship network. However, it is too easy to assume that nontraditional, the adjective applied to the families discussed in this volume, implies abnormal or unhealthy. Adoptive families will be served more effectively when research, writing, and advocacy on their behalf present a more balanced view of the range of functioning among adoptive families than one finds in the existing literature.

ACKNOWLEDGMENT

During the preparation of this chapter, the authors were supported by a research grant from the William T. Grant Foundation.

REFERENCES

Abidin, R. R. (1986). *Parenting stress index*. Charlottesville, VA: Pediatric Psychology Press.
AdoptioNetwork. (1996, April 14). Quick Stats [On-line]. Available: http://www.infi.net/adopt/ qfact/html
Barth, R. P., & Berry, M. (1988). *Adoption and disruption: Rates, risks, and responses*. New York: Aldine De Gruyter.
Barth, R. P., Berry, M., Yoshikami, R., Goodfield, R. K., & Carson, M. L. (1988). Predicting adoption disruption. *Social Work, 33*, 227–233.
Belbas, N. (1987). Staying in touch: Empathy in open adoptions. *Smith College Studies in Social Work, 57*, 184–198.
Benson, P. L., Sharma, A. R., & Roehlkepartain, E. C. (1994). *Growing up adopted: A portrait of adolescents and their families*. Minneapolis, MN: Search Institute.
Berry, M. (1993). Adoptive parents' perceptions of, and comfort with, open adoption. *Child Welfare, 72*, 231–253.
Bevan, C., & Pierce, W. (1994, November). *Privacy, secrecy, and confidentiality in adoption*. Paper presented at the Ethics in Adoption Conference, Minneapolis, MN.
Blanton, T. L., Deschner, J. (1990). Biological mother's grief: The postadoptive experience in open versus confidential adoption. *Child Welfare, 69*(6), 525–535.
Brinich, P. M. (1990). Adopton from the inside out: A psychoanalytic perspective. In D. M. Brodzin-

sky & M. D. Schechter (Eds.), *The psychology of adoption* (pp. 42–61). New York: Oxford University Press.

Brodzinsky, D. M. (1987). Adjustment to adoption: A psychosocial perspective. *Clinical Psychology Review, 7,* 25–47.

Caplan, A. L. (1994). The ethics of in vitro fertilization. In T. L. Beauchamp & L. Walters (Eds.), *Contemporary issues in bioethics* (pp. 198–201). Belmont, CA: Wadsworth.

Caplan, L. (1990). *An open adoption.* Boston: Houghton Mifflin.

Center for Adoption Research and Policy. (1997). *Case statement to explore a campaign for the Center for Adoption Research and Policy at the University of Massachusetts.* Worcester, MA: Author.

Chapman, C., Dorner, P., Silber, K., & Winterberg, T. (1986). Meeting the needs of the adoption triangle through open adoption: The birthmother. *Child and Adolescent Social Work, 3*(4), 203–213.

Chapman, C., Dorner, P., Silber, K., & Winterberg, T. (1987a). Meeting the needs of the adoption triangle through open adoption: The adoptee. *Child and Adolescent Social Work, 4,* 78–91.

Chapman, C., Dorner, P., Silber, K., & Winterberg, T. (1987b). Meeting the needs of the adoption triangle through open adoption: The adoptive parent. *Child and Adolescent Social Work, 4,* 3–12.

Child Welfare League of America. (1988). CWLA standards re sexual orientation of applicants. In *Standards for adoption service.* Washington, DC: Author.

Child Welfare League of America. (1995). CWLA policy re adoption by gay or lesbian individuals. In A. Sullivan (Ed.), *Issues in gay and lesbian adoption: Proceedings of the fourth annual Pierce-Warwick adoption symposium* (pp. 41–42). Washington, DC: Author.

Christian, C. L., McRoy, R. G., Grotevant, H. D., & Bryant, C. (1997). Grief resolution of birthmothers in confidential, time-limited mediated, ongoing mediated, and fully disclosed adoptions. *Adoption Quarterly, 1*(2), 35–58.

Cohen, N. J., Coyne, J. C., & Duvall, J. D. (1996). Parents' sense of "entitlement" in adoptive and nonadoptive families. *Family Process, 35,* 441–456.

Cohen, N. J., Duvall, J., & Coyne, J. C. (1994). *Characteristics of post-adoptive families presenting for mental health service* (Final Report). Newmarket, Ontario: Children's Aid Society of York Region.

Cole, E., & Donley, K. (1990). History, values, and placement policy issues. In D. Brodzinsky & M. Schechter (Eds.), *The psychology of adoption* (pp. 273–294). New York: Oxford University Press.

Corea, G. (1985). *The mother machine: Reproductive technologies from artificial insemination to artificial wombs.* New York: Harper & Row.

Curtis, P. (1986). The dialectics of open versus closed adoption of infants. *Child Welfare, 65*(5), 437–445.

Daly, K. J., & Sobol, M. P. (1993). Adoption as an alternative for infertile couples: Prospects and trends. In *The prevalence of infertility in Canada: Research studies of the royal commission on new reproductive technologies.* Ottawa: Minister of Supply and Services.

Demick, J. (1993). Adaptation of marital couples to open versus closed adoption: A preliminary investigation. In J. Demick, K. Burski, & R. DiBiase (Eds.), *Parental development.* Hillsdale, NJ: Lawrence Erlbaum Associates.

Demick, J., & Wapner, S. (1988). Open and closed adoption: A developmental conceptualization. *Family Process, 27,* 229–249.

Erikson, E. H. (1968). *Identity: Youth and crisis.* New York: Norton.

Etter, J. (1993). Levels of cooperation and satisfaction in 56 open adoptions. *Child Welfare, 72,* 257–267.

Festinger, T. (1990). Adoption disruption: Rates and correlates. In D. Brodzinsky & M. Schechter (Eds.), *The psychology of adoption* (pp. 201–218). New York: Oxford University Press.

Fisher, F. (1973). *In search of Anna Fisher.* New York: Ballantine.

Fravel, D. L. (1995). *Boundary ambiguity perceptions of adoptive parents experiencing various levels of openness in adoption.* Unpublished doctoral dissertation, University of Minnesota.

Glidden, L. M. (1991). Adopted children with developmental disabilities: Post-placement family functioning. *Children and Youth Services Review, 13,* 363–377.

Goebel, B. L. & Lott, S. L. (1986, August). *Adoptees' resolution of the adolescent identity crisis: Where are the taproots?* Paper presented at the meeting of the American Psychological Association, Washington, DC.

Golombok, S., & Tasker, F. (1996). Do parents influence the sexual orientation of their children? *Developmental Psychology, 32*(1), 3–11.

Gottman, J. S. (1989). Children of gay and lesbian parents. *Marriage and Family Review, 14*(3–4), 177–196.

Grotevant, H. D. (1997). Coming to terms with adoption: The construction of identity from adolescence into adulthood. *Adoption Quarterly, 1*(1), 3–27.

Grotevant, H. D., & McRoy, R. G. (1997). The Minnesota/Texas Adoption Research Project: Implications of openness in adoption for development and relationships. *Applied Developmental Science, 1,* 166–184.

Grotevant, H. D., & McRoy, R. G. (1998). *Openness in Adoption: Exploring family connections.* Newbury Park, CA: Sage.

Grotevant, H. D., McRoy, R. G., Elde, C. L., & Fravel, D. L. (1994). Adoptive family system dynamics: Variations by level of openness in the adoption. *Family Process, 33,* 125–146.

Grotevant, H. D., McRoy, R. G., & Jenkins, V. Y. (1988). Emotionally disturbed adopted adolescents: Early patterns of family adaptation. *Family Process, 27,* 439–457.

Grotevant, H. D., van Dulmen, M., & McRoy, R. G. (1997, April). Feelings and perceptions about face-to-face contact: Differing trajectories for adoptive parents and birthmothers? In H. D. Grotevant (Chair), *Openness in adoption: Diverging perspectives of adopted children, adoptive parents, and birthmothers.* Symposium conducted at the meeting of the Society for Research in Child Development, Washington, DC.

Groze, V. (1991). Adoption and single parents: A review. *Child Welfare, 70*(3), 321–331.

Groze, V., & Rosenthal, J. A. (1991). Single parents and their adopted children. *Families in Society, 72*(2), 67–77.

Hayes, P. (1992). Transracial adoption: Politics and ideology. *Child Welfare, 72*(3), 301–309.

Indian Child Welfare Act, 25 U.S.C. §VV1901, 1915(a). (1978).

Jenista, J. A., & Chapman, D. (1987). Medical problems of foreign born adopted children. *American Journal of Diseases and Children, 141*(3), 293–302.

Kagan, R. M., & Reid, W. J. (1986). Critical factors in the adoption of emotionally-disturbed youths. *Child Welfare League of America, 65,* 63–73.

Kaye, K. (1990). Acknowledgment or rejection of differences? In D. M. Brodzinsky & M. D. Schechter (Eds.), *The psychology of adoption* (pp. 121–143). New York: Oxford University Press.

Kaye, K., & Warren, S. (1988). Discourse about adoption in adoptive families. *Journal of Family Psychology, 1,* 406–433.

Kirk, H. D. (1964). *Shared fate: A theory of adoption and mental health.* New York: The Free Press.

Kirk, H. D. (1981). *Adoptive kinship: A modern institution in need of reforms.* Toronto, Canada: Butterworth.

Kirk, H. D. (1995, July). *Looking back, looking forward.* Keynote address presented at the meeting of Adoptive Families of America, Dallas, TX.

Klein, R. D. (1989). *Infertility: Women speak out about their experiences of reproductive medicine.* London: Pandora.

Kraft, A., Palombo, J., Mitchell, D., Woods, P. & Schmidt, A. (1985). Some theoretical considerations on confidential adoptions: Part II: The adoptive parent. *Human Science Press,* 69–81.

Kraft, A., Palombo, J., Mitchell, D., Woods, P., Schmidt, A., & Tucker, N. (1985). Some theoretical considerations on confidential adoption: Part III: The adopted child. *Human Science Press,* 139–153.

Kraft, A., Palombo, J., Woods, P., Mitchell, D., & Schmidt, A. (1985). Some theoretical considerations on confidential adoptions: Part I: The birthmother. *Human Science Press,* 13–21.

Kroger, J. (1996). *Identity in adolescence: The balance between self and other* (2nd ed.). London: Routledge.

Lamb, M. E., & Gilbride, K. E. (1985). Compatibility in parent–infant relationships: Origins and processes. In W. Ickes (Ed.), *Compatible and incompatible relationships* (pp. 33–60). New York: Springer-Verlag.

Lifton, B. J. (1994). *Journey of the adopted self: A quest for wholeness.* New York: Basic Books.

Marcenko, M. O., & Smith, L. K. (1991). Post-adoption needs of families: Adopting children with developmental disabilities. *Children and Youth Services Review, 13,* 413–424.

McDermott, M. T. (1993). The case for independent adoption. *Adoption: The Future of Children, 3(1),* 146–152.

McNamara, J. (1975). *The adoption adviser.* New York: Hathorn Books.

McRoy, R. G. (1988) An organizational dilemma: The case of transracial adoptions. *The Journal of Applied Behavioral Science, 25(2),* 145–160.

McRoy, R. G., Grotevant, H. D., & Ayers-Lopez, S. (1994). *Changing practices in adoption.* Austin, TX: Hogg Foundation for Mental Health.

McRoy, R. G., Grotevant, H. D. & Zurcher, L. A. (1988). *Emotional disturbance in adopted adolescents: Origins and development.* New York: Praeger.

McRoy, R. G., & Zurcher, L. (1983). *Transracial and inracial adoptees: The adolescent years.* Springfield, IL: Charles C. Thomas.

National Committee for Adoption. (1989). *Adoption factbook: United States data, issues, regulations, and resources.* Washington, DC: Author.

National Association of Black Social Workers. (1972, April). *Position statement on transracial adoptions.* A paper presented at the National Association of Black Social Workers Conference, Nashville, TN.

O'Hanlon, T. (1995). *Accessing federal adoption subsidies after legalization.* Washington, DC: Child Welfare League of America.

Oppenheim, E. & Bussiere, A. (1996). Adoption: Where do relatives stand? *Child Welfare, 75(5),* 471–487.

Partridge, S., Hornby, H., & McDonald, T. (1986). *Legacies of loss: Visions of gain, and inside look at adoption disruption.* Portland: University of Southern Maine.

Patterson, C. J. (1992). Children of lesbian and gay parents. *Child Development, 63(5),* 1025–1042.

Pinderhughes, E. E. (1996). Toward understanding family readjustment following older child adoptions: The interplay between theory generation and empirical research. *Children and Youth Services Review, 18,* 115–138.

Reiss, D. (1992, September). *Preliminary thoughts on the theoretical basis for family assessment.* Paper presented at the meeting of the National Institute of Mental Health Working Group on Methodological Issues in the Study of Family, Washington, DC.

Reitz, M. & Watson, K. W. (1992). *Adoption and the family system.* New York: Guilford.

Roland, R. (1992). *Living laboratories: Women and reproductive technologies.* Bloomington: Indiana University Press.

Rosenthal, J. A., & Groze, V. (1992). *Special needs adoption: A study of intact families.* New York: Praeger.

Ross, N. M. (1995). Adoptive family processes that predict adopted child behavior and self esteem. Unpublished masters thesis, University of Minnesota.

Shireman, J. F. (1995). Adoptions by single parents. *Marriage and Family Review, 20(3–4),* 367–388.

Siegel, D. H. (1993). Open adoption of infants: Adoptive parents' perceptions of advantages and disadvantages. *Social Work, 38(1),* 15–23.

Silber, K., & Dorner, P. M. (1990). *Children of open adoptions.* San Antonio, TX: Corona Publishing.

Simon, R. J., & Alstein, H. (1987). *Transracial adoptees and their families: A study of identity and commitment.* New York: Praeger.

Sorich, C., & Siebert, R. (1982). Toward humanizing adoption. *Child Welfare, 61*(4), 207–216.

Spar, K. (1997). *CRS Report for Congress: Foster care and adoption statistics.* Washington, DC: Congressional Research Service.

Stacey, J. (1996). *In the name of the family: Rethinking family values in the postmodern age.* Boston: Beacon.

Stein, L. M., & Hoopes, J. L. (1985). *Identity formation in the adopted adolescent.* New York: Child Welfare League of America.

Stolley, I. S. (1993). Statistics on adoption in the United States. *Adoption: The Future of Children, 3*(1), 26–42.

Sullivan, A. (1995). Policy issues. In A. Sullivan (Ed.), *Issues in gay and lesbian adoption: Proceedings of the fourth annual Pierce-Warwick adoption symposium* (pp. 1–10). Washington, DC: Author.

Tasker, F., & Golombok, S. (1995). Adults raised as children in lesbian families. *American Journal of Orthopsychiatry, 65*(2), 203–215.

U.S. Department of Health and Human Services, Office of Civil Rights, Administration for Children and Families (1995, April 25). Policy guidance on the use of race, color, or national origin as considerations in adoption and foster care placements. *Federal Register* [On-line], *60*(79). Available: http://www.infi.net/adopt/jdregs.htm

U.S. Department of State. (1996). Intercountry adoptions 1985–1995. *National Adoption Reports, January/February*, 11.

Vick, C. (1995). Out of sight, out of mind: The child welfare data collection problem. *Adoptalk* (Fall issue), 4.

Wilkenson, H. S. (1995). Psycholegal process and issues in international adoption. *The American Journal of Family Therapy, 23*(2), 173–183.

Wrobel, G. M., Ayers-Lopez, S., Grotevant, H. D., McRoy, R. G., & Friedrick, M. (1996). Openness in adoption and the level of child participation. *Child Development, 67*, 2358–2374.

Chapter 10

Families Headed by Lesbian and Gay Parents

Charlotte J. Patterson
Raymond W. Chan
University of Virginia

The notion of family has traditionally been intertwined with heterosexist assumptions. Not only does society generally presume children to be heterosexual unless otherwise specified, but also parents are presumed to be heterosexual. Only recently have gay and lesbian individuals begun to be acknowledged within the context of families. In the 1990s, research has focused on lesbian and gay couples (Kurdek, 1995; Peplau, Veniegas, & Campbell, 1996; Savin-Williams, 1996; Sherman, 1992; Weston, 1991) and on their families of origin (Allen & Demo, 1995; Newman & Muzzonigro, 1993). Research on lesbian mothers, gay fathers, and their children has also emerged, and a considerable research literature has accumulated (Patterson, 1995c, in press).

The most visible group of nonheterosexual parents are lesbian mothers. Many lesbian mothers conceived and gave birth to children within the context of heterosexual relationships, but adopted a lesbian identity later in life (Kirkpatrick, 1996). Observers have commented upon the increasing numbers of women who have chosen to have children after assuming a lesbian identity, and this trend has sometimes been called a lesbian baby boom (e.g., Patterson, 1994a; Weston, 1991). Similar trends can also be seen among gay fathers, many of whom had children within the context of heterosexual relationships, only later assuming a gay identity. Today, however, more and more gay men are taking part in what is sometimes called a gayby boom, and are having children after establishing their identities as gay men (Patterson & Chan, 1996).

Within the 1990s, many studies from both the United States and Europe have examined the well-being of gay and lesbian parents and their children. In this chapter, we present an overview of empirical research on lesbian and gay parents and their children, with particular attention to research that has emerged since the mid-1990s. First, we consider issues and perspectives relevant to research on lesbian and gay parents and their children. This is followed by a discussion of research on lesbian and gay parents themselves, and then by a review of research on children of lesbian and gay parents. The chapter ends with conclusions suggested by existing studies and with directions for future work.

ISSUES AND PERSPECTIVES

Research on lesbian mothers, gay fathers, and their children has arisen in an historical context that has helped to shape the issues believed to be worthy of study as well as the perspectives from which they have been explored. In this section, we describe three main standpoints from which interest in lesbian and gay parenting has emerged and identify some sources of diversity within lesbian and gay parenting communities.

Perspectives on Lesbian Mothers, Gay Fathers, and Their Children

Interest in lesbian and gay parents and their children has arisen from several perspectives. First, the phenomenon of large numbers of openly lesbian and gay parents raising children represents a sociocultural innovation that is specific to this historical era (D'Emilio, 1983; Faderman, 1991). Because many individuals identify themselves as lesbian or gay for the first time in adulthood, many have been married and given birth to children before assuming lesbian or gay identities. Others become parents after their lesbian or gay identities have become well established. Thus, lesbian and gay parented families can serve to focus attention on the ways in which, and the extent to which, social change affects children.

A second perspective asks the question, To what extent does growing up with lesbian or gay parents influence children's development? Lesbian and gay parents and their children raise questions about the kinds of home environments that can foster positive development (Patterson, 1992, 1994a; Tasker & Golombok, 1997). Because it is widely believed that family environments exert significant influences on children who grow up in them, and because it is believed by many that lesbian and gay parents may provide input that is different in important ways from that provided by heterosexual parents, it has often been suggested that the experience of growing up with a gay or lesbian parent may have significant effects on the children involved (e.g., Baumrind, 1995). Although feminists have sometimes imagined benefits that might accrue to mothers and children in a less patriarchal world (e.g., Gilman, 1915/1979), expectations based on many psychological theories are generally more negative (Patterson, 1992, 1995c). Thus, lesbian and gay parented families can provide unusual tests of deeply held ideas about psychological development.

A third perspective from which interest in lesbian and gay families with children has arisen is that of the law (Patterson & Redding, 1996). With few exceptions, the legal system in the United States has been relatively hostile to gay men and to lesbians who are or who wish to become parents (Editors of the Harvard Law Review, 1990; Falk, 1989; Flaks, 1994; Polikoff, 1990; Rivera, 1991). Judicial and legislative bodies in some states have found lesbians and gay men to be unfit as parents because of their sexual orientation, and lesbian mothers and gay fathers have often been denied custody or visitation with their children following divorce (Editors of the Harvard Law Review, 1990; Pershing, 1994). Lesbians' and gay men's opportunities to become foster or adoptive parents have similarly been curtailed by public policies and judicial decisions that embody a variety of negative expectations about the likely influences of lesbian and gay parents on the development of children in their care (Patterson, 1995a, Ricketts, 1991; Ricketts & Achtenberg, 1990). Because such negative assumptions have often been explicit in judicial determinations involving child custody and visitation, and because such assumptions are open to empirical test, they have provided an important impetus for research in this area (Patterson & Redding, 1996).

Sources of Diversity Among Lesbian and Gay Families

Reasons for interest in research on lesbian and gay families with children have thus emerged from a number of perspectives. In considering these, however, it is important not to overlook many sources of diversity among lesbian and gay families with children. To comprehend adequately the diversity that characterizes gay and lesbian families, it is important to examine some of the differences among them.

One important distinction among lesbian and gay families with children concerns the sexual identity of parents at the time of a child's birth or adoption. Probably the largest group of children with lesbian and gay parents today are those who were born in the context of heterosexual relationships between the biological parents, and whose parent or parents subsequently identified as gay or lesbian. These include families in which the parents divorce when the husband comes out as gay or the wife comes out as lesbian, as well as families in which one or both of the parents come out and the parents decide not to divorce. Gay or lesbian parents may be single, or they may have same-sex partners. A gay or lesbian parent's same-sex partner may or may not take up stepparenting or coparenting relationships with the children. If the partner has also had children, the youngsters may also assume stepsibling relationships with one another. Thus, gay and lesbian families with children born in the context of heterosexual relationships are themselves a relatively diverse group.

In addition to children born in the context of heterosexual relationships between parents, lesbians and gay men are having children (Brewaeys, Ponjaert, Van Hall, & Golombok, 1997; Chan, Raboy, & Patterson, 1997; Crawford, 1987; Golombok, Tasker, & Murray, 1997; Patterson, 1992, 1994a, 1994b, 1995b; Pies, 1985; 1990; Rohrbaugh, 1988; Steckel, 1987; Weston, 1991). The majority of such children are probably conceived through donor insemination (DI). Lesbians who wish to bear children may choose a friend, relative, or acquaintance to be the sperm donor, or may choose instead to use sperm from an unknown donor. When sperm donors are known, they may take parental, avuncular, or other roles relative to children conceived via DI, or they may not (Brewaeys et al., 1997; Patterson, 1994a, 1994b; Pies, 1985, 1990). Gay men may also become biological parents of children whom they intend to parent, whether with a single woman (who may be lesbian or heterosexual), with a lesbian couple, or with a gay male partner (Patterson & Chan, 1996). Options pursued by gay men and lesbians also include both adoption and foster care (Patterson, 1995a; Ricketts, 1991). Thus, given advances in reproductive technologies, children are today being brought up in a diverse array of lesbian and gay families, many of which simply did not exist as recently as 50 years ago.

Another important distinction among lesbian and gay parents is the extent to which family members are related biologically to one another (Pollack & Vaughn, 1987; Riley, 1988; Weston, 1991). Although biological relatedness of family members to one another is taken for granted in many heterosexual families, this is often not the case in lesbian and gay families with children. When children are born via DI into lesbian families, they are generally related biologically only to the birth mother, not to her partner. Similarly, when children are born via surrogacy to a gay couple, only the father who served as a sperm donor will be biologically related to the child. In heterosexual families, heavy cultural weight is traditionally placed on biological kinship, and expectations for relationships with blood kin are generally different than those for relationships with others (Henderson, Hetherington, Mekos, & Reiss, 1996). An important issue among lesbian and gay families concerns the extent to which biological relatedness does or ought to affect the experience of kinship (Chan, Brooks, Raboy, & Patterson, in press; Patterson, in press; Patterson, Hurt, & Mason, in press; Polikoff, 1990; Riley, 1988; Weston, 1991).

An additional distinction of particular importance for lesbian and gay parents concerns living arrangements for minor children. As in heterosexual families, children may be in the sole physical custody of one or both biological parents, or they may be in joint physical custody (i.e., spending part of their time in one parent's household and part of their time in another's). Because of the hostility of the legal system to gay and lesbian parents in some parts of the United States, many lesbian mothers and gay fathers have lost custody of their children to heterosexual spouses following divorce, and the threat of custody litigation looms larger in the lives of custodial divorced lesbian mothers than it does in the lives of custodial divorced heterosexual ones (Lyons, 1983; Pagelow, 1980; Pershing, 1994). It is almost certainly the case that a greater proportion of gay and lesbian parents has lost custody of their children against their will than is true of the heterosexual population. For this reason, many more lesbians and gay men are noncustodial parents (i.e., do not have legal custody of their children) and nonresidential parents (i.e., do not live in the same household with their children) than might otherwise be expected.

Beyond these basic distinctions, others may also be important. In addition to difficulties in defining sexual orientation (see Brown, 1995; Gonsiorek, 1995), there are a number of other important ways in which lesbian and gay families with children may differ among themselves. These include variations associated with income, education, race/ethnicity, gender, and culture. Such variability undoubtedly contributes to differences in the qualities of daily life in families with lesbian and gay parents.

In the next sections, we first describe research on lesbian and gay parents, followed by studies of their children. Within each of these two sections, we begin with work on families whose children were born or adopted in the context of heterosexual relationships and then describe studies of families whose children were born or adopted by lesbian and gay parents. Within each section, emphasis is placed on the most recent research findings.

RESEARCH ON LESBIAN MOTHERS AND GAY FATHERS

Despite the diversity of lesbian and gay parenting communities, much of the available research has been conducted with relatively homogeneous samples of participants. Samples of parents have most often been composed of White, middle-class or upper-middle-class, well-educated individuals living in major urban centers, generally in the United States and Western Europe. Exceptions to this trend are specifically noted. In this section, we first present research on those who became parents in the context of heterosexual relationships, before coming out as lesbian or gay. Following that, we describe studies of lesbians who became parents after coming out. Other reviews of this material can be found in Bigner and Bozett (1990), Bozett (1989), Cramer (1986), Falk (1989), Gibbs (1988), Kirkpatrick (1996), Patterson (1996a), and Patterson and Chan (1996).

Lesbians and Gay Men Who Became Parents in the Context of Heterosexual Relationships

An important impetus for research in this area has come from extrinsic sources, such as judicial concerns about the psychological health and well-being of lesbian as compared with heterosexual mothers. Other work has arisen from concerns that are more intrinsic to the families themselves, such as what and when children should be told about their parents' sexual orientation. In this section, the material arising from extrinsic concerns is reviewed first, followed by the material stemming from intrinsic concerns. Although some parents may not have been married to the heterosexual partner with whom they had children, it is likely that most were. To avoid the use of more cumbersome labels, then, we refer to "divorced lesbian mothers" and to "divorced gay fathers."

Divorced Lesbian Mothers.   Because it has often been raised as an issue by judges presiding over custody disputes (Falk, 1989; Hitchens, 1979/80; Kleber, Howell, & Tibbits-Kleber, 1986; Patterson & Redding, 1996; Pershing, 1994), a number of studies have assessed the overall mental health of lesbian as compared to heterosexual mothers. Consistent with data on the mental health of lesbians in general (Gonsiorek, 1991), research in this area reveals that divorced lesbian mothers score at least as high as divorced heterosexual mothers on assessments of psychological functioning and adjustment. For instance, studies find no differences between lesbian and heterosexual mothers on self-concept (Mucklow & Phelan, 1979; Rand, Graham, & Rawlings, 1982), happiness (Rand et al., 1982), or overall adjustment or psychiatric status (Golombok, Spencer, & Rutter, 1983; Thompson, McCandless, & Strickland, 1971).

Another area of judicial concern has focused on maternal sex-role behavior and its potential impact on children (Falk, 1989). Stereotypes cited by the courts suggest that lesbians might be overly masculine or that they might interact in inappropriate ways with their children, or both. In contrast to expectations based on the stereotypes, however, neither lesbian mothers' reports about their own sex-role behavior (Kweskin & Cook, 1982) nor their self-described interest in childrearing (Kirkpatrick, Smith, & Roy, 1981) have been found to differ from those of heterosexual mothers. Reports about responses to child behavior (Mucklow & Phelan, 1979) and ratings of warmth toward children (Golombok et al., 1983) are found not to differ significantly between lesbian and heterosexual mothers. Hoeffer (1981) described lesbian mothers in her sample as more likely to choose a mixture of masculine and feminine sex-typed toys for their children, whereas heterosexual mothers were more likely to choose sex-typed toys to the exclusion of others, but there was no suggestion of inappropriate behavior on the part of any of the mothers.

Some differences between lesbian and heterosexual mothers have also been reported. Lyons (1983) and Pagelow (1980) found that divorced lesbian mothers reported greater fear about loss of child custody than did divorced heterosexual mothers. Similarly, R. Green, Mandel, Hotvedt, Gray, and Smith (1986) reported that lesbian mothers were more likely than heterosexual mothers to be active in feminist organizations. Although findings of this sort are hardly surprising, other reported differences are more difficult to interpret. For instance, Miller, Jacobsen, and Bigner (1981) reported that lesbian mothers were more "child-centered" in their discipline techniques than heterosexual mothers. In a sample of African American lesbian mothers and African American heterosexual mothers, Hill (1987) found that lesbian mothers reported being more flexible about rules, more relaxed about sex play and modesty, and more likely to have nontraditional expectations for their daughters. Pending confirmation and replication with different samples, the overall significance of these findings remains unclear.

Several researchers have also examined the social circumstances and relationships of lesbian mothers. Divorced lesbian mothers are reported to be more likely than divorced heterosexual mothers to be living with a romantic partner (Harris & Turner, 1985/86; Kirkpatrick et al., 1981; Pagelow, 1980). Whether this represents a difference between lesbian and heterosexual mother-headed families, on the one hand, or reflects sampling biases of the research, on the other, cannot be determined on the basis of information in these cross-sectional studies. However, longitudinal research by Tasker and Golombok (1997) revealed that over a 16-year period, divorced lesbian mothers and divorced heterosexual mothers were equally likely to have lived with a romantic partner. Furthermore, no differences emerged on the degree of exclusiveness of these relationships as a function the women's sexual orientation.

Information is sparse about the impact of mothers' romantic relationships in lesbian mother families, but what has been published suggests that, like heterosexual stepparents, coresident lesbian partners of divorced lesbian mothers can be important sources of conflict as well as support in the family (Harris & Turner, 1985/86; Kirkpatrick et al., 1981). Tasker and Golombok (1997) reported that lesbian mothers' partners were more readily accepted as parent figures by the children than were the male partners of heterosexual mothers. Further research on the subsequent couple relationships of lesbian and heterosexual mothers would certainly be valuable.

Relationships with the fathers of children in lesbian mother homes have also been studied. Few differences in the likelihood of paternal financial support have been reported for lesbian and heterosexual families with children. Kirkpatrick and her colleagues (1981) reported, for example, that only about half of heterosexual and about half of lesbian mothers in their sample received any financial support from the fathers of their children. Findings about frequency of contact with the fathers are mixed, with some (e.g., Kirkpatrick et al., 1981) reporting no differences as a function of maternal sexual orientation and others (e.g., Golombok et al., 1983; Hare & Richards, 1993) reporting more contact with fathers among children of lesbian than among children of heterosexual mothers. In a comparison of contacts with friends and relatives among heterosexual and lesbian mothers, Green and his colleagues (1986) reported no differences.

Although most research to date has involved assessment of possible differences between lesbian and heterosexual mothers, a few studies have reported other comparisons. For instance, in a study of divorced lesbian mothers and divorced gay fathers, Harris and Turner (1985/86) found that fathers were more likely to report higher incomes and more likely to report that they encouraged sex-typed toy play among their children whereas mothers were more likely to see benefits for their children (e.g., increased empathy and tolerance for differences) as a result of having lesbian or gay parents. In comparisons of relationship satisfaction among lesbian couples who did or did not have children, Koepke, Hare, and Moran (1992) reported that couples with children scored higher on overall measures of relationship satisfaction and of the quality of their sexual relationship. These findings are intriguing, but further research will be needed before their interpretation will be clear.

Another important set of questions, as yet little studied, concerns the conditions under which lesbian mothers experience enhanced feelings of well-being,
support, and ability to care for their children. Rand and her colleagues (1982) reported that psychological health of lesbian mothers was associated with the mothers' openness about her sexual orientation with her employer, ex-husband, children, and friends, and with her degree of feminist activism. Kirkpatrick (1987)
found that lesbian mothers living with partners and children had greater economic and emotional resources than those living alone with their children. Much
remains to be learned about determinants of individual differences in psychological well-being among lesbian mothers.

A number of additional issues that have arisen in the context of divorced lesbian mother families are also in need of study. For instance, when a mother is in
the process of coming out as a lesbian to herself and to others, at what point in that
process should she address the topic with her child, and in what ways should she
do so—if at all? And what role ought the child's age and circumstances play in
such a decision? Some writers have suggested that early adolescence may be a
particularly difficult time for parents to initiate such conversations, and that disclosure may be less stressful at earlier or later points in a child's development
(Baptiste, 1987; Huggins, 1989; Lewis, 1980; Paul, 1986), but systematic research
on these issues is just beginning. For example, Tasker and Golombok (1997) reported that adult children of lesbian mothers felt better about their families if
their mothers were open about their lesbian identities, but did not study the timing of such disclosures. Similarly, many issues remain to be addressed regarding
stepfamily and blended family relationships that may emerge as a lesbian mother's
household seeks new equilibrium following her separation or divorce from the
child's father.

Divorced Gay Fathers.   There is relatively little empirical research on gay fathers.
A small handful of studies have addressed questions about possible differences
between gay and heterosexual fathers in psychological adjustment, parenting behavior, and other social relationships. Much of the existing work has been devoted
to efforts to conceptualize changes in gay fathers' identities over time (Patterson
& Chan, 1996).

It is interesting to note that, although considerable research has focused on the
overall psychological adjustment of lesbian mothers as compared to that of heterosexual mothers, no published studies of gay fathers make such comparisons
with heterosexual fathers. This fact may be attributable to the greater role of judicial decision making as an impetus for research on lesbian mothers. In jurisdic-
tions where the law provides for biases in custody proceedings, these are likely to
favor female and heterosexual parents. Perhaps because, other things being equal,
gay fathers are unlikely to win custody battles over their children after divorce,
fewer such cases seem to have reached the courts. Consistent with this view, only
a minority of gay fathers have been reported to live in the same households as

their children (Bigner & Bozett, 1990; Bozett, 1980, 1989; Crosbie-Burnett & Helmbrecht, 1993).

Research on the parenting attitudes of gay versus heterosexual divorced fathers has, however, been reported. Bigner and Jacobsen (1989a, 1989b) studied 33 gay and 33 heterosexual fathers, each of whom had at least two children. Their results revealed that, with one exception, there were no significant differences between gay and heterosexual fathers in their motives for parenthood. The single exception concerned the greater likelihood of gay than heterosexual fathers to cite the higher status accorded to parents as compared with nonparents in the dominant culture as a motivation for parenthood (Bigner & Jacobsen, 1989b). In another study, Bigner and Jacobsen (1992) also reported similar findings.

Bigner and Jacobsen (1989a, 1992) also asked gay and heterosexual fathers to report on their own behavior when interacting with their children. Although no differences emerged in the fathers' reports of involvement or intimacy, gay fathers reported that their behavior was characterized by greater responsiveness, more reasoning, and more limit setting than did heterosexual fathers. These reports by gay fathers of greater warmth and responsiveness, on the one hand, and greater control and limit-setting, on the other, would seem to raise the possibility that gay fathers are more likely than their heterosexual counterparts to exhibit authoritative patterns of parenting behavior such as those described by Baumrind (1967; Baumrind & Black, 1967). Caution must be exercised, however, in the interpretation of these results, which stem entirely from paternal reports about their own behavior.

In addition to research comparing gay and heterosexual fathers, a handful of studies have made other comparisons. For instance, Robinson and Skeen (1982) compared sex-role orientations of gay fathers with those of gay men who were not fathers and found no differences. Similarly, Skeen and Robinson (1985) found no evidence to suggest that gay men's retrospective reports about relationships with their own parents varied as a function of whether they were parents themselves. As noted above, Harris and Turner (1985/86) compared gay fathers and lesbian mothers, reporting that, although gay fathers had higher incomes and were more likely to report encouraging their children to play with sex-typed toys, lesbian mothers were more likely to believe that their children received positive benefits such as increased tolerance for diversity from having lesbian or gay parents. Studies like these begin to suggest the possibilities for research on gender, sexual orientation, and parenting behavior, and it is clear that there are many valuable directions that research could take.

Crosbie-Burnett and Helmbrecht (1993) identified predictors of happiness with family life among 48 divorced gay fathers, their gay partners, and their teenage offspring. Even though most of the teenagers lived primarily with their mothers and only visited in the gay fathers' households, predictors of family happiness were strongly related to the role of the fathers' partners. For teenagers as well as for their fathers and for the fathers' partners, psychological inclusion of the partners into the family and the quality of partners' relationships with the teenagers were important predictors of happiness with family life.

Much research in this area has also arisen from concerns about the gay father's identity and its transformations over time. Miller (1979) and Bozett (1980, 1981a, 1981b, 1987) described the processes through which a man who considers himself to be a heterosexual father may come to identify himself, both in public and in private, as a gay father. Based on interviews with gay fathers in the United States and in Canada, these authors emphasized the pivotal nature of identity disclosure itself and of reactions to disclosure by significant people in fathers' lives. Miller (1979) suggested that, although many factors (e.g., extent of occupational autonomy, amount of access to gay communities) may affect how rapidly a gay man is able to disclose his identity to others, the most important factor is likely to be the experience of falling in love with another man. It is this experience, more than any other, Miller argued, that leads a man to integrate the otherwise compartmentalized parts of his identity as a gay father. This hypothesis is clearly open to empirical evaluation, but such research has not yet been reported.

Overall, then, there is clearly a need for further research on gay fathers. In particular, questions about the sources of diversity among gay fathers have not yet been addressed by empirical research. For instance, one question concerns variations in the amount of contact that a divorced gay man has with his children and how his relationship with them may be affected by such variations. Another question concerns the ways in which a man's contacts with gay communities and with parenting communities may affect his views of himself as well as of his children. The research agenda here is extensive.

Lesbians and Gay Men Choosing to Become Parents

Although for many years lesbian mothers and gay fathers were generally assumed to have become parents in the context of previous heterosexual relationships, both men and women are increasingly choosing to undertake parenthood in the context of preexisting lesbian and gay identities (Brewaeys et al., 1997; Chan et al., 1997, in press; Crawford, 1987; Golombok, Cook, Bish, & Murray, 1993, 1995; Mitchell, 1996; Patterson, 1992, 1994a, 1994b, 1995c, 1996b; Pies, 1985, 1990). A substantial body of research addresses the transition to parenthood among heterosexuals (e.g., C. Cowan & Cowan, 1992; P. Cowan, Cowan, & Kerig, 1993), examining ways in which decisions to have children are made, normative changes during the transition to parenthood, and factors related to individual differences. Although many issues that arise for heterosexuals also face lesbians and gay men (e.g., concerns about how children will affect couple relationships, economic concerns about supporting children), lesbians and gay men must also cope with many additional issues because of their situation as members of stigmatized minorities (Patterson, 1994b). These issues are best understood by viewing them against the backdrop of pervasive heterosexism and antigay/antilesbian prejudice.

Antigay and antilesbian prejudice is evident in institutions involved with health care, education, and employment that often fail to support, and in many cases are openly hostile to, lesbian and gay parents and their children (Casper, Schultz, & Wickens, 1992; Polikoff, 1990; Pollack & Vaughn, 1987). Prospective lesbian and gay parents may encounter antigay prejudice and bigotry even from their families of origin (Pollack & Vaughn, 1987; Weston, 1991). Many if not most of the special concerns of prospective lesbian and gay parents arise from problems created by such hostility (Patterson, 1994b).

A number of interrelated issues are often faced by prospective lesbian and gay parents (Patterson, 1994b). Lesbians and gay men who want to become parents need accurate, up-to-date information on how they could become parents, how their children are likely to develop, and what supports are available to assist gay and lesbian parented families. In addition to these educational needs, lesbians and gay men who are seeking biological parenthood are also likely to encounter various health concerns, ranging from medical screening of prospective birth parents to assistance with DI techniques, prenatal care, and preparation for birth. As matters progress, a number of legal concerns about the rights and responsibilities of all parties emerge (Polikoff, 1990). There are also financial issues; in addition to the support of a child, auxiliary costs of medical and legal assistance can be considerable. Finally, social and emotional concerns of many different kinds are also likely to emerge. For instance, prospective parents may experience disappointment if family members and friends are not supportive of their desire to become parents (Crawford, 1987; Pies, 1985, 1990; Patterson, 1994b).

As this outline of issues suggests, numerous research questions are posed by the emergence of prospective lesbian and gay parents. What factors influence lesbians' and gay men's inclinations to make parenthood a part of their lives, and through what processes do they operate? What effects does parenting have on lesbians or gay men who undertake it, and how do these effects compare with those experienced by heterosexuals? How well do special services such as support groups serve the needs of lesbian and gay parents and prospective parents? What are the elements of a social climate that are supportive for gay and lesbian parents and their children? As yet, little research has addressed such questions.

The earliest studies of childbearing among lesbian couples were reported by McCandlish (1987) and by Steckel (1987). Both investigators reported research based on small samples of lesbian couples who had given birth to children by means of DI. Their focus was primarily on the children in such families, and neither investigator attempted systematic assessment of mothers. McCandlish, however, noted that, regardless of their degree of interest in parenting prior to birth of the first child, the nonbiological mothers in each couple unanimously reported an "unexpected and immediate attachment" to the child (1987, p. 28). Although both mothers took part in parenting, they reported shifting patterns of caretaking responsibilities over time, with the biological mother taking primary responsibility during the earliest months, and the nonbiological mother's role increasing in importance after the child was 12 or more months of age. Couples also reported changes in their own relationships following the birth of the child, notably a reduction or cessation in sexual intimacy. Results of these pioneering studies thus raise many intriguing issues and questions for further research.

Hand (1991) examined the ways in which 17 lesbian and 17 heterosexual couples with children under 2 years of age shared child care, household duties, and occupational roles. Hand's principal finding was that lesbian couples shared parenting more equally than did heterosexual couples. Lesbian nonbiological mothers were significantly more involved in child care and regarded their parental role as significantly more salient than did heterosexual fathers. Lesbian biological mothers viewed their maternal role as more salient than did any of the other mothers, whether lesbian or heterosexual. Fathers viewed their occupational roles as more salient than did any of the mothers, whether lesbian or heterosexual.

Another study (Osterweil, 1991) involved 30 lesbian couples with at least one child between 18 and 36 months of age. Consistent with Hand's results for parents of younger children, Osterweil reported that biological mothers viewed their maternal role as more salient than did nonbiological mothers. In addition, although household maintenance activities were shared about equally, biological mothers reported somewhat more influence in family decisions and somewhat more involvement in child care. Osterweil also reported that the couples in her study scored at about the mean for normative samples of heterosexual couples in overall relationship satisfaction. Taken together, results of the Hand and Osterweil studies thus suggest that lesbian couples who have chosen to bear children are likely to share household and child care duties to a somewhat greater degree than do heterosexual couples.

Patterson (1995b, 1996b) studied 26 families headed by lesbian couples who had children between 4 and 9 years of age living at home with them. Consistent with results of other investigators (Koepke et al., 1992; Osterweil, 1991), Patterson found that lesbian parents' relationship satisfaction was generally high relative to norms for relationship satisfaction among heterosexual couples. Although they reported sharing household tasks and decision making equally, the couples reported that biological mothers were more involved in child care and that nonbiological mothers spent longer hours in paid employment. Within this context, they also reported greater satisfaction with division of labor when child care was shared more equally between them.

Flaks and his colleagues (1995) studied 15 lesbian parenting couples and compared them with 15 heterosexual parenting couples. Results indicated that lesbian and heterosexual parents were similar in their levels of satisfaction with couple relationships. Lesbian couples showed more awareness of skills needed for effective parenting than did heterosexual couples, but this may have been attributable to gender rather than to sexual orientation as such, in that all mothers (whether lesbian or heterosexual) scored higher than fathers.

Chan and his colleagues (Chan et al., 1997, in press) studied 55 lesbian-headed families and 25 heterosexual-headed families with school-age children who had been conceived using DI. Families who participated in this study were recruited from among the clients of a single sperm bank that worked with health care providers across the United States; thus, families resided in many parts of the country. Results showed that lesbian parents reported sharing child-care tasks more equally than their heterosexual counterparts. Consistent with earlier reports (e.g., Cowan & Cowan, 1992), heterosexual fathers were less willing than nonbiological lesbian mothers to assume equal responsibility for the care of their children. Similar findings were reported by Mitchell (1996).

From Europe, two major studies have been reported (Brewaeys et al., 1997; Golombok et al., 1997). Brewaeys and her colleagues studied 30 lesbian mothers who conceived children using DI and compared them with 38 heterosexual mothers who conceived using DI and with 30 heterosexual mothers who conceived children in the conventional way. Parents in all three types of families were relatively satisfied in their couple relationships and there were no differences among family types in this regard. In terms of parenting, lesbian nonbiological mothers were reported to have more positive interactions with their children than were heterosexual fathers regardless of the mode of conception. Lesbian nonbiological mothers also participated in more child-care activities and were more active in disciplining children than were heterosexual fathers; but fathers of children who were conceived via DI showed a higher level of participation in child care than did fathers who had conceived children in the conventional way.

Golombok and her colleagues (1997) studied a group of 30 lesbian mothers (15 single lesbian mother and 15 lesbian couples) and 34 single heterosexual mothers and compared them with 41 heterosexual couples. Three major findings emerged: (1) single heterosexual mothers and lesbian mothers were reported to show more warmth and more positive interaction with their children than coupled heterosexual mothers; (2) lesbian mothers were also rated as having more positive interactions with their children than were single heterosexual mothers; and finally (3) single heterosexual mothers and lesbian mothers reported more serious (though not more frequent) disputes with their children than coupled heterosexual mothers.

Overall then, the results from research on lesbian mothers are quite clear. In independent studies from the United States and Europe, lesbian mothers have been found to express satisfaction with their couple relationships. Lesbian couples, by and large, reported being able to negotiate their division of labor equitably. In addition, lesbian nonbiological mothers were consistently described as more involved than heterosexual fathers with their children.

Two studies of men who became fathers after identifying themselves as gay have also been reported. Sbordone (1993) studied 78 gay men who had become parents through adoption or surrogacy arrangements and compared them with 83 gay men who were not fathers. Consistent with earlier findings for divorced gay fathers (Skeen & Robinson, 1985), there were no differences between fathers and nonfathers on reports about relationships with the men's own parents. Gay fathers did, however, report higher self-esteem and fewer negative attitudes about homosexuality than did gay men who were not fathers.

An interesting result of Sbordone's (1993) study was that more than half of the gay men who were not fathers indicated that they would like to rear a child. Those who said that they wanted children were younger than those who said they did not, but the two groups did not differ otherwise (e.g., on income, education, race, self-esteem, or attitudes about homosexuality). Given that fathers had higher self-esteem and fewer negative attitudes about homosexuality than either group of nonfathers, Sbordone speculated that gay fathers' higher self-esteem might be a result rather than a cause of parenthood.

Another study of gay men choosing parenthood was conducted by McPherson (1993), who assessed division of labor, satisfaction with division of labor, and satisfaction with couple relationships among 28 gay and 27 heterosexual parenting couples. Consistent with evidence from lesbian parenting couples (Hand, 1991; Osterweil, 1991; Patterson, 1995b), McPherson found that gay couples reported a more even division of responsibilities for household maintenance and child care than did heterosexual couples. Gay parenting couples also reported greater satisfaction with their division of child-care tasks than did heterosexual couples. Finally, gay couples also reported greater satisfaction than did heterosexual couples with their couple relationships, especially in the areas of cohesion and expression of affection.

As this brief review has revealed, lesbians and gay men who have chosen to become parents have received considerable research attention in the 1990s (Brewaeys et al., 1997; Chan et al., 1997, in press; Flaks et al., 1995; Golombok et al., 1997; Mitchell, 1996; Patterson, 1994a, 1995b, 1996a). Although many studies have been conducted on a relatively small scale and many important issues have yet to be addressed, the accumulated data clearly show that lesbian and gay couples tend to divide the duties of parenting more evenly than do heterosexual couples. However, the majority of the research has focused on lesbian mothers. Much remains to be learned about the determinants of parenting, especially among gay men.

RESEARCH ON CHILDREN
OF LESBIAN AND GAY PARENTS

Like research on parents, research on children of lesbian and gay parents with few exceptions has been conducted with relatively homogeneous groups of White, well-educated, middle-class, largely professional families living in or around urban centers in the United States or in other Western countries. Research on children born in the context of heterosexual relationships is presented first, followed by a description of work with children born to or adopted by lesbian and gay parents.

Research on Children Born
in the Context of Heterosexual Relationships

As with research on lesbian mothers, much of the impetus for research in this area has been generated by judicial concerns about the psychosocial development of children residing with gay or lesbian parents. Research in each of three main areas of judicial concern—namely, children's sexual identity, other aspects of children's personal development, and children social relationships—is summarized here. For other reviews of this material, see Falk (1989), G. Green and Bozett (1991), Patterson (1992, 1995c, 1996a), and Tasker and Golombok (1991, 1997).

Sexual Identity. Following Money and Ehrhardt (1972), we consider research on three aspects of sexual identity here. *Gender identity* concerns a person's self-identification as male or female. *Gender role behavior* concerns the extent to which a person's activities, occupations, and the like are regarded by the culture as masculine, feminine, or both. *Sexual orientation* refers to a person's attraction to and choice of sexual partners—for example, heterosexual, homosexual, or bisexual. To examine the possibility that children in the custody of lesbian mothers experience disruptions of sexual identity, we describe research findings relevant to each of these three major areas of concern.

Research on gender identity has failed to reveal any differences in the development of children as a function of their parents' sexual orientation. In one of the earliest studies, Kirkpatrick, Smith, and Roy (1981) compared the development of twenty 5- to 12-year-old children of lesbian mothers to that of twenty same-age children of heterosexual mothers. In projective testing, most children in both groups drew a same-sex figure first, a finding that fell within expected norms. Of those who drew an opposite-sex figure first, only 3 (1 with a lesbian mother and 2 with heterosexual mothers) showed concern about gender issues in clinical interviews. Similar findings have been reported in projective testing by other investigators (R. Green, 1978; R. Green et al., 1986). Studies using more direct methods of assessment (e.g., Golombok et al., 1983) have yielded similar results. In short, no evidence for difficulties in gender identity among children of lesbian mothers has been reported.

Research on gender role behavior has also failed to reveal difficulties in the development of children with lesbian mothers. R. Green (1978) reported that 20 of 21 children of lesbian mothers in his sample named a favorite toy consistent with conventional sex-typed toy preferences, and that all 21 children reported vocational choices within typical limits for conventional sex roles. Results consistent with those described by R. Green have also been reported for children by Golombok et al. (1983), Hoeffer (1981), Kirkpatrick et al., (1981), Rees (1979), and for adult daughters of lesbian mothers, by Gottman (1990). In interviews with 56 children of lesbians and 48 children of heterosexual mothers, R. Green and his colleagues (1986) found no differences with respect to favorite television programs, television characters, games, or toys. These investigators did, however, report that daughters of lesbian mothers were more likely to be described as taking part in rough and tumble play or as playing with masculine toys such as trucks or guns, but found no comparable differences for sons. Overall, research has failed to identify any notable differences in the development of sex-role behavior among children of lesbian mothers.

A number of investigators have also studied sexual orientation, the third component of sexual identity. For instance, Huggins (1989) interviewed 36 youngsters who were between 13 and 19 years of age; half were the offspring of lesbian mothers and half had mothers who were heterosexual in their orientation. No child of a lesbian mother identified as lesbian or gay, but one child of a heterosexual mother did; this difference was not statistically significant. Similar results have been reported by Golombok and her colleagues (1983), Gottman (1990), R. Green (1978), Paul (1986), and Rees (1979); a few children of lesbian mothers have identified themselves as gay, lesbian, or bisexual, but their numbers did not exceed expectations based on presumed population base rates or on rates in comparison groups of heterosexually parented children (Golombok & Tasker, 1996; Tasker & Golombok, 1995, 1997). Studies of the offspring of gay fathers have yielded similar results (Bozett, 1980, 1982, 1987, 1989; Miller, 1979).

Two studies have added to this literature. Pattatucci and Hamer (1995) studied a large sample of women, some of whom identified as lesbian or bisexual. They found that, of the 19 such women in their sample with daughters old enough to report sexual orientation, 6 daughters were identified as lesbian or bisexual. However, when more restrictive criteria were used to distinguish lesbian participants, only 1 of 7 adult daughters were identified as lesbian or bisexual. No significant results emerged for sons of nonheterosexual mothers in this sample. Bailey and his colleagues (1995) worked with 55 gay fathers, inquiring about the sexual orientations of their 75 adult sons. They reported that only 7 sons (9%) were identified as gay or bisexual. No information about the daughters of gay fathers was collected in this study. The clearest conclusion from these and the earlier studies would seem to be that, although the extent of possible genetic contributions to sexual orientation remains unknown, the great majority of children with lesbian and gay parents grow up to identify themselves as heterosexual (Bailey & Dawood, in press).

Other Aspects of Personal Development. Studies of other aspects of personal development among children and lesbian parents have assessed psychiatric and behavior problems (Golombok et al., 1983; Kirkpatrick et al., 1981; Tasker & Golombok, 1995, 1997), personality (Gottman, 1990), self-concept (Huggins, 1989;

Puryear, 1983), locus of control (Puryear, 1983; Rees, 1979), moral judgment (Rees, 1979), and intelligence (R. Green et al., 1986). As was true for sexual identity, studies of other aspects of personal development revealed no significant differences between children of lesbian or gay parents and children of heterosexual parents. From longitudinal data (Tasker & Golombok, 1997), adult children of lesbian and heterosexual parents did not differ in their mental health status, as indexed by anxiety, depression, or the need for professional consultations. Tasker and Golombok (1997) also reported no differences in regards to adult children's employment status or employment history as a function of maternal sexual orientation. On the basis of existing evidence, then, hypotheses that children of gay and lesbian parents suffer deficits in personal development seem to be without empirical foundation.

Social Relationships.   Studies assessing potential differences between children of lesbian and gay versus heterosexual parents have sometimes included assessments of children's social relationships. Studies in this area have consistently found that school-age children of lesbian mothers report a predominantly same-sex peer group and that the quality of their peer relations is described by their mothers and by the investigators as good (Golombok et al., 1983; R. Green, 1978; R. Green et al., 1986). Anecdotal accounts describe children's worries about being stigmatized as a result of their parents' sexual orientation (Pollack & Vaughn, 1987; Rafkin, 1990) but available research provides no evidence for the proposition that the development of children of lesbian mothers is compromised by difficulties in peer relations. Among adult children of lesbian mothers in Tasker and Golombok's (1997) sample, only 22% reported that their childhood friends did not know about their mothers. Most remembered their childhood friends as accepting or positive about their families, and only 3% recalled negative responses from their childhood friends.

One often-voiced concern regarding children of lesbian parents is that they will be exposed to teasing because of their families. Tasker and Golombok (1995, 1997) asked adult children of divorced lesbian and heterosexual mothers to recall teasing they had received as children and found no differences as a function of parental sexual orientation in the extent or duration of peer teasing during childhood. However, if adult children of lesbian mothers did recall being teased by peers, they were more likely than others to say that teasing concerned issues related to sexual orientation. Thus, although children of lesbian mothers did not, as adults, recall being teased more than other children, if they were teased, such comments were likely to focus on issues related to sexual orientation.

Research has also been directed toward description of children's relationships with adults, especially fathers. For instance, Golombok and her colleagues (1983) found that children of lesbian mothers were more likely than children of heterosexual mothers to have regular contact with their fathers. Most children of lesbian mothers had some contact with their father during the year preceding data collection, but most children of heterosexual mothers had not. Kirkpatrick and her colleagues (1981) also reported that in their sample lesbian mothers were more concerned than heterosexual mothers that their children have opportunities for good relationships with adult men, including fathers. Hare and Richards (1993) reported that the great majority (90%) of children living with divorced lesbian mothers in their sample also had regular contact with their fathers. Overall, results of the research suggest that children of divorced lesbian parents have satisfactory relationships with adults of both sexes.

Concerns that children of lesbian or gay parents are more likely than children of heterosexual parents to be sexually abused have also been voiced by judges in the context of child-custody disputes. Results of research in this area show that the great majority of adults who perpetrate sexual abuse are male; sexual abuse of children by adult women is very rare (Finkelhor & Russell, 1984; Jones & MacFarlane, 1980). Lesbian mothers are thus extremely unlikely to expose their children to sexual abuse. Moreover, the overwhelming majority of child sexual abuse cases involve an adult male abusing a young female (Jones & MacFarlane, 1980). Gay men are no more likely than heterosexual men to perpetrate child sexual abuse (Groth & Birnbaum, 1978). For example, Jenny and her colleagues (1994) studied 269 consecutive child sexual abuse cases in a large urban hospital and found that in only 2 cases (0.7%) was the offender identifiable as gay or lesbian. Fears that children in custody of gay or lesbian parents might be at heightened risk for sexual abuse are thus without empirical foundation.

Diversity Among Children With Divorced Lesbian or Gay Parents. Despite the tremendous diversity of gay and lesbian communities (Blumenfeld & Raymond, 1988; Savin-Williams & Cohen, 1996), research on differences among children of lesbian and gay parents is as yet very limited. Here we focus on the impact of parental psychological and relationship status as well as on the influence of other stresses and supports.

One important dimension of variability among gay and lesbian families concerns whether or not the custodial parent is involved in a romantic relationship, and if so, what implications this may have for children. Pagelow (1980), Kirkpatrick et al. (1981), and Golombok et al. (1983) all reported that divorced lesbian mothers were more likely than divorced heterosexual mothers to be living with a romantic partner. Huggins (1989) reported that self-esteem among daughters of lesbian mothers whose lesbian partners lived with them was higher than that among daughters of lesbian mothers who did not live with a partner. This finding might be interpreted to mean that mothers who are high in self-esteem are more likely to be involved in romantic relationships and to have daughters who are also high in self-esteem, but many other interpretations are also possible.. In view of the judicial attention that lesbian mothers' romantic relationships have received during custody proceedings (Falk, 1989; Hitchens, 1979/80; Kirkpatrick, 1987; Pershing, 1994), however, it is surprising that more research has not examined the influence of this variable on children.

Rand, Graham, and Rawlings (1982) found that lesbian mothers' sense of psychological well-being was related to the extent to which they were open about their lesbian identity with employers, ex-husbands, and children. In this sample, a mother who felt more able to disclose her lesbian identity was more likely also to express a greater sense of well-being. In light of the consistent finding that children's adjustment in heterosexual families is often related to maternal mental health (Rutter, Izard, & Read, 1986; Sameroff & Chandler, 1975), one might expect factors which enhance mental health among lesbian mothers also to benefit the children of these women. No research has yet been reported, however, that investigates this possibility.

Another area of great diversity among families with a gay or lesbian parent concerns the degree to which a parent's sexual identity is accepted by other significant people in children's lives. Huggins (1989) found a tendency for children whose fathers were rejecting of maternal lesbian identity to report lower self-esteem than those whose fathers were neutral or positive. Tasker and Golombok (1997) found that adult children who reported feeling more distant from their fathers were more likely to recall being teased about their mother's lesbian identity. Those who recalled their fathers' expressions of negative emotions about their mothers' lesbian identities were also more likely to remember difficulties with peers. Thus, reactions of other important adults in a child's life to a parent's lesbian or gay identity may shape the child's experience of that identity to some extent as well.

Effects of the age at which children learn of parents' gay or lesbian identities have also been a topic of study. Paul (1986) reported that those who were told either in childhood or in late adolescence found the news easier to cope with than did those who first learned of it during early to middle adolescence. Huggins (1989) reported that those who learned of maternal lesbian identity in childhood had higher self-esteem than did those who were not informed until adolescence. Some writers have suggested that early adolescence is a particularly difficult time for children to learn of their parents' lesbian or gay identities (Baptiste, 1987; Lewis, 1980).

As this brief review reveals, research on diversity among children with divorced lesbian and gay parents is just beginning (Freiberg, 1990; Martin, 1989). Existing data favor early disclosure of identity to children, positive maternal mental health, and a supportive milieu, but the available data are still limited. No information is as yet available on differences stemming from race or ethnicity, family economic circumstances, cultural environments, or related variables. One study (Golombok & Tasker, 1996; Tasker & Golombok, 1997) employed a longitudinal design and has revealed a wealth of information on the development of children growing up with divorced lesbian mothers. Nonetheless, it is clear that much remains to be learned about differences among gay father and lesbian mother families and about the influence of such differences on children growing up in these homes.

Research on Children Born to or Adopted by Lesbian Mothers

Although many writers have noted an increase in childbearing among lesbians, research with these families is as yet relatively new (Mitchell, 1996; Patterson, 1992, 1994a; Polikoff, 1990; Pollack & Vaughn, 1987; Riley, 1988; Tasker & Golombok, 1997; Weston, 1991). In this section, we summarize the research on children born to or adopted by lesbian mothers. Although some gay men are also undertaking parenthood after coming out, no research has yet been reported on these families.

In one of the first systematic studies of children born to lesbians, Steckel (1985, 1987) compared the progress of separation-individuation among 11 preschool children born via DI to lesbian couples with that among 11 same-age children of heterosexual couples. Using a variety of techniques, Steckel compared independence, ego functions, and object relations among children in the two types of families. Her main results documented impressive similarity in development among children in the two groups. Similar findings, based on extensive interviews with five lesbian mother families, were also reported by McCandlish (1987).

The first study to examine psychosocial development among preschool and school-age children born to or adopted by lesbian mothers was conducted by Patterson (1994a). She studied 37 children, ages 4 to 9, using a variety of standardized measures and found that children scored in the normal range for all measures. On the Achenbach and Edelbrock (1983) Child Behavior Checklist, for example, children of lesbian mothers' scores for social competence, internalizing behavior problems, and externalizing behavior problems differed significantly from those for a large clinical sample of (troubled) children used in norming the test, but did not differ from the scores for a large representative sample of normal children also used in norming the test (Achenbach & Edelbrock, 1983). Likewise, children of lesbian mothers reported sex-role preferences within the expected range for children of this age. On most subscales of the self-concept measure, answers given by children of lesbian mothers did not differ from those given by same-age children of heterosexual mothers studied in the standardization sample.

On two subscales of the self-concept measure, however, children of lesbian mothers reported not only feeling more reactions to stress (e.g., feeling angry, scared or upset), but also a greater sense of well-being (e.g., feeling joyful, content, and comfortable with themselves) than did the same-age children of heterosexual mothers in the standardization sample. One possible interpretation of this finding is that children of lesbian mothers reported greater reactivity to stress because, in fact, they experienced greater stress in their daily lives than did other children. Another possibility is that, regardless of actual stress levels, children of lesbian mothers were better able to acknowledge both positive and negative aspects of their emotional experience. Although this latter interpretation is perhaps more consistent with the differences in both stress reactions and well-being, clarification of these and other potential interpretations must await the results of further research.

Whereas results of Patterson's (1994a, 1996b) study addressed normative questions, another report (Patterson, 1995b) based on the same sample focused on individual differences. In particular, Patterson (1995b) studied the 26 families in her sample that were headed by a lesbian couple and assessed division of labor, satisfaction with division of labor, and satisfaction with couple relationships as predictors of children's adjustment. Results revealed that parents' satisfaction with their relationships, though generally high, was not associated with outcomes for children. Parents were, however, more satisfied and children were better adjusted when labor involved in child care was more evenly distributed between the parents. These results suggest the importance of family process variables as predictors of child adjustment in lesbian as well as in heterosexual families (Patterson, 1992).

Chan and his colleagues (Chan et al., 1997, in press) studied a group of 80 families formed by lesbian and heterosexual parents via DI and reported similar findings. Children's overall adjustment was unrelated to parents' sexual orientation. Regardless of parents' sexual orientation or relationship status, parents who were experiencing higher levels of parenting stress, higher levels of interparental conflict, and lower levels of love for each other had children who exhibited more behavior problems. Among lesbian couples, nonbiological mothers' satisfaction with the division of labor, especially in family decision making, was related to better couple adjustment, which was in turn related to children's positive psychological adjustment (Chan et al., in press), a result that is consistent with research on heterosexual families (P. Cowan, Cowan, & Kerig, 1993). Flaks and his colleagues (1995) also compared children from lesbian mother families with heterosexual families and found no differences in the children's level of psychological adjustment as a function of mother's sexual orientation.

From Europe, Brewaeys and her colleagues (1997) studied children's adjustment among a group of 4-to-8-year-old children who were conceived via DI by lesbian mother headed families ($N = 30$) and heterosexual parents ($N = 38$) and compared them to a group of children who were conceived by heterosexual parents in the conventional way ($N = 30$). When children were asked about their perceptions of parent–child relationships, all children reported positive feelings about their parents and there were no differences in children's reports as a function of family types. Children's behavior and emotional adjustment were also assessed, and results indicated that overall, children who were conceived via DI in heterosexual families exhibited more behavior problems than children who were naturally conceived. Furthermore, girls who were conceived via DI in heterosexual families exhibited more behavioral problems than girls from other family types. Brewaeys concluded that these difference observed in the heterosexual DI families may be attributable to issues of confidentiality and secrecy among heterosexual DI regarding the origin of the child whereas this type of concern is not relevant to lesbian parented families, who generally disclose information about DI. Further research on the role of secrecy regarding the origin of children conceived via DI could advance our understanding of family functioning among these families.

In another European study, Golombok, Tasker, and Murray (1997) reported on the psychological well-being of children raised since birth by lesbian mothers ($N = 30$), and by heterosexual single mothers ($N = 34$). These children were compared with children raised in two-parent heterosexual families ($N = 41$). Results indicated that these children did not show unusual emotional or behavior problems (as reported by parents or by teachers), and there were no differences as a function of family type. In terms of children's attachment relationships to their parents, children from mother-only families (lesbian mothers and heterosexual single mothers) scored higher on an attachment-related assessment than did children reared by heterosexual couples, suggesting the possibility that children from mother-only families had more secure attachment relationships with their mothers. With respect to children's perceived competence, children from mother-only families reported lower perceived cognitive and physical competence than those children from father-present families. Thus, key findings in this study seemed to depend on parents' gender rather than parental sexual orientation.

CONCLUSIONS

Research on lesbian mothers, gay fathers, and their children is a phenomenon of the 1980s and 1990s. Systematic study of lesbian and gay families with children began in the context of judicial challenges to the fitness of lesbian and gay parents. For this reason, much of the early research was designed to evaluate judicial presumptions about negative consequences for psychological health and well-being of parents and children in lesbian and gay families. Although much remains to be done to understand the conditions that foster positive mental health among lesbian mothers, gay fathers, and their children, the results of the research are exceptionally clear. Results of the empirical research provide no reason under the prevailing best interests of the child standard to deny or curtail parental rights of lesbian or gay parents on the basis of their sexual orientation, nor do systematic studies provide any reason to believe that lesbians or gay men are less suitable than heterosexuals to serve as adoptive or foster parents.

With these conclusions in mind, researchers are now beginning also to turn their attention to areas of diversity among gay and lesbian families and are starting to identify conditions that help gay and lesbian families to flourish. This transition, now well underway, appears to be gathering momentum, and it justifies the conclusion that research on lesbian and gay families has reached a significant turning point (Patterson, 1992, 1994c, 1995c). Having begun to address many of the negative assumptions represented in psychological theory, judicial opinion, and popular prejudice, researchers are now in a position to explore a broader range of issues.

From a methodological viewpoint, a number of directions seem especially promising. Longitudinal research has begun to follow families over time and illuminate how changing life circumstances affect both parents and children (Golombok & Tasker, 1996; Tasker & Golombok, 1997), but much more longitudinal work is needed. There is also a clear need for observational studies, and for research conducted with larger samples. A greater focus on family interactions and processes as well as on structural variables is also likely to be valuable (Patterson, 1992; Chan et al., 1997).

From a substantive point of view, many issues relevant to lesbian and gay families are in need of study. First and most obvious is that studies representing the demographic diversity of lesbian and gay families are needed. With few exceptions (e.g., Hill, 1987), existing research mostly involves White, well-educated, relatively affluent families who live in urban areas in the United States and Western Europe. More work is needed to understand differences that are based on race and ethnicity, family economic circumstances, and cultural environments. Research of this kind should explore differences as well as commonalities among lesbian and gay families with children.

Future research should also, insofar as possible, encompass a larger number of levels of analysis. Existing research has most often focused on children or on their parents, considered as individuals. As valuable as this emphasis has been, it will also be important to consider couples and families as such (e.g., Chan et al., in press; Patterson et al., in press). Assessments of dyadic adjustment or family climate can enhance understanding of individual-level variables, such as self-esteem. When families are considered at different levels of analysis, nested within the various contexts and communities in which they live, a more comprehensive understanding of lesbian and gay families will become possible.

In this effort, it will be valuable to devote attention to family process as well as to family structure. How do lesbian and gay families negotiate their interactions with institutional settings such as the school and the workplace (Casper et al., 1992; Victor & Fish, 1995)? How are family processes and interactions affected by economic, cultural, religious, and legal aspects of the contexts in which families live? How do climates of opinion that prevail in their communities affect lesbian and gay families, and how do families cope with prejudice and discrimination when these are encountered?

Gender is a matter deserving of special attention in this regard. Inasmuch as lesbian and gay relationships encourage the separation of gender and behavioral roles, one might expect to find considerable variability among families in the ways in which they carry out essential family, household, and child-care tasks (Chan et al., 1997; Hand, 1991; Mitchell, 1996; Osterweil, 1991; Patterson, 1995b). In what ways do nontraditional divisions of labor affect children who grow up in lesbian and gay homes? And in what ways does the performance of nontraditional tasks affect parents themselves? In general terms, it will be valuable to learn more about the relative importance of gender and behavioral roles in lesbian and gay families with children.

One additional issue that should be given special emphasis involves the conceptualization of parents' sexual identities. In the research literature on gay and lesbian parenting, scant attention has been devoted to the fluidity of sexual identities over time or to the implications of any such fluidity for children. For instance, many parents are probably bisexual to some degree, rather than exclusively heterosexual, gay, or lesbian, yet this is rarely noted, much less studied directly in the existing research literature. Increasing numbers of adults seem to be identifying themselves as bisexual (see Fox, 1995). Future research might benefit from closer attention to issues in assessment of parental sexual orientation.

In conclusion, although research on lesbian mothers, gay fathers, and their children has been fruitful, there is yet much important work to be done. Having addressed many widespread prejudices shared by jurists, theorists, and others, researchers are now in a position to examine a broader range of issues raised by the emergence of different kinds of lesbian and gay families with children. Results of future work in this area have the potential to enhance our knowledge of human development, contribute to the growth of psychological theory, and affect the evolution of law and policy relevant to lesbian mothers, gay fathers, and their children.

REFERENCES

Achenbach, T. M., & Edelbrock, C. (1983). *Manual for the Child Behavior Checklist and Revised Child Behavior Profile*. Burlington: University of Vermont.

Allen, K. R., & Demo, D. H. (1995). The families of lesbians and gay men: A new frontier in family research. *Journal of Marriage and the Family, 57,* 111–127.

Bailey, J. M., Bobrow, D., Wolfe, M., & Mikach, S. (1995). Sexual orientation of adult sons of gay fathers. *Developmental Psychology, 31,* 124–129.

Bailey, J. M., & Dawood, K. (in press). Behavioral genetics, sexual orientation, and the family. In C. J. Patterson & A. R. D'Augelli (Eds.), *Lesbian, gay, and bisexual identities in families: Psychological perspectives.* New York: Oxford University Press.

Baptiste, D. A. (1987). Psychotherapy with gay/lesbian couples and their children in "stepfamilies": A challenge for marriage and family therapists. In E. Coleman, (Ed.), *Integrated identity for gay men and lesbians: Psychotherapeutic approaches for emotional well-being* (pp. 223–238). New York: Harrington Park Press.

Baumrind, D. (1967). Childcare practices anteceding three patterns of preschool behavior. *Genetic Psychology Monographs, 75,* 43–88.

Baumrind, D., & Black, A. E. (1967). Socialization practices associated with dimensions of competence in preschool boys and girls. *Child Development, 38,* 291–327.

Bigner, J. J., & Bozett, F. W. (1990). Parenting by gay fathers. In F. W. Bozett & M. B. Sussman, (Eds.), *Homosexuality and family relations* (pp. 155–176). New York: Harrington Park Press.

Bigner, J. J., & Jacobsen, R. B. (1989a). Parenting behaviors of homosexual and heterosexual fathers. In F. W. Bozett, (Ed.), *Homosexuality and the family* (pp. 173–186). New York: Harrington Park Press.

Bigner, J. J., & Jacobsen, R. B. (1989b). The value of children to gay and heterosexual fathers. In F. W. Bozett, (Ed.), *Homosexuality and the family* (pp. 163–172). New York: Harrington Park Press.

Bigner, J. J., & Jacobsen, R. B. (1992). Adult responses to child behavior and attitudes toward fathering: Gay and nongay fathers. *Journal of Homosexuality, 23,* 99–112.

Blumenfeld, W. J., & Raymond, D. (1988). *Looking at gay and lesbian life.* Boston: Beacon.

Bozett, F. W. (1980). Gay fathers: How and why they disclose their homosexuality to their children. *Family Relations, 29,* 173–179.

Bozett, F. W. (1981). Gay fathers: Evolution of the gay father identity. *American Journal of Orthopsychiatry, 51,* 552–559.

Bozett, F. W. (1982). Heterogeneous couples in heterosexual marriages: Gay men and straight women. *Journal of Marital and Family Therapy, 8,* 81–89.

Bozett, F. W. (1987). Children of gay fathers. In F. W. Bozett, (Ed.), *Gay and lesbian parents* (pp. 39–57). New York: Praeger.

Bozett, F. W. (1989). Gay fathers: A review of the literature. In F. W. Bozett, (Ed.), *Homosexuality and the family* (pp. 137–162). New York: Harrington Park Press.

Brewaeys, A., Ponjaert, I., Van Hall, E. V., & Golombok, S. (1997, April). *Donor insemination: Child development and family functioning in lesbian mother families with 4 to 8 year old children.* Paper presented at the biennial meeting of the Society for Research in Child Development, Washington, DC.

Brown, L. S. (1995). Lesbian identities: Concepts and Issues. In A. R. D'Augelli & C. J. Patterson (Eds.), *Lesbian, gay, and bisexual identities over the lifespan: Psychological perspectives* (pp. 3–23). New York: Oxford University Press.

Casper, V., Schultz, S., & Wickens, E. (1992). Breaking the silences: Lesbian and gay parents and the schools. *Teachers College Record, 94,* 109–137.

Chan, R. W., Brooks, R. C., Raboy, B., & Patterson, C. J. (in press). Division of labor among lesbian and heterosexual parents: Associations with children's adjustment. *Journal of Family Psychology.*

Chan, R. W., Raboy, B., & Patterson, C. J. (1998). Psychosocial adjustment among children conceived via donor insemination by lesbian and heterosexual mothers. *Child Development, 69,* 443–457.

Cowan, C. P., & Cowan, P. A. (1992). *When partners become parents: The big life change for couples.* New York: Basic Books.

Cowan, P. A., Cowan, C. P., & Kerig, P. K. (1993). Mothers, fathers, sons, and daughters: Gender differences in family formation and parenting style. In P. A. Cowan, D. Field, D. Hansen, A. Skolnick, & G. Swanson (Eds.), *Family, self, and society: Toward a new agenda for family research* (pp. 165–195). Hillsdale, NJ: Lawrence Erlbaum Associates.

Cramer, D. (1986). Gay parents and their children: A review of research and practical implications. *Journal of Counseling and Development, 64,* 504–507.

Crawford, S. (1987). Lesbian families: Psychosocial stress and the family-building process. In Boston Lesbian Psychologies Collective, *Lesbian psychologies: Explorations and challenges* (pp. 195–214). Urbana: University of Illinois Press.

Crosbie-Burnett, M., & Helmbrecht, L. (1993). A descriptive empirical study of gay male stepfamilies. *Family Relations, 42,* 256–262.

D'Emilio, J. (1983). *Sexual politics, sexual communities: The makings of a homosexual minority in the United States, 1940–1970.* Chicago: University of Chicago Press.

Editors of the Harvard Law Review. (1990). *Sexual orientation and the law.* Cambridge, MA: Harvard University Press.

Faderman, L. (1991). *Odd girls and twilight lovers: A history of lesbian life in twentieth century America.* New York: Columbia University Press.

Falk, P. J. (1989). Lesbian mothers: Psychosocial assumptions in family law. *American Psychologist, 44,* 941–947.

Finkelhor, D., & Russell, D. (1984). Women as perpetrators: Review of the evidence. In D. Finkelhor (Ed.), *Child sexual abuse: New theory and research* (pp. 171–187). New York: Free Press.

Flaks, D. K. (1994). Gay and lesbian families: Judicial assumptions, scientific realities. *William & Mary Bills of Rights Journal, 3*(1), 345–372.

Flaks, D. K., Ficher, I., Masterpasqua, F., & Joseph, G. (1995). Lesbians choosing motherhood: A comparative study of lesbian and heterosexual parents and their children. *Developmental Psychology, 31*(1), 105–114.

Fox, R. C. (1995). Bisexual identities. In A. R. D'Augelli & C. J. Patterson (Eds.), *Lesbian, gay, and bisexual identities over the lifespan: Psychological perspectives* (pp. 48–86). New York: Oxford University Press.

Freiberg, P. (1990). Lesbian moms can give kids empowering role models. *APA Monitor, 21*, 33.

Gibbs, E. D. (1988). Psychosocial development of children raised by lesbian mothers: A review of research. *Women and Therapy, 8*, 55–75.

Gilman, C. P. (1979). *Herland*. New York: Pantheon. (Original work published 1915)

Golombok, S., Cook, R., Bish, A., & Murray, C. (1993). Quality of parenting in families created by the new reproductive technologies: A brief report of preliminary findings. *Journal of Psychosomatic Obstetrics and Gynecology, 14*, 17–22.

Golombok, S., Cook, R., Bish, A., & Murray, C. (1995). Families created by the new reproductive technologies: Quality of parenting and social and emotional development of the children. *Child Development, 66*, 285–298.

Golombok, S., Spencer, A., & Rutter, M. (1983). Children in lesbian and single-parent households: Psychosexual and psychiatric appraisal. *Journal of Child Psychology and Psychiatry, 24*, 551–572.

Golombok, S. & Tasker, F. L. (1996). Do parents influence the sexual orientation of their children? Findings from a longitudinal study of lesbian families. *Developmental Psychology, 32*(1), 3–11.

Golombok, S., Tasker, F. L., & Murray, C. (1997). Children raised in fatherless families from infancy: Family relationships and the socioemotional development of children of lesbian and single heterosexual mothers. *Journal of Child Psychology & Psychiatry, 38*, 783–791.

Gonsiorek, J. C. (1995). Gay male identities: Concepts and issues. In A. R. D'Augelli & C. J. Patterson (Eds.), *Lesbian, gay, and bisexual identities over the lifespan: Psychological perspectives* (pp. 24-47). New York: Oxford University Press.

Gottman, J. S. (1990). Children of gay and lesbian parents. In F. W. Bozett & M. B. Sussman, (Eds.), *Homosexuality and family relations* (pp. 177–196). New York: Harrington Park Press.

Green, G. D., & Bozett, F. W. (1991). Lesbian mothers and gay fathers. In J. C. Gonsiorek & J. D. Weinrich (Eds.), *Homosexuality: Research implications for public policy*. Beverly Hills, CA: Sage.

Green, R. (1978). Sexual identity of 37 children raised by homosexual or transsexual parents. *American Journal of Psychiatry, 135*, 692–697.

Green, R., Mandel, J. B., Hotvedt, M. E., Gray, J., & Smith, L. (1986). Lesbian mothers and their children: A comparison with solo parent heterosexual mothers and their children. *Archives of Sexual Behavior, 15*, 167–184.

Groth, A. N., & Birnbaum, H. J. (1978). Adult sexual orientation and attraction to underage persons. *Archives of Sexual Behavior, 7*, 175–181.

Hand, S. I. (1991). *The lesbian parenting couple*. Unpublished doctoral dissertation, The Professional School of Psychology, San Francisco.

Hare, J., & Richards, L. (1993). Children raised by lesbian couples: Does the context of birth affect father and partner involvement? *Family Relations, 42*, 249–255.

Harris, M. B., & Turner, P. H. (1985/1986). Gay and lesbian parents. *Journal of Homosexuality, 12*, 101–113.

Henderson, S. H., Hetherington, E. M., Mekos, D., & Reiss, D. (1996). Stress, parenting, and adolescent psychopathology in nondivorced and stepfamilies: A within-family perspective. In E. M. Hetherington & E. A. Blechman (Eds.), *Stress, coping, and resiliency in children and families* (pp. 36–66). Mahwah, NJ: Lawrence Erlbaum Associates.

Hill, M. (1987). Child-rearing attitudes of black lesbian mothers. In Boston Lesbian Psychologies Collective, *Lesbian psychologies: Explorations and challenges* (pp. 215–226). Urbana: University of Illinois Press.

Hitchens, D. J. (1979/1980). Social attitudes, legal standards, and personal trauma in child custody cases. *Journal of Homosexuality, 5*, 1–20, 89–95.

Hoeffer, B. (1981). Children's acquisition of sex-role behavior in lesbian-mother families. *American Journal of Orthopsychiatry, 5,* 536–544.

Huggins, S. L. (1989). A comparative study of self-esteem of adolescent children of divorced lesbian mothers and divorced heterosexual mothers. In F. W. Bozett, (Ed.), *Homosexuality and the family* (pp. 123–135). New York: Harrington Park Press.

Jenny, C., Roesler, T. A., & Poyer, K. L. (1994). Are children at risk for sexual abuse by homosexuals? *Pediatrics, 94,* 41–44.

Jones, B. M., & MacFarlane, K. (Eds.). (1980). *Sexual abuse of children: Selected readings.* Washington, DC: National Center on Child Abuse and Neglect.

Kirkpatrick, M. (1987). Clinical implications of lesbian mother studies. *Journal of Homosexuality, 13,* 201–211.

Kirkpatrick, M. (1996). Lesbians as parents. In R. P. Cabaj & T. S. Stein (Eds.), *Textbook of homosexuality and mental health* (pp. 353–370). Washington, DC: American Psychiatric Press.

Kirkpatrick, M., Smith, C., & Roy, R. (1981). Lesbian mothers and their children: A comparative survey. *American Journal of Orthopsychiatry, 51,* 545–551.

Kleber, D. J., Howell, R. J., & Tibbits-Kleber, A. L. (1986). The impact of parental homosexuality in child custody cases: A review of the literature. *Bulletin of the American Academy of Psychiatry and Law, 14,* 81–87.

Koepke, L., Hare, J., & Moran, P. B. (1992). Relationship quality in a sample of lesbian couples with children and child-free lesbian couples. *Family Relations, 41,* 224–229.

Kurdek, L. A. (1995). Lesbian and gay couples. In A. R. D'Augelli & C. J. Patterson (Eds.), *Lesbian, gay, and bisexual identities over the lifespan: Psychological perspectives* (pp. 243–261). New York: Oxford University Press.

Kweskin, S. L., & Cook, A. S. (1982). Heterosexual and homosexual mothers' self-described sex-role behavior and ideal sex-role behavior in children. *Sex Roles, 8,* 967–975.

Lewis, K. G. (1980). Children of lesbians: Their point of view. *Social Work, 25,* 198–203.

Lyons, T. A. (1983). Lesbian mothers' custody fears. *Women and Therapy, 2,* 231–240.

Martin, A. (1989). The planned lesbian and gay family: Parenthood and children. *Newsletter of the Society for the Psychological Study of Lesbian and Gay Issues, 5, 6,* 16–17.

McCandlish, B. (1987). Against all odds: Lesbian mother family dynamics. In F. Bozett, (Ed.), *Gay and lesbian parents* (pp. 23–38). New York: Praeger.

McPherson, D. (1993). *Gay parenting couples: Parenting arrangements, arrangement satisfaction, and relationship satisfaction.* Unpublished doctoral dissertation, Pacific Graduate School of Psychology at Palo Alto, CA.

Miller, B. (1979). Gay fathers and their children. *Family Coordinator, 28,* 544–552.

Miller, J. A., Jacobsen, R. B., & Bigner, J. J. (1981). The child's home environment for lesbian versus heterosexual mothers: A neglected area of research. *Journal of Homosexuality, 7,* 49–56.

Mitchell, V. (1996). Two moms: Contribution of the planned lesbian family to the deconstruction of gendered parenting. In J. Laird & R. J. Green (Eds.), *Lesbians and gays in couples and families: A handbook for therapists* (pp. 343–357). San Francisco: Jossey-Bass.

Mucklow, B. M., & Phelan, G. K. (1979). Lesbian and traditional mothers' responses to adult responses to child behavior and self concept. *Psychological Reports, 44,* 880–882.

Money, J., & Ehrhardt, A. A. (1972). *Man and woman, boy and girl: The differentiation and dimorphism of gender identity from conception to maturity.* Baltimore: Johns Hopkins University Press.

Newman, B. S., & Muzzonigro, P. G. (1993). The effects of traditional family values on the coming out process of gay male adolescents. *Adolescence, 38,* 213–226.

Osterweil, D. A. (1991). *Correlates of relationship satisfaction in lesbian couples who are parenting their first child together.* Unpublished doctoral dissertation, California School of Professional Psychology, Berkeley.

Pagelow, M. D. (1980). Heterosexual and lesbian single mothers: A comparison of problems, coping, and solutions. *Journal of Homosexuality, 5,* 198–204.

Pattatucci, A. M. L., & Hamer, D. H. (1995). Development and familiality of sexual orientation in females. *Behavior Genetics, 25,* 407–420.

Patterson, C. J. (1992). Children of lesbian and gay parents. *Child Development, 63,* 1025–1042.

Patterson, C. J. (1994a). Children of the lesbian baby boom: Behavioral adjustment, self-concepts, and sex-role identity. In B. Greene & G. Herek (Eds.), *Psychological perspectives on lesbian and gay issues: Vol. 1. Lesbian and gay psychology: Theory, research, and clinical applications* (pp. 156–175). Thousand Oaks, CA: Sage.

Patterson, C. J. (1994b). Lesbian and gay couples considering parenthood: An agenda for research, service, and advocacy. *Journal of Gay and Lesbian Social Services, 1*(2), 33–55.

Patterson, C. J. (1994c). Lesbian and gay families. *Current Directions in Psychological Science, 3,* 62–64.

Patterson, C. J. (1995a). Adoption of minor children by lesbian and gay adults: A social science perspective. *Duke Journal of Gender, Law, and Policy, 2,* 191–205.

Patterson, C. J. (1995b). Families of the lesbian baby boom: Parents' division of labor and children's adjustment. *Developmental Psychology, 31*(1), 115–123.

Patterson, C. J. (1995c). Lesbian mothers, gay fathers, and their children. In A. R. D'Augelli & C. J. Patterson (Eds.), *Lesbian, gay, and bisexual identities over the lifespan: Psychological perspectives* (pp. 262–292). New York: Oxford University Press.

Patterson, C. J. (1996a). Lesbian and gay parents and their children. In R. C. Savin-Williams & K. M. Cohen (Eds.), *The lives of lesbians, gays, and bisexuals: Children to adults* (pp. 274–304). Fort Worth, TX: Harcourt Brace.

Patterson, C. J. (1996b). Lesbian mothers and their children: Findings from the Bay Area Families Study. In J. Laird & R. J. Green (Eds.), *Lesbians and gays in couples and families: A handbook for therapists* (pp. 420–438). San Francisco: Jossey-Bass.

Patterson, C. J. (in press). Family lives of children with lesbian mothers. In C. J. Patterson & A. R. D'Augelli (Eds.), *Lesbian, gay, and bisexual identities in families: Psychological perspectives.* New York: Oxford University Press.

Patterson, C. J., & Chan, R. W. (1996). Gay fathers. In M. E. Lamb (Ed.), *The role of the father in child development* (3rd ed., pp. 245–260). New York: Wiley.

Patterson, C. J., Hurt, S., & Mason, C. (in press). Families of the lesbian baby boom: Children's contacts with grandparents and other adults. *American Journal of Orthopsychiatry.*

Patterson, C. J., & Redding, R. E. (1996). Lesbian and gay families with children: Implications of social science research for policy. *Journal of Social Issues, 52*(3), 29–50.

Paul, J. P. (1986). *Growing up with a gay, lesbian, or bisexual parent: An exploratory study of experiences and perceptions.* Unpublished doctoral dissertation, University of California at Berkeley.

Peplau, L. A., Veniegas, R. C., & Campbell, S. M. (1996). Gay and lesbian relationships. In R. C. Savin-Williams & K. M. Cohen (Eds.), *The lives of lesbians, gays, and bisexuals: Children to adults* (pp. 250–273). Fort Worth, TX: Harcourt Brace.

Pershing, S. B. (1994). "Entreat me not to leave thee": Bottoms v. Bottoms and the custody rights of gay and lesbian parents. *William & Mary Bill of Rights Journal, 3*(1), 289–326.

Pies, C. (1985). *Considering parenthood.* San Francisco: Spinsters/Aunt Lute.

Pies, C. (1990). Lesbians and the choice to parent. In F. W. Bozett & M. B. Sussman (Eds.), *Homosexuality and family relations* (pp. 137–154). New York: Harrington Park Press.

Polikoff, N. (1990). This child does have two mothers: Redefining parenthood to meet the needs of children in lesbian mother and other nontraditional families. *The Georgetown Law Review, 78,* 459–575.

Pollack, S., & Vaughn, J. (Eds.). (1987). *Politics of the heart: A lesbian parenting anthology.* Ithaca, NY: Firebrand Books.

Puryear, D. (1983). *A comparison between the children of lesbian mothers and the children of heterosexual mothers.* Unpublished doctoral dissertation, California School of Professional Psychology, Berkeley.

Rafkin, L. (1990). *Different mothers: Sons and daughters of lesbians talk about their lives.* Pittsburgh, PA: Cleis Press.

Rand, C., Graham, D. L. R., & Rawlings, E. I. (1982). Psychological health and factors the court seeks to control in lesbian mother custody trials. *Journal of Homosexuality, 8*, 27–39.

Rees, R. L. (1979). *A comparison of children of lesbian and single heterosexual mothers on three measures of socialization.* California School of Professional Psychology, Berkeley.

Ricketts, W. (1991). *Lesbians and gay men as foster parents.* Portland: National Child Welfare Resource Center, University of Southern Maine.

Ricketts, W., & Achtenberg, R. (1990). Adoption and foster parenting for lesbians and gay men: Creating new traditions in family. In F. W. Bozett & M. B. Sussman (Eds.), *Homosexuality and family relations* (pp. 83–118). New York: Harrington Park Press.

Riley, C. (1988). American kinship: A lesbian account. *Feminist Issues, 8*, 75–94.

Rivera, R. (1991). Sexual orientation and the law. In J. C. Gonsiorek & J. D. Weinrich (Eds.), *Homosexuality: Research implications for public policy* (pp. 81–100). Newbury Park, CA: Sage.

Robinson, B. E., & Skeen, P. (1982). Sex-role orientation of gay fathers versus gay nonfathers. *Perceptual and Motor Skills, 55*, 1055–1059.

Rohrbaugh, J. B. (1988). Choosing children: Psychological issues in lesbian parenting. *Women and Therapy, 8*, 51–63.

Rutter, M., Izard, C. E., & Read, P. B. (Eds.). (1986). *Depression in young people: Developmental and clinical perspectives.* New York: Guilford.

Sameroff, A. J., & Chandler, M. (1975). Reproductive risk and the continuum of caretaking casualty. In F. D. Horowitz (Ed.), *Review of child development research* (Vol. 4). Chicago: University of Chicago Press.

Savin-Williams, R. C. (1996). Dating and romantic relationships among gay, lesbian, and bisexual youths. In R. C. Savin-Williams & K. M. Cohen (Eds.), *The lives of lesbians, gays, and bisexuals: Children to adult* (pp. 166–180). Fort Worth, TX: Harcourt Brace.

Savin-Williams, R. C. & Cohen, K. M. (Eds.). (1996). *The lives of lesbians, gays, and bisexuals: Children to adult.* Fort Worth, TX: Harcourt Brace.

Sbordone, A. J. (1993). *Gay men choosing fatherhood.* Unpublished doctoral dissertation, City University of New York, New York.

Sherman, S. (Ed.). (1992). *Lesbian and gay marriage: Private commitments, public ceremonies.* Philadelphia: Temple University Press.

Skeen, P., & Robinson, B. (1985). Gay fathers' and gay nonfathers' relationships with their parents. *Journal of Sex Research, 21*, 86–91.

Steckel, A. (1985). *Separation-individuation in children of lesbian and heterosexual couples.* Unpublished doctoral dissertation, The Wright Institute Graduate School, Berkeley, CA.

Steckel, A. (1987). Psychosocial development of children of lesbian mothers. In F. W. Bozett (Ed.), *Gay and lesbian parents* (pp. 75–85). New York: Praeger.

Tasker, F. L., & Golombok, S. (1991). Children raised by lesbian mothers: The empirical evidence. *Family Law, 21*, 184–187.

Tasker, F. L., & Golombok, S. (1995). Adults raised as children in lesbian families. *American Journal of Orthopsychiatry, 65*(2), 203–215.

Tasker, F. L., & Golombok, S. (1997). *Growing up in a lesbian family: Effects on child development.* New York: Guilford.

Thompson, N., McCandless, B., & Strickland, B. (1971). Personal adjustment of male and female homosexuals and heterosexuals. *Journal of Abnormal Psychology, 78*, 237–240.

Victor, S. B., & Fish, M. C. (1995). Lesbian mothers and their children: A review for school psychologists. *School Psychology Review, 24*(3), 456–479.

Weston, K. (1991). *Families we choose: Lesbians, gays, kinship.* New York: Columbia University Press.

Chapter 11

Black Families in Intergenerational and Cultural Perspective

Vivian L. Gadsden
University of Pennsylvania

Black[1] families have been the focus of research and policy discussions since the 1950s. Considerable attention in these discussions has centered on the impact of social isolation and poverty experienced by many Black families, the resulting violence and despair, and the implications of intergenerational hardship for child and family welfare. Most noticeable is the rarity with which studies focus on middle-class Black families. Because many Black families have structures and exhibit patterns different from those of Whites, they have been criticized for deviating in culture and practices rather than being examined as equally valuable models to explore the meaning of family and nature of family development.

Since the 1970s, research studies on Black families have diverged from early work in at least three notable ways: their focus on (1) Black cultural heritage and practices as positive contributors to Black family life, (2) the different contexts in which Black families function and the salience of these social settings in understanding and supporting Black child and family development, and (3) direct attention to issues of race and racial socialization. Despite increased research, the study of Black families continues to be situated on the periphery or margins of research on families in general; the most expansive analyses on Black families are not to be found in child development or family studies research but in research on poverty and family dysfunction. Conspicuously lacking from most research discussions, across disciplines, are frameworks that consider seriously the diversity within and among families of African descent (including but not limited to families in poverty); that examine critically the relationship among Black family life, children's development, and culture; that include Black family research in the dominant discourses in the field, rather than append it; and that identify and interrogate issues that define, mediate, or enhance Black families' life-course development.

---

[1] *Black* is used to capture the range of families of African descent who reside in the United States and is not intended to minimize the significance of the concept, *African American*.

221

Comparative models continue to dominate studies on Black families. Although such comparisons may be a necessary feature of studies focused on equity and socioeconomic structural disparities, they often bear the residual effects of cultural-deficit perspectives. Researchers such as McDaniel (1994) argued that a subtle or implicit danger of comparative models, including socioeconomic structural frameworks, is that they create a continuum of legitimacy: at the low end, common practices in Black families and at the high end, common practices within White families. Changes in Black family formation patterns are examined in relation to how well they cohere with or how much they differ from traditional or nuclear family forms associated with White families in the United States. These traditional family forms are depicted typically as middle-class, well-educated, and having access to educational and employment opportunities; living in married, two-parent households in which the nuclear family (father, mother, and children) provides an insular and self-sustaining structure; and having specific gender roles assigned to mothers and fathers.

Definitions of nuclear families reflect changes in gender roles and dominant social mores, such as increased mother employment outside the home and out-of-wedlock births by middle-income, White women; however, disciplines such as developmental psychology typically adhere to nuclear family models in which mothers are primary caregivers and fathers are breadwinners. The changing definitions and the frameworks that result from them function, with modest exceptions, as a fundamental model against which researchers and policymakers measure not only Black families but also other culturally diverse families who deviate from the triadic (mother–father–child) relationship. Studies using comparative frameworks yield important data on the position of Black families within larger societal identities and on the impact of structural features within society that militate against the efficacy of Black families. Still, their current uses do relatively little to enhance either our ability to contextualize and understand the experiences of Black families across different generations or our capacity to support their development through effective public policies.

In this chapter, I focus on Black families within an intergenerational, life-course perspective and present a framework for exploring multiple domains of Black family life: that is, the experiences that influence family members' responses to societal demands and the ways that these influences shape the nature of familial expectations and the course of family life itself. An intergenerational, life-course perspective provides a convenient and useful umbrella under which to locate distinctive and diverse features of Black families who, more than any cultural family group in the United States, have been exposed to disruption, hardship, and inequalities of access, social options, and resources. Intergenerational, life-course perspectives assume variability within families and in the strategies that the family unit and individual family members use to manipulate life events and negotiate changes that promote or threaten healthy child and family development. In the case of Black families, intergenerational, life-course frameworks and approaches allow both researchers and practitioners to examine short-term and long-term implications of cultural heritage; family beliefs, practices, and choices; and the impact of institutional discrimination and racism. In addition, they encourage larger and provocative discussions among researchers, practitioners, and policymakers about the nature of the problems facing Black families and children and the possibilities for them.

I have developed this chapter around two assumptions that allow me to cross the traditional boundaries of research, practice, and policy. The first is that there is no appropriate, prototypical model of Black family structure. In fact, significant changes in family formation patterns have occurred from the Industrial Period to the present, resulting in a vast range of family constellations. The second is that like other ethnic family groups, Black families' past and contemporary experiences have dictated or defined the family structures in which they function, with varying degrees of socially valued success. Each family brings a repertoire of beliefs, knowledge, skills, and experiences that are as likely to strengthen as to debilitate its members, depending upon the family's access to resources and upon the family's ability to rise above the constraints, social practices, and laws that circumscribe opportunities.

I begin this chapter with a summary of the historical and social contexts of Black family research and the challenges to contemporary Black families, including issues around Black family formation patterns, poverty, and debates on Black family structure and cultural variation. In the second part, I examine current issues in Black family structure and the vulnerability of Black children. In the third, I use intergenerationality and life-course family development as a context to present my own family cultures framework which was developed, in large part, from my continuing work with 25 four-generation Black families, originally from the rural south. I conclude the chapter by revisiting the complex issues facing Black families and the implications of intergenerational, life-course models for increasing our understanding of the cultural significance of practices within Black families.

HISTORICAL CONTEXTS OF RESEARCH
ON BLACK FAMILIES

What one hears when one speaks to Black families is often a high level of expectation of and from parents and other family members—for example, expectations of themselves, their children, and society; discontent and concern about poverty and being poor; mild hysteria, public perception, or real experience around disorder in families; reliance upon strong practices and intergenerational activities; and learning and teaching across different generations to remedy social and familial problems or to improve family life and opportunities for children. What one finds in research studies about Black families is a range of cultural and structural competing orientations and an attempt to find a mesh within and across disciplinary lines such as sociology, psychology, family studies, anthropology, education, and history.

The Origins of Competing Perspectives on Black Families

From the 1900s to the present, social scientists have vacillated on the conceptual and methodological frameworks that should be used to study and situate Black families' cultural identities and social needs within dominant institutional and structural frameworks. Up to the mid-1950s, race-based models of pathology and deviance dominated research. More recent models (e.g., strengths and resilient-adaptive models, cultural-deficit models, and structural models) represent an expansion of old frameworks and call attention to the complexity of inserting new ones (Taylor, Chatters, Tucker, & Lewis, 1990).

Much of the scholarly debate on Black families has its origins in sociology and anthropology and has focused on the legitimacy of the term *culture* to describe the beliefs and practices associated with Black family life. In *The Philadelphia Negro* (1899) and *The Negro American Family* (1908), DuBois provided the first social science studies of Black families, drawing from the African and slave background of Blacks to explain the cultural differences of Blacks from White society. In the 1920s, genetic theories of scientific racism and racial superiority gained attention and prominence over all other explanations of difference. They dismissed the idea of culture as a conceptual or theoretical framework to understand or study Black family life. Respected researchers of the time did not regard the continent of Africa as a possible source and location of culture or civilization and used eugenic racial essentialism coupled with biological notions of race and family to obscure ethnicity (*ethnicity* is associated with culture and places of origin; McDaniel, 1994; Model, 1993). Alternative explanations from anthropology challenged the view that Africa was not a source of culture and raised the question of cultural *survivals*, that is, language, religion, folktales, and practices that survived the Middle Passage of African slaves to the United States and that were embedded in the daily life of Black people.

A pivotal point in this early history was the publication of Frazier's (1939) *The Negro Family in the United States*, based upon the analytic structure and disorganization theme made popular by the Thomas and Znaniecki (1918) study, *The Polish Peasant*. In Thomas and Znaniecki's work, *disorganization* served as a metaphor for the disarray of traditions and change experienced by Polish immigrants to the United States; *reorganization* became a metaphor for "the production of new schemes of behaviors and new institutions [that are created to adapt better] to the changed demands of the group" (Thomas & Znaniecki, 1918, p. 130).

Like the model from which it was adapted, Frazier's (1939) framework was equally concerned with migration. Frazier addressed the growing concern attached to Black migration from the south to the north (i.e., the problems that Black migration to the urban north created) and the negative consequences of social welfare measures as antidotes to the resulting poverty. He suggested that the ravages of Black slavery in the United States were too pervasive and culturally intrusive to allow for a cohesive Black family. He recommended that Blacks eliminate from their daily practices and interactions the African traditions that were associated with Black rural, southern life in order to progress in the urban north. If Blacks failed to divest themselves of this legacy, he warned, "black family life which evolved within the isolated world of the Negro folk [would] become increasingly disorganized" (Frazier, 1939).

Although his assessment was cutting, Frazier's analysis was rigorous and not irrelevant to the debates of his time or current discussions. Its limitations were in the conceptual framework. First, Frazier compared Blacks to Whites in the United States and minimized the distinctive pathways to change available to each group and the ways in which each group's progress might be proscribed in a race-structured society. Second, he treated as pejorative family networks, systems, and social supports that mediated the difficulties of Black transition to the north.

Conceptual and Theoretical Shifts in the 1960s and 1970s

In the 1960s and 1970s, increased visibility of and discontent about the social inequalities experienced by Blacks created a shift in sociological and psychological studies. Considerable attention was given to educational and social problems faced by Black families and to their adaptive approaches. At least two categories of research studies became prominent. One group focused on the barriers to social mobility; explored approaches to improving the quality of Black family life; or attempted to respond to policy and racial dilemmas associated with the civil rights movement and the War on Poverty (e.g., Clark, 1965; Coleman et al., 1966; Kerner Commission Report, 1968; Moynihan, 1965). For the most part, these studies offered a critical lens on the circumstances and conditions that obstructed Black social mobility. However, a few, such as Moynihan's (1965) commissioned essay, *The Negro Family: Case for National Action,* were thought by some social scientists to marginalize the experiences of Black families and the practices within them. Moynihan's essay was concerned with the implications of Black family disorder for the growing social and racial discontent. His essay revived Frazier's disorganization explanation as a framework to understand the hardship experienced by Black families whose deterioration Moynihan described as inherent to the deterioration of Black society. Thus, although calling much needed attention to intrinsic inequities in opportunity during the times, Moynihan's analysis, and others of less national note, promoted frameworks that unfailingly cast the Black families studied as pathological and distanced from normative family structures in the United States (Jaynes & Williams, 1989).

A second group of studies offered a strengths model as an alternative to cultural-deficit or deviant frameworks in the study of Black families. These studies (e.g., Aschenbrenner, 1975; Billingsley, 1968; Blassingame, 1972; Gutman, 1976;

Hill, 1972; Stack, 1975), along with developing structural and economic models (Rainwater, 1970; W. Wilson, 1973), created new and expansive analytic frameworks to locate and respond to the experiences of Black families. Allen (1978) suggested that in cultural variant perspectives Black families represent a social form distinct from that of the White family, influenced by culture and socioeconomic environment.

The emergence of the term *underclass* as an all-encompassing concept to describe the plight of Black families not only was both an asset and detractor to the credibility of structural models but also drew attention to macrostructural changes in the economy. The decline in entry-level jobs, the relocation of jobs away from the inner city, and the mismatch between job requirements and employee skills were compared against parallel declines in rates of male employment, marriage, and childbearing within and outside of marriage (Furstenberg, Hershberg, & Model, 1975). Issues around migration were recast to examine the points between disorganization and reorganization. Life-course studies highlighted the nature of social support and the kin ties that insulated migrating and transplanted families; they illustrated the reciprocity of support, goods, and services that transpired within and among Black families in transition.

In describing the developments in the field during the 1960s and 1970s, Elder (1985) asserted that the changes in research paradigms from pathology to resilience reflect a more radical transformation than accounted for in perspectives on cultural variations. He argued that the changes also have been part of a general conceptual transformation of family studies and that research on Black families should be located within the evolving field of family studies, rather than scholarly tensions about social disorganization and reorganization.

The Emergence of Structural Explanations and the Focus on Marriage Rates

The confluence of research in different disciplines and public discussions from the 1960s through the early 1970s was reflected in new emphases on Black family research in the 1980s to the 1990s. A wave of studies representing interdisciplinary perspectives and structural explanations examined issues facing Black families living in poverty, single-parent homes, and declines in marriage (e.g., Bumpass & McLanahan, 1989; Dornbusch et al., 1985; W. Wilson, 1987). Increasing negative public sentiment toward welfare and impending political initiatives to reform public assistance to families with children overshadowed the successes of Black families and thrust into the public discourse deepening problems such as father absence and intergenerational hardship.

Studies that included any data on racial differences—and on Blacks, across domains in the social sciences, education, and public policy—were applied to discussions of Black families, from those focused on genetic tracking to those describing the pervasiveness and impact of apparent racist or discriminatory practices (Massey & Denton, 1993; Oliver & Shapiro, 1995). Some studies attempted to create new theoretical frameworks that combined cultural features of Black families and structural frameworks within society. Staples (1985), for example, used exchange theory to examine the conflict between family ideology and structural conditions. He noted that Black women do not marry or do not remain married when they perceive the costs of marriage (e.g., continued alliances to a low wage earner) to outweigh the benefits of such an arrangement.

Research on Black families in the 1990s took a decisive turn to focus on female-headed households and poverty, ranging from studies on adolescent mothers to a slowly emerging body of work on Black fathers (Bowman, 1990; Burton & Dilworth-Anderson, 1991; Chase-Lansdale & Brooks-Gunn, 1991; Furstenberg, 1991; Maynard, 1997; McLanahan & Sandefur, 1994; McLoyd, 1990; Scott-Jones, 1991). These bodies of work, with a few exceptions, mirrored previous studies and continued to focus on the differences between White and Black families and the persistence of a gap between the two over time, particularly in educational attainment, income, and marriage rates. This has led some researchers, such as McDaniel (1994), to suggest that research on Black families has been obsessed with marriage and household leadership as determinants of family form and stability and, thus, has been unproductively emulative of earlier work in the field.

The research design of studies on Black families has changed modestly in both the conceptual and methodological frameworks used. Greater interest in family life-course development has required expanded notions of intergenerationality and more integrative frameworks to explain the complex relationships between individual family members and the family unit (Gadsden & Hall, 1996). Many studies have relied heavily on analyses from large datasets (e.g., The National Study of Family Households or the National Longitudinal Study of Youth). However, others use a combination of field and secondary analytic approaches to identify the scope of problems facing poor Black families (Jackson, 1991; M. Wilson, Kohn, Curry-El, & Hinton, 1995). An increasing number of studies use ethnographic or qualitative approaches that attempt to connect family constructions of life events and to locate the development, strengths, and exigencies of Black families within age, contextual, and temporal frameworks (e.g., Stack & Burton, 1993). As a result, we have more information, not simply about the incidence of positive or negative life events typically available in U.S. Census reports, but also about the ways in which some of these life events shape and are shaped by the experiences, expectations, and images of and within Black families.

A persistent area of concern in research and policy discussions is the declining rate of marriage, particularly among young Black adults. In 1970, 68% of Blacks were married; 28% of households were headed by women, with no spouse present; and 4% were headed by men, with no spouse present. By 1994, 47% of Blacks were married; 48% of households were female-headed, with no spouse present;

and 6% of households were headed by men, with no spouse present (U.S. Bureau of the Census, Current Population Reports, 1995, pp. 60–187). In 1994, children were present in 69% of Black families, with 50% of families having one to two children. Five percent of Black families had four or more children.

Declining marriage rates are associated with increases in female-headed households, among the fastest growing groups of impoverished families since the 1960s. Less than 40% of Black children grew up in two-parent homes in the 1980s (U.S. Bureau of the Census, 1990, pp. 20–480), and approximately 3 out of 4 young Black children can expect to grow up with their fathers absent from the home (but not necessarily from the children's lives). In 1960, out-of-wedlock births accounted for 22% of all births to Black families; by the mid-1980s, 53% of female-headed households were in poverty; and in 1990, out-of-wedlock births accounted for 60% of all births in Black families (U.S. Bureau of the Census, Current Population Reports, P20–480 1990). At least some of the increase in mother heads of households can be found in the increases in the number of adolescent mothers.

Two demographic trends have been identified to explain the increase in the percentage of out-of-wedlock births. The first indicates that the age at which Black women marry has risen at the same time that the length of time they are married has shortened. This enlarges the window of time in which a nonmarital birth can occur and shortens the period during which marital childbearing is possible. The second shows that the fertility rate of married Black women has declined more significantly than the fertility rate of unmarried Black women. This difference, Taylor and his colleagues (1990) suggested, results in an increase in the percentage of total births to unmarried Black women. Based upon data from the 1970s and 1980s, Farley and Allen (1987) showed that the birth rates of unmarried Black women actually declined, not that the percentage of births increased.

In the midst of alarm over female-headed households and declining marriage rates, several issues are taken for granted, and other trends are overlooked. For example, empirical evidence has changed neither the public's perception that public assistance is an incentive to young Black women to bear children out of wedlock (or at least a disincentive to delayed child bearing) nor the public's perception that the women resist work. In fact, the reasons for early childbearing or childbearing outside of marriage are more complex than the desire of young women to collect small sums of money (Fernandez-Kelley, 1995). Even when intolerance for public welfare might lead one to argue that the young mothers resist work, data from recent studies reveal that the ability or desire of many young mothers to work is constrained by poor educational preparation, limited work skills, and lack of affordable child care. Fernandez-Kelley (1995) and Jarrett (1994) both delivered compelling accounts of Black adolescent and young adult mothers who are personally motivated to work but educationally unprepared (after several years of schooling) and distrustful of institutions designed to improve their lives.

CURRENT ISSUES IN BLACK FAMILIES

Black Extended Families

Social scientists throughout the 20th century have been reticent to expand the theoretical basis for their arguments about Black families. In current discussions about family support, there is considerable emphasis on marriage. The institution of marriage is seen as the point at which families are formed and the medium to ensure the healthy development of children. However, several social scientists, anthropologists primarily, who study Black families and the continuities and patterns within them assert the importance of African traditions to Black family formation in which the child, not the conjugal unit, create a family.

One measure of family structure that distinguishes Black and White families is the family form called the extended family. The term *extended*, which is used to describe these families, is based upon the presumption that families that diverge from the triadic, nuclear family model (mother–father–child) represent a nontraditional family form. Although children in nuclear families have access to family members outside of the nuclear structure, their social development and the daily concern over and attention to their welfare are considered to be the responsibility of parent(s) primarily.

The nature of extendedness differs in its content and generational focus. Ethnographic work on families suggest that in White extended families, nonnuclear members usually live within the same households and include the elderly parents of the conjugal parents. On the other hand, Black extended families often embrace several households in which children are not the possessions of a single, private family. The extended family takes place in the exchange of consanguineous children (Hill, 1972; Shimkin, Shimkin, & Frate, 1978). Data on the role(s) of extended families are not available from popular analyses of Black family structure based upon the U.S. Census alone. These families, nevertheless, paint a picture of family constellations with depth and breadth, not reflected in private, triadic relationships.

An alternative perspective on the role of Black extended families is that they, in fact, are not extended forms at all but represent a different form of nuclear or centered family. Extended families serve a variety of purposes within Black life and offer young women and men a range of supports around child and adult development. In a report by the early Childcare Research Network of the National Institute for Child Health and Human Development (NICHD), researchers found that in the lowest income quartile of the Black families studied, 60% included unmarried, adult, single parents (NICHD, in press). Fifty percent of these parents (typically mothers) were embedded within extended family households. They had access to and relied heavily upon the family community to support them and their children, from monetary assistance, to childcare and childrearing, to emotional support. Data from earlier studies such as *Who's Minding the Kids* (U.S. Government Printing Office, 1988); Shimkin, Shimkin, and Frate (1978), and Stack and Burton (1993) agree with this finding, although the particular examples each study uses differ based upon the context of the study, class status of the informants, and the purposes of the researchers.

Black families become extended through a range of other ways, particularly in relation to the treatment and nurturing of children. Perhaps less pervasive now than in the early part of the century, Black families extended themselves through informal *child fosterage*, the informal conventions of placing dependent children in homes other than those of their biological parents. Miller (1993) asserted that examinations of fosterage as an extended family form allow us to use a model based upon cultural variance sensitive to the centrality of children to family definitions in the African heritage and not tied to the traditional social science model of a private, Western nuclear family. Fosterage has never replaced nuclear families but is identified with practices concerned with the consequences for children when the nuclear family is not viable. Because children are at the center of family formation in many segments of the Black community, Black people, both unmarried and married, assume the responsibilities for kith and kin in a way that differs from most Whites. McDaniel (1994) suggested that Whites do not redistribute children to make families but to add to them, whereas Blacks simply tend to increase the number of homes caring for children.

Vulnerability Among Black Children

The analyses in the earlier sections of this chapter and conceptions of Black extended families as safe nests for children and relatives beg the question of why there is greater incidence and prevalence reportedly of vulnerability among Black children (National Commission on Children, 1991). There is no single answer. However, several longstanding circumstances and experiences of Black children and their families may contribute to the hardship to which many Black children are exposed. First, increasing numbers of Black children live in homes where parents and other family members are poor and where there is an intergenerational context of poverty and little access to jobs and education. Although access to resources has increased for many Black people, for others, the ability to be self-sufficient and self-sustaining has diminished. The nature and quality of extendedness has changed as families are less likely to live in the same neighborhoods or cities and, in some instances, are more likely to be influenced by White, middle-class concepts of family in which the nuclear family is only loosely linked to the extended family. Community networks have become more formalized, less accessible, and operated by people who are not familiar to Black residents. In addition, jobs and workplaces have relocated outside of urban communities where there are the highest concentrations of Black children and families. Thus, as the number of job opportunities has dwindled, so has the ability of families to support their children.

Second, poor Black families, particularly in urban areas, are often trapped by their limited exposure to good schools for their children; the result is that subsequent generations are locked out of meaningful job opportunities. Children who grow up in poor homes also are at enormous risk, not only for poor schooling but also for poor treatment in schools and other social contexts (Gadsden, Smith, & Jordan, 1996; McLoyd, 1990). They often are exposed to school experiences that focus more on making them happy in the short term than on either ensuring their achievement and cognitive development or preparing them for successful entry into the workforce. The quality of their school experiences differs dramatically from that of other Black children who are middle-class and from that of White middle-class children in urban or suburban schools (Gadsden, Smith, and Jordan, 1996; Johnson, 1988). Although many teachers are generally dedicated, some share the larger societal tendency to seek simplistic solutions to the problems that poor Black families face, blaming the children and families rather than critically examining and rethinking institutional barriers.

Third, for many other children, both parents are socially vulnerable, and neither parent is available to assume caregiving responsibilities. Grandparents, particularly grandmothers, long have assumed these responsibilities, for example, when the parent moved to a new city, remarried, or chose the security of the grandparent to that of latch-key status for children. Grandparents and their children once entered into informal agreements for the care of the child. However, many of the custodial grandparents in recent times have assumed parenting because of the personal crises of their children who are unable to make decisions or to enter into agreements. As a result, grandparents often forfeit the possibility of receiving public support for the child, and all (grandparents and grandchildren) may succumb to even greater poverty and shrinking resources.

Black Fathers

The issue that has received the most attention, however, in studying poor Black families focuses on the oppressive fear that U.S. society has held of Black males—apprehension that distorts these men's ability to participate in family life. This is particularly striking when one seeks out research on Black fathers. With a few exceptions, Black fathers, irrespective of social class, marital status, or involvement with their families, are studied apart from other fathers whose portraits in the literature are typically of White, married, middle-class, and well-educated men. The significance of race is demonstrated in the few studies that focus on Black, middle-class fathers, and the emphasis on class is reflected in the limited number of studies on poor fathers and poor, noncustodial fathers across diverse ethnic groups.

As Bowman (1995) suggested, Black father presence and responsibility were the norm on both southern tenant farms under Jim Crow laws and during the Industrial Period within working class families in northern cities. More recent work on Black fathers has focused primarily on poor, noncustodial, nonresidential fathers who represent a growing subset of Black fathers and who are implicated in discussions about female-headed households. Analyses by Darity and Myers (1995), Anderson (1990), Testa (1990), and W. Wilson (1996), though premised on different conceptual and methodological models, attribute much of the rise in female-headed households and the rise in the fraction of never-married African Americans to their economic marginalization—what Mason (1996) described as their social unwantedness and economic redundancy, particularly among Black males. Bowman (1990, 1995) and Sum and Fogg (1990) suggested that the lack of employment for and oppressive fear of African American men serve as obstacles to their assuming the provider role that is associated with middle-class family patterns.

Although economists (e.g., Brien & Willis, 1997) suggest that these fathers—like employed, middle-class fathers—should be able to replace the financial support lost from welfare, their simulations are based upon U.S. Census data that often do not include many poor Black men. The simulations also ignore the pervasiveness of unemployment among Black men, both nonresidential and residential fathers, and limited job skills to obtain employment, even when their desire to be providers is great. Practitioners who work with these young fathers daily note that despite the importance of father presence, the strain of inadequate income complicates family life, particularly among the working poor, and that many of the young men who most need to assume responsibility for their children are the least educationally ready or work-prepared to assume it (Gadsden, Pouncy, & Brenner, 1997).

It is because of the urgency around children's well-being and the potential for intergenerational hardship that the issue of father absence has gained substantial attention; however, the issues are far from resolved. Poor children typically have poor fathers, and the problems facing these men, despite considerable public discussion, have been explored only minimally (Kane, Gadsden, & Armorer, 1997). Fathers' physical presence alone in the home may not change substantially the poverty that their children experience.

The challenges facing Black families exist not because of a lack of success within many Black families but because neither work from the field nor public policy has improved the quality of life for many others. Although the most challenging issue facing contemporary Black families has been described as the increase in female-headed households and the decrease in marriage, the most pressing problem for disproportionately high numbers of families is poverty, the bleak outlook for children growing up in poverty, and the slow untangling of inequality and inequity. The consequences on children are threaded through every part of their lives, from the quality of neighborhood life to access to good schools. Parents' responses to their children's needs and children's understanding of family behaviors and societal demands contribute to the intergenerational construction of family beliefs and practices.

INTERGENERATIONAL FAMILY DEVELOPMENT: THE CONTEXT OF FAMILY CULTURES

Family Life-Course

Research on Black families has been constrained by at least three elements: (1) a failure to examine interrelationships among factors that operate at varying levels and that sometimes manifest themselves in diverse behaviors and phenomena, (2) the need for research within expanded disciplinary frameworks, and (3) a broadening of the study of Black families to consider not only the problems and challenges they face but also the ways they achieve success and the basic issues of family function, beliefs, structure, and relationships (Taylor et al., 1990). These issues are located in several cultural, social, and temporal domains in which families construct, develop, and transfer life views. Intergenerational and life-course frameworks offer a way to explore these domains critically and the traditions that are linked to and emerge from them.

At each point in our history, we have focused on different generations of Black families and have either through data or assumptions assigned different values to their family structure, beliefs, and experiences. According to McLanahan and Sandefur (1994), Black children who grow up in low-income, mother-headed households do less well on several social indicators than children who grow up with two parents. They found that these children are more likely to drop out of school and to become adolescent mothers. Adolescent girls from father-absent families are more likely to have a teenage birth, to have a premarital birth, and to experience marital disruption.

Stack and Burton (1993) explored many of the complexities of Black family life in their multigenerational research that led to the development of *kinscripts*. Kinscripts are developed upon the premise that families have their own agenda, their own interpretation of cultural norms, and their own histories. Stack and Burton's model examined the temporal nature of the life-course (e.g., lifetime, social time, family time, and historical time) and life-course independence (e.g., the ways in which individual transitions and trajectories are affected by or are contingent upon the life stages of others). The framework is developed around three critical issues: (1) temporal and interdependent factors in family role transitions, (2) creation and intergenerational transmission of family norms, and (3) negotiation, exchange, and conflict within families over the life-course.

In similar intergenerational studies, parents and grandparents share with children a range of positive learnings that they translate into effective survivals. The spoken and written legacies within these families suggest that children manipulate these teachings in ways that are extremely productive but that are challenged continually by society. The ways in which parents, both fathers and mothers, convey messages about manhood, womanhood, parenting, learning, schooling, and persistence are part of a difficult communicative mechanism that may be affected by people and factors outside the family. For Black families, social experiences and life circumstances are complicated by exclusion or marginalization within society. They serve to remind Black children and their parents of the two worlds in which they live and the incongruence often seen in the expectations of these two worlds.

In my own ethnographic-focused, intergenerational work, Black adult children, both men and women, often reported having difficulty enacting the messages of their parents about parent responsibility and persistence. Despite their stated acceptance of and belief in their family's values, they wrestled with cultural messages from peers and societal messages that were in stark contrast to those of the family. Adult children reported that they were less likely to discuss these "hard" issues, which were reminders of the intractability of social barriers.

Family Cultures and Intergenerational Learning in Edgerton

The field lacks frameworks that capture the scope and development of strengths within Black families or across different generations. There are relatively little data about Black families who are thriving (either financially or emotionally) and about how they sustain themselves over time. Even when there are discussions about successful Black families, the analyses more often than not attempt to explain why some families make it and others do not, which invariably leads to ideological struggles over the definitions of success. Like other families, however, Black families vary, even within the same family line and nuclear or extended family (Spencer & Markstrom-Adams, 1990).

The work on kin ties has offered us multiple ways to locate individuals within and outside their larger family constellations. However, it still tells us relatively little about how each family constructs its placement—the pervasive or shared feelings among family members about the family unit, its meaning, and its personal impact on the life definitions and life views that people develop; that they convey; and that geographic distance from or proximity to the family of origin challenges. Where there is little knowledge specifically about African cultural survivals, how do family members think of culture, the structure or immutability of family bonds, the passages that transcend time, and the permeability of traditions?

I, along with a research team, have been exploring these and other questions with four generations of Black families, the first cohort (73 to 87 years) of which resides in Edgerton[2] (a small rural community in South Carolina) whose progeny is spread throughout rural southern and urban northern communities. The generations represented a wide cross section in level of education, gender, income, number of children, and marital status, with social mobility becoming more apparent

---

[2] Edgerton is a pseudonym.

in each generation. Family is defined within kin networks and includes siblings, nieces, nephews, and cousins who contribute in some way to the household.

Each of the family lines, the lineages, is defined by a set of behaviors, accomplishments, and expectations both internal and external to the family. Family oral and written discourses contribute to family definitions and meld the cultural traditions of African Americans, community practices, personal experiences, family needs and goals, and social and educational access. These familial ways of seeing, constructing, and negotiating the world are combined into a framework that I call *family cultures*. Rather than focusing on either the hardships or the successes of the families, we were interested in exploring how they defined themselves and how individual family members translated or used those definitions across the different generations, within and outside of family contexts. This section describes the evolution of the framework, using commentaries from the four generations to highlight salient intergenerational and life-course perspectives.

Family cultures are developed around the meanings and roles of family units and the individuals in them. They are sustained, changed, or eliminated through their intersection with larger cultural and social institutions such as schools; they encompass family paradigms, family histories, kin-time, and social and societal variants. In the formation of identity, the family member uses one of several approaches to behaving within and interacting with the family. A family member simply may accept, without question, home, cultural, or community practices, teachings, and beliefs; accept some and reject others; or reject all. He or she may engage in an ongoing critique of the family unit and cultural context but by middle age embrace and promote the very practices and beliefs that were rejected in youth.

In family cultures, individual family members and the collective family unit assess their identities within the context of known and imagined possibilities, constantly reconciling the limitations of their immediate contexts with a view of the future. For historically oppressed individuals and groups, these cultures are developed and given credibility through memories and legacies often associated with historical successes and real and contrived explanations for apparent failures and shortcomings within families. School, community, and society are perceived as complicit in offering and denying opportunity. This is implied in the common statement, "I would have gotten more grades if times hadn't been so hard" mapped against the expectations for children in the family, "That's why I made sure that I worked . . . so my children could have a better time of it," or "The opportunities were there, I just didn't use them." In Edgerton, these perceptions are found in the identities that are formed, the sense of family and community caring, the idea of education as a cultural and community tradition, issues of race, and kin networks.

Identity.   Each family member forms an identity by locating his or her role in relationship to personal, familial, and cultural frames of reference that are influenced by kin-ties, ethnic traditions and mores, temporal space, and context. Pat, a second-generation northerner, remembers:[3]

> There was always a past in our house that I resisted that used to make what was happening in the house real and that related the expectations of us children. The talks were about being nice girls or boys, getting your schoolwork, and showing the world how far we had come. It seemed like a burden, sometimes. But, it worked. This doesn't mean that it would work for all families or all children, say, Black children, but it worked for us. Even when we didn't quite think everything [we heard] was accurate, we thought maybe our parents had a purpose . . . , and we basically liked each other as sisters and brothers. So, we saw the success of one being the success of all.

The family unit constructs meaning but does not determine solely how that meaning is interpreted within larger cultural frameworks and how it is affected by external factors such as educational access, racism and discrimination, and persistence. The families in each generation portray the tensions in negotiating Markus' (1987) concept, *possible selves*, or our construct, *real versus ideal selves*. Sherry, a third-generation northerner, describes the reconciliation of these different selves in her daughter's storywriting:

> How children think about the next step has little to do with how they are doing now. . . . If you notice children though, they write about things sometimes that they have never seen or what they read in their storybooks. My daughter used to read the stories and used to write some, too. It used to make me think and laugh because she would take the whole family and put us in a different place, sometimes in Edgerton. The place looked different, usually nicer, but usually the people from the neighborhood were in the stories and the family stayed the same. You see what I'm saying; the conditions changed, but the way people did things and the family didn't changed. I knew she just wanted things to be better, and I worked to give my children the things that other people had, like my mom and dad.

Family Culture and Community Caring.   Unlike family development frameworks based upon the norms of White middle-class families, the family cultures framework begins with cultural frames of reference in which the experiences of a group such as Black U.S. citizens are accounted for within different social and societal contexts, from home to school. Family cohesion, at the same time, may support the individual in new efforts or debilitate him or her in activities requiring increasingly greater separations from the family. Lana, a second-generation transplanted southerner, noted:

> You know, the idea of leaving home and all the kin folks was hard. My husband and I were going up north with not much. Then, I found out I was pregnant. My parents wanted us to move back home, but we thought we needed the distance. So, we struggled up north, but although we didn't ask for the help, we knew that we had close kin here we could count on, and they came through. But, you know, we knew

---

[3]At the request of the informants, I have made a few modest grammatical corrections to their commentaries.

my parents were keeping up with us and knew everything that we *didn't* bother to tell them. When my children were born, we used the same approaches, mainly because they were the ones we knew.

Alicia, a third-generation southern urban resident and single mother, asserts the importance of family line and its linkages to community and caring:

> My son said to me the other day, "I'm my own person, my own man." I corrected him, told him, "Sorry, son, you'll always be a Lenlie—my son, Ida and Pierce's grandson, Laura Jean and Henry's great-grandson." The older I get, the more sense things make!

The concept of culture is basic to the discussion of families and life-course issues and to the formation of individual and group identity. Culture here extracts from modern analyses in which long-held ethnic traditions, heritages, and beliefs are seen as central to a group but in which individuals construct, refine, and re-define manipulable life events periodically. In other words, a framework may be offered by early generations but over time members of society and subsequent generations assume their roles as the active agents in determining the parameters and limit(lessness) of culture—who is in, who is out, whose practices are valued, and what issues assume prominence. Each new generation demonstrates respect for older generations and negotiates and barters certain practices, as Efraim, a second-generation Edgerton resident, points out:

> There's a way of doing things down here that don't disrespect the older people in the community. . . . You know, in the Sunday School, some of the older heads just come. You don't see them as useless, and you see them coming in that class every Sunday for the learning, just like the little children. They show children learnin's important, no matter where it is and no matter how old.

Caring for children was at the heart of all discussion about family and the meaning of culture. Miss Marlis, a great-grandmother from the first generation, noted about the community and the families:

> Two things seemed to make a difference, and to tell the truth, I'm not sure what came first. One was that maybe some of our children could become the ruling people around here with some learning. Another was that people liked to see children have families. I don't know about slavery but as far back as I can remember, people were married and most of the children around here were born to married people, except in a few cases. Sometimes somebody had one or two children before they married. I think that when we emphasized the book learning and the parents kept the children busy with their chores, to tell you the truth, the children who took it seriously didn't have much time for much else. Some of them just started thinking that maybe they could marry or get an education first. We loved all the babies now, even when the children weren't married, but people wanted their children to have it better than the old heads, and so most watched their girl children and made sure that they could be taken care of by a decent boy or make it on their own if they ever had to.

Families believed that their own emphasis on schooling and education within the homes provided children with a way of thinking that resulted in the children choosing alternative behaviors and planning for the future or that family practices and mandates such as harsh warnings were successful.

Family time provides a dominant construct that enables the development of family cultures and is complemented by both lifetime and cultural contexts that include temporal and social factors. Family time, as Hareven suggested, is defined by the "timing of events such as marriage, birth of a child, leaving home, and the transition of individuals into different roles as the family moves through its life course" (1982, p. 580). How one progresses is influenced by historical and social contexts, although individuals and families may disagree about the timing of these events. Hagestad (1987) interpreted family time in terms of cultural units. Family members devise timetables that chart the movement of the family unit through "predictable phases of development and changing generational structures." These family timetables, Stack and Burton (1993) indicated, represent shared understandings and interdependencies within family structures and are recorded in written, mental, or oral scripts among kin.

Education as Tradition.   Education is central to the concept of culture in the family and in family traditions studied. In the more financially prosperous of the five family lines studied, more than one third of the second-generation members completed college; in the third generation, more than 60% attended college or completed degrees; and in the fourth generation, 80% of those of college age were attending or had completed college degrees. In the less financially prosperous lines, at least a small percentage of second-generation members attended college and up to 25% attended or completed a college degree in the third and fourth generations.

Family members reportedly monitored the achievements of the second generation and used these achievements as a way to motivate other children. One first-generation informant noted:

> When a child in the family made it through the grades or went on to college, it meant that the other children saw themselves as doing the same . . . you could use that child as an example. The same was true when a girl or boy didn't make it or when one of these children here got pregnant and had a baby. The parents used to talk and talk to make sure that the other children didn't get any ideas. The church helped out, too.

The more financially prosperous lines developed family traditions around the assumption that, over time and with support, the quality of life within and for subsequent generations would improve. In the first generation, support was given to children who wanted to pursue a path different from paths chosen by other family members, as long as they respected and revered the family unit. Family members expected that with more education life would be different: "We never knew where education would lead our children and what their success might be, but we got them the education anyway" (First-Generation Male).

In the second generation, informants had an explicit expectation that their children would go to college and would be successful. They had more knowledge than their parents about and exposure to opportunities and choices. Despite their respect for teaching and preaching as honorable professions, they no longer expected that their children would be teachers or preachers only; instead, they anticipated that children would be able to choose from a range of other professions also. A second-generation grandfather of a fourth-generation member who is an aspiring artist said, "My grandson wants to draw pictures. Don't know how long that learning will take him. Hard to imagine someone from my line just drawing pictures. Think he can earn a livin' out of it?" while his daughter more eagerly accepts the uncertainty, "My son is going to have a career as an artist. He has always been good at art and has always had an imagination. We're going to help him until he makes it."

Some families who had fewer of the advantages of the other family lines also held high expectations but were more fearful of the ways that the family would change if children had multiple options and suspicious about whether children would return to the family: "The children sometimes get their education and then they all go up north. They're not much help to me, but they send me help and try to visit." Family cohesion was often measured by the choices children made to stay in the community. In some families, children often went up north even when they had not acquired the literate or educational preparation. Second and third generations within these families have returned to their southern community in the greatest numbers compared to the other family lines.

For many, the north provided a harsh experience that motivated them to seek a better life in their small rural community of origin. In general, the exposure to the north has had two effects on these families. Some developed a greater reliance upon the family of origin when they returned, having felt the absence of family closeness and often social dependency in the north; others returned with noticeable cynicism about what education means for Blacks in the long term. In both cases, they talk about family building even when the physical evidence is lacking, and typically their hopes and fears about family cohesion resemble those of their parents.

The temporal nature of family development forms one critical thrust from the interviews. As individuals seek their own identity and as the family unit matures, family members' practices change as do their expectations and tolerance for new ideas within the family. One second-generation male commented:

> I knew early that I didn't want to go to college . . . didn't know how to tell my parents. So, I wrote a letter to them. In the letter, I said things that I would never have been able to say out loud. I knew that I could never achieve my parents' goals for me, and they didn't really have much money to do all the things they had hoped for me. So, I made a decision that I'm sometimes sorry about. My mother kept that letter I sent them.

Race. Familial and societal messages about race were often in conflict. Northerners with fewer support systems and with higher incomes talked more about race and inequities. Southern family members seemed to acknowledge race by their deliberate ignoring of it. A fourth-generation southern woman noted,

> These people around here pick and choose. They want to hear what other people are doing in other communities like theirs. They don't give too many points just because White people are doing it . . . only if they can see some real advantage for the community or themselves. That's a little different from what you see, say, on the tv. Not every Black girl is pregnant, on drugs . . . !

There were four ways in which parents interacted around race. One, they gave explicit messages in which parents, typically fathers talking to sons, shared with their children the realities of racism in their attempts to succeed. This was as likely to occur in low-income homes as middle-income homes and across the four generations. Young male children were prepared for poor or unfair treatment. The frequency of the messages seemingly changed, although the content did not. Second, parents gave indirect or subtle messages conveyed through larger conversations about the importance of schooling and learning as the primary means to overcoming institutional barriers. Third, some parents provided examples of ways in which race was an obvious barrier to a specific family member's achieving. Fourth, parents' verbal recognition of race was replaced by their emphasis on the responsibilities of children to become prepared to advance the community. In only two families was there little to no discussion about race.

Kin Networks. The kin networks also mandated a sense of identity within family lines, as this interchange at a meeting in Edgerton indicates and as Mr. Irvin, an 83-year-old in the first generation demonstrates when he skillfully tries to locate Ware, a young adult family member within the intergenerational constellation:

Mr. I: Whose line are you in?
Ware: My parents are Jerry and Sally Parker.
Mr. I: Whose child are you exactly?
Ware: (confused) I am Jerry and Sally Parker's son.
Mr. I: (showing a little frustration) Oh, shucks, boy, who are your grandparents, I mean? Make me know who you are!!
Ware: On my father's side, Mr. Edward Parker and Mrs. Audra Parker and on my mother's side Mr. Artis Lenlie and Mrs. Ida Lenlie.
Mr. I: (wearing a smile) Do you know who I am?
Ware: No sir.
Mr. I: (appearing incredulous that Ware would not know who he is) Well, I'm your Uncle. I'm your grandmama, Ida, middle brother. Come here boy! (Ware comes over and receives a hug).
Mr. I: Where do you live?
Ware: New York.
Mr. I: Do you know Sherry, Sherry Ediston?
Ware: Yes sir.

Mr. I: (speaking with pride) Well she my granddaughter. You know her from where now?
Ware: I met her when I was in middle school, I think.
Mr. I: Uh, huh. You doing alright? What you doing for yourself up there?
Ware: Working and getting ready to go back to college.

As this conversation between a first-generation and fourth-generation member indicates, a person may be defined by intergenerational connections that link people across geographic distance ("Where do you live?") or to biological relationships ("Whose child are you exactly?") or to age cohorts ("Do you know Sherry. Well, she's my granddaughter"). Ware understood that he had to make connections between historical and individual time in order to construct the social space for a conversation with relatives such as Mr. Irvin. Mr. Irvin's demand, "Make me know who you are" is commonly heard in Edgerton. Ware's conversation with his granduncle suggests that a name is not enough, that one is identified by genealogy at such gatherings and valued as a family member when he or she acknowledges or understands where and how to locate his or her space. Moments of encouragement permeate the conversation as do reminders that despite the travails of your life experiences in New York, the larger family offers the safe space for growth.

Kin networks were also evident in the willingness of family members to raise children for varying periods of time. Second- and third-generation members in the south and north often brought their children home for their parents to raise for short periods—until the parents were able to gain stability in the north or until the child entered school. This was typically true of single parents in the north and two-parent families with insufficient income to make ends meet. Parents in the first generation took pleasure in rearing their grandchildren, but few first-, second-, or third-generation members reported that these children gave their lives meaning or that they experienced pleasure when an adolescent child became a parent, particularly prior to completing high school.

There were distinctive features of the first three generations that demonstrate the kin networks and the nature of intergenerational meanings. First, members of all three generations in the north and south framed much of their belief about self around the spoken goals of the family. Second, when first- and second-generation members talk about and transmit perceptions of these contexts, their perceptions may be microcosmic in their original construction or may represent a more selective process in which family members are expected to extract from or ignore the larger society, as culturally and socially useful and appropriate. Third, the Edgerton community, the communities of the northern relatives, and larger social settings contribute to certain practices and beliefs being sustained. Edgerton residents and their northern relatives assume responsibility for kin who are unable to care for themselves and their children and were generous in their appraisals of family members' abilities to survive on their own. Fourth, what seemed to be a simple transmission of hope is a complex myriad of possibilities and limitations that second- and third-generation informants experience in surviving and achieving.

CONCLUDING CONSIDERATIONS

Black families, similar to other families, are biological and social structures, providing the first intersection between individual and society. However, as Hewitt
noted, "family structures and the social structures within which they function differ and, in fact, may be at odds" (1994, p. 2). Families respond to environmental
and social structures in varied ways, based upon the life needs of their members
and the survival of family cultures and family organization. The question that
persists is how do researchers capture these responses and understand within cultural history and social contexts?

There is a persistent push-pull in both research and policy discussions about
Black families. This is particularly true of those who look to standardize family
forms upon the Western notion of nuclear families and who ignore the salience of
other culturally embedded family forms such as extended family networks. Black
families, whether middle-class, two-parent, or female-headed families, identify
disproportionately with kin networks, although middle-class families may have
access to more goods and services for which they can pay. When the rates of marriage were highest within Black families, kin networks functioned as immeasur-
able resources. Thus, the sustained failure of research and policy to acknowledge
or explore kin networks, not simply as placid survivals but important family
structures, is counter to efforts on behalf of Black children. Until we study kin networks, not as unique features of Black families but as central to their life-course
development, a critical discourse about Black families will be denied.

In the discussion on family cultures and Edgerton, we have been intent on not
isolating the families as one of two extremes—in large part, both the families and
the research team see the families as part of a long story of life views and family
relationships over time. What is shared, for example, by the generations in Edgerton and their northern counterparts is the struggle for education and equality;
what differs are the particularities of the struggle and of families, experiences with
hardship, and discrimination. Their sense of struggle, their daily experiences, and
their family histories combine in distinctive ways to determine how people form,
think about, and use hope as a metaphor for persistence and survival, whether in
learning literacy or securing their families. Academically and socially successful
children talk about glass ceilings that they attempt to explain away using the for-
mulas of their parents and grandparents. Those living in relative poverty cling to a
belief that if they reconfigure a few environmental factors and build upon personal strengths, they can rise above the obstacles they face. Others hold on to an
idealistic view that their life circumstances are better in the north than those of
Blacks in the south and hold to an image of the south as less modern and civilized
than the urban labyrinths and markets through which they maneuver daily. Yet,
others move between a sense of possibility, gauging the probabilities for success,
and the vestiges of despair. They seek the ideal selves that they often present as

their real selves when talking to outsiders such as researchers and teachers about life circumstances, personal goals, literacy, education, and family. In almost a century of research on Black families in the United States, we have more statistical information about them but may understand the connections across context, process, and time only minimally. Intergenerational and life-course approaches, while not the cure-all for the field, offer a more expansive perspective that allows us potentially to examine the range of possibilities and limitations within families, based upon their own analyses of history, expectations, identity, and cultural embeddedness of family practices. The challenges with which a growing segment of Black families and the children in them grapple are indicators of the need for different conceptual and empirical frameworks—for Black families, frameworks that seek to identify the nexus between family and culture; the ways in which the two are situated against public expectations; the constructions of struggle, survival, and persistence; and the human ideologies and social histories used to convey knowledge across multiple generations.

REFERENCES

Allen, W. R. (1978). Black family research in the United States: A review, assessment, and extension. *Journal of Comparative Family Studies, 9,* 167–189.

Anderson, E. (1990). *Streetwise.* Philadelphia, PA: University of Pennsylvania Press.

Aschenbrenner, J. (1975). *Lifelines: Black families in Chicago.* New York: Holt, Rinehart, & Winston.

Billingsley, A. (1968). *Black families in White America.* Englewood, NJ: Prentice-Hall.

Blassingame, J. (1972). *The slave community: Plantation life in the antebellum South.* New York: Oxford University Press.

Bowman, P. (1995). Coping with provider role strain: Adaptive cultural resources among Black husband-fathers. *Journal of Black Psychology, 16*(2), 1–21.

Bowman, P. (1995). Education and responsible fatherhood among African Americans: Socialization, mobilization, and allocation challenges. In V. L. Gadsden & W. Trent (Eds.), *Transitions in the life-course of African American males: Issues in schooling, adulthood, fatherhood, and families* [Monograph WP-95-2], National Center on Fathers and Families. Philadelphia: University of Pennsylvania.

Brien, M. J., & Willis, R. J. (1997). The partners of welfare mothers: Potential earnings and child support. *The Future of Children, 7*(1), 65–73.

Bumpass, L. L., & McLanahan, S. (1989). Unmarried motherhood: Recent trends, composition, and Black-White differences. *Demography, 26,* 279–286.

Burton, L. M., & Dilworth-Anderson, P. (1991). The intergenerational family roles of aged Black Americans. *Marriage and Family Review, 16,* 311–330.

Chase-Lansdale, P. L., & Brooks-Gunn, J. (1991). Research and programs for adolescent mothers: Missing links and future promises. *Family Relations, 40,* 396–403.

Clark, K. B. (1965). *Dark ghetto: Dilemmas of social power.* New York: Harper & Row.

Coleman, J. S., Campbell, E. Q., Hobson, C. J., McPartland, J. M., Mood, A., Weinfeld, F. D., & York, R. L. (1966). *Equality of educational opportunity.* Washington, DC: U.S. Government Printing Office.

Darity, W. A., Jr., & Myers, S. L., Jr. (1995). Family structure and the marginalization of Black men: Policy implications. In M. B. Tucker & C. Mitchell-Kernan (Eds.), *The decline in marriage among*

African Americans: Cause, consequences, and policy implications. New York: Russell Sage Foundation.

Dornbusch, S. M., Carlsmith, J. M., Bushwall, S. J., Ritter, H. L., Hastorf, A. H., & Gross, R. T. (1985). Single parents, extended households, and the control of adolescents. *Child Development, 56,* 326–341.

DuBois, W. E. B. (1899). *The Philadelphia Negro.* Philadelphia: University of Pennsylvania.

DuBois, W. E. B. (1908). *The Negro American Family.* Atlanta, GA: Atlanta University Press.

Elder, G. (1985). Household kinship and the life course: Perspectives on Black families. In M. B. Spencer, G. K. Brookins & W. R. Allen (Eds.), *Beginnings: The social and affective development of Black children* (pp. 29–44). Hillsdale, NJ: Lawrence Erlbaum Associates.

Farley, R., & Allen, W. R. (1987). *The color line and the quality of life in America.* New York: Russell Sage Foundation.

Fernandez-Kelly, M. P. (1995). Social and cultural capital in the urban ghetto: Implications for the economic sociology of immigration. In A. Portes (Ed.), *The economic sociology of immigration: Essays on networks, ethnicity, and entrepreneurship.* New York: Russell Sage Foundation.

Frazier, E. F. (1939). *The Negro family in the United States.* Chicago: University of Chicago Press.

Furstenberg, F. F., Jr., Hershberg, T., & Model, J. (1975). The origins of the female-headed Black family: The impact of the urban experience. *Journal of Interdisciplinary History, 6*(2), 211–233.

Furstenburg, F. (1991). *Divided families: What happens to children when parents part.* Cambridge, MA: Harvard University Press.

Gadsden, V. L., & Hall, M. (1996). *Intergenerational learning: A review of the literature on fathers and families* [Monograph LR-96-7], National Center on Fathers and Families. Philadelphia: University of Pennsylvania.

Gadsden, V., Pouncy, H., & Brenner, E. (1997). Unemployment and father involvement among low-income, noncustodial fathers. *Workforce Investment Quarterly, National Governors' Association, 4,* 26–34.

Gadsden, V. L., Smith, R. R., & Jordan, W. J. (1996). The promise of desegregation: Tendering expectation and reality in achieving quality schooling. *Urban Education, 31*(4), 381–402.

Gutman, H. G. (1976). *The Black family in slavery and freedom 1750–1925.* New York: Vintage Books.

Hagestad, G. O. (1987). Problems and promises in the social psychology of intergenerational relations. In R. Fogel, E. Hatfield, S. Kiesler, & J. March (Eds.), *Stability and change in the family* (pp. 11–46). New York: Academic Press.

Hareven, T. K. (1982). The life course and aging in historical perspective. In T. K. Hareven & K. J. Adams (Eds.), *Aging and life course transitions: An interdisciplinary perspective* (pp. 1–26). New York: Guilford.

Hewitt, P. (1994). Families in flux. *The Political Quarterly, 65*(2), 168–178.

Hill, R. (1972). *The strengths of Black families.* New York: Emerson-Hall.

Jackson, J. (Ed.). (1991). *Life in Black America.* Newbury Park, CA: Sage.

Jaynes, G. D., & Williams, R. M. (1989). *A common destiny: Blacks and American society.* Washington, DC: National Academy Press.

Jarrett, R. L. (1994). Living poor: Family life among single-parent, African American women. *Social Problems, 41*(1), 30–49.

Johnson, D. J. (1988). Parental racial socialization strategies of Black parents in three private schools. In D. P. Slaughter & D. J. Johnson (Eds.), *Visible now: Blacks in private schools* (pp. 251–267). Westport, CT: Greenwood.

Kane, D., Gadsden, V., & Armorer, K. (1997). *The fathers and families core learnings: An update from the field.* Philadelphia: National Center on Fathers and Families, University of Pennsylvania.

Kerner Commission Report. (1968). *The National Advisory Commission on Civil Disorders.* New York: Bantam.

Markus, H. (1987). Dynamic self-concept: A social psychological perspective. *Annual Review of Psychology, 38,* 299–337.

Mason, P. L. (1996). *Joblessness and unemployment among African American men and fathers: A review of the literature* [Monograph LR-96-3], Philadelphia: University of Pennsylvania.

Massey, D. S., & Denton, N. A. (1993). *American apartheid: Segregation and the making of the underclass.* Cambridge, MA: Harvard University Press.

Maynard, R. A. (Ed.). (1997). *Kids having kids: Economic costs and social consequences of teen pregnancy.* Washington, DC: Urban Institute.

McDaniel, A. (1994). Historical racial differences in living arrangements of children. *Journal of Family History, 19*(1), 57–77.

McLanahan, S., & Sandefur, G. (1994). *Growing up with a single parent: What hurts, what helps.* Cambridge, MA: Harvard University Press.

McLoyd, V. C. (1990). The impact of economic hardship on Black families and children: Psychological distress, parenting, and socioemotional development. *Child Development, 61,* 311–346.

Miller, A. (1993). Social science, social policy, and the heritage of African American families. In M. B. Katz (Ed.), *The "Underclass" debate: Views from history* (pp. 254–289). Princeton, NJ: Princeton University Press.

Model, S. (1993). Ethnic niche and the structure of opportunity: Immigrants and minorities in New York. In M. B. Katz (Ed.), *The "Underclass" debate: Views from history* (pp. 161–193). Princeton, NJ: Princeton University Press.

Moynihan, D. P. (1965). *The Negro family: Case for national action.* Washington, DC: Department of Labor, Office of Policy, Planning, and Research.

National Commission on Children. (1991). *Beyond rhetoric: A new American agenda for children and families.* Washington, DC: U.S. Government Printing Office.

National Institute of Child Health and Human Development. (in press). *The NICHD study of early childcare.* Bethesda, MD: Author.

Oliver, M., & Shapiro, T. (1995). *Black wealth/White wealth: A new perspective on racial inequality.* New York: Routledge.

Rainwater, L. (1970). *Behind ghetto walls: Black families in a federal slum.* Chicago: Aldine.

Scott-Jones, D. (1991). Educational levels of adolescent childbearers at first and second births. *American Journal of Education, 99*(4), 461–480.

Shimkin, D. B., Shimkin, E. M., & Frate, D. A. (Eds.). (1978). *The extended family in Black societies.* The Hague, The Netherlands: Mouton.

Spencer, M. B., & Markstrom-Adams, C. (1990). Identity processes among racial and ethnic minority children in America. *Child Development, 61*(2), 290–309.

Stack, C. B. (1975). *All our kin.* The Hague, The Netherlands: Mouton.

Stack, C. B., & Burton, L. (1993). Kinscripts. *Journal of Comparative Family Studies, 24*(Summer), 157–170.

Staples, R. (1985). Changes in Black family structure: The conflict between family ideology and structural conditions. *Journal of Marriage and the Family, 47,* 1005–1013.

Sum, A., & Fogg, N. (1989). *The changing economic fortunes of young Black men in the new American economy of the 1980s.* Boston, MA: Northeastern University, Center for Labor Market Studies.

Sum, A., & Fogg, N. (1990). The changing economic fortunes of young Black men in America. *Black Scholar,* January-March, 47–53.

Taylor, R. J., Chatters, L. M., Tucker, M. B., & Lewis, E. (1990). Developments in research on Black families: A decade review. *Journal of Marriage and the Family, 52,* 993–1014.

Testa, M. (1990, August). *Joblessness and absent fatherhood in the inner city.* Paper presented at the annual meeting of the American Sociological Association, Washington, DC.

Thomas, W. I., & Znaniecki, F. (1918). *The Polish peasant in Europe and America: Monograph of an immigrant group.* Boston: G. Badger.

U.S. Bureau of the Census. (1990). *The Black Population of the United States: March 1994 and 1993* (Current Population Reports). Washington, DC: U.S. Government Printing Office.

U.S. Bureau of the Census. (1995). *Child Support for Custodial Mothers and Fathers: 1991* (Current Population Reports). Washington, DC: U.S. Government Printing Office.

U.S. Government Printing Office (1988). *Who's minding the kids.* Washington, DC: Author.

Wilson, M. N., Kohn, L. P., Curry-El, J., & Hinton, I. D. (1995). The influence of family structure characteristics on the childrearing behaviors of African American mothers. *Journal of Black Psychology, 21*(4), 450–462.

Wilson, W. J. (1973). *Power, racism, and privilege: Race relations in theoretical and sociohistorical perspectives.* New York: Macmillan.

Wilson, W. J. (1987). *The truly disadvantaged: The inner city, the underclass, and public policy.* Chicago: University of Chicago Press.

Wilson, W. J. (1996). *When work disappears.* Chicago: University of Chicago Press.

Chapter 12

Latino Families

BIRGIT LEYENDECKER
MICHAEL E. LAMB
National Institute of Child Health and Human Development

Latino families represent the third largest, but the fastest growing, demographic segment of the U.S. population. If current rates of legal and illegal immigration as well as natural domestic population growth continue, Latino or Hispanic-American families will overtake Black or African American families as the second largest group by early in the next century. This fact alone suggests the Latino families merit more attention from sociologists and developmental psychologists than they have been accorded in the past. As we attempt to show in this chapter, such an examination would reveal that Latino families face some unique challenges and have several strengths and characteristics that distinguish them from the mainstream Euro-American culture whose practices and characteristics are typically (and often unthinkingly) viewed as traditional. Further examination would also reveal that Latinos constitute a remarkably heterogeneous group, united by their ancestral language (Spanish), origins in Central and South America, and a variety of general characteristics, the best understood of which define some important differences between Latino families and their Euro-American counterparts. The former are the focus of the present chapter.

The majority of Latino families differ from the traditional or prototypical Euro-American families in a variety of respects and we focus here on three dimensions that we consider crucial for the understanding of Latino families. First, although some Latino families have lived in the southwest for many centuries, the majority of Latino families immigrated within the last two generations. Demographic projections indicate that immigration will remain common (Buriel & De Ment, 1997), thus ensuring that the immigration experience, characterized by such factors as changes in social networks, socioeconomic circumstances, and processes of acculturation (Rogler, 1994), will continue to influence everyday life and decision making for most Latino families. As befits a heterogeneous population of individuals from many different countries of origin and with differing immigration histories, social networks, and socioeconomic characteristics, Latino

247

families deal with these issues in diverse ways. Second, Latino families tend to differ from Euro-American families with regard to their sociocentric rather than individualistic cultural values. These broad cultural orientations, which are evident in many aspects of life, reflect the importance of the extended family as the primary source of social contact and support, as well as childrearing attitudes that emphasize interdependence and reciprocity rather than independence. Third, the acculturation processes experienced by contemporary Latino immigrants are likely to differ from those experienced by yesterday's Euro-American immigrants. Although Euro-Americans might have viewed themselves as Italian-Americans or Irish-Americans for many generations after immigration, they tended to substitute the cultural beliefs, values, skills, and language of the United States for their own, easily and rapidly. By contrast, Latino families are more likely to add the skills, cultural values, and behaviors of their new host country to their repertoire, only partially replacing the Spanish language and the practices and values that remain important components of their identities.

LATINO FAMILIES IN THE UNITED STATES: THE IMPACT OF IMMIGRATION

Immigration and Heterogeneity

> *Immigration to the United States is largely a family affair.*
> —Rumbaut (1997, p. 6)

By definition, the Latino population of the United States includes all those who can trace their origin to one of the former Spanish colonies in Latin America. Latinos thus have roots in Mexico, Puerto Rico, Cuba, Central America, or South America and are a demographically, socioculturally, and socioeconomically diverse population. They are further differentiated within and across their countries of origin along racial and ethnic lines, timing of immigration to the United States, socioeconomic and legal status, social networks, family structure, and geographic concentration within the United States. Latinos do, however, share such common characteristics as familiarity with the Spanish language and broad cultural values that emphasize the extended family, cooperative rather than individualistic efforts, and a concept of time focused on the here and now, with people being more important than schedules (e.g., Suarez-Orozco & Suarez-Orozco, 1994). In addition, apart from groups such as the Mexican Americans who have lived in the Southwest for centuries and the first wave of immigrants from Cuba, Latinos on average have lower socioeconomic status and poorer educational and professional backgrounds than the average U.S. citizen.

Most Latinos have migrated from developing countries mired in poverty and war to an industrialized nation characterized by a different hierarchical distribution of power, privilege, and prestige (Rogler, 1994). Indeed, with the exception of the Mexicans who lived in the Southwest and became U.S. citizens by annexation in 1848, and the Puerto Ricans who obtained citizenship in 1917 (19 years after the colonial conquest of 1898), immigration has been central to the experiences of Latinos in the United States. Mexican Americans have been migrating continuously for more than one hundred years, whereas the numbers of people migrating from other Hispanic countries to the United States has increased just recently. Based on the 1994 Current Population Survey of a nationally representative sample of 150,000 individuals, Jensen and Chitose (1997) reported that only 4.2% of those whose parents were both born in the United States were of Hispanic origin, whereas nearly half (44.3%) of the first-generation immigrants in the United States were of Hispanic origin, making this the largest group of immigrants. According to 1996 U.S. Census Bureau data, two million immigrants came from Latin American countries to the United States between 1990 and 1994.

Time of Arrival

Time of arrival is an important source of diversity within and among the Hispanic subgroups. Consider the Cuban-American population, for example. Cuban Americans did not migrate in substantial numbers until Fidel Castro's ascent to power in 1959. Many of the Cubans who joined the first wave of immigration in the early 1960s were highly trained professionals and their families who fled Cuba for political reasons. The disproportionate number of elderly immigrants who were allowed to leave Cuba between 1965 and 1973 helped create a large number of three generation Cuban-American households. By contrast, large groups, such as the Marielitos in 1980 and the Balseros in the 1990s predominantly comprised young males of lower socioeconomic status. Thus, Rumbaut stated, there "is no single 'Cuban American family type' in the United States; but rather, family outcomes have shaped and have been shaped by immigrants' reactions to specific contexts and contingencies" (1997, p. 13). Using official U.S. statistics, Rumbaut (1997) showed that the Cuban immigration pattern ("first the wealthy, later the poor") is typical of immigrants from less developed countries and contributes to the diversity of immigrant populations.

Mexico remains the main source of both legal and illegal immigrants to the United States (U.S. Bureau of the Census, 1993), with its citizens migrating largely in search of economic opportunities. Immigrants from Central America, particularly from El Salvador, Nicaragua, and Guatemala, predominantly sought to escape economic hardship, political persecution, and civil war. Although immigrants from Central America constitute the fastest growing subgroup of Latinos, they are also the least educated and have the highest poverty rates.

Poverty and the Immigrant Family

The absence of visas and working permits, poor knowledge of the English language, and relatively low levels of formal education are some of the factors that increase the likelihood of poverty for Hispanic-American families. "Hispanic households struggle as poorest of the poor in U.S." read the headline on the front page of *The New York Times* on January 30, 1997, and the Census Bureau statistics presented in the article were indeed alarming (Goldberg, 1997). Median household income rose for every other ethnic and racial group in the United States but dropped 5.1% among the nation's 27 million Hispanics, ensuring that, for the first time, poverty was more common among Hispanics than among Blacks. Whereas high school dropout rates have declined steadily to 12.7% and 15.5% for White and Black teenagers, respectively, drop out rates among Hispanic-American students have remained at a troubling 34.7% in 1994, even though high school graduation rates increased between 1970 and 1990 for all ethnic groups, including Hispanics (Ortiz, 1995). Education remains problematic for many Latino families for a number of reasons: The children must attend inadequate schools ill equipped with the resources needed to address the special needs of immigrant Hispanic-American families; the parents themselves are prevented from helping by their own lack of education and unfamiliarity with English; crime-ridden neighborhoods both harass and tempt; poverty fosters an urgent need to earn money rather than study; and it is widely perceived that investment in education is not rewarded (Ogbu, 1978; Suarez-Orozco & Suarez-Orozco, 1994; Suarez-Orozco, 1989; Vigil, 1988). Ninety percent of the Hispanic-American population lives in urban areas where they tend to encounter underfinanced school systems such as the Los Angeles Unified School District, which is 70% Hispanic. Many immigrants have little choice but to live in affordable yet crime-ridden and gang-infested neighborhoods where teenagers are tempted by the obvious rewards of crime and unimpressed by the dubious benefits of education. For most Hispanic-American adolescents in inner-city neighborhoods, of course, gangs serve as models of attitude and dress while family ties and support buffer them from more insidious effects. By contrast, youths from troubled families and marginal adolescents alienated from both their ancestral culture and Euro-American society are particularly likely to join gangs or engage in delinquent behavior (Buriel & De Ment, 1997; Gil, Vega, & Dimas, 1994; Horowitz, 1983; Vigil, 1988).

Surprisingly, the likelihood of school failure appears to increase among Hispanic-American immigrants over succeeding generations. On average, for example, immigrants from Mexico are a highly self-selected group of individuals with more education and more skilled or semiskilled professional training than the average Mexican citizen as well as a better ability to save the money needed for immigration (Portes & Bach, 1985). These characteristics suggest that first-generation Mexican immigrants represent a segment of the Mexican population striving to attain middle-class status by moving to another country and by working hard (Buriel & De Ment, 1997). Despite language barriers, their children tend to perform better in school than their U.S.-born Mexican-American peers, who represent the failure of later generations to maintain the upward mobility. Massey, Zambrana, and Bell attributed this phenomenon to "the chronic stressors of poor socioenvironmental conditions, poverty, institutional discrimination, and limited access to quality health and human services" (1995, p. 198). Although Latino families provide high levels of support for other families, these support networks cannot outweigh all the adversities associated with poverty.

Immigration and Resources

Like the accouterments of social class (e.g., financial resources and education) and legal entry status, social networks and family structure have a substantial influence on the social and psychological successes of immigrant families (Rumbaut, 1997). Legal and illegal immigration often depends on a network of friends and family who can provide some support, although marriage to a U.S. citizen remains the most common form of legal immigration. Family networks and job opportunities at the time of immigration have promoted serial migration and concentrations of Latino groups in certain areas. In 1993, 90% of all Hispanics lived in just ten states, particularly in their urban metropolitan areas. California and Texas were home to more than one third (34.4%) and one fifth (19.4%) of the Hispanic-American population, respectively (U.S. Bureau of the Census, 1993). Cuban Americans in southern Florida have stayed close to their former home country, whereas many Puerto Ricans live in metropolitan New York. Many recent immigrants from Central America have settled in the Washington, DC, area such that, according to Schoultz (1992), 20% of the inhabitants of Intipuca, El Salvador, were living in the Adams-Morgan section of Washington, DC, by 1985. Within the larger metropolitan areas, particularly New York City, the network of help-giving kin and friends is reflected in ethnically segregated (e.g., Dominicans, Puerto Ricans, Cuban) neighborhoods (Rogler, 1994). These neighborhoods play an important role for new immigrants attempting to establish new social networks after emigrating. As Buriel and De Ment (1997) described, many Latino families live in extended households with relatives and nonfamily members for the first 10 years after immigration. Later, they tend to live as nuclear families in close proximity to their relatives and friends.

Family Cohesion and Resources

Successful immigration demands enormous resourcefulness and flexible adaptation to new and changing circumstances. The strains these impose can lead either to further family cohesion or disintegration. Despite the enormous heterogeneity of the Hispanic-American population, *familism*—a deeply ingrained sense of being rooted in the family to which one is oriented and obligated—is one core feature of Hispanic-American culture. Although the family and familial obligations tend to decline in importance over time in the United States, familial support and extensive contact tend to remain high relative to other U.S. citizens despite acculturation (Sabogal, Marin, Otero-Sabogal, Marin, & Perez-Stable, 1987). Nevertheless, migration to another culture forces contrasts between traditional values, gender roles, and parent–child relationships and those of the new culture. The traditional roles and hierarchical structure of a family may also be challenged by circumstances that provide jobs for mothers and teenage daughters while fathers remain unemployed (Vega, 1995). "In given circumstances, however, because families are nested in and shaped by the larger structural, cultural, and historical contexts, the shared adversity of the migration and the subsequent adaptation experiences can motivate the family to close ranks cohesively and productively, honing in social solidarity an adaptive ethos of effort and efficacy and providing fertile soil for often remarkable achievement in the new country" (Rumbaut, 1997, p. 9).

Census data indicate that the extended family structures of most Hispanics in the United States differ greatly from those that are typical in their home countries because most families are cut off from the older generation. In comparison to the overall population, in fact, Latino families are more likely to have young children and less likely to have grandparents living in the United States. In 1993, 12.1% of all U.S. residents but only 5.4% of the resident Latinos, and only 3.9% of those from Central American backgrounds, were 65 years of age and older, although more than 20% of the Cuban-American population were older than 64 years (U.S. Bureau of the Census, 1993). By contrast, in comparison to the national average of 7.8%, Cuban-American families tend to have fewer and Hispanics in general tend to have more young children under the age of 5 than U.S. families in general (4.5%, 11.1%, and 7.8%, respectively). Obviously, these demographics will change over time, such that second- and third-generation Hispanic-American families will have richer kin networks but until then, first-generation Latino families must accommodate family networks lacking in multigenerational support.

Despite such adversities, family cohesion appears to be high, particularly in first-generation immigrant families, and the cohesion of Latino families can be a protective force (Buriel & De Ment, 1997; Vega, 1995). Family cohesion is of special importance because the social bonds that characterized home countries are no longer available, and even after serial migration, it takes time and effort to establish larger social networks. Two-parent households provide more family support which in turn fosters parent–child relationships of higher quality, reduced family conflict, and higher school achievement. Although divorce rates in the third generation of Mexican Americans match the U.S. averages, they are very low (less than 10%) among first-generation immigrants (Rumbaut & Weeks, 1996). Unlike the United States as a whole, there is no direct correspondence between poverty and father-absence in Hispanic-American families. Whereas 30% of the Mexican Americans in the United States live in poverty, only 14% live in female-headed households. By contrast, 25% of the Salvadorans live in poverty and 21% live in female-headed households (Rumbaut, 1997), perhaps because Salvadoran networks broke down in response to multiple stresses and the weakened support from relatives and friends in El Salvador (Dorrington, 1995; Rumbaut, 1997). Overall, however, most Latino families appear to adapt well to the challenges of establishing new social networks.

The Individual as the Family's Resource

The deeply rooted sense of family obligations is also illustrated by the efforts made by many Latinos to provide financial support to family members in their home countries. Unlike contemporary immigration from European countries, Latino migration to the United States is less an effort to better an individual's circumstances than a family affair. Many immigrants from Latin American countries thus support family members in the United States as well as family members still living in Latin American countries.

In the case of recent immigrants from war-torn Latin American countries, the emotional connections and obligations to those left behind can be particularly burdensome. In a study of 14- to 19-year-olds from Central America, Suarez-Orozco (1989; Suarez-Orozco & Suarez-Orozco, 1994) found that most had left some or all the members of their nuclear families behind because the entire families could not afford to leave these economically troubled and politically dangerous countries. In contrast to many native-born ethnic populations, teachers reported that these adolescents were more disciplined and harder working, even though many worked full-time jobs after school. Sending money home was one way for these adolescents to deal with a sense of guilt because their families sacrificed to send them to the United States while they still faced terror and scarcity. Studying hard in school was motivated by desires both for better material circumstances than their parents had experienced and to help improve their families' current circumstances. Instead of the individualistic search for self-advancement and independence associated with other Western-oriented U.S. citizens, the achievement motivation of these Hispanic-American immigrants was closely linked to familial interdependence and affiliation. Such a concern with familial interdependence, demonstrating that achievement motivation need not have an individualistic orientation, is shared by Hispanics of all national and ethnic origins (Suarez-Orozco & Suarez-Orozco , 1994).

Immigration and Acculturation

Responses to change and processes of acculturation in Hispanic-American families are as diverse and multifaceted as the heterogeneity of this population would lead one to expect. The process of acculturation, involving changes in Latino cultural beliefs and values in response to those of the United States, is not independent of changes in their legal status, and the continuous changes in social network and socioeconomic status are likely to differ within and between families. To assess these dynamics, it is also necessary to differentiate between the access to new cultural experiences (influenced, for example, by language proficiency, contact with others outside of the Hispanic-American community, and exposure to mass media), and the acquisition and internalization of mainstream cultural values and beliefs (Rogler, 1994). In the latter case, it is important to differentiate further between cultural values and beliefs that (a) that are added to the ancestral values, (b) replace the ancestral values, and (c) lead to the creation of new and uniquely integrated values. Paths to acculturation may be influenced by the dynamics of psychosocial and developmental processes as well as by each individual's cognitive structure and coping mechanisms (Laosa, 1989, 1997), age at immigration, gender, and motivation for immigration. Family units face the task of adapting to and blending with a strange and at times hostile environment while at the same time maintaining a sense of cultural and family identity. As Garcia Coll and Magnusson (1997) pointed out, most immigrant children are able to cope with their new environments, although there has been little research on normative adjustment and development among Latino children and much research on the behavior problems associated with maladjustment among immigrants. "[T]he way in which researchers have approached the study of immigrant children has led them to chart the adjustment of children based on measurable negative outcomes and has disposed them to overlook measurements of normative outcomes inclusive of the experiences and processes involved in acculturation and adjustment" (Garcia Coll & Magnusson, 1997, p. 93).

Chances of Biculturalism

The goal of assimilating into the United States melting pot might have characterized those immigrating from Europe a century ago but does not characterize most contemporary immigrants. Buriel and De Ment (1997) proposed a unidirectional model of change from ethnic Euro-culture to the mainstream Euro-American culture for European immigrants and a bidirectional model of sociocultural change for the Latino population. Whereas giving up a native language within a generation or two did not appear to threaten the cultural identity of most immigrants from Europe, mastering the Spanish language appears to be a very important symbolic feature of the Latino culture and is closely associated with cultural identity (Suarez-Orozco & Suarez-Orozco, 1994). Assimilation into the dominant Euro-American culture thus threatens the cultural identity of Hispanics, whereas adding a second frame of cultural reference allows the mastery of English and the acquisition of behavioral norms and values primarily as tools for success at school and in the job market. Biculturalism allows Latinos to acquire instrumental skills and an additional language without giving up their own culture (Delgado-Gaitan, 1994; Garcia Coll & Magnusson, 1997; Ogbu, 1994) although it is frequently misunderstood and misrepresented as a position exactly between two cultures (Rogler, Cortes, & Malgady, 1991). Biculturalism does not require either balanced involvement in two cultures or an identity as one who feels equally comfortable in two cultures. The term encompasses quite a range of processes, both additive (e.g., mastering the challenges posed by a new country) and transformational (e.g., modifying or replacing some values or behavioral norms). Measures of bicultural change thus require independent scales designed to capture dynamic processes of addition, modification, and replacement of cultural values although most measures of acculturation actually involve single scales and implicitly represent acculturation as a process of mutual exclusion (Rogler et al., 1991).

Beyond its everyday instrumental functions, biculturalism and bilingualism can be enormous assets in the modern world. "As the immediate strains of the immigration experience subside, a more gradual process of acculturation and adaptation begins, and the individual child is faced with both greater challenges and greater rewards. Thus, research on immigrant children should inform how the process of immigration can increase an individual's repertoire of coping skills, facilitate the acquisition of new and different skills, and broaden opportunities as well as world views" (Garcia Coll & Magnusson, 1997, p. 105). Of course, the benefits cannot be fully realized unless mainstream society recognizes multiculturalism rather than assimilation as the desired norm.

Generational and Cultural Gaps Within Families

Often, the developmentally normal generational gap occurring in all families with adolescents is worsened by a "cultural gap."
—Suarez-Orozco & Suarez-Orozco (1994)

Age at the time of immigration has a major impact on the acculturation process. Within Latino families, acculturation proceeds more rapidly for children than for parents (Vega, 1995) and perceptions of the United States have changed across successive waves of immigration. Although early idealization of the United States may be replaced by a more sober and realistic view, first-generation immigrants still tend to maintain their country of origin as a point of reference and are less likely to compare their experiences and situations with those of the dominant society. In addition, immigrants on the whole represent a highly self-selected, upwardly mobile, and achievement-oriented group. Contrary to popular belief, Mexican immigrants hope to attain middle-class status through hard work and endurance and are often willing to accept employment below their occupational skills in the process (Buriel & De Ment, 1997). "The selectivity of the migration stream from Mexico to California tends to create a psychologically robust first-generation immigrant population who feels less deprived because migration has increased their standard of living; in contrast, the Mexican Americans born in the United States feel more deprivation because of their much higher but unrealized aspirations" (Rogler et al., 1991, p. 589). Members of the second generation and the so-called 1.5 generation (comprising those who immigrated as children) incorporate the country of their families' origin into their frames of reference as well, although they may romanticize the old world, which they do not know, and have little idea of the hardships that motivated their parents to move. They are also more likely to compare their situations with those of peers living in the suburbs (Waters, 1997). Again, family cohesion and a sense of the ancestral culture foster biculturalism and a dual sense of reference, whereas the contrary state, marginalization, involves discomfort in both cultures and distorted perceptions of ancestral values. Proximity to the Mexican border, residence in those parts of the Southwest that maintain Hispanic-American culture, frequent visits to relatives in the ancestral country, and school curricula that incorporate and respect the Latino culture all help to keep ancestral cultures visible and alive.

INTERDEPENDENCE VERSUS INDEPENDENCE

Individuality and independence as opposed to sociocentrism and interdependence are terms frequently used to describe contrasting socialization goals in differing childrearing environments (Greenfield & Cocking, 1994; Harwood, Schölmerich, & Schulze, in press; Markus & Kitayama, 1991). *Individuality* refers to a view of oneself as unique and distinctive whereas *interdependence* refers to a view of one self interconnected with other human beings. The values of the Euro-American middle class are often described as individualistic and the values of Latino families as more sociocentric. In fact, social interdependence and an emphasis on the extended family are considered central features of Latino culture. Connections to extended family networks involve intensive contacts as well as mutual support and are evident in many aspects of daily life. Costa Rican children have more frequent contact with their relatives than with their peers (DeRosier & Kupersmidt, 1991), many Latinos are willing to sacrifice individual comfort for the well-being of their families (Triandis, Marin, Betancourt, Lisansky, & Chang, 1982; Vega, 1990), and Cuban teenage mothers receive extensive support from their families (Field, Widmayer, Adler, & De Cubas, 1990), for example. Beyond providing mutual support, however, family networks also provide frames of reference and orientation. Although the individualistic values of the Euro-American tend to be incorporated over time, particularly by those from more economically advantaged families (Rumbaut, 1997), sociocentric orientations are widely maintained by Latinos after immigration to the United States (Harrison, Wilson, Pine, Chan, & Buriel, 1990; Sabogal et al., 1987; Schumm et al., 1988; Slonim, 1991).

Interdependence and Maternal Socialization Goals

Socialization goals and childrearing practices in part reflect the parents' conceptions of what is required in order for their children to become socially competent and successful members of society, and thus parents are likely to view their efforts and goals in relation to the expectations and demands of the larger community. Individual goals may vary depending on the country of origin, length of stay in the

United States, acculturation, personal circumstances and preferences, and socioeconomic status, but some core socialization goals are widely shared within the Latino community. Studies involving both lower and middle-class mothers in Puerto Rico, low socioeconomic status Puerto Rican mothers in the United States, mothers who migrated recently from Central America to the United States, and several samples of Euro-American mothers have repeatedly shown that the broad sociocentric and individualistic values of these groups are evident in the mothers' long-term socialization goals (Harwood, 1992; Harwood, Schölmerich, Ventura-Cook, Schulze, & Wilson, 1996; Leyendecker, Lamb, Harwood, & Schölmerich, 1997). Whereas the Euro-American mothers emphasized qualities such as independence, self-confidence, and achievement, the Latina mothers strove to instill qualities (such as respectfulness and proper demeanor in the presence of others) that promote integration into the family and the larger community and expressed concern that disobedience and disrespectfulness might hamper this integration. These socialization goals were also evident in the description of desirable and undesirable everyday situations (Leyendecker et al., 1997). Latina immigrants from Central America identified appropriate and cooperative behavior as the single most important determinant of successful and unsuccessful interactions and perceived their children as partners in daily interactions who were expected to cooperate and behave appropriately. By contrast, Euro-American mothers were more likely to focus on external factors, rather than on the behavior of the interactional partners, particularly when evaluating undesirable situations.

Family Is More Important Than Schedules

Emphasis on the extended family is likely to have two implications for the social experiences of children: fostering multiple significant relationships within the extended family (not only within the nuclear family) and assuring a supportive network of adult family members. Mindel (1980) also speculated that Hispanics were more likely to migrate toward family networks whereas Euro-Americans were more likely to migrate away from their families and to maintain long distance relationships. For various reasons, Euro-American families in urban areas tend to live as isolated nuclear families, and they are less likely than Hispanics to rely on relatives for emotional support or child care (e.g., Sampson, 1985, 1988; Spence, 1985). Thus, individualism and connectedness are likely to affect the structure of children's everyday lives.

Leyendecker, Lamb, Schölmerich, and Fracasso (1995) found that immigrant families from Central America and middle-class Euro-American families indeed provided different every day experiences and daily structures for their 8- and 12-month-old first-born infants. Overall, the social worlds of the Central American children were characterized by the simultaneous presence of several people and thus by multiple social partners, whereas the social worlds of the Euro-American children were characterized by more opportunities for dyadic interactions and by exposure to fewer partners. During a 24 hour period on weekdays, Central American fathers spent more time with their children than the Euro-American fathers (35% and 23% of their waking time, respectively), although they were less likely to be alone with their infants (5% and 11%, respectively). Most of the people encountered by the Central American infants were relatives, who were present for 30% of the infants' waking time. By contrast, most of the people the Euro-American infants met were babysitters or friends of their parents. In the Central American families, nonparental care was provided by relatives and friends rather than by paid babysitters and this assured an important degree of flexibility when job opportunities and schedules changed suddenly. Broad social networks and extended family arrangements thus facilitated the sharing of limited resources (Harrison et al., 1990) and also shaped everyday experiences from early in life.

The Central American parents also included the infants in their own lives and routines and did not seek to establish special schedules and environments for them. Infants in the Euro-American families experienced relatively structured days, for example, with feeding on a tripartite (morning-noon-evening) schedule and midday naps. The Central American infants were fed as often, but at times when the entire family was together rather than on a schedule established exclusively for the infants. Thus, depending on the parents' work schedules, infants were fed late at night or early in the morning when the entire (extended) family was together. Many of the Central American infants thus started their overnight sleep quite late or woke up quite early in the mornings, making up for this with extensive daytime naps, and they were more likely to co-sleep with their parents. The weekday and weekend social lives of Central American 1-year-olds did not differ, whereas the Euro-American infants spent more time with their fathers, as well as more time with both parents, on weekends than on weekdays. In addition, contacts with friends and relatives were much more likely to occur on weekends than on weekdays, whereas in the Central American families friends and relatives were present throughout the week.

The flexible integration of Central American infants into daily routines reflects the relaxed concept of time often ascribed to Hispanic-American cultures, in which people are more important than schedules (e.g., Suarez-Orozco & Suarez-Orozco, 1994), and is probably more common internationally than is the Western pattern of living by the clock. As Cole (1992) suggested, these differences probably influence later life as well, enabling the children of the Central American immigrants to adopt more flexible sleeping habits as adults than their Euro-American counterparts.

Although these differences in everyday experiences and social structures were evident, the two samples studied did not differ with respect to the amount of time infants and their care providers spent engaged in feeding, caretaking, social play, and object play. Lengthy observations covering a 12 hour period when the infants were 3 months of age also showed that care providers in both groups were equally attentive and responsive to the infants' needs and signals (Leyendecker, Lamb, &

Schölmerich, 1997). Overall, the social ecology of the two groups differed substantially, however, suggesting that familism and individualism are appropriate descriptions not only for different adult lifestyles but also for infants' social worlds. It is likely that the differing early experiences of infants growing up in these two rearing environments will also affect their development, perhaps shaping their tolerance for intense social interaction, their relative desires to be with others or alone, and their dependence on and preference for time-structured lifestyles. High variability was evident within each of the groups, however, suggesting that familism and individualism permit a multitude of variations.

SUMMARY AND CONCLUSION

The extant literature on Latino families in the United States focuses on the experience of living as an impoverished minority population in an often hostile Anglo-American environment. Themes such as the trauma of immigration, the harsh and pervasive effects of poverty, high levels of fertility, low levels of education, high school dropout rates, and adolescent engagement in gangs, drugs, and violence are frequently and prominently addressed. Although poverty is indeed a pressing problem, it is important not to confuse the effects of culture and poverty (Massey et al., 1995), particularly as this ignores the enormous heterogeneity of the Hispanic-American population and prevents consideration of the uniqueness and strengths of Hispanic-American families and of biculturalism.

Three features of Latino families deserve special emphasis. First, despite great heterogeneity, Latino families are more likely than Euro-American families to embrace cultural values of interdependence rather than independence. This is evident in maternal socialization goals and evaluations that stress the importance of appropriate, cooperative, and respectful behavior as well as in the social world children experience. Although only part of the extended family is available after immigration, contact with these family members is extensive and shapes the social experiences of children from early in their lives even after several generations in the United States. In addition, Hispanic-American children are less likely than Anglo-American children to experience special and separate schedules, routines, and environments. They are more likely to be integrated into family routines and to share bedrooms with parents or siblings or both. In contrast, Euro-American parents are more likely to emphasize their children's uniqueness and individuality from early in their lives.

Second, immigration is a central element in the lives of most Latino families and tends to remain central well after the first generation. Latino families adapt to life in the United States in many different ways, however. Differences within families are attributable to gender, age at immigration, and generational status. Differences between families are influenced by time of arrival, socioeconomic and legal status, and social support networks, as well as by culture-specific aspects of the immigrants' national origins. Although many Latino values, such as respect for authority, proper demeanor, and mutual support are associated with old traditional values, Latino families who have migrated to the United States are far from traditional when compared to compatriots who stayed behind. Migration is a radical process that requires daily adjustment and considerable flexibility on the part of every family member. Old cherished values are juxtaposed against those of the new host society, and every family member must decide which traditions to retain and which to modify or to exchange. Adaptation to these new challenges produces further diversity within the Latino population. Migration can marginalize some individuals whereas others are able to learn the English language and acquire new skills, norms, and values without losing their ethnic identity.

Third, many Latino-American families, including middle-class Mexican-American families in the Los Angeles area and Cuban-American families in southern Florida, have found their ecological and economic niches, are financially secure, and have adopted bicultural life styles that allow them to be "American" without giving up their cultural identity. Unfortunately, many others, particularly those who immigrated recently from impoverished and war-torn Latin American countries, face poverty and inadequate support and schooling for their children. Although family cohesion often helps protect members of the first generation, the strains faced by these families may become overwhelming and be reflected in the increased high school dropout rates, the increased vulnerability to illicit drug use, and increases in the numbers of single-parent, female-headed households. Extensive support within and from other Latino families serves as a buffer against the adversities of migration, but these families also need outside support in the form of social policy programs (adequate schooling, health care, job and language training) that address rather than ignore their specific needs.

REFERENCES

Buriel, R., & De Ment, T. (1997). Immigration and sociocultural change in Mexican, Chinese, and Vietnamese American families. In A. Booth, A. C. Crouter, & N. Landale (Eds.), *Immigration and the family* (pp. 165–200). Mahwah, NJ: Lawrence Erlbaum Associates.

Cole, M. (1992). Culture in development. In M. H. Bornstein & M. E. Lamb (Eds.), *Developmental psychology: An advanced textbook* (3rd ed., pp. 731–789). Hillsdale, NJ: Lawrence Erlbaum Associates.

Delgado-Gaitan, C. (1994). Socializing young children in Mexican-American families. In P. M. Greenfield & R. R. Cocking (Eds.), *Cross-cultural roots of minority child development* (pp. 55–86). Hillsdale, NJ: Lawrence Erlbaum Associates.

DeRosier, M. E., & Kupersmidt, J. B. (1991). Costa Rican children's perceptions of their social networks. *Developmental Psychology, 27*, 656–662.

Dorrington, C. (1995). Central American refugees in Los Angeles: Adjustment of children and families. In R. E. Zambrana (Ed.), *Understanding Latino families: Scholarship, policy, and practice* (pp. 107–156). Thousand Oaks, CA: Sage.

Field, T. M., Widmayer, S., Adler, S., & De Cubas, M. (1990). Teenage parenting in different cultures, family constellations, and caregiving environments: Effects of infant development. *Infant Mental Health Journal, 11,* 158–174.

Garcia Coll, C., & Magnusson, K. (1997). The psychological experience of immigration: A developmental perspective. In A. Booth, A. C. Crouter, & N. Landale (Eds.), *Immigration and the family* (pp. 91–131). Mahwah, NJ: Lawrence Erlbaum Associates.

Gil, A. G., Vega, W. A., & Dimas, J. M. (1994). Acculturative stress and personal adjustment among Hispanic adolescent boys. *Journal of Community Psychology, 22,* 43–53.

Goldberg, C. (1997, January 30). Hispanic households struggle as poorest of the poor in the U.S. *The New York Times,* pp. A1, A16.

Greenfield, P. M., & Cocking, R. R. (Eds.) (1994). *Cross-cultural roots of minority development.* Hillsdale, NJ: Lawrence Erlbaum Associates.

Harrison, A. O., Wilson, M. N., Pine, C. J., Chan, S. Q., & Buriel, R. (1990). Family ecologies of minority children. *Child Development, 61,* 347–362.

Harwood, R. L. (1992). The influence of culturally derived values on Anglo and Puerto Rican mothers' perceptions of attachment behavior. *Child Development, 63,* 822–839.

Harwood, R. L., Schölmerich, A., & Schulze, P. (in press). *New Directions for Child Development.* San Francisco: Jossey-Bass.

Harwood, R. L., Schölmerich, A., Ventura-Cook, E., Schulze, P., & Wilson, S. P. (1996). Culture and class influences on Anglo and Puerto-Rican mothers' beliefs regarding long-term socialization goals and child behavior. *Child Development, 67,* 2446–2461.

Horowitz, R. (1983). *Honor and the American dream: Culture and identity in a Chicano community.* New Brunswick, NJ: Rutgers.

Jensen, L., & Chitose, Y. (1997). Immigrant generations. In A. Booth, A. C. Crouter, & N. Landale (Eds.), *Immigration and the family* (pp. 47–62). Mahwah, NJ: Lawrence Erlbaum Associates.

Laosa, L. M. (1989). *Psychosocial stress, coping, and the development of Hispanic immigrant children.* Princeton, NJ: Educational Testing Service.

Laosa, L. M. (1997). Research perspectives on constructs of change: Intercultural migration and developmental transitions. In A. Booth, A. C. Crouter, & N. Landale (Eds.), *Immigration and the family* (pp. 133–148). Mahwah, NJ: Lawrence Erlbaum Associates.

Leyendecker, B., Lamb, M. E., Harwood, R. L., & Schölmerich, A. (1997). *External factors versus internal factors: Parental evaluations of desirable and undesirable everyday situations in two diverse cultural niches.* Manuscript submitted for publication.

Leyendecker, B., Lamb, M. E., & Schölmerich, A. (1997). Studying mother-infant interaction: The effects of context and length of observation in two subcultural groups. *Infant Behavior and Development, 20,* 325–338.

Leyendecker, B., Lamb, M. E., Schölmerich, A., & Fracasso, M. P. (1995). The social worlds of 8- and 12 month-old infants: Early experiences in two subcultural contexts. *Social Development, 4,* 194–208.

Markus, H. R., & Kitayama, S. (1991). Culture and the self: Implications for cognition, emotion, and motivation. *Psychological Review, 98,* 224–253.

Massey, D. S., Zambrana, R. E., & Bell, S. A. (1995). Contemporary issues in Latino families: Future directions for research, policy, and practice. In R. E. Zambrana (Ed.), *Understanding Latino families: Scholarship, policy, and practice* (pp. 109–204). Thousand Oaks, CA: Sage.

Mindel, C. H. (1980). Extended familism among urban Mexican-Americans, Anglos, and Blacks. *Hispanic Journal of Behavioral Sciences, 2,* 21–34.

Ogbu, J. U. (1978). *Minority education and caste: The American system in cross-cultural perspective.* Orlando, FL: Academic.

Ogbu, J. U. (1994). Cultural frame of reference. In P. M. Greenfield & R. R. Cocking (Eds.), *Cross-cultural roots of minority child development* (pp. 365–391). Hillsdale, NJ: Lawrence Erlbaum Associates.

Ortiz, V. (1995). The diversity of Latino families. In R. E. Zambrana (Ed.), *Understanding Latino families: Scholarship, policy, and practice* (pp. 18–39). Thousand Oaks, CA: Sage.

Portes, A., & Bach, R. (1985). *Latin journey*. Berkeley: University of California Press.

Rogler, L. (1994). International migrations: A framework for directing research. *American Psychologist, 49*, 710–708.

Rogler, L., Cortes, D., & Malgady, R. (1991). Acculturation and mental health status among Hispanics. *American Psychologist, 46*, 585–597.

Rumbaut, R. G. (1997). Ties that bind: Immigration and immigrant families in the United States. In A. Booth, A. C. Crouter, & N. Landale (Eds.), *Immigration and the family* (pp. 3–46). Mahwah, NJ: Lawrence Erlbaum Associates.

Rumbaut, R. G., & Weeks, J. R. (1996). Unraveling a public health enigma: Why do immigrants experience superior perinatal health outcomes? *Research in the Sociology of Health Care, 13*, 337–391.

Sabogal, F., Marin, G., Otero-Sabogal, R., Marin, B. V., & Perez-Stable, E. (1987). Hispanic familism and acculturation: What changes and what doesn't? *Hispanic Journal of Behavioral Sciences, 9*, 379–412.

Sampson, E. E. (1985). The decentralization of identity. *American Psychologist, 40*, 1203–1211.

Sampson, E. E. (1988). The debate on individualism. *American Psychologist, 43*, 15–22.

Schoultz, L. (1992). Central America and the politicization of the U.S. immigration policy. In C. Mitchell (Ed.), *Western hemisphere immigration and United States foreign policy* (pp. 157–220). University Park: Pennsylvania State University Press.

Schumm, W. R., McCollum, E. E., Bugaighis, M. A., Jurich, A. P., Bollman, S. R., & Reitz, J. (1988). Differences between Anglo and Mexican-American family members on satisfaction with family life. *Hispanic Journal of Behavioral Sciences, 10*, 39–53.

Slonim, M. B. (1991). *Children, culture, and ethnicity: Evaluating and understanding the impact*. New York: Garland.

Spence, J. T. (1985). Achievement American style: The rewards and costs of individualism. *American Psychologist, 40*, 1285–1295.

Suarez-Orozco, C., & Suarez-Orozco, M. M. (1994). The cultural psychology of Hispanic immigrants. In T. Weaver (Ed.), *Handbook of Hispanic cultures in the United States: Vol. 2. Anthropology* (pp. 129–146). Houston, TX: Arte Publico Press.

Suarez-Orozco, M. M. (1989). *Central American refugees and the U.S. high schools: A psychosocial study of motivation and achievement*. Stanford, CA: Stanford University Press.

Triandis, H. C., Marin, G., Betancourt, H., Lisansky, J., & Chang, B. H. (1982). *Dimensions of familism among Hispanic and mainstream Navy recruits* (Tech. Rep. No. 14). Champaign: Department of Psychology, University of Illinois.

U.S. Bureau of the Census. (1993). *Current Populations Reports, Hispanic Americans Today*. Washington, DC: U.S. Government Printing Office.

Vega, W. A. (1990). Hispanic families in the 1980s: A decade of research. *Journal of Marriage and the Family, 52*, 1015–1024.

Vega, W. A. (1995). The study of Latino families: A point of departure. In R. E. Zambrana (Ed.), *Understanding Latino families: Scholarship, policy, and practice* (pp. 3–17). Thousand Oaks, CA: Sage.

Vigil, J. D. (1988). *Barrio gangs: Street life and identity in southern California*. Austin: University of Texas Press.

Waters, M. C. (1997). Immigrant families at risk: Factors that undermine the chances for success. In A. Booth, A. C. Crouter, & N. Landale (Eds.), *Immigration and the family* (pp. 79–90). Mahwah, NJ: Lawrence Erlbaum Associates.

Chapter 13

Multiracial Families

Paul C. Rosenblatt
University of Minnesota

Gregory: I know enough about interracial relationships to know that they are not socially condoned in America. (p. 121)[1]

Barb: I think that overall people aren't really accepting of interracial relationships. And I think that my friends who are black and in black families have some prejudiced feelings against my family, but nothing that is really harmful. . . . You do have trouble being taken seriously sometimes because of the fact of being interracial, . . . people having questions about your sexuality, and is that why you chose across racial lines. (p. 121)

This chapter is about families with members of more than one race. Most such families come about when a person joins a partner who considers self or is considered to be of a different race or when a monoracial individual or couple adopts a child of another race.

Race is not a scientific concept but one that has served and continues to serve racism in the domination and control of people of color. *Racism* can be defined as "the assumption of inherent superiority of one race coupled with discrimination, prejudice, and stereotyping directed at people of at least one other race" (Rosenblatt, Karis, and Powell, 1995, p. 1) and as "hostile actions with the intent to harm, based on the skin color of the intended victim" (Rosenblatt et al., p. 2). Anyone who uses the concept of race is at risk of being drawn into the oppressive system in which race is a central concept. At the very least, talk of race invites some sort of talk about difference, which then invites some sort of ranking based on the difference, which then becomes a basis for thinking less well of those who are ranked lower, which then becomes a basis for discrimination. It seems that the world would be a better place if race could be ignored, yet race cannot be ignored, because the way race has been defined, dealt with in legislation, and acted on in the United States has had an enormous impact on everyone—harming people of color im-

---

[1]All page numbers following quotes that are not otherwise identified refer to pages in Rosenblatt, Karis, and Powell, 1995. Reprinted with permission of Sage Publications, Inc.

mensely, harming Euro-Americans in real but more subtle ways (Frankenberg, 1993), and benefiting Euro-Americans in economic and other ways.

When reading about multiracial families as nontraditional, it is very important to keep track of how racial labels and the label nontraditional could be used against a family or a member of that family. It is important to ask who is defining whom and for what purpose. As steps toward avoiding racism, it is helpful to learn how people define themselves and what that definition means to them, to avoid stigmatizing people, and to be aware of how a person's racial self-label can become somebody else's label for hurting that person.

From a systems theory perspective (Rosenblatt, 1994), what may be most significant about multiracial families is not their internal dynamics but what the larger society makes of them. Although this chapter focuses on multiracial families, most of what is written in this chapter reflects the ways in which people of color and multiracial families have been ill treated in the larger society.

HISTORICAL CONTEXT

The history of multiracial families in the United States is complex (Spickard, 1989) because of the diversity of multiracial families, because in ordinary U.S. thinking the line between race and ethnicity is often unclear, because many different historical forces have been at work over the history of the United States, because of the ways historical records and the writing of history reflect the interests and perspectives of dominant groups, and because that history is quite variable across places, times, and social situations. This brief overview of a few significant historical underpinnings to the contemporary situation for multiracial families cannot do justice to the enormous range of particulars of who was involved, what the social context was, the nature of the relationship, and much more. Consider the range involved in relationships early in the 19th century between Mexicans in what is now the U.S. southwest and White immigrants from the United States to that part of what was at the time Mexico, of the relationships between Chinese field hands in Mississippi at the end of the 19th century and Black families only recently free of slavery, or of the relationship since the 1970s of Sikhs from India and Mexican Americans in the central valley of California.

One of the challenges in talking about the history of multiracial families is to decide what is family. At times what might be called a multiracial family was not considered a family by the standards of many in the community or those in the larger society who count families. Historically and even in the present there are relationships that could be called familial, based on coresidence, commitment, patterns of sharing, and feelings, but are not legally or socially recognized by many in the surrounding community.

A related challenge in looking at the history of multiracial relationships stems from the fact that slavery in the United States frequently included the sexual exploitation of Black women by White men. Even after the end of slavery and in the experience of some contemporary people, the economic and political power of White men has allowed them to exploit Black women sexually (Funderburg, 1994, pp. 32–34). Those exploitive relationships may not have been familial in any modern sense of the term, but they often produced children with parents of different races. Furthermore, there were relationships that occurred under slavery or in other contexts that were extremely oppressive to people of color but that created relationships that by some criteria could be considered familial—relationships that were enduring, emotionally intimate, and economically and socially interdependent (Spickard, 1989, ch. 9).

Although multiracial marriages and families have often been taboo or illegal, at certain times and in certain places they have been tolerated or even encouraged—for example, in the 18th century, French fur traders were encouraged by their employers to marry Native-American women as a connection that would support fur trading and survival.

Far more often in U.S. history, and from the 1600s on (Takaki, 1993, pp. 41–42, 55, 67), multiracial relationships, even merely friendly contacts, were discouraged and punished. Until the *Loving v. Virginia* decision by the U.S. Supreme Court in 1967, marriage between Blacks and Whites was illegal in many states. There were similar laws in some states blocking marriage between White partners and Chinese, Native American, or people of color in general (Takaki, p. 205). Since intermarriage became legal throughout the United States the intermarriage rate has increased substantially (Kalmijn, 1993)

That there were laws suggests that some people under some circumstances were inclined to partner across racial lines. Making multiracial relationships illegal meant that they were less likely to occur, but also that if they did occur they were defined as other things or were hidden. That makes it hard to know how many multiracial partnerships and families there have been at various times and in various places. Even now, to the extent that there are taboos or penalties, people may not disclose a relationship or their full understanding of the racial identity of self, partner, or other family member on a census form, to neighbors, or to members of the family of origin.

Why there were laws can be understood in many different ways. To the extent that lawmakers were White men, perhaps the question is why White men wanted such laws. Were laws passed to control the reproductive capacities and relationship choices of White women or to keep land and other forms of wealth from moving from White men to men of color? Were the laws about multiracial relationships key in legislative thinking or were they not more important than laws restricting property owning, the right to vote, the right to testify at civil trials, the right to attend public schools, and other rights denied to some or all people of color in many states and localities? Or were state or local lawmakers simply trying to show that they had the same standards as people in other states or localities who already had laws against such relationships?

There are many reasons why people might enter a partnership with somebody of another race. Despite the significance of race in U.S. thinking, for many people race might not be an important compatibility factor in comparison to other factors. Some immigrant populations had an enormous gender role imbalance—for example, although Chinese men were brought to the United States to work on the railroads, Chinese women were not and were for the most part legally barred from entering the United States (Takaki, 1993, ch. 8). Although many Chinese workers had wives and families back in China, to the extent that a man from China wanted a wife in the United States, bridging the gap of race was almost the only alternative. Taboos may themselves create an interest in violation of taboo. And sometimes taboos on marriage can allow people to develop an emotional intimacy that would be harder to develop if they saw each other as potential marital partners. Then, having developed an intimacy made easy by the sense that they could not possibly become partners, they might want the relationship to be legitimated in a way that is taboo.

DEMOGRAPHY

To the extent that censuses define people and their relationships for them or limit their choices to options that do not capture their reality, the census data that are available on multiracial families are suspect. Still, they say some things. For whatever it is worth, in the United States, multiracial marriages have increased markedly since 1967 but still are far less frequent than if people were partnering randomly (Waters, 1990, pp. 103–104). According to U.S. Census data, as of April, 1995, there were 1,392,000 married couples in the United States with partners from different races, 328,000 of them Black-White couples (U.S. Bureau of the Census, 1996).

Multiracial marriages are not randomly distributed across the United States but are found predominantly in cities and on the east and west coasts. Further, in different parts of the country, different constellations of multiracial relationship are found. For example, far more Asian or Asian American with White relationships are found on the west coast and far more Mexican or Mexican American with White relationships in the southwest, including California. Similarly, interracial adoptions are not randomly distributed but reflect, among many things, the connections of major adoption agencies of a geographic area to certain countries (for example, there is a Minnesota connection with Korea) and the proximity of a middle-class White population to a substantial population of people of color.

TRANSRACIAL ADOPTION

In the United States in 1990 there were approximately 119,000 adoptions. There are estimates that 8% of adoptions are interracial, with the most common involving children who are neither White nor Black being adopted into households with a White mother (Simon, Altstein, & Melli, 1994, p. 3). Many children who are transracially adopted come from Asia or Latin America. Native-American children were, until 1978, relatively likely to be removed from their family of origin and were much more likely than children of other racial groups to be transracially adopted (Simon et al., p. 8). Since 1978, the Indian Child Welfare Act has virtually stopped transracial adoption of Native-American children (Simon et al., p. 8). The states of the United States are diverse in laws dealing with interracial adoption, from explicitly giving priority to same-race adoption to mandating that race shall not be a factor (Simon et al., p. 17).

State statutes and adoption agency policies focus on the best interests of the child, so the issue of transracial adoption is usually dealt with as a question of where a child can best be nurtured and brought up. Those who are opposed to transracial adoption often focus on the limited capacity of a White family to help a child of color to deal with racism and discrimination and their limited capacity to help a child to know her or his own birth heritage, to develop an appropriate racial identity, to function in a society that will attach a racial label to the child, to be connected to members of her or his own racial community, and to know how to get along in that community. Some see White adoption of children of color as an expression of White racism—of Whites taking from people of color that to which they are not entitled. Some see the collateral issue of whether there are sufficient families of color to adopt available children of color as tied up in a battle between racial groups over whose standards should be applied, with critics of transracial adoption saying that White standards and values close the door to many potentially excellent adopters in communities of color (Simon et al., ch. 3).

Those who favor transracial adoption or who are neutral about it say that loving parents who can meet a child's needs for nurturance, guidance, and material well-being will do a good job whether or not of the same race. They also say that being of a different race is not an insurmountable block to appreciating a child's birth heritage and to bringing up a child to face adversity, including adversity from racism and discrimination. For additional discussion of interracial adoption, see the Grotevant and Kohler chapter in this volume.

MARITAL AND FAMILY ISSUES
FOR BLACK-WHITE MULTIRACIAL COUPLES

There are many different constellations of multiracial couples. There is reason to believe that cultural and socioenvironmental differences are important, so a study of Black-White couples in Minnesota will miss important issues that a Filipino and White couple in Hawaii, a Korean American and White couple in California, or a Black and White couple in southern Alabama will experience. Still, there are issues that seem common across situations. In the remainder of this chapter, those common issues are addressed based largely on a qualitative interview study of Black-White heterosexual couples in Minnesota (Rosenblatt et al., 1995; see Lockman, 1984, for a study on interracial gay male couples.) The Rosenblatt, Karis, and Powell study drew on intensive interviews of 21 couples living in the Minneapolis–St. Paul metropolitan area. This chapter is based so much on this qualitative study in part because, as of this writing, there is not a quantitative literature on multiracial family experiences and dynamics, and even qualitative research is still sparse.

Self-Perception as Ordinary

Most people in the 21 multiracial couples said that they considered themselves ordinary, that they were not together because they wanted to create a sociopolitical revolution and were not living a different life from other couples. Most people talked about themselves as similar to and compatible with their partner, not seeing race as the wide gulf that it can appear to be to people in the larger society.

Donna: You look for a person to be with, not a race or color. . . . A relationship is based on a few basic things, has nothing to do with color at all. . . .
Henry: I don't think we ever viewed ourselves as an interracial couple. (p. 25)

Flora: When I met [him] I didn't look at him as a white man. I looked at him as somebody there for me when I needed to go out. . . . We live and breathe and pay taxes and do . . . and everything else, just like anybody else. Have a home and work. (p. 25)

Experiences of Racism and Discrimination

It is often challenging to know, when an interracial couple is a target of racism or discrimination, how much the discrimination is because one partner is a person of color or because they are an interracial couple (Frankenberg, 1993, pp. 112–113). Although couples differed markedly in how much they had experienced being targets of racism and discrimination, how much they felt injured by racism and discrimination, and how much they organized their daily lives to defend themselves against racism and discrimination, all couples reported experiences of what seemed like racism or discrimination.

Stares. All reported stares from strangers in public. Although some experienced stares as intrusive and hostile, many had come to experience stares as either generally benign or beneath notice.

Joyce: Sometimes in restaurants, people just staring. . . . There really hasn't been any . . . kind of racially harmful things; it's been more just people's sort of awkwardness of staring, not quite knowing how to react. (p. 132)

That most couples said they had so few adverse experiences may mean that there was not much overt racism or discrimination in the Twin Cities metropolitan area, or that couples had learned how to navigate their environment so they stayed away from danger. However, having only a few adverse experiences to report may not mean that a couple feels safe. People can be traumatized for life by a single adverse experience or even the fear of one. For that reason, and because adverse experiences tell a lot about racism, it is useful to know some of the forms of racism and discrimination experienced by the couples. What follows describes areas of racism or discrimination that were commonly reported.

Institutional Racism—Real Estate. Institutional racism involves a pattern of racism that comes from and is supported by a larger social institution, like the government, real estate dealers, or a corporation. When couples encountered what seemed like racism, it sometimes seemed to express racism rooted in and sustained by a larger institution. Some couples talked about problems in renting or purchasing a place to live or in getting a mortgage loan.

> *Eve:* We used to live . . . in [a suburb]. . . . We lived in the first building, the one closest to the road. . . . The second building behind us was real quiet, and everyone [who] kind of looked like us . . . [was in the first building]. . . . Everybody in the front building that we lived in was either
>
> *Houston:* Chinese (he laughs)
>
> *Eve:* Hmong, black, interracial, or like
>
> *Interviewer:* Minority groups.
>
> *Eve:* Yeah. I felt like they had put all the misfits and . . . the . . . younger kids . . . in there. We were all thrown into one building, and this second building was like a whole different world. . . . That really bothered me, that they . . . separated us. . . . That means they were really looking at . . . what we were when we stepped into that office. (pp. 141–142)

Institutional Racism—Government Forms. Some people experienced racism in the assumption underlying government and university forms that presumed everybody could be classified into one of a small number of discrete racial categories.

> *Wanda:* The census doesn't allow for you to put down that your child is of more than one culture. . . . Those are probably the things that anger me the most. . . . That even goes to schools, and that's why I try to be involved in schools. . . . There are lots of kids out there who are aware of interracial couples, . . . and yet within the school that's not something that's put out there. (p. 143)

Institutional Racism—Church.

> *Eve:* At church, they were talking about once again the big question, which is blacks and whites and marry. And they always try to use that verse, that you shouldn't be on an unequal yoke. (p. 143)

Institutional Racism—Police.

> *Dot:* Police pulled us over. I was driving, got out. Him and [my step son] had to put their hands up, and I had to show my license and [the officer] said [we] could go. Now I have had enough experience . . . with the police that I didn't even question that man. We came home, and I called the . . . police station. And I said, "You have to understand that a certain amount of humiliation was suffered here. At least two neighbors drove by and looking at the (name) family with their hands on top of their head." And the man said, ". . . There has . . . been a rash of stolen checks cashed and . . . it is a black man and a white woman in a navy blue Cadillac or Lincoln. . . ." And I said, ". . . We were a black man, a white woman, a black boy in a black Oldsmobile. And I understand the police have to do their job. I want them to do some soul-searching too." But we looked suspicious and the thing that identified us as suspicious was once they heard that it was an interracial couple driving around with these checks it really didn't matter if it was Oldsmobile or Pinto. . . . [Another] time we were stopped by the police. They took us in separate cars, put a gun to my head. . . . I was subjected to many many many horrible remarks on the way downtown. . . . They used the "n" word repeatedly. . . . Then on the way down there they just said horrible icky ugly things about our [being] interracial. . . . [They were] looking for drugs. And they didn't find anything, of course. (pp. 145–146)

Racism in the neighborhood.

> *Kate:* We had a [racial] incident with our daughter last summer, with a little white girl. And this little girl's dad about had a fit. . . . I was at work and the dad of this little girl ended up coming over and having a long conversation with Robert. And what did he say about 200 times during that conversation, "But I'm not a racist! But I'm not a racist!" (laughs). And Robert just said, "Look, you're entitled to teach your children what you want to teach them. You're entitled to believe what you want to believe and . . . think what you want to think; however, when it infringes on my family . . . then it becomes my business. If your child ever bites my daughter again because she doesn't like black people, we're going to have a serious problem." (p. 199)

Identity Issues

Being in a multiracial relationship can raise questions for oneself or others about one's identity.

> *William:* I've been reading people who talk about how consorting with white people compromises one. . . . I can see that it does kind of weaken your position. . . . I'm writing a history of Africans in America, . . . so I've been thinking about this a lot. . . . It's an interesting position to be in. . . . As far as I know it doesn't matter between Laura and me. But when I'm reading certain authors, for instance, . . . militant black nationalists . . ., it makes me think . . . about how, for instance, I would make much more sweeping generalizations if I weren't married to Laura. . . . I have

thought more about what other people might think because when I write about . . . black things . . . I wonder how [my marriage] would be received. I wonder how people will read me differently because of that. (pp. 181–182)

> *Gregory:* There've been some . . . events that Joyce has wanted to do, and I just said . . . I'm not gonna do it. I've just had too much of a European focus this week. . . . Joyce [has] been understanding, and [said], "Oh yeah, okay. Say you've got your basic European overload, right. . . ."
>
> *Interviewer:* What are those events?
>
> *Joyce:* . . . Like being totally away from black people, going and spending a week away from the city, or going to [a town where everyone is white] (laughs).
>
> *Gregory:* . . . I don't want to look around at an event and see I'm the only African-American. . . . It's . . . sort of like a psychological type of oppression when you're the only person from your race somewhere. (pp. 187–188)

At least in Minnesota, racial identity issues can be much more salient for people of color than for White people, who live where they can take whiteness as so ordinary and so dominant that it isn't experienced as part of identity, that it's only "the others" who have identity.

> *Dot:* As little as white people think about their race . . . I never defined myself as a white person growing up. Unlike black people who have to think of their race everyday. . . . It isn't something I think about daily. When outside forces come into play then I do think about it. . . . As far as society's concerned, I need to be ever mindful that I am in an interracial marriage. Society views me differently because of my interracial marriage.
>
> *Wilson:* . . . Just growing up in the United States as a black child, I was aware that I was different. . . . I understood that I had to be conscious of what's going on about me. . . . It becomes a burden, which I think affects most black people as far as hypertension, stress. It becomes a heavy burden to carry from day to day. When you get up . . . in the morning and look in mirror, the first thing that comes in my mind, "I'm still black. I'm still beautiful, but I've got to [go] out there and deal with these ignorant people."
>
> *Dot:* That's what I mean by the white people don't think about their race. Never a day in my life that I look in the mirror and think, "You're white," because I was surrounded by white people. (pp. 189–190)

Children in multiracial families deal with matters of identity—perhaps not so much because of competing loyalties but because of the need of the larger society to define them and because, by common societal standards, one cannot define oneself as being of more than one of the simple racial categories with which most of society operates. If a child is going to be defined as a person of color in the larger society, that means that the child will benefit enormously from being socialized to know what that means and how to exist safely with that identity.

> *Lorenzo:* When the black partner in a couple has a really weak or undeveloped sense . . . self as a black person, as a member of the African-American community,

I think that's a real set up for all kinds of problems. It's a set up for problems with them as a couple, and . . . for . . . everybody's spoken or unspoken fears about what about the kids, which the in-laws always bring up. . . . If the African-American parent can't carry the ball in terms of helping those kids mold their self identity . . ., choices don't get made in the family then that support the children's need to build a strong self identity, because ostensibly it doesn't matter to either parent. Families like that tend to build and strengthen this very insular and false notion that it's okay to shut out the rest of the world and forget that people are going to see their children as black children and forget that race does matter very, very much in the United States and instead cling to this kind of creative little bubble world within the family that because we say . . . we love each other that race doesn't matter . . . .

We say within our family that everybody should accept everybody for who and what they are. . . . But if the kids are brought up expecting, because this is what they've heard at home, that this is what they should also demand and respect outside, it's a recipe for disaster. And I've seen so much unhappiness on the part of both the broader families involved and . . . the kids that I would very, very passionately and specifically counsel families who think this way to . . . reexamine where they are. . . . There are 28,000,000 black people in the United States and . . . 28,000,000 different ways of . . . being black . . ., so you can't tell somebody who just doesn't feel culturally black and doesn't feel that they have much of a connection with the African-American community that . . . they better go out and get that for themselves, but . . . you certainly have to be aware of it and take responsibility for the fact that . . . it's your job as the . . . black parent to help your kids get ready to deal with the world that you find offensive and didn't create. (pp. 185–186)

To many African American parents of multiracial children, it is of crucial importance that the White partner support the socialization of their child to be knowledgeable about African American heritage and able to function well in a world of racism.

Gloria: I'm . . . on Kent to be aware of black history and to convey to [our daughter] his interest in my culture along with his culture. [Before], if he didn't sit down and watch a program with me . . . on TV, I wouldn't give him a hard time. . . . But . . . I don't want to give mixed messages to our child (laughs), and so I want him to also watch things, or attend things, so that she feels as proud of both sides of her heritage. . . . If Kent is not aware of when things are going on, . . . who's going to pick up on it for [her]? So I feel the need to, that he's as conscious of it all as I am. . . . I don't know if I should relate this story, but . . . it reminded me of the difference between being black and white in this society. . . . He doesn't have that kind of paranoia that I think black folks in this country (chuckles) just have to have because you *don't know* sometimes what . . . the motivations for saying or doing . . . things are; you don't know whether it's based on your color or based on something you actually did. . . . Something simple like I tell him like if he walks into a store without a receipt, he doesn't bother carrying a bag in (laughs) with the merchandise, and I just would be afraid to do that. . . . In fact I've felt people following me in stores. And it's a constant reminder to me as a black person that no matter how I dress or how I look or what I accomplish that there are gonna be people who're gonna be looking out for me because I'm black. And I don't think he has to experience that as a white male. (p. 200)

Lorenzo: There has never been any social or cultural meaning to being a so-called "mixed" person. . . . It didn't matter what percentage of black blood you had by state law in state after state. If you had one drop of black blood you were black. . . . Since that is still very much where we are, it doesn't really make sense to encourage a group of people, just because they have mixed racial heritage, to . . . carve out [a] niche for themselves that makes them different from the rest of the community of color to which they ultimately, because of how things are, . . . belong. Now that's why I'm saying that family mythology and the family trip about who we are is different, and you are going to know because you've encouraged your kids to develop radar too, and they just kind of have, just by you modeling that to them, they will know, increasingly who it's okay to talk about these things with, and who it's not. And you just know those things and go on with your life. . . .

Virginia: I think that part of our responsibility as parents is to teach our children to survive in the world, and that's on all levels. And with racially mixed children that includes dealing with the broader world on racial issues, and that they get from identifying with those who are black and not by playing games or expecting the white community not to see them different. The white community will see them as different, and . . . they just need to get that stuff straight early on. . . . I never felt like I've heard other white women say they felt like they were left out. . . . I never felt that. I just see that the survival skill that they need to understand how to function in the world, and I can't teach them that. And if they tell me that something's happening and that they think it has something to do with race, I'm sure it does. They would know that more than I do, but in terms of who they are as an identity I think it is a saner and more useful thing in terms of how they see themselves to identify themselves as black. . . . The black community has had a history forever of accepting people of all shades, and that's a much easier thing to deal with than to be thinking that somehow they're different. I think that any ambivalence the kids have has more to do with not feeling like they really came out of a hard core black community. (pp. 209–210)

In school, there can be intense pressures on multiracial children to have a monoracial identity.

Gregory: While [our children] are in grade school it seems like . . . things are fine. . . . They walk into high school. Things aren't fine! Things change when you go to high school! Whoa! They change, and then kids are made to choose. Okay, so one parent's black and one parent's white, what are you? Which group you gonna be with? Can't have both! You can't be with white people one day and black people the next. . . . Here's the line drawn down the middle; choose up. (p. 213)

Opposition from Family of Origin

Paralleling findings of Kouri and Lasswell (1993), some people said that there were no problems with their family of origin, others that the opposition soon melted away, and others that there were problems (though in most cases there were also family members who were supportive). The opposition seemed to be greater from the White partner's family of origin than the African American partner's family of origin. But often the opposition would lessen with time or with the birth of children.

> *Liz:* We had it out that one time about he wasn't gonna talk to me anymore if I came home with a black man, rethought it and said, "No matter what," and they've just kind of stuck with that. They really love the kids. . . . He had a heart attack in . . . January. . . . I think he thought he was going to die, and he kept calling and asking for [our son] to come stay with him. So the kids are really important to my parents. (p. 194)

> *Virginia:* My mother, once we got married and it was apparent that she couldn't do anything about it, then she kind of switched sides, and she will now get very intense with relatives . . . and she'll confront people. . . . She's very protective of the kids, particularly when they were little. Somebody would be sitting next to her on the bus would say something and she'd . . . say, "Well, you're talking about my grandchildren." (pp. 194–195)

Opposition in the Black Community

It is not easy to generalize about how the Black community was experienced by the multiracial couples we interviewed. As has been reported in other studies (e.g., See, 1989) and in the popular press, what seemed most clear was that some African American women were critical of African American men partnering with White women.

> *Nora:* The most negativity towards me personally because I was dating and am now married to a black man comes from black women. There seems to me this kind of thing of like, "Well, you've taken one out of circulation, and that means there's one less good one for me." (p. 150)

BAD AND GOOD OUTCOMES

The Stereotypes Are Wrong

Questions about the outcomes experienced in any category of nontraditional family play off the stereotypes others apply to those families. In a very real sense, the first thing to be said about outcomes for such families is that the stereotypes are simplistic and wrong.

> *Eve:* Everybody always tells me that interracial couples don't work. I always hear negative things. The children are mixed up. . . . In that respect it *is* important to me that we . . . project a positive image for interracial couples. . . . The larger commu-

nity, I still don't think that they accept it yet. But I think it's because they don't understand it. . . . I don't see the larger community as seeing us in a very positive way. (pp. 123–124)

The More Important Questions May Be about Experiences

Questions about pathology and negative outcomes in multiracial families are politically charged. Who defines pathology? What does it mean to identify a statistical pattern that suggests possible pathology? Does it mean that families need treatment or that society does? It is certainly possible for racism, discrimination, and stereotyping to set up processes that can make life difficult for people in multiracial families and that may even create health problems for some targets of racism, discrimination, and stereotyping (Burke, 1984). But it seems less respectful to look for pathology in such families than to ask questions about the experience of people in such families.

Beyond experiences addressed in this chapter, it may be useful to ask, What is it like, in terms of identity, self-esteem, and psychological adjustment to be a person with more than one racial background? What are the consequences of identifying oneself as biracial or multiracial? There are interesting and enlightening first steps in exploring that question (e.g., Kerwin, Ponterotto, Jackson, & Harris, 1993; Root, 1992, 1996), with a sense of there being great variation in identity, self-esteem, and adjustment and also there being situational variability in how people think of themselves and act. There are also interesting and enlightening beginnings to answering questions about racial or cultural combinations other than Black-White that address how cultural differences and differences in group history and demography play out—for example, Sung's (1990) work on Chinese-American intermarriage.

Learning about Partner's Culture and Experience

A positive outcome often reported in multiracial relationships is learning about the experience and culture of the other. In Black-White multiracial couples, the White partner, who may have lived in ignorance of the experience of being Black in the United States, may learn an enormous amount from the Black partner.

Patricia: I was . . . raised . . . to understand that as a black person [racism] is part of the experience in this country. And it doesn't matter. My mother used to say to us, "I don't care how much money you have, how many fur coats you own. You can drive up to the biggest hotel in town, and the man who parks your car will find some way to remind you that you're black." And I used to think, "God, that's really silly." But I think it prepared me so much for life. . . .

Gary: I think part of the education for me was if the discrimination was not absolutely blatant and in my face, I would often not notice it. And Patricia would point something out. "Did you see that this happened?" "Let's see, yeah, I remem-

ber that." And she'd say, "You know what that means." And then I, "Oh, I sup-
pose." (pp. 216, 218)

Eve: I am more aware of the struggles that he as a black male faces. And I realize
that my life if I were married to a white male would be very different. And I am
thankful that I am married to him because I can see that. I am more aware of it because I see everyday the things that he has to go through. . . . I try to share with
people that it's important, that issues that affect him really affect all of us, and I try
to share with my friends . . . things like that, but they don't understand me because
they are not living with it. . . . Just subtle things. The way that I've been treated differently. Just like for example going to the grocery store and getting the third
degree when I'm trying to write a check with him. You always wonder, "Is this
racism? . . . Am I feeling what it's like . . .? And he always say, "It is, it is." But I
really don't know what racism is, so I'm learning. (p. 220)

Rosemary: The [neatest] thing for me has been . . . the cultural difference and
learning something about Ed's [world]. We're like soul mates, and yet . . . we've
come into the relationship with a lot of experiences that the other hasn't had. . . .
One of my favorites, that I would never have experienced, is going up to the bar-
bershop on Fourth Avenue and 38th. . . . You have to come first come first served.
And people just wait, and so you can go in there, and you're like maybe 20th in
line. So you sit there all day . . . not minding it one bit, because I'm learning something . . . and you're listening to these people talk. . . . They're not that different
than me. And yet there *is* a cultural, there's just something. And they're yelling
back and forth, and so part of it's . . . their cultural stuff . . . and then watching them
get their hair cut. . . . I can remember one time when a woman . . . had fallen asleep
while she was getting her hair cut, and it was a woman cutting her hair, a woman
barber. The woman woke up, and looked at her hair, and she was just like, "Oh, girl
friend! Girl friend!" . . . Experiences like that are enriching. Or if you haven't gone
to Detroit with Ed and meeting . . . musician friends of his. . . . There's this one guy
[who is] just the coolest guy in the world, a trumpet player. . . . Meeting his mother.
I would sit and listen to her until three in the morning telling me stories. (pp.
257–258)

Bridging

People in multiracial relationships may not want the responsibility of bridging the
gulf between races in the United States and may not think of their own relationship as more than just a relationship. And yet it is possible to see the relationship
or children of the relationship as in some sense a bridge.

Adam: The [multiracial] kids that succeed . . . often develop skills so that they
can sort of live in both worlds. . . . It's . . . a strength. It's like learning another
language. . . .
Wanda: There are . . . things that you give to your child that [couples who are in
the same culture] may not be able to do. (pp. 195–196)

CONCLUSIONS

Judging by what 21 intensively interviewed Black-White couples had to say and judging by the growing literature in this area, cultural and experiential differences can challenge a multiracial couple, and they can also be challenged by all the issues that arise for same race couples. But the greatest challenge seems to be that created by racism in the United States. For some multiracial couples the challenges from racism are many and intense; for others, the challenges are fewer. A couple may have to deal with stares, discrimination, institutional racism, catcalls in public places, and family and community opposition. There is also a knowledge gap, typically one that is asymmetrical, with the White partner knowing less about the world of the Black partner than the reverse, because Whites are often not well informed about what it means to be a person of color in the United States. It is not the responsibility of people of color or of multiracial families to educate others, and yet learning about their experience may be helpful not only in knowing who they are, but also in understanding racism in the United States and the challenge of repairing the damage that racism creates.

REFERENCES

Burke, A. W. (1984). Racism and psychological disturbance among West Indians in Britain. *International Journal of Social Psychiatry, 30*(1/2), 50–68.

Frankenberg, R. (1993). *White women, race matters: The social construction of Whiteness.* Minneapolis: University of Minnesota Press.

Funderburg, L. (1994). *Black, White, other: Biracial Americans talk about race and identity.* New York: Morrow.

Kalmijn, M. (1993). Trends in Black/White intermarriage. *Social Forces, 72,* 119–146.

Kerwin, C., Ponterotto, J. G., Jackson, B. L., & Harris, A. (1993). Racial identity in biracial children: A qualitative investigation. *Journal of Counseling Psychology, 40,* 221–231.

Kouri, K. M., & Lasswell, M. (1993). Black-White marriages: Social change and intergenerational mobility. *Marriage and Family Review, 19*(3/4), 241–255.

Lockman, P. T., Jr. (1984). Ebony and ivory: The interracial gay male couple. *Lifestyles: A Journal of Changing Pattern, 7,* 44–55.

Root, M. P. P. (Ed.). (1992). *Racially mixed people in America.* Newbury Park, CA: Sage.

Root, M. P. P. (Ed.). (1996). *The multiracial experience.* Thousand Oaks, CA: Sage.

Rosenblatt, P. C. (1994). *Metaphors of family systems theory.* New York: Guilford.

Rosenblatt, P. C., Karis, T. A., & Powell, R. D. (1995). *Multiracial couples: Black and White voices.* Thousand Oaks, CA: Sage.

See, L. A. L. (1989). Tensions between Black women and White women. *Affilia, 4*(2), 31–45.

Simon, R. J., Altstein, H., & Melli, M. S. (1994). *The case for transracial adoption.* Washington, DC: American University Press.

Spickard, P. (1989). *Mixed blood: Intermarriage and ethnic identity in twentieth-century America.* Madison: University of Wisconsin Press.

Sung, B. L. (1990). *Chinese American intermarriage.* New York: Center for Migration Studies.

Takaki, R. (1993) *A different mirror: A history of multicultural America.* Boston: Little, Brown.

U.S. Bureau of the Census. (1996). *Statistical abstract of the United States.* Washington, DC: U.S. Government Printing Office.

Waters, M. C. (1990). *Ethnic options: Choosing identities in America.* Berkeley: University of California Press.

Chapter 14

Struggling to Make Ends Meet
Poverty and Child Development

JEANNE BROOKS-GUNN
PIA REBELLO BRITTO
CHRISTY BRADY
Columbia University

The proportion of families in the United States struggling to make ends meet is very high. Child poverty has increased from about 15% in the 1970s to more than 20% in the late 1990s. In the late 1990s, about 14 million children (over one in five of all U.S. children) are living in families below the poverty threshold. Another one in five are members of families whose incomes are not more than twice the poverty threshold. This additional 20% translates into another 14 million children living in families struggling to make ends meet. Although children under the age of 18 represent only 27% of the total population, they make up 40% of the poverty population (U.S. Bureau of the Census, 1996).

Income poverty is defined by the poverty threshold in the United States. Poverty thresholds in the United States take into account household size and are adjusted each year for cost of living (Consumer Price Index). The threshold was originally developed in 1959, based on expected food expenditures (thrifty food basket) for families of particular sizes (Orshansky, 1988). The U.S. poverty line is absolute, not relative. In 1996, the poverty threshold was $12,516 for a family of three people and $16,036 for a family of four.

An unprecedented rise in the divorce rate since the mid-1960s and the dramatic increase in the number of children born out-of-wedlock gave rise to an increase in the number of female-headed households. In 1990, nearly one fifth of White and two thirds of Black children were born to unmarried mothers (Ventura, 1995). Of children born to married parents, approximately 45% are expected to experience parental divorce before the age of 18 (Bumpass, 1984). These households represent the largest proportion of poor families in which poor children reside. Approximately 60% of poor children under the age of 6 live in female-headed households compared to 12% of such children in married-couple families. The current economic and demographic trends suggest that an even higher proportion of children

279

born in the 1990s will be raised by single mothers. A rise in single motherhood due to divorce can be attributed to higher divorce than remarriage rates. The poverty level for children living in families in which divorce has occurred is high because incomes for custodial mothers tend to drop by more than one third after marital disruption (Duncan, 1991; McLanahan & Sandefur, 1994). Poverty rates are high for children in families with unmarried mothers, particularly because these mothers have low rates of employment, often combined with ineffective child support enforcement (Cherlin, 1992; Edin & Lein, 1997; Furstenberg, Brooks-Gunn, & Morgan, 1987). About half of all never-married mother households have incomes below the poverty line compared to 6% of married-couple households.

A rise in children's poverty rates can also be attributed to changes in employment patterns and wage inequality. Additionally, a decline in manufacturing, relocation of jobs to the suburbs, and increasing polarization of the labor market into high and low wage sectors has lead to an increase in the level of unemployment and stagnation of wages among semiskilled adults in the cities (Danzinger & Goltschalk, 1995; Sampson & Morenoff, 1997; Wilson, 1987). These employment and economic factors are considered to be prime determinants of family income, or lack thereof, and the resultant rates of childhood poverty.

A salient issue in understanding poverty experiences is knowing how long bouts of poverty last. It is difficult to report on a single time point of experiencing poverty because family incomes fluctuate periodically, moving families in and out of poverty (Duncan & Brooks-Gunn, 1997). The dynamic nature of poverty experiences can be attributed to multiple factors such as changes in life situations (divorce, death of earning member of family, changes in employment) and changes in the social and economic climate of the country (economic recessions and expansions; Corcoran & Chaudry, 1997; Elder, 1974; Haveman, Wolfe, & Spaulding, 1991).[1] With respect to duration, family poverty can be transient (lasting only for a short period of time), occasional, recurrent, or persistent (continuing for many years) (Ashworth, Hill, & Walker, 1994). Data from the Panel Study of Income Dynamics, an ongoing survey since 1968 of more than 5,000 families, indicates that 15% of poor children have spent more than 10 years in poverty (Duncan & Rogers, 1988).

Researchers have been paying more attention to another issue related to child and family poverty, that is, how do poor families make ends meet. Most families or mothers who are living at the poverty line are unable to make ends meet by either relying on their Temporary Assistance to Needy Families (TANF) stipend, formerly known as Aid to Families with Dependent Children (AFDC), or by working. Most mothers use a variety of strategies, including augmenting their AFDC stipend by working off the books, receiving child support through informal rela-

---

[1] The literature does not typically distinguish among reasons for low income, that is, disability (physical or mental) of parent that prevents working, child with a disability, job loss, low wage earner, part-time work. The most notable exceptions are work by Elder (1974, 1979), McLoyd (1990), McLoyd & Wilson (1991), and Conger and colleagues (Conger et al., 1992) on the effects of income loss on families.

tionships with the absent father, by augmenting or adding low wages with informal child support, doubling up, and receiving assistance from friends or agencies (Edin & Lein, 1997). We have little information on how mothers who have a little more income (i.e., are not hovering at the poverty threshold, but still have incomes less than twice the poverty threshold) make ends meet.

We have organized our chapter around four central questions related to family poverty and child development in the United States (for review, see Brooks-Gunn & Duncan, 1997; Duncan & Brooks-Gunn, 1997):

1. What are the consequences of income poverty on child development?
2. How strong are income effects?
3. What are the pathways through which poverty operates?
4. What are the policy implications of family and childhood poverty?

WHAT ARE THE CONSEQUENCES OF INCOME POVERTY ON CHILD DEVELOPMENT?

Research has documented the consequences of poverty on child development. Undoubtedly, low income has substantial detrimental effects on child and adolescent well-being. However, of interest is a more detailed and nuanced examination of the effects of poverty on specific child outcomes such as physical health, academic achievement, emotional and behavioral functioning, and the developmental stage at which income poverty influences these outcomes. Based on specific indicators of well-being, poor children suffer higher incidences of adverse health, and developmental, emotional, and behavioral outcomes than nonpoor children. However, the size of these effects is in question, due to the fact that many studies do not control for other family characteristics that may account, in part, for associations between family income and child outcomes.

Table 14.1 presents findings (summarized in a 1997 volume of *Futures of Children*) from large nationally representative surveys on the physical health, academic achievement, and emotional and behavioral functioning of poor and nonpoor children. However, the data presented in this table are based on simple cross-tabulations and do not control for factors that might be important for child outcomes other than poverty status, at the time of data collection.

In a volume by Duncan and Brooks-Gunn (1997), the effects of poverty on infants, children, and youth were analyzed, taking into account omitted-variable bias, expanded-measurement models, and comparing effect sizes across studies. We review results of income poverty on domain specific outcomes for children and youth from both U.S. and Canadian large multisite developmental studies, such as the Panel Study of Income Dynamics (PSID), the National Longitudinal Survey of Youth (NLSY), Children of the NLSY (the follow-up of the children born to women in the original NLSY cohort), the National Survey of Families and Households (NSFH), the Infant Health and Development Program (IHDP), and

TABLE 14.1
Selected Population-Based Indicators of Well-Being
for Poor and Nonpoor Children in the United States

Indicator	Percentage of Poor Children (unless noted)	Percentage of Nonpoor Children (unless noted)	Ratio of Poor to Nonpoor Children
Physical Health Outcomes (for children between 0 and 17 years unless noted)			
Low birth weight (less than 2,500 grams)[a]	1.0	0.6	1.7
Deaths during childhood (0 to 14 years)[b]	1.2	0.8	1.5
Stunting (being in the fifth percentile for height for age for 2 to 17 years)[c]	10.0	5.0	2.0
Number of days spent in bed in past year[d]	5.3	3.8	1.4
Number of short-stay hospital episodes in past year per 1,000 children[d]	81.3	41.2	2.0
Achievement Outcomes (5 to 17 years)			
Learning disability (defined as having exceptional difficulty in learning to read, write, and do arithmetic) (3 to 17 years)[d]	8.3	6.1	1.4
Grade repetition (reported to have ever repeated a grade)[d]	28.8	14.1	2.0
Ever expelled or suspended[d]	11.9	6.1	2.0
High school dropout (percentage 16- to 24-year-olds who were not in school or did not finish high school in 1994)[e]	21.0	9.6	2.2
Emotional/Behavioral Outcomes (3 to 17 years)			
Parent reports child has ever had an emotional or behavioral problem that lasted three months or more[f]	16.4	12.7	1.3
Parent reports child ever being treated for an emotional problem or behavioral problem[d]	2.5	4.5	0.6
Parent reports child has experienced one or more of a list of typical child behavioral problems in the last three months (5 to 17 years)[g]	57.4	57.3	1.0

Note: From "The Effects of Poverty on Children," by J. Brooks-Gunn and G. J. Duncan, 1997, *Futures of Children,* 7(2), pp. 58–59. Copyright 1997 by the Center for the Future of Children, the David and Lucile Packard Foundation. Adapted with permission.

[a]Data from the National Maternal and Infant Health Survey, collected in 1989 and 1990, with 1988 as the reference period. Percentages were calculated from the number of low birth weight births per 1,000 live births as reported in Federman et al., (1996).

[b]Percentages include only Black and White youths. Percentages calculated from Table 7 in Rogot (1992).

[c]Data from NHANES II, 1976–1980.

[d]Data from the 1988 National Health Interview Survey Child Health Supplement (NHIS-

(Continued)

TABLE 14.1 *(continued)*
CHS), a nationwide household interview survey. Children's health status was reported by the adult household member who knew the most about the sample child's health, usually the child's mother. Figures calculated from Dawson (1991), and Coiro, Zill & Bloom (1994).

[e]National Center for Educational Statistics. *Dropout rates in the United States: 1994.* Table 7, Status dropout rate, ages 16–24, by income and race ethnicity: October 1994, Available online at: http://www.ed.gov/NCES/pubs/r9410t07.html

[f]Data from the NHIS-CHS. The question was meant to identify children with common psychological disorders such as attention deficit disorder or depression, as well as more severe problems such as autism.

[g]Data from the NHIS-CHS. Parents responded "sometimes true," "often true," or "not true" to a list of 32 statements typical of children's behaviors. Each statement corresponded to one of six individual behavior problems—antisocial behavior, anxiety, peer conflict/social withdrawal, dependency, hyperactivity, and headstrong behavior. Statements included behaviors such as cheating or lying, being disobedient in the home, being secretive, and demanding a lot of attention. For a more complete descriptions, see Section P-11 of the NHIS-CHS questionnaire.

the Quebec Longitudinal Studies of Behavior. Table 14.2 (adapted from the volume, *Consequences of Growing Up Poor;* Duncan & Brooks-Gunn, 1997) illustrates the effects of income on the physical health, achievement, and emotional and behavioral functioning of children, adolescents, and young adults by the stage at which the outcome was measured. The results presented in Table 14.2 control for mother's education, family structure, and other demographic variables. Three rough sizes of income effects are presented for the ability and achievement measures for each developmental period. A *large* effect is one in which the effect sizes are significant at the .05 level and are almost always one third of a standard deviation or larger. A *moderate to small* effect is one in which the income coefficient, although significant at the .05 level, is less than one third of a standard deviation. *No effect* means that the income coefficients were not statistically significant.

Table 14.2 illustrates that family income has large effects on measures of children's ability and achievement. The table also illustrates that family income effects are greater during childhood than adolescence or young adulthood. For instance, income appears to have a large effect on children's verbal ability, reading, and math scores during early childhood. However, based on studies reported in *Consequences of Growing Up Poor* (Duncan & Brooks-Gunn, 1997), family income appears to have little or no effect on children's motor and social development, behavior, or mental and physical health (but see Duncan et al., 1994; Korenman, Miller, & Sjaastad, 1995; McLeod & Shanahan, 1993).

In the following subsections we provide a brief review of the results for three outcomes: physical health; school achievement and cognitive ability; and emotional and behavioral outcomes (for a more complete discussion of these findings see Brooks-Gunn & Duncan, 1997; Duncan & Brooks-Gunn, 1997).

Physical Health Outcomes

Poor children, compared to nonpoor children in the United States, experience diminished physical health as measured by a number of health status indicators,

TABLE 14.2
Summary Analysis: Effects of Family Income on Children's Performance
on Measures of Ability and Achievement

	Size of Effect[a]		
Stage of Outcome	*Large*	*Small or Moderate*	*None*
Childhood	−IQ Score (age 3, 5)[b] −Verbal Score (age 3, 5, 7)[b,c] −Math & Reading Achievement (age 5, 7)[c]	−Behind in grade for age (age 6–12)[e]	
Adolescence		−AFQT score[h] −Odds of completing high school[g]	−Self-reported grades[k] −Odds of high school graduation[k]
Young adulthood	−Family income[f] −Men's labor income[g] −Men's hourly earnings[f] −Men's work hours[f]	−Completed schooling[d] −Odds of attending college[j] −Status of first job[j]	−Completed schooling[i] −Odds of attending college[i]

Note: From *Consequences of Growing Up Poor* (ch. 5, 7, 10–17), by G. J. Duncan and J. Brooks-Gunn (Eds.), 1997, New York: Russell Sage Foundation Press. Copyright 1997 by the Russell Sage Foundation. Adapted by permission.

[a] *Large:* all income coefficients from income-based models were significant at the .05 level or below; the effect size was almost always one-third of a standard deviation or larger. *Small to moderate:* most income coefficients from income-based models were significant at the .05 level or below; the effect size was consistently less than one-third of a standard deviation. *None:* few or no income coefficients from income-based models were significant at the .05 level.

[b] Smith, Brooks-Gunn, and Klebanov (1997). Data from the Infant Health and Development Program.

[c] Smith, Brooks-Gunn, and Klebanov (1997). Data from the National Longitudinal Survey of Youth (NLSY).

[d] Axinn, Duncan, and Thornton (1997). Data from the Detroit Longitudinal Study of Mothers and Children. Income measured five times from birth to age seventeen years.

[e] Pagani, Boulerice, and Tremblay (1997). Data from the Quebec Longitudinal Studies of Behavior.

[f] Corcoran and Adams (1997). Data from the Panel Study of Income Dynamics (PSID). Income measured as early as age three and as late as age sixteen years, but mostly during adolescence.

[g] Haveman, Wolfe, and Wilson (1997). Data from the PSID. Income measured between ages six and eighteen years.

[h] Peters and Mullis (1997). Data from the NLSY.

[i] Teachman, Paasch, Day, and Carver (1997). Data from the National Longitudinal Surveys of Young Men and Women.

[j] Hauser and Sweeney (1997). Data from the Wisconsin Longitudinal Survey.

[k] Conger, Conger, and Elder (1997). Data from the Iowa Youth and Family Project.

such as low birth weight, infant mortality, growth stunting, and number of hospitalizations (see Table 14.1). Estimating effects of poverty on birth outcomes is complicated by the fact that adverse birth outcomes are more prevalent for unmarried women, those with low levels of education, and Black mothers—all groups with high poverty rates (Brooks-Gunn & Duncan, 1997; Brooks-Gunn, Klebanov, & Duncan, 1996).

Deficits in children's nutritional status are also associated with poverty. Growth stunting or low height for age, though not a nutritional status measure per se, is a physical health outcome. Studies using the data from the NLSY show that differentials in height for age between poor and nonpoor children are greater when long-term rather than single-year measures of poverty are used in models to predict stunting (Miller & Korenman, 1994). However, these effects are relatively small, most likely due to the availability of food stamps (Currie, 1997).

Children also suffer from health problems due to exposure to lead in the environment. However, the magnitude of the health problems varies not only by length and intensity of exposure to lead in the environment but also by the developmental stage of the child. A study using the National Health and Nutrition Examination Survey (NHANES III, 1988–1991) found that the level of lead in children's blood declined as family income increased. All other things being equal, the average blood lead levels were 9% lower for 1-to-5-year-olds in families with income twice the poverty level compared to poor families (Brody et al., 1994).

School Achievement and Cognitive Ability Outcomes

Children's cognitive development and school achievement during early childhood is susceptible to income poverty (Duncan, Brooks-Gunn, & Klebanov, 1994; Klebanov, Brooks-Gunn, McCarton, & McCormick, in press; Korenman et al., 1995; Smith, Brooks-Gunn, & Klebanov, 1997). The effects of income poverty on children's verbal ability standardized test scores during the early childhood years are approximately one fourth to one third of a standard deviation. These income effects are clearly seen as early as age 2 (Klebanov et al., in press). The test score differences are further amplified for children who are living in homes with incomes less than half of the poverty threshold and in persistent poverty (Smith et al., 1997).

Measures of child well-being after entrance into school typically include school achievement test scores, grade failure, and learning and attention problems (Brooks-Gunn, Duncan, & Maritato, 1997). Results on the effects of income poverty on test scores for children between 7 and 8 years of age are parallel to those obtained for children 3 years of age (Smith et al., 1997). Other research has found modest effects of household income on child and adolescent school performance and grade point average (Hanson, McLanahan, & Thomson, 1997). In Canada, effects of persistent poverty have also been found for academic failure as assessed by grade placement (Pagani, Boulerice, & Tremblay, 1997). Children who were categorized as always poor were twice as likely not be to placed in an age appropriate classroom compared to their never poor peers.

Academic measures of adolescent well-being typically include high school graduation or school dropout or both, school engagement, grades, and, to a lesser extent, achievement test scores. The effect of income poverty on school completion is quite modest. In general, studies suggest that a 10% increase in family income is associated with a 0.2% to 2% increase in number of school years completed (Haveman & Wolfe, 1994, 1995; Teachman, Paasch, Day, & Carver, 1997). Income poverty in the early childhood years is more strongly associated with school completion than is income poverty in the middle childhood and adolescent school years. In addition, income effects are most pronounced for those families in deep poverty (Duncan, Yeung, Brooks-Gunn, & Smith, 1998).

Emotional and Behavioral Outcomes

Emotional problems are usually grouped along two dimensions: externalizing (aggression, tantrums, acting out), and internalizing (depression, anxiety, moodiness). Based on maternal reports of children's behavior problems, in the Infant Health and Development Program data set found that children who were persistently poor had more behavior problems than nonpoor children (Duncan et al., 1994). Research on both the Infant Health and Development Program and the National Longitudinal Survey of Youth data sets has found that persistent poverty is associated with internalizing behavior problems (Brooks-Gunn, Smith, Berlin, & Lee, in press; Korenman et al., 1995; McLeod & Shanahan, 1993).

Emotional and behavioral outcomes during adolescence typically include the onset of sexual intercourse, drug and alcohol use, and smoking (Brooks-Gunn, Duncan, & Maritato, 1997). In terms of teenage pregnancy, even though the rate of out-of-wedlock childbearing for poor teens is nearly three times that of nonpoor teens, these results are often accounted for by demographic factors other than poverty (Brooks-Gunn & Duncan, 1997). The data from the Panel Study of Income Dynamics indicate that the likelihood of a teenager giving birth out-of-wedlock declined as the family income levels rose above the poverty threshold. The duration and timing of poverty had no effect on this association, however (Haveman, Wolfe, & Wilson, 1997).

Summary of Findings on the Consequences of Growing Up Poor

Our brief review of the effects of income poverty suggests the following points. First, income poverty appears to have a greater influence on children's academic achievement compared to emotional functioning. Second, the strength of the influence appears to weaken during the adolescent years. One explanation for these findings could be that during the adolescent years extrafamilial environments (schools, neighborhoods, peer groups) begin to take on importance, decreasing the influences of family conditions (Brooks-Gunn & Duncan, 1997). A second explanation could be related to the timing of the measurement of poverty. Even though family income fluctuates over time, few studies collect information on the family's income over time, from early childhood to adolescence. In one of the few studies to look at academic outcomes in the context of poverty across the epochs of early childhood through adolescence, a negative association between high school completion and poverty was found, but only for poverty experienced during the early childhood years (Duncan et al., 1998). Third, emotional and behavioral well-being may be linked to family income. The lack of findings, however, may be due to measure reliability.

Among the several other family factors related to children's well-being, maternal education, family structure, and the effects of cumulative risk have received considerable attention. Maternal education is often considered a poverty cofactor and, in some earlier developmental studies, has been used as a measure for income. Low levels of maternal education have been associated with low socioeconomic status, and maternal education is often confounded with low income. In most studies, maternal education and family income are equally predictive of children's ability and achievement (Duncan & Brooks-Gunn, 1997).

Family structure is also associated with family income. McLanahan (1997) questioned what matters more, parent absence or poverty. Looking across a set of developmental longitudinal studies, she examined the impact of family structure —intact, nonintact, single-parent, never-married families—on six domains of child well-being. Her conclusion is that family structure does influence child well-being, in that children from nonintact families are at risk for poorer developmental outcomes compared to children from intact families. The findings are stronger for emotional outcomes than for cognitive and achievement outcomes (in regression equations when income usually accounts for most of the effects of family structures). Thus, income is a stronger correlate of children's achievement and ability than is family structure, but family structure seems to influence emotional well-being more.

Poverty often co-occurs with a host of other factors that place a child at risk for lower levels of well-being. The accumulation of adversity is detrimental for children. Cumulative risk models developed by Sameroff and colleagues (Sameroff, Seifer, Baldwin, & Baldwin, 1993; Sameroff, Seifer, Barocas, Zax, & Greenspan, 1987) tested the premise that the accumulation of risks, rather than individual risk factors, accounts for developmental delays in children. Through their work, they have demonstrated that the effects of 10 socioenvironmental risk factors account for 16% of the variance in children's IQ scores at age 4. Work by Liaw and Brooks-Gunn (1994) examined the effects of cumulative risks on poor and nonpoor children in the Infant Health and Development Program sample. Analogous to the risk factors examined by Sameroff and colleagues, Liaw and Brooks-Gunn looked at the effects of 13 risks—biological (e.g., birthweight, neonatal status), socioeconomic (e.g., race/ethnicity, employment of head of household), maternal characteristics (e.g., maternal education, verbal ability), and family structure (e.g., teenage motherhood, father absence)—on the IQ scores of 36-month-old low

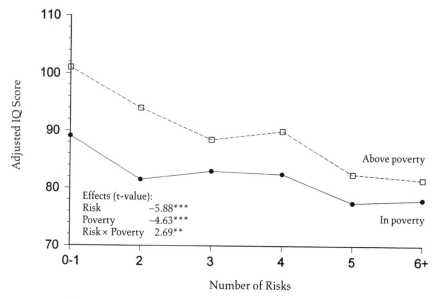

FIG 14.1.   Adjusted IQ score by risk group and poverty status. From F. Liaw and J. Brooks-Gunn (1994a). Copyright 1994 by Lawrence Erlbaum Associates. **p.01; ***p.001

birth weight children. They found that as the number of risks increased, IQ scores declined for both the low birth weight 3-year-old poor and nonpoor children (see Fig. 14.1). When the nonpoor children were exposed to high cumulative risks, their IQ scores were quite similar to those of the poor children with multiple risks. However, poor children who had no risk factors had IQ scores which were lower than those of the nonpoor children with no risk factors. Thus, children living in poor families appear to be doing worse on measures of cognitive ability, even if no other risk factors are present (at least the ones measured in most studies).

HOW STRONG ARE INCOME EFFECTS?

Family income appears to be a strong predictor of child outcomes after accounting for other family characteristics known to be associated with poverty. Most studies of family characteristics typically included education (e.g., high-school completion) and family structure (e.g., single parenthood). However, other family characteristics not typically included in analyses may also account for the poverty and well-being link. For example, some social scientists believe that family income is mostly a proxy for other characteristics, such as a strong work ethic or genetic endowment. Susan Mayer (1997), in her book, *What Money Can't Buy: The Effect of Parental Income on Children's Outcomes,* has made this argument. In her book she estimated the effects on child well-being of various components of income (for instance, asset income) that are independent of the actions of the family. Although her tests provide some support for her hypothesis that family income may not matter as much for child outcomes as earlier studies suggest, even Mayer admits that these statistical tests are not without their problems. Duncan and colleagues (1998) further test the hypothesis that income effects have been overestimated, by looking at associations between family income and achievement for siblings (parental genetic endowment and parental work ethic are held constant in such comparisons). Because families vary in yearly income, one child might have experienced poverty at age 5, whereas her siblings, when they were age 5, did not. Duncan and colleagues found that sibling differences in family income were related to sibling differences in years of completed schooling. Putting sibling controls did reduce the income effects, even though these effects remained significant. Consequently, from a selection point of view, even though the Duncan and Brooks-Gunn models might be overestimating the effects of income, just as the Mayer models might be underestimating these effects, we interpret these different sets of findings as a demonstration that income does matter. The question is the degree to which it matters.

More convincing evidence that income matters comes from the Income Maintenance/Negative Income Tax Experiment conducted in the 1960s and 1970s, which had some components based on randomized designs (see Currie, 1997). Families in the experimental group received a guaranteed minimum income. Positive effects of the income were seen in some sites, but not others. Benefits resulting from increased income effects were found for some child outcomes, such as child nutrition, early school achievement, and high school completion in some sites, but not in others. Since the site with the largest effects for younger children (North Carolina) was also the poorest site, one might surmise that income effects are most important for the very poorest families (Salkind & Haskins, 1982).

WHAT ARE THE PATHWAYS THROUGH WHICH POVERTY OPERATES?

There are a variety of pathways through which poverty influences children's well-being. In this section we discuss five pathways: health and nutrition, parental mental health, parent–child interactions, the home environment, and neighborhood conditions. Even though the focus of this volume is the family unit, we think that ignoring other contextual influences, such as the neighborhood, may give an incomplete picture of the pathways through which poverty operates, especially during the adolescent years. We define *pathways* as mechanisms through which poverty can influence child outcomes. By implication, this is a causal pathway between income and child outcomes (Brooks-Gunn & Duncan, 1997).

Health and Nutrition

Although health is itself an outcome, it can also be viewed as a pathway through which poverty influences other child outcomes, such as cognitive ability and school achievement. As discussed previously, poor children experience increased rates of low birth weight and growth stunting when compared to nonpoor children. These conditions have, in turn, been associated with reduced IQ and other measures of cognitive functioning in young children and, in the case of low birth weight, with increased rates of learning disabilities, grade retention, and school dropout in older children and youths (Brooks-Gunn & Duncan, 1997).

Parents' Mental Health

Parents who are poor are less likely to be healthy, both emotionally and physically, than those who are not poor (Adler, Boyce, Chesney, Folkman, & Syme, 1994). McLoyd (1990), and McLoyd and Wilson (1991) argued that psychological distress derived from negative life events is the major mediator between economic hardship and parenting behavior. The stressful conditions associated with poverty, such as inadequate housing, lack of money, and unsafe neighborhoods, lead to mental health problems and elevated levels of psychological distress. Their work with African American poor single mothers living under conditions of chronic poverty demonstrates how the burdens and responsibilities of solo parenting coupled with the social isolation of low-income neighborhoods predisposes these young mothers to anxiety, depression, and other mental health problems (McLoyd & Wilson, 1991). In many studies, maternal mental health is associated with competent parental functioning as depressed mothers are often times unresponsive, disengaged from their children, less affectionate, and emotionally unavailable (Crnic & Greenberg, 1987; Patterson, 1986; Teti, Gelfand, & Pompa, 1990). A few studies have established that parental mental health accounts for some of the effect of economic circumstances on child health and behavior (McLoyd, Jayaratne, Ceballo, & Borquez, 1994).

Poverty also has deleterious effects on adult marital relationship. Loss of earnings and inadequate sums of money can put a strain on marital bonds either through fueling spousal conflict or then through poor mental health or depression (Ray & McLoyd, 1986). In two-parent families, loss of father's income and increased maternal responsibility in decision making is predictive of marital discord and low family integration. Marital discord can influence parenting behavior (Elder, 1974).

Other research has examined the effects of job loss or income loss, as opposed to long-term poverty, on parental mental health. The experience of job loss or temporary economic hardship is quite different from experiencing the chronic stressors associated with unemployment or long standing poverty. Adults experiencing job loss or income loss, compared to adults who are employed, show some signs of anxiety, hostility towards others, and dissatisfaction with themselves, as well as higher rates of alcoholism (Buss & Redburn, 1983; Galambos & Silbereisen, 1987). During the period of job loss, the parents often compensate for their lack of income by making all sorts of adaptations, such as reducing consumption, borrowing money, relocating to less expensive neighborhoods, and other family members taking up employment. It is interesting that more frequent and intensive adaptations of this nature are associated with higher levels of psychological and mental health problems (Conger et al., 1992; Elder, Nguyen, & Caspi, 1985; McLoyd, 1989).

Families experiencing chronic or persistent poverty are confronted with a different set of issues. Unlike job loss or temporary income loss, they are faced with a situation of ongoing and cumulative stressors. In such acute situations, adults have higher rates of mental health problems and psychological distress compared to their counterparts experiencing transient poverty (McAdoo, 1986; McLoyd, 1990). Changes in parenting behavior due to the cumulative effects of stress are similar to those experiences by depressed mothers (Elder, Nguyen, & Caspi, 1985; Jackson Gyamfi, & Brooks-Gunn, in press; McLoyd, 1990; McLoyd et al., 1994). The constellation of life stressors, poor mental health, and social isolation often makes these adults vulnerable to the negative influence of other life events. Chronic poverty weakens these adults' ability to cope with the situation and consequently makes new problems and challenges increasingly debilitating (Conger et al., 1992; Elder et al., 1985; McLoyd, 1989).

Researchers who have examined the effects of sudden economic hardship during the Great Depression (Elder, 1979) or more recently in the rural midwest (Conger et al., 1992) demonstrated how loss of income is associated with parental irritability, ill temper, and punitiveness towards the children. Further, parent irritability and depressive symptoms are associated with more conflictual interactions with adolescents, leading to less satisfactory emotional, social, and cognitive development (Brooks-Gunn & Duncan, 1997).

Parenting Behavior

Parenting behavior is another pathway or mechanism through which poverty or income influences child well-being. Unemployment, stressful life events, and female-headed households are all expressions of poverty that influence children through parenting behaviors. Poverty and economic loss have been associated with parenting behavior that is less consistent, supportive, and involved, and more punitive and coercive (Conger et al., 1992; Elder, 1979; McLoyd et al., 1994). Research using the National Longitudinal Survey of Youth data found that poor mothers spanked their children more than nonpoor mothers and that this harsh behavior was an important component of the effect of poverty on children's mental health (McLeod, & Shanahan, 1993). Using data from the Infant Health and Development Program, poverty status and poverty cofactors such as low maternal education and living in a female-headed household were all found to be associated with a 3-year-old child's likelihood of receiving harsh discipline (Smith & Brooks-Gunn, 1997). The effects of poverty were particularly strong for boys—those male children living in poverty were four times more likely to be hit by their mothers and boys living in families with total income in the near-poor category were six times more likely to be hit, compared to the nonpoor families. These findings control for maternal age, race, education level, and female-headship of families.

Another study on parenting behavior and child outcomes using the Infant Heath and Development Program sample demonstrated the mediating role played by parenting behavior. The effects of family income and maternal education on child IQ were mediated by firm and controlling (authoritarian) parenting behavior as well as maternal depressive affect (Kohen, 1997; Linver, Brooks-Gunn, & Kohen, 1998). Low ratings of authoritarian behavior were associated with lower cognitive test scores at age 3.

The influence of poverty on parenting may also be mediated by factors such as values and beliefs (Ogbu, 1981). For instance, in order to ensure survival and success for their children living in economically impoverished environments, parents may adopt more power-assertive parenting behaviors (Garcia Coll et al., 1996; Garcia Coll, Meyer, & Brillon, 1995; Ogbu, 1981; 1988). However no studies have directly tested this premise.

The parenting behavior pathway is not always found to have a strong mediating effect between income and child outcomes. One possible explanation is that parenting behaviors are measured differently across studies. The findings are stronger in studies that involve an observational methodology of assessing parenting behavior than for other studies that have assessed parenting behavior via survey or interview data (see Berlin et al., 1995; Hanson et al., 1997). Additionally, as indicated in the section on the influence of poverty on child well-being, stronger effects of low income are noted for young children compared to their older counterparts. Future research needs to address the issue of timing of poverty in order to improve our understanding of the link between income and child outcomes mediated via parent-child interactions and parenting behavior.

The Home Environment

The *home environment* is the immediate environment within which a child's development takes place, especially during infancy and early childhood years. Physical aspects of the home, such as the rooms being perceptually varied and bright, the absence of structurally dangerous objects, and the presence of cognitively stimulating materials are linked to child well-being. The home environment, however, is often a reflection of the availability of financial resources. Family income appears to influence the cognitive development of preschoolers through the provision of a richer learning environment.

In many research studies, the child's home environment has been assessed used the Home Observation of Measurement of the Environment Inventory (HOME; Bradley et al., 1989; Caldwell & Bradley, 1984). This scale assesses learning materials in the home, the experiences offered by the mother, and the amount of warmth expressed toward the child. The full inventory consists of 55 items that include both mother reports and interviewer ratings of cognitive stimulation and emotional support available in the home. The HOME scale is correlated with family income, poverty, and cumulative risk, with higher levels of income associated with more enriching home environments (Klebanov et al., in press; Garrett, Ng'andu, & Ferron, 1994).

The child's home environment, which includes opportunities for learning, warmth of mother and child interactions, and the physical condition of the home, accounts for a substantial portion of the effects of family income on the cognitive outcomes of children. The provision for learning experiences in the home (as measured by specific subscales of the HOME scale) have been shown to account for up to half of the effect of poverty status on the IQ scores of 5-year-olds (Smith et al., 1997). It is interesting that links between children's IQ scores and home environment scores are stronger for children of more educated mothers than for children of mothers who had not completed high school (Brooks-Gunn et al., 1996). Thus, the child's home environment is another pathway through which family income or poverty influences child outcomes.

Neighborhood Conditions

A fifth possible pathway through which family income operates is the neighborhood in which a poor family resides. Poor parents are constrained in their choice of neighborhoods and schools. Low income may lead to residence in extremely poor neighborhoods characterized by social disorganization (crime, many unemployed adults, neighbors not monitoring the behavior of adolescents) and few resources (playgrounds, child care, health care facilities, parks, after school programs) for child development (Sampson & Morenoff, 1997; Wilson, 1987). The affluence of neighborhoods is positively associated with child and adolescent outcomes (intelligence test scores at ages 3 and 5 and high school graduation rates by age 20) over and above family poverty (Brooks-Gunn, Duncan, & Aber, 1997; Brooks-Gunn, Duncan, Klebanov, & Sealand, 1993). Neighborhood residence also seems to be associated with parenting practices, over and above family income and education. Neighborhood effects on intelligence scores are, in part, mediated by the learning environment in the home (Klebanov, Brooks-Gunn, Chase-Lansdale, & Gordon, 1997).

WHAT ARE THE POLICY IMPLICATIONS OF FAMILY AND CHILDHOOD POVERTY?

The daunting reality of poverty in the United States, particularly among children, is cause for concern. With the implementation of new welfare reforms, such as the Family Support Act of 1988 and the 1996 Personal Responsibility and Work Opportunity Reconciliation Act (PRWORA), the question now is whether the overhaul of the welfare system will prove beneficial, detrimental, or result in no change for poor families and their children.

Family Support Act and PRWORA

Although touted as an end to welfare as we know it, these new reforms are viewed by some, rather, as an incremental change in welfare policy. Prior to the passage of the PRWORA in 1996, more than half of all states had already begun implementing experimental welfare plans to move recipients off welfare and into the job market. The essential difference of the PRWORA, however, is that it marks the end of federal entitlement programs and the beginning of greater state control over welfare disbursement (Duncan & Brooks-Gunn, 1998).

Moving individuals from welfare dependence to work is not a new concept. Historically, in fact, poor mothers have been more likely to seek employment than middle-class mothers (Chase-Lansdale & Vinovskis, 1995). A four-fold increase in maternal employment from the 1960s to the 1980s (U.S. Bureau of the Census, 1988) further strengthened the opinion in Congress that mothers receiving economic aid should also be expected to work (see *Welfare: Reform or Replacement?*, 1987). In addition to this demographic change in U.S. society, Chase-Lansdale and Vinovskis (1995) also cited bipartisan support for welfare change in Congress, a better understanding of patterns of welfare dependence, and program innovations at the state level as other factors leading to the passage of the Family Support Act of 1988.

The primary objective of the Family Support Act was to assist recipients of Aid to Families with Dependent Children (AFDC) in becoming financially independent. At its core was the establishment of the Job Opportunity and Basic Skills Training Program (JOBS), which required states to provide welfare recipients with job training and educational opportunities. Along with the general trend to make work mandatory, many states had already begun welfare to work demonstration programs, with mixed results (see Cohen, 1997; Gueron & Pauly, 1991; Wiseman, 1996). In 1996, the PRWORA replaced the JOBS program and ended the state requirement to provide training and basic education, moving the focus from job training to immediate job placement, regardless of skill or educational level. Notably missing in both reforms, however, is a serious consideration of how the new changes will affect the well-being of children. At the time of the Family Support Act, Ron Haskins, staff director of the Subcommittee on Human Resources, U.S. House of Representatives, attributed this oversight, in part, to the fact that, "nobody [knew] much about the impact of either welfare or welfare reform on children" (1995, p. 243).

What do we know about children and welfare reform? Does the new welfare reform policy address issues vital to child well-being? Are the policies undergirded by an understanding of the pathways through which poverty affects children? How will the newly changed structure of welfare delivery direct future research investigations?

Children and Welfare Reform

Although sufficient time has not elapsed for researchers to measure the impact of the new welfare reforms on child outcomes, one can make reasonable predictions about a program's potential efficacy by examining what is known about poverty and its effects on child well-being. Research shows that poverty's effects are most pronounced for children who are very poor, persistently poor, or poor during their first five years of life (Brooks-Gunn & Duncan, 1997). The most effective reforms for child well-being would intervene at these levels.

In an analysis of governmental benefit programs (both cash and noncash benefits), a comparison was made between the number of poor individuals before ("pre-transfer poverty") and after ("post-transfer poverty") program benefits were counted. The study found that in 1995, the number of children in poor families would have been 17.1 million (pre-transfer) had governmental programs not reduced it to 11.4 million (post-transfer) (Primus, 1997). This indicates that 33% of children who would have been poor without governmental aid were removed from poverty. Despite these results, 20.5% of U.S. children under 18 are still living in poverty (U.S. Bureau of the Census, 1996). Clearly, governmental programs are not doing enough.

The PRWORA of 1996 replaces the 60-year-old Aid to Families with Dependent Children (AFDC) with block grants controlled by each state. Whereas AFDC was an entitlement program (i.e., all eligible families received assistance), the new block grants (also referred to as Temporary Aid to Needy Families or TANF) end this entitlement, giving each individual state the authority to decide who receives benefits. Critics of the new reforms predict that benefits under TANF will likely be lower than they were under AFDC. Plotnick (1997) cited three rationales for this prediction. First, financial incentives no longer favor raises in benefit levels. Under the new reforms, a raise in benefits is paid out of state funds, whereas a decrease in benefits results in savings for the state. Prior to the reforms, increases were subsidized by the federal government and decreases were returned to the federal government. Second, TANF funds will grow slowly and are more susceptible to fluctuations in the economy, especially in the event of a recession. Third, some poor families may no longer qualify for service delivery programs, thus decreasing overall benefits even if cash benefits remain the same.

The TANF block grant also carries stipulations, the most publicized of which are a cancellation of cash benefits for those who do not obtain employment within a certain time limit (usually two years) and a 5-year lifetime limit on total welfare receipt. The time limits for obtaining allowable work activities under TANF vary between states, with Texas imposing the shortest time limit (12 months) and other states allowing recipients as much as five years or more to find employment. Although states may exempt 20% of their caseloads from the lifetime limits, Duncan, Harris, and Boisjoly (1997) predicted that close to 50% of the states' caseloads—more than twice the allowed exemption—will exceed their lifetime limits within 8 years.

These new dimensions of the welfare system will have a direct effect on both the depth and persistence of poverty in many U.S. households. Duncan and Brooks-Gunn (1998) predicted that the new reforms may have more of an impact on the distribution of poverty than on the average level of poverty. Two diverging groups are expected to emerge: those who make the transition from welfare to work and those who do not. The result of this change will be a larger gap between the poorest and better-off low-income children. Although some will benefit from increased economic opportunities, others will be pushed even deeper into poverty. As employment options diminish and welfare limits are reached, the children in families of the hard core jobless will most likely face a double jeopardy: both deep and persistent poverty.

The TANF time limits and sanctions will also influence the number of children experiencing poverty at a young age. Mothers of children as young as one year are not exempt from the work requirement in most states. Some states grant more lenient provisions (until the child's third birthday), whereas others are more stringent (granting an exemption only until the child is three months old). The entry of these mothers into the work place will likely create added economic hardships with regard to child care and transportation. Due to financial constraints, some may be forced to enroll their children in substandard child care. Even then, employment is not always a ticket out of poverty. In fact, a significant portion of year-round, full-time workers earn less than the poverty threshold for a four-person family. In 1989, among White and African American full-time workers, 39% and 42% (respectively) between the ages of 18 and 24, and 15% and 22% between the ages of 25 and 34, had low earnings, according to this definition (Kaplan, 1997). Further, a study by Edin and Lein (1997) reported that nearly all welfare recipients are working in some form, yet all remained below the poverty threshold (see Brooks-Gunn, Smith, Berlin, & Lee, in press). In a recent analysis, the outcomes of young children whose mothers left welfare were similar to those whose mothers did not leave welfare, except for the group whose mothers had mothers above the poverty threshold (Smith, Brooks-Gunn, Kohen, & McCormick, 1998).

It is also important to note that the drive to enlist single mothers in the workforce is often fueled by the assumption that working conditions faced by parents living in poverty are similar to those faced by middle-income parents. This assumption is quite false. In an analysis of data from the National Longitudinal Survey of Youth (NLSY), working parents who had received welfare in the past were significantly more likely to lack paid sick leave, paid vacation leave, and job flexibility in their jobs than working parents who had never received welfare (Heymann & Earle, 1997). This finding is underscored by the fact that it describes working conditions at a time when the move from welfare to work was voluntary, rather than mandated.

Policies and Pathways

Clearly, childhood poverty will not be eliminated through governmental programs and welfare reforms alone. As stated previously, the strongest links found between poverty and poor child outcomes are in the domains of physical health (Miller & Korenman, 1994; Brody et al., 1994) and cognitive ability (Brooks-Gunn & Duncan, 1997). Therefore, the most comprehensive and effective plan would couple programs designed to move children out of poverty with programs designed to mitigate poverty's effects, especially in the physical and cognitive domains.

Governmental aid to poor families falls into two broad categories: cash transfer and service (in-kind) benefit programs. *Cash programs* are designed to provide cash assistance directly to poor families, thus increasing household income. *Service delivery programs*, on the other hand, target a child's basic needs for food, housing, medical care, and early education in the form of vouchers, coupons, and services, rather than through cash allocation.

The Earned Income Tax Credit (EITC) grants income tax credit to low-income families with children. It has been effective in moving 1.4 million people (approximately one million of whom were children) out of poverty (Primus, 1997) and alleviating the depth of poverty for about 18 million families (Plotnick, 1997). It is unknown how the new welfare laws will affect EITC benefits; however, critics predict that the negative effects wrought by PRWORA benefit decreases may override the positive impact of the EITC.

Also essential in the endeavor to improve child outcomes is an understanding of the pathways through which poverty influences child well-being. These pathways, as discussed previously, are health and nutrition, parent mental health, parenting behavior, home environment, and neighborhood.

Service delivery programs, such as Women, Infants and Children (WIC), Medicaid, Head Start, Food Stamps, and the National School Lunch Program, have been shown to mitigate some of the ill effects of poverty in the realm of health and nutrition (Devaney, Ellwood, & Love, 1997). There are few large governmental programs, however, specifically geared toward improving the home environment, parent–child interactions, or the neighborhoods of low-income families (the exception is Head Start, which serves about one third of those children who are eligible). Due to the more private and personal nature of these domains, grassroots and community-based interventions may have a stronger impact than those imposed by the government.

Interventions addressing both home environment and parent–child interactions through modeling and teaching parenting skills, such as the Learning Games curriculum (see Sparling & Lewis, 1984) and others, have been shown to improve parenting behavior and child language and school readiness (Benasich, Brooks-

Gunn, & Clewell, 1992; Brooks-Gunn, Berlin, & Fuligni, in press). Home interventions are most effective when they are frequent (several times per month), extensive (several years in duration), and focused on specific behaviors and interactions (Barnett, 1995; Ramey & Ramey, 1992; Berlin, O'Neal, & Brooks-Gunn, 1998; Weiss, 1993).

Other programs designed to improve child well-being take into account parent health and education. As more parents enter the workforce, however, their physical and mental health may not necessarily improve due to a lack of social support, increased time and financial pressures, and lack of insurance benefits. Analyses of the National Survey of Midlife Development in the United States (MIDUS) revealed that low-income working parents in the United States were less likely to have friends, family, neighbors, and coworkers on whom they could rely for help (Heymann & Earle, 1997). Low-income working parents are also less likely to have savings on which they can draw in times of unexpected emergencies. To compound the situation, a reported 52% of poor, full-time workers lack health insurance (U.S. Bureau of the Census, 1996).

With the current publicity that welfare reform is receiving, it is difficult to ignore the information regarding the status of children and welfare. Emerging areas of research, in light of the new welfare reforms, are state-level comparisons and program analyses. TANF block grants are based on past welfare expenditures by states. As the funding for each state varies, we are likely to see vast differences between states in the quality and comprehensiveness of service and aid delivery. We are also likely to see more private, nonprofit, or community-level programs compete for federal grants. It will be years before we have a definitive account of the effects of welfare reform on children. The challenge now is to identify and aid those children slipping through the new holes in the safety net.

CONCLUSION

Poverty is a more normative situation for children in the United States than we would like. One in five children (and one in four under the age of six) live at or below the poverty threshold. The proportions are even higher if one looks at basic needs budgets (Ruggles, 1990), illustrating how many families struggle to make ends meet. Hernandez (1997), using 50% of the median income (a measure more akin to that used in other Western countries), estimated that one in three of all children live in families having difficulty making ends meet. The children in these families enter the world at a disadvantage. They are more likely to be low birth weight, exhibit growth stunting, live in high-risk neighborhoods, lack positive parental interactions, and have poorer school achievement than their nonpoor counterparts. Although there is more broad-based support for programs that offer benefits directly to children (bypassing the caretaker), a consideration of the pathways through which poverty effects children makes it impossible to disentangle the two groups; poor children do not grow up independently from their families.

In order to create lasting changes for children in poverty, their parents must be included in the equation. For many parents currently on welfare, aid will come in the form of employment. Yet as the split between employed and unemployed poor families widens, new efforts must be made to meet the needs of the emerging class of deeply poor.

ACKNOWLEDGMENT

The authors were supported by grants from the National Institute of Child Health and Human Development (NICHD) Research Network on Child and Family Well-being, the Spencer Foundation, the W.T. Grant foundation, the Canadian Institute for Advanced Research (CIAR), the Russell Sage Foundation, and the MacArthor Network on Family and Work during the writing of this chapter. We also are deeply appreciative of our collaboration with Greg Duncan.

REFERENCES

Adler, N. E., Boyce, T., Chesney, M. A., Cohen, S., Folkman, S., Kahn, R. L., & Syme, S. L. (1994). Socioeconomic status and health: The challenge of the gradient. *American Psychologist, 49*(1), 15–24.

Ashworth, K., Hill, M., & Walker, R. (1994). Patterns of childhood poverty: The dynamics of spell. *Journal of Policy Analysis and Management, 13*(4), 658–680.

Axinn, W., Duncan, G. J., & Thorton, A. (1997). The effects of parents' income, wealth, and attitudes on children's completed schooling and self esteem. In G. J. Duncan & J. Brooks-Gunn (Eds.), *Consequences of growing up poor* (pp. 518–540). New York: Russell Sage Foundation Press.

Barnett, W. S. (1995). Long-term effects of early childhood programs on cognitive and school outcomes. *The Future of Children, 5*(3), 25–50.

Benasich, A. A., Brooks-Gunn, J., & Clewell, B. C. (1992). How do mothers benefit from early intervention programs? *Journal of Applied Developmental Psychology, 13*, 311- 362.

Berlin, L. J., Brooks-Gunn, J., Spiker, D., & Zaslow, M. J. (1995). Examining observational measures of emotional support and cognitive stimulation in black and white mothers of preschoolers. *Journal of Family Issues, 16*(5), 664–686.

Berlin, L. J., O'Neal, C. R., & Brooks-Gunn, J. (1998). What makes early intervention programs work? The program, its participants, and their interaction. In L. J. Berlin (Ed.), Opening the black box: What makes early child and family development programs work? [Special issue]. *Zero to three, 18,* 4–15.

Bradley, R. H., Caldwell, B. M., Rock, S. L., Ramey, C. T., Barnard, K. E., Gray, C., Hammond, M. A., Mitchell, S., Gottfried, A. W., Siegel, L., & Johnson, D. L. (1989). Home environment and cognitive development in the first three years of life: A collaborative study involving six sites and three ethnic groups in North America. *Developmental Psychology, 25,* 217–235.

Brody, D. J., Pirkle, J. L., Kramer, R., Flegal, K. M., Matte, T. D., Gunter, E. W., & Paschal, D. C. (1994). Blood levels in the U.S. population. *Journal of the American Medical Association, 272*(4), 277–283.

Brooks-Gunn, J. (1995). Children and families in communities: Risk and intervention in the Bronfenbrenner tradition. In P. Moen, G. H. Elder, & K. Lusher (Eds.), *Examining lives in context: Perspective on the ecology of human development* (pp. 467–519). Washington DC: American Psychological Association Press.

Brooks-Gunn, J., Berlin, L. J., & Fuligni, A. S. (in press). Early childhood intervention programs:

What about the family? In J. P. Shonkoff & S. J. Meisels (Eds.), *Handbook on early childhood intervention* (2nd ed.). New York: Cambridge University Press.

Brooks-Gunn, J., & Duncan, G. J. (1997). The Effects of poverty on children. *Futures of Children, 7*(2), 55–71.

Brooks-Gunn, J., Duncan, G. J., & Aber, J. L. (Eds.). (1997). *Neighborhood Poverty: Context and consequences for children: Vol. 1. Six studies of children in families in neighborhoods.* New York: Russell Sage Foundation Press.

Brooks-Gunn, J., Duncan, G. J., Klebanov, P. K., & Sealand, N. (1993). Do neighborhoods influence child and adolescent development? *American Journal of Sociology, 99*(2), 353–395.

Brooks-Gunn, J., Duncan, G. J., & Maritato, N. (1997). Poor families, poor outcomes: The well-being of children and youth. In G. Duncan & J. Brooks-Gunn (Eds.), *Consequences of growing up poor* (pp. 1–17). New York: Russell Sage Foundation Press.

Brooks-Gunn, J., Klebanov, P. K., & Duncan, G. J. (1996). Ethnic differences in children's intelligence test scores: Role of economic deprivation, home environment, and maternal characteristics. *Child Development, 67,* 396–408.

Brooks-Gunn, J., Smith, J., Berlin, L. J., & Lee, K. (in press). Familywork: Welfare changes, parenting and young children. In G. K. Brookins (Ed.), *Exits from poverty.* New York: Cambridge University Press.

Bumpass, L. (1984). Children and marital disruption: A replication and update. *Demography, 21,* 71–82.

Buss, T., & Redburn, F. S. (1983). *Mass unemployment: Plant closings and community mental health.* Beverly Hills, CA: Sage.

Caldwell, B. & Bradley, R. H. (1984). *Home Observation for Measurement of the Environment.* Little Rock: University of Arkansas, Center for Research on Teaching and Learning.

Chase-Lansdale, P. L., & Vinovskis, M. A. (1995). Whose responsibility? An historical analysis of the changing roles of mothers, fathers, and society. In P. L. Chase-Lansdale & J. Brooks-Gunn (Eds.), *Escape from poverty: What makes a difference for children?* (pp. 11–37). New York: Cambridge University Press.

Cherlin, A. (1992). *Marriage, divorce, remarriage.* Cambridge, MA: Harvard University Press.

Cohen, S. (1997). What's working? Lessons from the front lines of welfare reform. *Manhattan Institute, 1,* 1–19.

Coiro, M. J., Zill, N., & Bloom, B. (1994). Health of our nation's children. *Vital Health and Statistics* (Series 10, no. 191). Hyattsville, MD: U.S. Department of Health and Human Services, Public Health Service.

Conger, R., Conger, K., & Elder, G. H. (1997). Family economic hardship and adolescent adjustment: Mediating and moderating processes. In G. J. Duncan & J. Brooks-Gunn (Eds.), *Consequences of growing up poor* (pp. 288–310). New York: Russell Sage Foundation Press.

Conger, R., Conger, K., Elder, G., Lorenz, F., Simons, R., & Whitbeck, L. (1992). A family process model of economic hardship and adjustment of early adolescent boys. *Child Development, 63,* 526–541.

Corcoran, M. E., & Adams, T. (1997). Race, sex, and the inter-generational transmission of poverty. In G. J. Duncan & J. Brooks-Gunn (Eds.), *Consequences of growing up poor* (pp. 461–517). New York: Russell Sage Foundation Press.

Corcoran, M. E., & Chaudry, A. (1997). The dynamics of childhood poverty. *Futures of Children, 7*(2), 40–54.

Crnic, K., & Greenberg, M. (1987). Maternal stress, social support, and coping: Influences on early mother–child relationships. In C. Boukydis (Ed.), *Research on support for parents and infants in the postnatal period* (pp.25–40). Norwood, NJ: Ablex.

Currie, J. M. (1997). Choosing among alternative programs for poor children. *The Future of Children, 7*(2), 113–131.

Danzinger, S., & Goltschalk, P. (1995). *America unequal.* Cambridge, MA: Harvard University Press.

Dawson, D. A. (1991). Family structure and children's health: United States, 1988. *Vital Health and*

Statistics (Series 10, no. 178). Hyattsville, MD: U.S. Department of Health and Human Services, Public Health Service.

Devaney, B. L., Ellwood, M. R., & Love, J. M. (1997). Programs that mitigate the effects of poverty on children. *The Future of Children, 7*(2), 88–112.

Duncan, G. J. (1991). The economic environment of childhood. In A. C. Huston (Ed.), *Children in poverty: Child development and public policy* (pp. 23–50). New York: Cambridge University Press.

Duncan, G. J., & Brooks-Gunn, J. (Eds.). (1997). *Consequences of growing up poor.* New York: Russell Sage Foundation Press.

Duncan, G. J., & Brooks-Gunn, J. (1998). Welfare's new rules: A pox on children. *Issues in Science and Technology, 14*(2), 67–72.

Duncan, G. J., Brooks-Gunn, J., & Klebanov, P. K. (1994). Economic deprivation and early-childhood development. *Child Development, 65*(2), 296–318.

Duncan, G. J., Harris, K. M., & Boisjoly, J. (1997). *Time limits and welfare reform: New estimates of the number and characteristics of affected families* [On-line]. Available: http://ww.spc.uchicago.edu/PovertyCenter.htm

Duncan, G. J., & Rogers, W. (1988). Longitudinal aspects of childhood poverty. *Journal of Marriage and the Family, 50*(4), 1007–1021.

Duncan, G. J., Yeung, W., Brooks-Gunn, J., & Smith, J. R. (1998). How much does childhood poverty affect the life chances of children? *American Sociological Review, 63*(3), 406–423.

Edin, K., & Lein, L. (1997). *Making ends meet: How single mothers survive welfare and low-wage work.* New York: Russell Sage Foundation.

Elder, G. H., Jr. (1974). *Children of the great depression: Social change in life experience.* Chicago: University of Chicago Press.

Elder, G. H., Jr. (1979). Historical change in life patterns and personality. In P. Baltes & O. Brim (Eds.), *Life span development and behavior* (Vol. 2, pp. 117–159). New York, Academic Press.

Elder, G. H., Jr., Nguyen, T., & Caspi, A. (1985). Linking family hardship to children's lives. *Child Development, 56,* 361–375.

Federman, M., Garner, T., Short, K., Cutter, W. B., Kiely, J., Levine, D., McGough, D., & McMillen, M. (1996). What does it mean to be poor in America? *Monthly Labor Review, 119*(5), 3–17.

Furstenberg, F. F., Jr., Brooks-Gunn, J., & Morgan, S. P. (1987). *Adolescent mothers in later life.* New York: Cambridge University Press.

Galambos, N., & Silbereisen, R. (1987). Influences of income change and parental acceptance on adolescent transgression proneness and peer relations. *European Journal of Psychology of Education, 1,* 17–28.

Garcia Coll, C., Meyer E., & Brillon, L. (1995). Ethnic and minority parenting. In M. Bornstein (Ed.), *Handbook of parenting* (pp. 189–209). Hillsdale, NJ: Lawrence Earlbuam Associates.

Garcia Coll, C., Lamberty, G., Jenkins, R., McAdoo, H. P., Crnic, K., Wasik, B. H., & Vásquez García, H. (1996). An integrative model for the study of developmental competencies in minority children. *Child Development, 67,* 1891–1914.

Garrett, P., Ng'andu, N., & Ferron, J. (1994). Poverty experiences of young children and the quality of their home environments. *Child Development, 65,* 331–345.

Gueron, J. M., & Pauly, E. (1991). *From welfare to work.* New York: Russell Sage Foundation.

Hanson, T. L., McLanahan, S., & Thomson, E. (1997). Economic resources, parental practices, and children's well-being. In G. Duncan & J. Brooks-Gunn (Eds.), *Consequences of growing up poor* (pp. 190–238). New York: Russell Sage Foundation Press.

Haskins, R. (1995). Losing ground or moving ahead? Welfare reform and children. In P. L. Chase-Lansdale & J. Brooks-Gunn (Eds.), *Escape from poverty: What makes a difference for children?* (pp. 241–271). New York: Cambridge University Press.

Hauser, R. M., & Sweeney, M. M. (1997). Does poverty in adolescence affect the life chances of high school graduates? In G. J. Duncan & J. Brooks-Gunn (Eds.), *Consequences of growing up poor* (pp. 190–238). New York: Russell Sage Foundation Press.

Haveman, R., & Wolfe, B. (1994). *Succeeding generations: On the effects of investments in children.* New York: Russell Sage Foundation.

Haveman, R., & Wolfe, B. (1995). The determinants of children's attainments: A review of methods and findings. *Journal of Economic Literature, 33*(4), 1829–1878.

Haveman, R., Wolfe, B., & Spaulding, J. (1991). Childhood events and circumstances influencing high school completion. *Demography, 28*(1), 133–157.

Haveman, R., Wolfe, B., & Wilson, K. (1997). Childhood poverty and adolescent schooling and fertility outcomes: Reduced-form and structural estimates. In G. J. Duncan & J. Brooks-Gunn (Eds.), *Consequences of growing up poor* (pp. 419–460). New York: Russell Sage Foundation Press.

Hernandez, D. J. (1997). Poverty trends. In G. J. Duncan & J. Brooks-Gunn (Eds.), *Consequences of growing up poor* (pp. 18–34). New York: Russell Sage Foundation Press.

Heymann, S. J., & Earle, A. (1997). *Working conditions: What do parents leaving welfare and low income parents face?* (Working paper No. H-97-01). Boston: Harvard University, Malcolm Weiner Center for Social Policy.

Jackson, A., Gyamfi, P., & Brooks-Gunn, J. (in press). Employment status, social support, and physical discipline practices of single black mothers. *Journal of Marriage and Family.*

Kaplan, T. (1997). *Welfare policy and caseloads in the United States: Historical background* (Special Report No. 70). Madison: University of Wisconsin-Madison, Institute for Research on Poverty.

Klebanov, P. K., Brooks-Gunn, J., Chase-Lansdale, L., & Gordon, R. (1997). Are neighborhood effects on young children mediated by features of the home environment? In J. Brooks-Gunn, G. J. Duncan, & J. L. Aber (Eds.), *Neighborhood poverty: Context and consequences for children: Vol. 1* (pp. 119–145). New York: Russell Sage Foundation Press.

Klebanov, P. K., Brooks-Gunn, J., McCarton, C. & McCormick, M. M. (in press). The contribution of neighborhood and family income upon developmental test scores over the first three years of life. *Child Development.*

Kohen, D. E. (1997). *Parenting behaviors: Associated characteristics and child outcomes.* Unpublished doctoral dissertation, Teachers College, Columbia University, New York.

Korenman, S., Miller, J. E., & Sjaastad, J. E. (1995). Long term poverty and child development: Evidence from the NLSY. *Children and Youth Services, 17*(1–2), 127–155.

Liaw, F. R., & Brooks-Gunn, J. (1994). Cumulative risk and low-birth weight children's cognitive development and their determinants. *Developmental Psychology, 29,* 1024–1035.

Linver, M., Brooks-Gunn, J., & Kohen, D. (1998). *Effects of poverty and of intervention group on children's cognitive and socioemotional development.* Manuscript submitted for publication.

Mayer, S. E. (1997). *What money can't buy: Family income and children's life chances.* Cambridge, MA: Harvard University Press.

McAdoo, H. P. (1986). Strategies used by Black single mothers against stress. In M. Simms & J. Malveaux (Eds.), *Slipping through the cracks: The status of Black women* (pp. 153–166). New Brunswick, NJ: Transaction Books.

McLanahan, S. (1997). Parent absence or poverty: Which matters more? In G. J. Duncan & J. Brooks-Gunn (Eds.), *Consequences of growing up poor* (pp. 35–48). New York: Russell Sage Foundation Press.

McLanahan, S., & Sandefur, G. D. (1994). *Growing up with a single parent: What hurts, what helps?* Cambridge, MA: Harvard University Press.

McLeod, J. D., & Shanahan, M. J. (1993). Poverty, parenting, and children's mental health. *American Sociological Review, 58*(3), 351–366.

McLoyd, V. C. (1989). Socialization and development in a changing economy: The effects of paternal job and income loss on children. *American Psychologist, 44,* 293–302.

McLoyd, V. C. (1990). The impact of economic hardship on Black families and children: Psychological distress, parenting, and socioemotional development. *Child Development, 61,* 311–346.

McLoyd, V. C., Jayaratne, T., Ceballo, R., & Borquez, J. (1994). Unemployment and work interruption among African-American single mothers: Effects on parenting and socio-emotional functioning. *Child Development, 65,* 562–589.

McLoyd, V. C., & Wilson, L. (1991). The strain of living poor: Parenting, social support, and child mental health. In A. C. Huston (Ed.), *Children in poverty: Child development and public policy* (pp. 105–135). New York: Cambridge University Press.

Miller, J., & Korenman, S. (1994). Poverty and children's nutritional status in the United States. *American Journal of Epidemiology, 140*(3), 233–243.

National Center for Educational Statistics. (1994, October). *Dropout rates in the United States: 1994* [On-line]. Available: http://www.ed.gov/NCES/pubs/r9410t07.html

National Health and Nutrition Examination Survey III. (1988/1991). Bethesda, MD: U.S. Department of Health and Human Services.

Ogbu, J. (1981). Origins of human competence: A cultural-ecological perspective. *Child Development, 52*, 413–429.

Ogbu, J. (1988). Cultural diversity and human development. In D. T. Slaughter (Ed.), Black children and poverty: A developmental perspective [Special issue]. *New Directions for Child Development, 42*, 11–28.

Orshansky, M. (1988). Counting the poor: Another look at the poverty profile. *Social Security Bulletin, 51*(10), 25–51.

Pagani, L., Boulerice, B., & Tremblay, R. E. (1997). The influence of poverty on children's classroom placement and behavior problems. In G. J. Duncan & J. Brooks-Gunn (Eds.), *Consequences of growing up poor* (pp. 311–339). New York: Russell Sage Foundation Press.

Patterson, G. (1986). Performance models for antisocial boys. *American Psychologist, 41*, 434–444.

Peters, H. E., & Mullis, N. C. (1997). The role of family income and sources of income in adolescent achievement. In G. J. Duncan & J. Brooks-Gunn (Eds.), *Consequences of growing up poor* (pp. 340–381). New York: Russell Sage Foundation Press.

Plotnick, R. D. (1997). Child poverty can be reduced. *The Future of Children, 7*(2), 72–87.

Primus, W. (1997, November 15). The safety net delivers. *Center on Budget and Policy Priorities* [On-line]. Available: http://www.cbpp.org/SAFETY.htm

Ramey, C. T. & Ramey, S. L. (1992). Early educational intervention with disadvantaged children and low income families: To what effect? *Applied and Preventive Psychology, 1*(3), 131–140.

Ray, S. A., & McLoyd, V. C. (1986). Fathers in hard times: The impact of unemployment and poverty on paternal and marital relations. In. M. Lamb (Ed.), *The father's role* (pp. 339–383). New York: Wiley.

Rogot, E. (1992). *A mortality study of 1.3 million persons by demographic, social, and economic factors: 1979–1985 follow-up.* Rockville, MD: National Institutes of Health.

Ruggles, P. (1990). *Drawing the line: Alternative poverty measures and their implications.* Washington, DC: Urban Institute Press.

Salkind, N. J., & Haskins, R. (1982). Negative income tax: The impact on children from low-income families. *Journal of Family Issues, 3*(2), 165–180.

Sameroff, A. J., Seifer, R., Baldwin, A., & Baldwin, C. (1993). Stability of intelligence from preschool to adolescence: The influence of social and family risk factors. *Child Development, 64*, 80–97.

Sameroff, A. J., Seifer, R., Barocas, R., Zax, M., & Greenspan, S. (1987). Intelligence quotient scores of 4-year-old children: Social and environmental risk factors. *Pediatrics, 79*, 343–350.

Sampson, R., & Morenoff, J. (1997). Ecological perspectives on the neighborhood context of urban poverty: Past and present. In J. Brooks-Gunn, G. J. Duncan, & J. L. Aber (Eds.), *Neighborhood poverty: Context and consequence for children: Vol. 2. Conceptual, methodological, and policy approaches to studying neighborhoods* (pp. 1–23). New York: Russell Sage Foundation Press.

Smith, J. R., & Brooks-Gunn, J. (1997). Correlates and consequences of mother's harsh discipline with young children. *Archives of Pediatric and Adolescent Medicine, 151*, 777–786.

Smith, J. R., Brooks-Gunn, J., & Klebanov, P. K. (1997). The consequences of living in poverty for young children's cognitive and verbal ability and early school achievement. In G. J. Duncan & J. Brooks-Gunn (Eds.), *Consequences of growing up poor* (pp. 132–189). New York: Russell Sage Foundation Press.

Smith, J., Brooks-Gunn, J., Kohen, D., & McCarton, C. (1998). *Transitions on and off welfare: Implications for parenting and children's cognitive development.* Manuscript under review.

Sparling, J. J., & Lewis, J. (1984). *Partners for learning.* Lewisville, NC: Kaplan.

Teachman, J. D., Paasch, K. M., Day, R. D., & Carver, K. P. (1997). Poverty during adolescence and subsequent educational attainment. In G. J. Duncan & J. Brooks-Gunn (Eds.), *Consequences of growing up poor* (pp. 382–418). New York: Russell Sage Foundation Press.

Teti, D., Gelfand, D., & Pompa, J. (1990). Depressed mothers' behavioral competence with their infants: Demographic and psychosocial correlates. *Development and Psychopathology, 2,* 259–270.

U.S. Bureau of the Census. (1988). *Fertility of American women: June 1987* (Current Population Reports, Series P-20, No. 427). Washington, DC: U.S. Government Printing Office.

U.S. Bureau of the Census (1996). *Poverty in the United States: 1995* (Current Population Survey, No. P60-194). Washington, DC: U.S. Government Printing Office.

Ventura, S. J. (1995). *Births to unmarried mothers: United States, 1980–1992* (NCHS Series 21, No. 53). U.S. Department of Health and Human Services, Washington, DC: U.S. Government Printing Office.

Weiss, H. (1993). Home visits: Necessary but not sufficient. *The Future of Children, 3*(3), 113–128.

Welfare: Reform or replacement? (Work and welfare): Hearing before the Subcommittee on Social Security and Family Policy of the Committee on Finance, United States Senate, 100th Cong. (February 23, 1987).

Wilson, W. J. (1987). *The truly disadvantaged: The inner city, the underclass, and public policy.* Chicago: University of Chicago Press.

Wiseman, M. (1996). Some strategies for welfare reform: The Wisconsin story. *Journal of Policy Analysis and Management, 15*(4), 526–540.

Chapter 15

Violent Families

Kathleen J. Sternberg
Michael E. Lamb
National Institute of Child Health and Human Development

Although we prefer not to think about it, family violence is a remarkably common occurrence. The statistics reported later in this chapter reveal that between 0.5% and 10% of the children and 16% of the parents or parent-surrogates in the United States experience violence at the hands of intimates every year (Frieze & Browne, 1989; Straus & Gelles, 1990). Some children and adults are victimized year after year, whereas isolated incidents may characterize other families, making it difficult to estimate exactly how many children are exposed to some form of family violence at any time during their childhoods. Clearly, however, the numbers are considerable.

Of course, violence does not occur continuously even in the most violence-ridden families. It is important that we recognize and understand the ways in which these families function at times when overt physical abuse is not occurring because these nonviolent experiences may shape children's development in important ways. The goal of this chapter is to review the available evidence—neither comprehensive nor coherent—on the associations among family violence, interactional dynamics, parent–child relationships, and major aspects of child development.

Since the 1970s, there has been increased public awareness of child and spouse abuse and their impact on children's development and mental health. These concerns have fostered a body of research that began with case studies and clinical reports and is developing into a field characterized by careful and systematic scientific inquiry. Unfortunately, however, the study of family violence has been hampered by logistic, ethical, and sociopolitical issues that complicate research and necessitate a number of methodological compromises. Although research designs have improved considerably in recent years, a number of problems still exist, including the failure to document all types of abuse in families being studied, lack of specificity about the perpetrators of the various types of violence in the family, and reliance on single informants (usually mothers) for information about both family history and the effects on children (Fantuzzo & Lindquist, 1988; Sternberg, 1997; Sternberg, Lamb, & Dawud-Noursi, 1998; Weis, 1989).

The chapter begins with a discussion of incidence and prevalence statistics concerning child maltreatment, spouse abuse, and their co-occurrence. This information is important not only because it underscores how many children may be exposed to family violence, but also because closer examination of incidence figures illustrates how difficult it is to understand the phenomenon of family violence in its full complexity. We then review studies designed to compare parent–child interactions in violent and non-violent families. In this section, we emphasize research depicting children's perceptions of their parents and highlight the need to discriminate between perpetrating and non-perpetrating parents.

THE INCIDENCE OF FAMILY VIOLENCE

Many researchers have attempted to determine how many children are victims of child abuse or witnesses of spousal violence. Obviously, estimates of the incidence of child and spouse abuse differ as a function of how these behaviors are defined, the source of information (e.g., victim, parent, service records), the research design, and a variety of other factors. Unfortunately, however, these nuances are frequently overlooked as statistics are selectively used by advocates and policy makers to support their positions. In this section we review survey-based estimates of children's exposure to child and spouse violence.

Incidence of Physical Child Abuse

Diverse strategies have been employed in attempts to estimate the incidence of child abuse. The National Center on Child Abuse and Neglect (NCCAN) has commissioned three national incidence studies—NIS-1 (NCCAN, 1981), NIS-2 (NC-CAN, 1988), and NIS-3 (Sedlack & Broadhurst, 1996)—to assess the incidence of child maltreatment using information collected from nationally representative samples of county service agencies (schools, Child Protective Services [CPS] agencies, etc.). In the NIS-1, the definition of maltreatment was based on a standard of harm (whether the child was actually injured) whereas in NIS-2 and NIS-3 the definition was based on a standard of harm and endangerment (whether the child was at risk of harm). By the latter definition, in 1986, approximately 0.5% of the children under 18 were physically abused, 0.2% were sexually abused, and 0.3% were neglected. Data reported in 1993 in the NIS-3 indicated that 0.9% of children were at risk for physical abuse, 0.5% were at risk for sexual abuse, and 0.8% were at risk for emotional abuse. The numbers reflect a significant increase between 1986 and 1993 in all types of maltreatment. The authors attributed both heightened rates of reporting by community professionals and actual increases in the number of children being abused (Sedlack & Broadhurst, 1996).

Arguing that data collected from agency records are likely to underestimate the incidence and prevalence of family violence, meanwhile, researchers at the Universities of Rhode Island and New Hampshire conducted a series of nationally representative telephone surveys (Gelles & Straus, 1988; Straus & Gelles, 1986; Straus, Gelles, & Steinmetz, 1980). In the second such survey, conducted in 1985, 2.3% of the parents contacted reported they had punched, kicked, bit, burned, beaten, or threatened with a knife or gun a child between ages 3 and 17 in their household in the preceding twelve months. If one includes such incidents, as well as those in which children were hit with objects (sticks, belts, etc.), then a remarkable 11% of the parents admitted abusing their children in the previous year (Straus & Gelles, 1990). Based on the stricter definition of abuse, there were no age differences in the incidence of child abuse.

Finkelhor and Dziuba-Leatherman (1994) subsequently used a similar methodology when interviewing 2,000 10-to-16-year-old children about victimization within and outside the family. Twenty-seven percent of the girls and 30% of the boys reported that their parents used corporal punishment in the previous year, whereas 71% percent of the girls and 78% percent of the boys reported experiencing corporal punishment at some time in their lives. With respect to more serious parent–child maltreatment, 0.9% of the children reported an incident (punching, slapping, kicking, hitting with an object, or threatening with a weapon) in the past year, and 2.2% reported at least one incident of maltreatment ever. It is interesting that children were more likely to be assaulted by nonparent family perpetrators (5%) and nonfamilial perpetrators (22%) than by parents. In addition, although two thirds of the youngsters disclosed the assault to someone, only one fourth reported the assaults to authorities.

It is difficult to compare the results of these different studies because the age of the target children, the source of data, and the definitions of abusive events vary across studies. Children in the Finkelhor and Dziuba-Leatherman (1994) sample reported lower rates of parent–child violence than parents in the Straus and Gelles surveys, for example, but the children's ages differed substantially (Gelles and Straus, 1988, focused on violence toward 0-to-17-year-old children, whereas Finkelhor and Dziuba-Leatherman focused on 10-to-17-year-old children). The discrepancies between the results of these two surveys, along with the discrepancies between their findings and those reported by the agencies surveyed for the NIS studies, illustrate how difficult it is to develop accurate estimates of incidence and underscore the importance of reading the fine print when evaluating statistics about child abuse and other types of violence in the family. Clearly, differences in sampling methodology influence the estimates obtained.

Differences Between Mothers and Fathers. Results of the major surveys indicate that female caretakers are more likely than male caretakers to be identified as perpetrators of physical child abuse (American Association for Protecting Children 1986; Gil, 1973; National Center on Child Abuse and Neglect [NCANN]

1988; Straus, Gelles, & Steinmetz, 1980; Wolfner & Gelles, 1993). Of course, female caretakers on average spend more time with children than male caretakers do, and some have estimated that fathers are more likely to be perpetrators of abuse than mothers when such differences in availability are taken into account (Lennington, 1981; Lightcap, Kurland, & Burgess, 1982; Malkin & Lamb, 1994). Using data collected from 11 states by the American Humane Society, Malkin and Lamb (1994) also reported that fathers engaged in more minor acts of abuse, whereas mothers engaged in more serious acts of abuse. These findings suggest that it is difficult to determine whether children are at greater risk of abuse by mothers or fathers and that the severity of abusive acts should also be considered.

Associations With Family Composition. Results of the Second Family Violence Survey suggested that, although overall rates of violence were the same in single-parent and two-parent households, single parents were significantly more likely to admit serious acts of violence directed toward their children than were parents from two-parent families (Gelles, 1989). Single fathers and single mothers were equally likely to behave violently toward their children, but single fathers were more likely to admit severe violence. In households headed by single mothers (but not single fathers), abuse was significantly correlated with poverty, although severe child abuse was most likely in families headed by single fathers earning less than $10,000 a year.

Differences Between Parents and Parent-Surrogates. In widely cited studies, Daly and Wilson (1984, 1996) reported that children living with stepfathers were significantly more likely to be abused and even killed than children living with their biological fathers. Because they focused on household composition rather than perpetrator identity, however, Daly and Wilson could not determine whether children were at heightened risk of being abused by their biological mothers, their stepfathers, or both. Malkin and Lamb (1994) found that biologically related caretakers were more likely to engage in major physical and fatal acts of child abuse whereas nonrelated caretakers were more likely to engage in minor acts of abuse. Although they reported that 28% of the children in this sample lived in families with one biological parent and one stepparent, however, Malkin and Lamb did not discuss differences between family units that included biological mothers and stepfathers as opposed to those that included stepmothers and biological fathers.

In sum, the available data suggest that between 1% and 10% of the children in the United States may be victims of physical abuse. Questions about the relative risks of abuse by mothers and fathers, nonrelated caretakers, and single parents cannot yet be answered with any confidence, however. In addition, specificity about the severity of violence appears crucial.

Incidence of Children Exposed to Spousal Violence

Depending on the operational definitions and the methodologies employed, somewhere between 10% and 30% of the families living in the United States experience spouse abuse (Geffner & Pagelow, 1990; Hughes, in press; Straus & Gelles, 1986). In the Second National Violence Study (Straus & Gelles, 1986), for example, 16% of U.S. couples reported experiencing a violent assault in 1985. Six percent of the reported incidents involved serious violence (e.g. kicking, punching, biting, or choking).

Although researchers did not systematically inquire about the whereabouts of children during violent fights between their parents until the late 1980s, there is now accumulating evidence that children often witness or overhear these events. Hughes, Parkinson, and Vargo (1989) reported that children were either in the same room or a room adjacent to the assault 90% of the time, whereas O'Brien, John, Margolin, and Erel (1994) reported that 25% of the 8- to 11-year-old children studied had witnessed husband-wife violence and wife-husband violence at least once in their lives. Fifty-eight percent of the women studied by Dobash and Dobash (1984) reported that children were present during assaults by their husbands.

Recognizing that many children are exposed to violence between their parents or parent figures raises many additional questions about the context of these violent experiences and their meaning for children. In order to understand how children are affected by these experiences, for example, researchers need to know more about the perpetrators' and victims' relationships with the children. Although most researchers have focused on female victims and male perpetrators, a review of the survey data suggests that men and women are equally likely to be victimized. In the Second National Violence Survey, approximately 3.4% of the women and men in the sample reported being severely assaulted (e.g., punched, bitten, burned, kicked, choked) by their partners in the previous year (Straus & Gelles, 1990), although women are presently much more likely to be injured in these incidents (Kurz, 1993; Straus, 1993). Indeed, a recent analysis of emergency room admissions indicated that women were nearly 10 times more likely than men to seek treatment following assault by their partners ("Study Finds," 1997). These differences in vulnerability may in turn moderate the effects on children of observing the victimization of mothers as opposed to fathers.

It may be important to consider the child's relationship with the violent adult as well. Quite possibly, children will be affected less when the violent adults are transient boyfriends rather than biological fathers or boyfriends with whom their mothers have had a long-term relationship. The National Crime Victimization Survey conducted by the Department of Justice (Bachman & Salzman, 1995) showed that women were more likely to be abused by boyfriends or ex-husbands than by husbands. In the 1992–1993 Survey, approximately 29% of simple and aggravated assaults were committed by intimates: 5% by spouses, 5% by ex-spouses, and 17% and 15% by boyfriends and girlfriends, respectively. It is interesting that most simple (41%) and aggravated (36%) assaults were committed by acquaintances or friends rather than by intimates. These results suggest that the most common perpetrators of violence against women may be transient or former figures in the women's lives rather than their children's father figures. It is important to keep this in mind when discussing the potential consequences for children.

Developmental Trends in Children's Exposure to Spousal Violence

Recent evidence suggests that exposure to parental violence often begins early in life, with a substantial number of children exposed to violence in utero. Sixteen percent of the women questioned in public prenatal health clinics in two large U.S. cities reported being abused during their pregnancy, usually by an intimate partner, and over half the women reported multiple incidents of violence during pregnancy (McFarlane, Parker, & Soeken, 1995). Severe abuse was correlated with a variety of other risk factors during pregnancy, including drug and alcohol abuse, smoking, and low maternal weight gain (McFarlane, Parker, & Soeken, 1996). Women who reported being abused during pregnancy were twice as likely to delay prenatal care until the third trimester of pregnancy and to deliver babies who weighed less at birth than those women who did not report abuse. These results confirm that spousal violence poses serious risk for pregnant women and their unborn infants and raise questions about the associations between abuse and other prenatal risk factors.

Fantuzzo and his colleagues (1997) later examined 2,400 substantiated reports of domestic violence in five major cities in the United States. Children were disproportionally represented in households where violence against women occurred and this was particularly true for children under five years of age, who were more likely to be exposed to multiple incidents of violence and other risks, including poverty and substantiated abuse. Many of the children in this sample were not passive observers but were reportedly involved in the violent incidents. Whether they are involved, many children apparently are exposed to risks associated with violence between the adults with whom they live.

Do Spouse and Child Abuse Tend to Co-Occur?

Are children from households where spouse abuse occurs more likely to be victims of child abuse? If so, are these children more likely to be abused by the parent who perpetrated the spousal violence, the nonperpetrating parent, or both? Answers to these questions would be extremely valuable to researchers, policymakers, and counselors, but unfortunately they are not yet available.

Based on data from the First and Second Family Violence Surveys, Straus and Gelles suggested that different types of family violence tended to co-occur (Straus et al., 1980; Straus & Gelles, 1990). Ordinary marital violence (pushing, slapping, or shoving) by husbands toward their wives was associated with an increase in violence by both fathers and mothers toward their children. In the Second National Family Violence Survey, Straus and Gelles (1990) extended this inquiry by exploring the roles of female perpetrators of spousal violence as well. They examined whether male and female perpetrators of spouse abuse were more likely to perpetrate child abuse than parents who were not violent with their partners. Their examination of the co-occurence of child and spouse abuse revealed interesting findings. Men who used any violent tactics toward their wives in the previous year (*n* = 357) were 40% more likely to slap or spank their children and 150% more likely to use severe violence (e.g., kicking, biting, punching, beating up, scalding, attacking with a weapon) with their children than men who were not violent with their wives. Women who used violence with their husbands in the previous year (*n* = 395) were 30% more likely to slap or spank their children and 145% more likely to use serious violence toward their children than women who did not beat their husbands. After examining whether perpetrating spouse abuse was related to perpetrating child abuse, Straus and Gelles proceeded to explore whether adult victims of spouse abuse were more likely to perpetrate child abuse when compared with adults who were not victims of spousal violence. The authors found that both male and female victims of spousal violence were approximately one and one half times more likely to abuse their children than parents who had not been abused by their spouses. Overall, the data from the Second Family Violence Survey suggest that when spousal violence occurs, children are at a higher risk of child abuse. It is interesting, furthermore, that children are as likely to be beaten by the perpetrators of spousal violence as by the victims.

Although some researchers have estimated that the co-incidence of child and spouse abuse ranges from 40 to 60% (for a review of these data, see Edelson, 1997), such estimates are problematic. In most of the studies used to estimate this range of co-occurrence, subjects were selected because child or spouse abuse had been reported (e.g. Hughes, 1988; Sun & Abel, 1990; Walker, 1984) and thus the data should not be used to estimate co-incidence in the population. Instead, nonselected population studies are needed to evaluate the co-incidence of child abuse and spouse abuse. Studies addressing this question would be extremely useful to researchers and policymakers alike.

Summary

Clearly, substantial numbers of children in the United States are exposed to family violence every year. Family violence takes a number of forms (e.g., child abuse, spouse abuse, both child and spouse abuse), however, with multiple possible variations in the children's relationship with both the perpetrators and victims. Family violence also varies with respect to its severity and chronicity, although we know little about chronicity and its impact. These variations are seldom taken into account when the correlates and consequences of domestic violence are studied. It seems likely that chronic but not severe abuse by both parents throughout childhood would have different effects on child development than would a single incident in which a child was injured severely when coming to the aid of his mother during a violent struggle with her boyfriend, for example.

Because it is so difficult to study family violence, we are only beginning to understand how children are affected by child and spouse abuse. In the future, researchers need to document the possible co-ocurrence of diverse types of mal-treatment and employ varied research methodologies to explore the effects on children.

EFFECTS OF DOMESTIC VIOLENCE
ON PARENT–CHILD RELATIONSHIPS

It is widely believed that both child abuse and the exposure to parental violence profoundly and adversely affect children's relationships with their parents, al-though the pattern of effects is not as consistent as readers might expect. In this section, we briefly summarize the reported effects and identify some sources of variation in the magnitude of these effects.

Parent–Child Relationships in Physically Abusive Families

Prompted by the belief that inappropriate parenting and hostile or abusive par-ent–child relationships foster deviant developmental outcomes, investigators be-gan examining the effects of physical abuse on children's relationships with their parents in the 1980s. According to attachment theory (Crittenden & Ainsworth, 1989), repeated experiences with abusive parents should make abused children mistrustful and predispose victims to form insecure attachment relationships. Re-searchers have indeed reported that abusive mothers are more hostile and intru-sive than nonabusive mothers from similar socioeconomic backgrounds (Critten-den, 1981; Lyons-Ruth, Connell, & Zoll, 1989) and that abused infants are often insecurely attached to their abusive parents (Carlson, Cicchetti, Barnett, & Braun-wald, 1989; Crittenden, 1988; Lamb, Gaensbauer, Malkin, & Schultz, 1985). Ac-cording to Cassidy and Kobak (1988), however, abused children may protect them-selves from the effects of inconsistent parenting by processing information about intimate relationships in ways that minimize their feelings of rejection, and this may result in the formation of somewhat inaccurate representations of their par-ents. Such defensive processes may help children cope in the short term, but they may foster distorted interpersonal relationships in the long run.

Many clinicians believe that physically abused children hold their nonperpe-trating parents partially responsible for the behavior of abusive parents and gen-eralize negative perceptions of abusive parents to nonabusive parents. Although abused children were often insecurely attached to abusive parents, however, Lamb, Gaensbauer, et al. (1985) reported that they commonly established secure attach-ments to nonabusive care providers. Similarly, Lynch and Cicchetti (1991) re-ported that older abused children developed representational models of relation-ships with specific social partners. Unfortunately, little is known about abused children's attachments to nonabusive fathers. Presumably, it is especially benefi-cial for a child to have at least one healthy or secure attachment when one parent is abusive and the relationship with her or him insecure (Werner, 1989). The evidence suggests that, in the absence of such buffering relationships, insecure attachments foster less healthy psychosocial development than secure parent–child attachments do (Lamb & Hwang, in press; Lamb, Thompson, Gardner, & Charnov, 1985; Thompson, 1988).

Observational studies of parent–child interactions involving older children have focused on disciplinary tactics, attempts to achieve compliance, and the joint solution of problem-solving tasks. In the first study of physically abusive and neglectful families, Burgess and Conger (1978) reported that abusive mothers had fewer verbal interactions with their children than nonabusive mothers but did not differ with respect to rates of physical interaction, positive and negative behaviors, and maternal compliance with child requests. Although the fathers of abused children complied with their children's requests less frequently than did nonabusive fathers, they spoke to their children more often than either the other fathers or abusive mothers did. Unfortunately, Burgess and Conger did not distinguish between perpetrators and nonperpetrators, and it was thus not possible to examine differences between abusive and nonabusive parent–child dyads within the same families.

Herrenkohl, Herrenkohl, Toedter, and Yanushefski (1984) later asked whether abused children interacted more provocatively with their parents than nonabused children did and whether abusive parents responded more aggressively to their children's behavior. They found that maltreating parents directed more hostile and negative behaviors, as well as fewer positive verbal behaviors, toward their children than did parents in the comparison group. It is interesting that Herrenkohl et al. found that socioeconomic status accounted for a greater proportion of the variance in their sample than child abuse did.

Reviewing the observational research of parent–child interaction in abusive families, Mash (1991) underscored how much more we need to learn about the differences between abusive and nonabusive parent–child interactions if we are to understand their possible influence on developmental processes:

> It is not yet known whether the primary interactional risks to the child stem from a lack of affectionate care, actively hostile, cruel, or punitive parenting, the general effects of social impoverishment or, as is likely, from some combination of all of these factors. (p. 204)

The data make clear, however, that abusive and nonabusive parents behave differently and evince different relationship styles. These differences are likely to affect the children's conceptions of their parents as well as their behavior and adjustment.

Children's Perceptions of Their Parents

Although observations of parent–child interactions and parental reports of childrearing and disciplinary practices can provide insight into the style and quality of interactions within abusive and nonabusive dyads, they do not help us understand how children who are victims of child abuse or witnesses of spousal violence interpret their parents' behavior. Children's perceptions and interpretations of their relationships with their parents provide unique insights, which can be overlooked when researchers focus only on observational data or reports by others (e.g., Bryant, 1985; R. Dubin & E. R. Dubin, 1965; Finkelhor & Dziuba-Leatherman, 1994; Garbarino, Sebes, & Schellenbach, 1984; Grych & Fincham, 1993).

In one early study, Herzberger, Potts, and Dillon (1981) asked a small number of abused boys living in a group home to describe their parents' disciplinary techniques and their feelings of acceptance and rejection. The responses of boys who had been abused by one or both parents were compared with those of children who had not been abused. The abused children reported being more fearful of and negative in their descriptions of their parents than the other children were. Approximately 40% of the father-abused and 70% of the mother-abused children believed that they had been punished undeservedly, leading the authors to conclude that, "Perceptions of abusive and non-abusive fathers did not differ from each other as strongly or as often as did perceptions of abusive and non-abusive mothers" (p. 88). These findings thus underscore how important it is to distinguish between perpetrating and nonperpetrating parents. As noted before, it would be particularly important to learn whether children's relationships with their nonabusive parents can buffer the negative effects of abuse.

In an ongoing longitudinal study, Sternberg et al. (1994) studied 8- to 12-year-old Israeli children who were victims of physical abuse, witnesses of spousal violence, both victims and witnesses, or neither victims nor witnesses. When the children described relationships with their parents using the Family Relations Test (Bene & Anthony, 1957), we found that physically abused children more frequently reported negative perceptions of their abusive parents, but did not differ from comparison children with respect to the number of positive items reported. Although they were able to express negative feelings about violent parents, therefore, abused children also acknowledged some positive features of their relationships with abusive parents. More detailed analyses comparing fathers and mothers who were sole perpetrators of abuse with their nonabusive spouses revealed that children differentiated between their perpetrating and nonperpetrating parents, perceiving their abusive parents more negatively. Meanwhile, abused children rated the quality of their relationships with nonperpetrating parents like children in the comparison group viewed parents of the same gender. When we examined the adolescents' relationships with their mothers and fathers four years later using the Inventory for Peer and Parent Attachment (IPPA; Armsden & Greenberg, 1987), however, we found that child abuse prior to the first assessment had little apparent influence on these adolescents' current relationships with their parents (Dawud-Noursi, Sternberg, Lamb, Kaufman, & Larson, 1996). More recent experiences of child abuse appeared to have an important influence on these adolescents' perceptions of their relationships with their parents, however.

Although much remains to be learned about the effects of child abuse on children's relationships with their parents, it appears that the relationships between physically abusive parents and their children are less nurturant and supportive overall and that children's perceptions of their parents are affected accordingly. It is important, however, that these perceptions are selective and discriminating, such that children develop insecure and more negative relationships with abusive parents but do not generalize these negative perceptions to nonabusive parents. This suggests that nonabusive parents could be an important resource buffering children from the harmful effects of violence (Werner, 1989).

Parent–Child Interactions in Families With Spousal Violence

Although there is ample evidence that children are affected by angry arguments between their parents (Cummings & O'Reilly, 1997; Cummings, Zahn-Waxler, & Radke-Yarrow, 1981, 1984; Davies & Cummings, 1994; Fincham, Grych, & Osborne, 1994), researchers have only begun to examine systematically how more serious spousal violence affects children's relationships with their parents. Research on family conflict has been guided by two major explanatory models. These explanatory models differ in their relative emphasis on how direct (e.g., observing arguments or violent fights between parents) and indirect (e.g., living in stressful and chaotic family circumstances, which are the outcome of marital conflict) exposure to conflict affects children's mental health. Children who overhear or witness violent interactions between their parents may experience heightened levels of fear or anger regarding the violent parent, the victim, or both. They might feel responsible for the arguments, particularly if the disagreement involves childrearing issues, and may even be drawn into these arguments or fights. Children can also be influenced indirectly by their parents' violent interactions. It has been suggested, for example, that families characterized by domestic violence are more chaotic than nonviolent families (Holden & Ritchie, 1991) and that this influences the quality of parent–child interactions. Furthermore, the stresses associated with being an abused spouse may adversely affect parenting skills (Fauber, Forehand, Thomas, & Wierson, 1990).

Family violence takes many forms, and the types of families included in studies of spousal violence thus vary. In a study of families who were referred because of custody disputes, Johnston and Campbell (1993) found that 75% of the families had histories of domestic violence. Detailed information about violent incidents provided by both parents allowed Johnston and Campbell to identify five different profiles: ongoing/episodic male battering, female-initiated violence, male-controlling violence, separation/divorce violence, and psychotic/paranoid reactions. Families thus differed with respect to the initiator of the violence, how the violence progressed, how the victims reacted, how severe and frequent the violence was, and the amount of restraint involved. Moreover, the patterns of parent–child relationships differed depending on the type of violence. In cautioning researchers about the dangers of viewing spousal violence as a simple construct, Johnston and Campbell (1993) thus noted:

> Domestic violence appears to be a behavior or set of behaviors arising from multiple sources, which follow different patterns in different families, rather than being a syndrome with a single underlying cause. Parent–child relationships are likely to vary with the different patterns of violence, and children of different ages and gender are affected differently. There are also several trajectories for recovery and the reconstitution of family relationships and for the potential of future violence. (p. 296)

Unfortunately, these factors are seldom taken into account.

The initial studies of children exposed to spousal violence focused primarily on children in battered women's shelters. Holden and Ritchie (1991), for example, examined the disciplinary styles of abused women who lived in shelters with their children. Mothers in the shelters reported greater discrepancies between their and their partners' disciplinary styles than did mothers in a matched comparison group. The shelter mothers also reported altering their disciplinary practices when their husbands were present and felt that fathers spanked children too frequently and too harshly. The abused women further reported that their husbands were less involved in childrearing tasks than were fathers in the comparison families, that they were less affectionate toward the children, and that they were less likely to use inductive reasoning when disciplining the children. These data raise interesting questions about the parenting skills of battered women, although it is important to remember that information was collected only from mothers.

Prompted by the notion that violence begets violence, other researchers have asked whether violent spouses and their victims are more likely to be violent parents. In two studies, Jouriles and his colleagues (Jouriles & LeCompte, 1991; Jouriles & Norwood, 1995) examined parental aggression toward children whose mothers had requested counseling or shelter protection because they were battered by their husbands. In the first study (Jouriles & LeCompte, 1991), mothers described their violence toward their husbands and children and their husbands' violence toward the mothers and children in the last year ($n = 73$). According to the mothers, both parents were more aggressive toward boys than toward girls. Severity and frequency of husband-to-wife aggression was associated with the severity of aggression against sons by both mothers and fathers.

Jouriles and Norwood (1995) attempted to explore gender differences further by including a male and female child from each family. Twenty mothers from a battered women's shelter described levels of family violence while male and female children from each family also described their mothers' and fathers' aggression toward them. According to the mothers, boys whose fathers were extremely violent toward the mothers were more likely to be victimized by both of their parents. Boys, however, reported that their mothers were more aggressive toward them than their fathers were. It is interesting that the level of father-to-son aggression was higher when there was less extreme husband-to-wife aggression.

Of course, as residents of temporary shelters, the children in these studies had been exposed to multiple stressors, including separation from potential attachment figures, making it difficult to disentangle the effects of exposure to violence from other negative life circumstances. Furthermore, because no information was obtained from fathers, reporting biases are a concern. The results of several studies underscore the importance of obtaining information from multiple informants when studying family violence (Margolin, John, Ghosh, & Gordis, 1997; Sternberg, Lamb, & Dawud-Noursi, 1998).

Margolin and her colleagues (1997) examined whether physical aggression in the marriage was associated with impaired parenting in a community sample of families with children ranging from 8 to 11 years of age. Spousal violence in the past year was reported by approximately half of the couples whose parental behavior was assessed using a cooperative play activity. Spousal interaction during a triadic discussion was also observed so that the authors could determine whether the parents resolved conflicts with their partners and children in similar ways. Men who were violent with their wives were more authoritarian, less authoritative, and displayed more negative affect toward their sons than nonviolent men did, and their sons were less active. By contrast, maternal behavior was unrelated to reports of the mothers' aggressiveness toward their husbands. Spousal aggression was unrelated to the observed quality of parent–child interaction during the observed discussions although the sons' behavior during the discussion was predicted by histories of mother-to-father violence and father-to-mother violence. Boys with spousally aggressive fathers were more withdrawn, anxious, and distracted than comparison boys. Boys with aggressive mothers were also more withdrawn and distracted than boys with nonaggressive mothers, and girls seemed largely unaffected by the violence and aggressiveness of their parents. As the authors point out, this study is limited by its cross-sectional nature, but it remains one of the few studies to include multiple informants about violence and its effects on children.

Summary

Clearly, it is not easy to study the quality of parent–child relationships in spousally violent families. Although our understanding of these families is slowly improving, all of the studies reviewed here raised as many new questions as they answered. It is still unclear whether violent parents, or their victimized partners, consistently behave differently with their children or even whether children's perceptions of their parents are systematically affected by knowing that the adults are either victims or perpetrators of domestic violence. Attempts to oversimplify research findings in this area using cliches like "intergenerational transmission of violence" will only hinder our understanding of the process. Longitudinal studies, with information obtained from multiple informants, are needed to enhance our understanding of the ways in which children are affected by violence between their parents. Preliminary hints of gender differences also underscore the need to plan studies large enough to determine whether the gender of perpetrators and victims might differentially affect boys and girls.

EFFECTS OF VIOLENCE
ON CHILDREN'S BEHAVIOR PROBLEMS

Although it is widely believed that children who are victims of child abuse or witnesses of spouse abuse or both are more likely to manifest developmental problems than their nonabused peers, the effects are not as consistent as one might expect. For example, some researchers have found that physically abused children have more behavior problems than children in comparison groups (Aber, Allen, Carlson, & Cicchetti, 1989) whereas others report no such differences (Kravic, 1987; Wolfe & Mosk, 1983). Similarly, some researchers have reported that witnesses of domestic violence have more behavior problems than children in comparison groups (Jaffe, Wolfe, Wilson, & Zak, 1986) but in other studies have found no such differences (Wolfe, Zak, Wilson, & Jaffe, 1986). Variations in the effects of maltreatment may in part reflect individual differences in temperament and probably reflect variations in the actual forms and context of violence experienced. In addition, methodological differences among studies—such as variations in the definitions of child abuse, the failure to account for multiple types of maltreatment (e.g., neglect, witnessing violence), the poor selection of comparison groups, and ignorance of protective factors (such as supportive relationships with other relatives or friends)—may also play a role.

In North America, child maltreatment is associated with a variety of social and demographic characteristics. Domestic violence tends to be more prevalent in areas characterized by high crime rates and tolerance for ownership of weapons (Garbarino, Kostelny, & Dubrow, 1991). High rates of single parenthood, divorce, poverty, substance abuse, shelter residence, and institutionalization typically characterize the samples studied, and all have been identified as conditions that increase children's vulnerability to negative developmental outcomes. As a result, some scholars have suggested that such factors, not simply family violence, may be responsible for many of the effects of abuse (Elmer, 1977; Emery, 1989; Gelles, 1989; Hart & Brassard, 1987; Jaffe, Wolfe, & Wilson, 1990; Starr, 1979). In addition, studies examining the effects of witnessing violence on children initially involved mothers and children in battered women's shelters (Jaffe et al., 1990). Although the results of these studies suggest that children who witness violence may be at risk for a variety of developmental problems, the conclusiveness of the research is limited by the fact that these children have experienced other stressful life events, like separation from their fathers and familiar neighborhoods, as well as transitions to the often chaotic lifestyle of the shelters. Studies focused on community samples of children exposed to spousal violence may help disentangle the contributions of shelter residence and other risk factors from exposure to spousal violence, (McCloskey, Figueredo, & Koss, 1995; O'Keefe, 1996; Sternberg et al., 1993, 1994). The recent trend to include information from fathers in studies of family violence promises to be very informative (Jouriles & Norwood, 1995; Margolin et al., 1997; Sternberg et al., 1998).

Indeed, although both child and spouse abuse are believed to affect children's behavior problems and psychological well-being, researchers have only begun systematically inquiring about multiple types of family violence and child maltreatment (O'Keefe, 1996; Sternberg, 1997; Sternberg et al., 1993; Wolfe & McGee, 1994).

Interpretation of the evidence regarding the effects of violence on children's behavioral adjustment is also complicated by a growing body of evidence that the reported effects vary depending on the source of information about the effects. In the first phase of our longitudinal study (Sternberg et al., 1993), for example, the Child Behavior Check List and Youth Self-Report (Achenbach & Edelbrock, 1983, 1987) were completed by mothers, fathers, and their 8-to-12-year-old children in order to assess the effects of various types of domestic violence on children's behavior problems. According to their mothers, children had high levels of problematic behavior when spouse abuse had occurred, whereas children reported higher levels of problematic behavior when they themselves had been abused. Fathers reported no significant differences across the four groups. Since the mid-1990s, researchers have begun to include information from multiple informants about children's violent experiences and how they are affected by these experiences (Feldman, Salzinger, & Kaplan, 1995; Kaufman, Jones, Steiglitz, Vitalano, & Mannariono, 1994; Kinard, 1995; McGee, Wolfe, Yuen, Wilson, & Carnochan, 1995; O'Brien, Margolin, & John, in press; Sternberg et al., 1998). Unfortunately, only a few researchers have attempted to incorporate information from fathers as informants (e.g., Jouriles & Norwood, 1995; Margolin et al., 1997; Sternberg et al., 1998). By including information from and about fathers in studies focused on domestic violence, it should be possible to improve the overall quality of research on the effects of child and spouse abuse on children (Sternberg, 1997). Although information from multiple informants often complicates the interpretation of research findings, researchers are learning to explore the value of different perspectives in predicting children's adjustment.

Finally, various types of maltreatment may affect children differently depending on their age or developmental status (Aber et al., 1989; Crittenden, 1985; Egeland & Sroufe, 1981; Schneider-Rosen, Braunwald, Carlson, & Cicchetti, 1985; Wolfe & McGee, 1994). In order to better understand the relationship between domestic violence and developmental outcomes, therefore, studies must be designed to assess developmental differences in exposure to different types of maltreatment in order to explore how various types of maltreatment affect children at different developmental stages.

Summary

As expected, experiencing child abuse affects children's development adversely. However, the nature of the effects may vary depending on the children's ages, and their magnitude may vary depending on the extent to which children experience other traumatic or pathogenic events, including poverty, unpredictable housing, extended separations from their parents, and so forth. It is unclear how enduring these effects are and whether they can be ameliorated by individual therapy, supportive attachment relationships, or by changes over time in the behavior of the abusive parents.

A review of the empirical research evaluating the effects of family violence on children reveals a somewhat less consistent picture than researchers and clinicians might have predicted. Although it is possible to conclude that violence is not good for children, it is much more difficult to describe in a parsimonious fashion how children are affected by child abuse and violence between their parents.

CONCLUSION

Family violence is certainly not normative but it is a fact of life in many contemporary U.S. families. Unfortunately, although researchers have begun to develop a nuanced understanding of the ways in which nonviolent marital conflict may affect family processes and child development, they have tended in the past to view family violence simplistically as a pathogenic phenomenon. In addition, the paucity of data from and about fathers leaves many unanswered questions in this complicated puzzle. Family violence is almost certainly harmful, of course, but we are only now becoming aware of the many faces of family violence, and this knowledge is forcing psychologists to begin addressing more complex questions about its effects on family functioning and child development. How do family processes differ when there are unidirectional as opposed to bidirectional forms of partner violence? When spousal violence is or is not accompanied by child abuse? When one or both parents abuse their children? When children witness, are aware of, or remain ignorant of violent disputes between their parents or parent substitutes? When the perpetrators of violence are parents, stepparents, or transient adults moving through the lives of adults and children in the family? When the children have close supportive relationships with other individuals, inside and outside their families? Answers to these and similar questions are absolutely essential as we seek an understanding of family violence and its implications for parenting and child development.

REFERENCES

Aber, J. L., Allen, J. P., Carlson, V., & Cicchetti, D. (1989). The effects of maltreatment on development during early childhood: Recent studies and their theoretical, clinical, and policy implications. In D. Cicchetti & V. Carlson (Eds.), *Child maltreatment: Theory and research on the causes and consequences of child abuse and neglect* (pp. 579–619). Cambridge, England: Cambridge University Press.

Achenbach, T. M., & Edelbrock, C. (1983). *Manual for the Child Behavior Checklist and Revised Child Behavior Profile,* Burlington: University of Vermont.

Achenbach, T. M., & Edelbrock, C. S. (1987). *Manual for the Youth Self-Report and Profile.* Burlington: University of Vermont.

American Association for Protecting Children. (1986). *Highlights of official child neglect and abuse reporting: 1984.* Denver, CO: American Humane Association.

Armsden, G. C., & Greenberg, M. T. (1987). The Inventory of Parent and Peer Attachment: Individual differences and their relationship to psychological well-being in adolescence. *Journal of Youth and Adolescence, 16,* 427–454.

Bachman, R., & Salzman, L. E. (1995). *Violence against women: Estimates from the redesigned survey.* Bureau of Justic Statistics (Special Report NCJ–154348).

Bene, E., & Anthony, E. J. (1957). *Manual for the Family Relations Test.* London: National Foundation for Educational Research.

Bryant, B. K. (1985). The neighborhood walk: Sources of support in middle childhood. *Monographs of the Society for Research in Child Development, 50*(Serial No. 210).

Burgess, R. L., & Conger, R. D. (1978). Family interactions in abusive, neglectful, and normal families. *Child Development, 49,* 1163–1173.

Carlson, V., Cicchetti, D., Barnett, D., & Braunwald, K. G. (1989). Finding order in disorganization: Lessons from research on maltreated infants' attachments to their caregivers. In D. Cicchetti & V. Carlson (Eds.), *Child maltreatment* (pp. 494–528). New York: Cambridge University Press.

Cassidy, J., & Kobak, R. R. (1988). Avoidance and its relationship to other defensive processess. In J. Belsky & T. Nezworski (Eds.), *Clinical implications of attachment* (pp. 300–323). Hillsdale, NJ: Lawrence Erlbaum Associates.

Crittenden, P. M. (1981). Abusing, neglecting, problematic, and adequate dyads: Differentiating by patterns of interaction. *Merrill Palmer Quarterly, 27,* 1–18.

Crittenden, P. M. (1985). Social networks, quality of child-rearing, and child development. *Child Development, 56,* 1299–1313.

Crittenden, P. M. (1988). Relationships at risk. In J. Belsky & T. Nezworski (Eds.), *Clinical implications of attachment* (pp. 136–174). Hillsdale, NJ: Lawrence Erlbaum Associates.

Crittenden, P. M. & Ainsworth, M. D. S. (1989). Child maltreatment and attachment theory. In D. Cicchetti & V. Carlson (Eds.), *Child maltreatment* (pp. 432–463). New York: Cambridge University Press.

Cummings, E. M., & O'Reilly, A. W. (1997). Fathers in family context: Effects of marital quality on child adjustment. In M. E. Lamb (Ed.), *The role of the father in child development* (3rd ed. pp. 49–65). New York: Wiley.

Cummings, E. M., Zahn-Waxler, C., & Radke-Yarrow, M. (1981). Young children's responses to expressions of anger and affection by others in the family. *Child Development, 52,* 1274–1282.

Cummings, E. M., Zahn-Waxler, C., & Radke-Yarrow, M. (1984). Developmental changes in children's reactions to anger in the home. *Journal of Child Psychology and Psychiatry, 25,* 63–74.

Daly, M., & Wilson, M. (1984). A sociobiological analysis of human infanticide. In G. Hausfater & S. B. Hray (Eds.), *Infanticide: Comparative and evolutionary perspectives* (pp. 487–502). Hawthorne, NY: Archive Publishing Co.

Daly, M., & Wilson, M. I. (1996). Violence against stepchildren. *Current Directions in Psychological Science, 5,* 77–81.

Davies, P. T., & Cummings, E. M. (1994). Marital conflict and child adjustment: An emotional security hypothesis. *Psychological Bulletin, 116,* 387–411.

Dawud-Noursi, S., Sternberg, K., Lamb, M. Kaufman, A., & Larson, C. (1996, March). *The effects of domestic violence on adolescents' attachment relationships and conflicts.* Poster presented to the Society for Research on Adolescence, Boston.

Dobash, R. E, & Dobash, R. P. (1984). The nature and antecedents of violent events. *British Journal of Criminology, 24,* 269–288.

Dubin, R., & Dubin, E. R. (1965). Children's social perceptions: A review of research. *Child Development, 36,* 809–838.

Edleson, J. L. (1997). The overlap between child maltreatment and woman battering [On-line]. Available http://www.mincava.umn.edu/papers/overlap.htm

Egeland, B., & Sroufe, L. A. (1981). Developmental sequaelae of maltreatment in infancy. In R. Rizley & D. Cicchetti (Eds.), *Developmental perspectives in child maltreatment* (pp. 77–92). San Francisco: Jossey-Bass.

Elmer, E. (1977). A follow-up study of traumatized children. *Pediatrics, 59,* 273–279.

Emery, R. E. (1989). Family violence. *American Psychologist, 44,* 321–328.

Fantuzzo, J., Boruch, D. R., Beriama, A., Atkins, M., & Marcus, S. (1997). Domestic violence and children: Prevalence and risk in five major U.S. cities. *Journal of the American Academy of Child and Adolescent Psychiatry, 36,* 116–122.

Fantuzzo, J., & Lindquist, C. (1988). Violence in the home: The effects of observing conjugal violence on children. *Journal of Family Violence, 4,* 77–90.

Fauber, R., Forehand, R., Thomas, A. M., & Wierson, M. (1990). A mediational model of the impact of marital conflict on adolescent adjustment in intact and divorced families: The role of disrupted parenting. *Child Development, 61,* 1112–1123.

Feldman, R. S., Salzinger, S., & Kaplan, S. J. (1995, April) *Perspectives on physically abused children's and adolescent's behavior: Rater effects.* Paper presented to the Society for Research on Child Development, Indianapolis, IN.

Fincham, F. D., Grych, J. H., & Osborne, L. N. (1994). Does marital conflict cause child maladjustment? Directions and challenges for longitudinal research. *Journal of Family Psychology, 8,* 128–140.

Finkelhor, D., & Dziuba-Leatherman, J. (1994). Children as victims of violence: A national survey. *Pediatrics, 91,* 413–420.

Frieze, I. H., & Browne, A. (1989). Violence in marriage. In L. Ohlin & M. Tonry (Eds.), *Family violence* (pp. 163–218). Chicago: University of Chicago Press.

Garbarino, J., Kostelny, K., & Dubrow, N. (1991). *No place to be a child: Growing up in a war zone.* Lexington, MA: Lexington Books.

Garbarino, J., Sebes, J., & Schellenbach, C. (1984). Families at risk for destructive parent–child relations in adolescence. *Child Development, 55,* 174–183.

Geffner, R., & Pagelow, M. D. (1990). Victims of spouse abuse. In R. T. Ammerman & M. Hersch (Eds.), *Treatment of family violence* (pp. 113–135). New York: Wiley.

Gelles, R. J. (1989). Child abuse and violence in single parent families: Parent-absent and economic deprivation. *American Journal of Orthopsychiatry, 59,* 492–501.

Gelles, R. J. & Straus, M. A. (1988). *Intimate violence.* New York: Simon & Schuster.

Gil, D. (1973). *Violence against children: Physical child abuse in the United States.* Cambridge, MA: Harvard University Press.

Grych, J. H., & Fincham, F. D. (1993). Children's appraisals of marital conflict: Initial investigations of the cognitive-contextual framework. *Child Development, 64,* 215–230.

Hart, S. N., & Brassard, M. R. (1987). A major threat to children's mental health: Psychological maltreatment. *American Psychologist, 42,* 160–165.

Herrenkohl, E. C., Herrenkohl, R. C., Toedter, L., & Yanushefski, D. (1984). Parent–child interactions in abusive and nonabusive families. *Journal of the American Academy of Child Psychiatry, 23,* 641–648.

Herzberger, S., Potts, D. A., & Dillon, M. (1981). Abusive and non-abusive parental treatment from the child's perspective. *Journal of Consulting and Clinical Psychology, 49,* 81–91.

Holden, G. W., & Ritchie, K. L. (1991). Linking extreme marital discord, child rearing, and child behavior problems: Evidence from battered women. *Child Development, 62,* 311–327.

Hughes, H. (1988). Psychological and behavioral correlates of family violence in child witnesses and victims. *American Journal of Orthopsychiatry, 58,* 77–90.

Hughes, H. (in press). Research concerning children of battered women: Clinical implications. In R. Geffner, S. F. Sorenson, & P. K. Windberg-Love (Eds.), *Violence and sexual abuse at home: Current issues, interventions, and research in spousal battering and child maltreatment.* Binghamton, NY: Haworth.

Hughes, H. M., Parkinson, D. L., & Vargo, M. C. (1989). Witnessing spouse abuse and experiencing physical abuse: A "double whammy?" *Journal of Family Violence, 4,* 197–209.

Jaffe, P. G., Wolfe, D. A., & Wilson, S. K. (1990). *Children of battered women.* Newbury Park, CA: Sage.

Jaffe, P., Wolfe, D. A., Wilson, S. K., & Zak, L. (1986). Family violence and child adjustment: A comparative analysis of girls' and boys' behavioral symptoms. *American Journal of Psychiatry, 143,* 74–77.

Johnston, J. R., & Campbell, L. E. G. (1993). Parent–child relationships in domestic violence families disputing custody. *Family and Conciliation Courts Review, 31,* 282–298.

Jouriles, E. N., & LeCompte, S. H. (1991). Husbands' aggression toward wives and motehrs'and fathers' aggression toward children: Moderating effects of child gender. *Journal of Consulting and Clinical Psychology, 59,* 190–192.

Jouriles, E. N., & Norwood, W. D. (1995). Physical aggression toward boys and girls in families characterized by the battering of women. *Journal of Family Psychology, 9,* 69–78.

Kaufman, J., Jones, B., Steiglitz, E., Vitalano, L., & Mannariono, A. P. (1994). The use of multiple informants to assess children's maltreatment experiences. *Journal of Family Violence, 9,* 227–248.

Kinard, M. E. (1995). Mother and teacher assessments of behavior problems in abused children. *Journal of the American Academy of Child and Adolescent Psychiatry, 34,* 1043–1053.

Kravic, J. N. (1987). Behavior problems and social competence of clinic-referred abused children. *Journal of Family Violence, 2,* 111–120.

Kurz, D. (1993). Physical assaults by husbands: A major social problem. In R. J. Gelles & D. R. Loeske (Eds.), *Current controversies on family violence* (pp. 88–103). Newbury Park, CA: Sage.

Lamb, M. E., Gaensbauer, T. J., Malkin, C. M., & Schultz, L. A. (1985). The effects of abuse and neglect on security of infant–adult attachment. *Infant Behavior and Development, 8,* 35–45.

Lamb, M. E., & Hwang, C. P. (in press). Parent–child relationships. In M. H. Bornstein & M. E. Lamb (Eds.), *Developmental psychology: An advanced textbook* (4th ed.). Mahwah, NJ: Lawrence Erlbaum Associates.

Lamb, M. E., Thompson, R. A., Gardner, W., & Charnov, E. L. (1985). *Infant–mother attachment: The origins and developmental significance of individual differences in Strange Situation behavior.* Hillsdale, NJ: Lawrence Erlbaum Associates.

Lennington, S. (1981). Child abuse: The limits of sociobiology. *Ethology and Sociobiology, 2,* 17–29.

Lightcap, J. L., Kurland, J. A., & Burgess, R. L. (1982). Child abuse: A test of some predictions from evolutionary theory. *Ethology and Sociobiology, 3,* 61–67.

Lynch, M., & Cicchetti, D. (1991). Patterns of relatedness in maltreated and nonmaltreated children: Connections among multiple representational models. *Development and Psychopathology, 3,* 207–226.

Lyons-Ruth, K., Connell, D. B., & Zoll, D. (1989). Patterns of maternal behavior among infants at risk for abuse: Relations with infant attachment behavior and infant development at 12 months of age. In D. Cicchetti & V. Carlson (Eds.), *Child maltreatment* (pp. 464–493). New York: Cambridge University Press.

Malkin, C. M., & Lamb, M. E. (1994). Child maltreatment: A test of sociobiological theory. *Journal of Comparative Family Studies, 25,* 121–133.

Margolin, G., John, S. J., Ghosh, C. M., & Gordis, E. B. (1997). Family interaction process: An essential tool for exploring abusive relations. In D. D. Cahn & S. A. Lloyd (Eds.), *Family abuse: A communication perspective* (pp.37–58). Thousand Oaks, CA: Sage.

Mash, E. J. (1991). Measurement of parent–child interaction in studies of child maltreatment. In R. H. Starr & D. A. Wolfe (Eds.), *The effects of child abuse and neglect* (pp. 203–256). New York: Guilford.

McCloskey, L. A., Figueredo, A. J., & Koss, M. P. (1995). The effects of systematic family violence on children's mental health. *Child Development, 66,* 1239–1261.

McFarlane, J., Parker, B., & Soeken, K. (1995). Abuse during pregnancy: Frequency, severity, perpetrator, and risk factors of homicide. *Public Healthy Nursing, 12,* 284–289.

McFarlane, J., Parker, B., & Soeken, K. (1996). Abuse during pregnancy: Associations with maternal health and infant birth weight. *Nursing Research, 45,* 37–42.

McGee, R. A., Wolfe, D. A., Yuen, S. A., Wilson, S. K. & Carnochan, J. (1995). The measurement of maltreatment: A comparison of approaches. *Child Abuse and Neglect, 19,* 223–249.

National Center on Child Abuse and Neglect. (1981). *National study of the incidence and severity of child abuse and neglect* (81-30325). Washington, DC: U.S. Department of Health and Human Services.

National Center on Child Abuse and Neglect. (1988). *Study findings: Study of national incidence and prevalence of child abuse and neglect.* Washington, DC: U.S. Department of Health and Human Services.

O'Brien, M., John, R. S., Margolin, G., & Erel, O. (1994). Reliability and diagnostic efficacy of parents' reports regarding children's exposure to marital aggression. *Violence and Victims, 9,* 45–62.

O'Brien, M., Margolin, G., & John, R. (1995). Relation among marital conflict, child coping, and child adjustment. *Journal of Clinical Child Psychology, 24,* 346–361.

O'Keefe, M. (1996). The differential effects of family violence on adolescent adjustment. *Child and Adolescent Social Work Journal, 13,* 51–68.

Schneider-Rosen, K., Braunwald, K. G., Carlson, V., & Cicchetti, D. (1985). Illustrations from the study of maltreated infants. In I. Bretherton & E. Waters (Eds.), Growing points in attachment theory and research (pp.194–210). *Monographs of the Society for Research on Child Development, 72*(Serial No. 209).

Sedlack, A. J. & Broadhurst, D. D. (1996). *Third national incidence study of child abuse and neglect: Final report.* Washington, DC: U.S. Department of Health and Human Services.

Starr, R. H. (1979). Child abuse. *American Psychologist, 34,* 872–878.

Sternberg, K. J. (1997). Fathers, the missing parent in research on family violence. In M. E. Lamb (Ed.), *The role of the father in child development* (3rd Ed.). New York: Wiley.

Sternberg, K. J., Lamb, M. E., & Dawud-Noursi, S. (1998). Understanding domestic violence and its effects: Making sense of divergent reports and perspectives. In G. W. Holden, R. Geffner, & E. W. Jouriles (Eds.), *Children exposed to family violence* (pp. 121–156). Washington, DC: American Psychological Association.

Sternberg, K. J., Lamb, M. E., Greenbaum, C., Cicchetti, D., Dawud, S., Cortes, R. M., Krispin, O., & Lorey, F. (1993). Effects of domestic violence on children's behavior problems and depression. *Developmental Psychology, 29,* 44–52.

Sternberg, K. J., Lamb, M. E., Greenbaum, C., Dawud, S., Cortes, R. M., & Lorey, F. (1994). The effects of domestic violence on children's perceptions of their perpetrating and nonperpetrating parents. *The International Society for the Study of Behavioral Development, 17,* 779–795.

Straus, M. A. (1993). Physical assaults by wives: A major social problem. In R. J. Gelles & D. R. Loseke (Eds.), *Current controversies on family violence* (pp. 67–87). Newbury Park, CA: Sage.

Straus, M. A., & Gelles, R. J. (1986). Societal change and change in family violence from 1975 to 1985 as revealed by two national surveys. *Journal of Marriage and the Family, 48,* 465–479.

Straus, M. A. & Gelles, R. J. (1990). How violent are American families? Estimates from the national family violence resurvey and other studies. In M. A. Straus & R. J. Gelles (Eds.), *Physical violence in American families* (pp.95–108). New Brunswick, NJ: Transaction Books.

Straus, M. A., Gelles, R. J., & Steinmetz, S. (1980). *Behind closed doors: Violence in the American family.* New York: Doubleday/Anchor.

Study finds half of victims know attackers. (1997, August 25). *New York Times,* 16.

Sun, E., & Abel, E. M. (1990). The impact of spousal violence on the children of the abuser. *Journal of Independent Social Work, 4,* 27–34.

Thompson, R. A. (1988). Early sociopersonality development. In W. Damon & N. Eisenberg (Eds.), *Handbook of child psychology: Volume 3. Social, emotional, and personality development.* New York: Wiley.

Walker, L. E. (1984). *The battered woman syndrome.* New York: Springer.

Weis, J. G. (1989). Family violence research methodology and design. In L. Ohlin & M. Tonry (Eds.), *Family violence* (pp. 117–162). Chicago: University of Chicago Press.

Werner, E. E. (1989). High-risk children in young adulthood: A longitudinal study from birth to 32 years. *American Journal of Orthopsychiatry, 59,* 72–81.

Wolfe, D. A., & McGee, R. (1994). Dimensions of child maltreatment and their relationship to adolescent adjustment. *Development and Psychopathology, 6,* 165–182.

Wolfe, D. A., & Mosk, M. (1983). Behavioral comparisons of children from abusive and distressed families. *Journal of Consulting and Clinical Psychology, 51,* 702–708.

Wolfe, D. A., Zak, L., Wilson, S. K., & Jaffe, P. (1986). Child witnesses to violence between parents: Critical issues in behavioral and social adjustment. *Journal of Abnormal Child Psychology, 14,* 95–104.

Wolfner, G. D., & Gelles, R. J. (1993). A profile of violence toward children: A national study. *Child Abuse & Neglect, 17,* 197–212.

Chapter 16

The Families of Neglected Children

HOWARD DUBOWITZ
University of Maryland

Families have the primary responsibility to nurture and protect their children. Historically, families in the United States have been free to carry out this responsibility as they saw fit, with little outside interference. But there has been mounting attention to the rights of children and the recognition that some families may not adequately nurture and protect their children. Accordingly, the legal principle of *parens patriae* whereby the state has a responsibility to ensure the well-being of its citizens, including children, has been established in the United States. Since the 1960s this has been implemented mostly via the child welfare system and designated state agencies mandated to protect children who are being abused or neglected. The framework for this effort has been quite narrow, focusing on acts of commission and omission by parents or caregivers, with little attention to the contributory problems underlying the maltreatment of their children (e.g., few community resources for new parents). Even less attention has been paid to other aspects of our society and its institutions that may directly abuse or neglect children (e.g., seriously inadequate public schools); instead, families have been the primary concern and target. This is not to infer that intervening at the family level is inappropriate. Rather, the intent is to place the phenomenon of child neglect in context.

Neglect is the most prevalent form of child maltreatment in the United States. Over half of all reports to child protective services (CPS) each year are for neglect (U.S. Department of Health and Human Services, 1995). The Third National Incidence Study of Child Abuse and Neglect, not limited to cases reported to CPS, estimated that almost two million or 3% of children were neglected in the United States in 1993 (U.S. Department of Health and Human Services, 1996). Neglect accounted for two thirds of the maltreatment identified, and the rate had more than doubled from that in the previous such study in 1986.

Neglect is defined in the National Incidence Study, and in the child welfare system, as a parental (or caregiver) omission of care that harms a child or poses a significant risk of harm. Although state laws generally include the issue of potential harm or endangerment, the threshold for intervening in the absence of actual

327

harm is high (e.g., when a child is abandoned or left alone overnight). The three main areas of neglect are physical (e.g., inadequate attention to clothing, food, and health care needs), emotional (e.g., inadequate affection, inadequate attention to a child's emotional or developmental needs), and educational (e.g., failure to enroll a child in school in violation of state law, permitting chronic truancy, refusing to allow needed attention to a diagnosed educational problem). Using this framework, clinicians and researchers have been reluctant to consider situations as neglectful unless responsibility and blame can reasonably be attributed to parental omissions of care. For example, a child may be poisoned from lead paint chips in the home, but neglect would only be a consideration if the parents refused treatment. Inadequate low income housing, minimal resources for lead abatement programs, and a landlord's indifference may contribute to this problem, but these factors are rarely construed as child neglect.

Although often in the shadow of abuse (Dubowitz, 1994), the influence of neglect on children is substantial. Neglect has been associated, for example, with impaired attachment between mother and child (Lamb, Gaensbauer, Malkin, & Schultz, 1985; Crittenden & Ainsworth, 1989), increased aggression (Bousha & Twentyman, 1984), academic problems (Kendall-Tackett & Eckenrode, 1996), and risk for arrest for delinquency, adult criminality, and violent criminal behavior (Rivera & Widom, 1992). In addition to the morbidity associated with neglect, almost half the estimated annual fatalities due to child maltreatment result from neglect (Wiese & Daro, 1995), involving mostly children drowning or dying in fires due to a lack of supervision.

Before describing what is known about families in which child neglect occurs, a few cautionary caveats are needed. Despite its prevalence and harmful results, there has been relatively little research on neglect (Wolock & Horowitz, 1984; Dubowitz, 1994). Much of the research consists of small samples, uses retrospective or cross-sectional designs, and is based on cases substantiated by CPS. CPS cases are prone to biases concerning who gets identified, reported, investigated, and substantiated. Professional biases have been well documented (Hampton & Newberger, 1985; O'Toole, Turbett, & Nalepka, 1983). CPS interventions may cause differences in family functioning, which are then described as characterizing neglect. For example, it is feasible that the stigma of being reported for neglect leads to a family being ostracized; their social isolation may then be considered a contributor to the neglect. The cross-sectional designs make it difficult to discern cause from effect; mostly, we have correlates. Research on neglect has also focused primarily on maternal, demographic, and social network characteristics; little work has been done examining fathers and families.

Varying definitions of child neglect is another concern; there is still no consensus (Dubowitz, Black, Starr, & Zuravin, 1993; Erickson & Egeland, 1996). Most of the research, however, is based on definitions of neglect as serious omissions in care of a child by a parent or caregiver. This conforms with state legal definitions and child welfare practice. Still, state laws and clinical practice vary greatly, making it difficult to compare findings from different studies. Despite these shortcomings, we have learned a good deal about child neglect.

The ecological theory has been widely accepted as explaining child maltreatment (Belsky, 1980; Belsky & Vondra, 1989). Single factor theories (e.g., parental psychopathology, stress), have been replaced by the recognition that multiple and interacting factors usually contribute to abuse and neglect. These factors operate at different levels: the individual (e.g., a child's disability, maternal depression), the family (e.g., conflict, father absence), the community (e.g., lack of social supports, inadequate child care), and society at large (e.g., view of children, tolerance of poverty). A single mother who has lost her job, has a disabled child, and lives in an impoverished, violent neighborhood is an example of a high-risk situation for child maltreatment. This chapter focuses on the family members and families in which neglect is identified, but it is clear that the context in which families function and neglect occurs is crucial. This context cannot be ignored. In keeping with the ecological theory, each of the major levels of contributors to child neglect is described.

A view of the context in which the phenomenon of neglect occurs is followed by an examination of the research on families in which neglect has been identified. Important aspects of family functioning, such as conflict, social skills, and social isolation, as well as the relationships between mothers and their children are included in this section. Some of these areas are difficult to categorize. For example, social isolation involves aspects of the community and the family as well as the individual. The focus then turns to individual family members beginning with mothers on whom most of the research has been done. Finally, the limited research on fathers and neglected children is described. To understand the etiology of neglect, it is helpful to keep in mind the relationships among these factors, and the varied pathways to children's basic needs not being met.

THE CONTEXT OF CHILD NEGLECT

Child neglect has been strongly and repeatedly associated with poverty (Wolock & Horowitz, 1979; U.S. Department of Health and Human Services, 1996). Indeed, this has posed difficult legal, definitional, and clinical dilemmas. For example, state laws may explicitly exclude omissions in care that are clearly due to poverty, concerned instead with situations in which parents can reasonably be held accountable, for example, a family living in a terribly deteriorated and hazardous home. The child welfare system has followed suit with attention usually confined to parental omissions of care, for reasons other than poverty (Dubowitz et al, 1993). In studies of low-income families, neglect has been found to be most common in the most impoverished families (Dunst, Trivette, & Gowen, 1994; Giovannoni & Billingsley, 1970). A similar finding occurs throughout much of the research, most of it done on very poor families (e.g., Polansky, Gaudin, Ammons, & Davis, 1985).

Of all the correlates with child neglect, extreme poverty is the strongest (Besharov, 1990; Giovannoni & Billingsley, 1970), even after taking into account that many instances of inadequate care are excused by the child welfare system as due to poverty rather than parental negligence. In the Third National Incidence Study, neglect was 44 times more likely to be identified in families with annual incomes less than $15,000 compared to those earning more than $30,000 (U.S. Department of Health and Human Services, 1996).

In addition to the obvious financial burdens associated with poverty, there are also related stressors such as unemployment (American Humane Association, 1988), single parenthood (Nelson et al., 1994), housing instability or frequent moves (Gaudin, Polansky, Kilpatrick, & Shilton, 1993), and depleted communities or living in high-risk neighborhoods (Zuravin, 1989). Zuravin (1986) also found that household crowding was more strongly associated with neglect than with abuse. In addition to the impact of poverty on parents' abilities to care for their children, there are many other ways that poverty results in children's basic needs not being met (Parker, Greer & Zuckerman, 1988). These include, for example, limited access to health care due to a lack of insurance coverage, exposure to environmental hazards such as lead, poor schooling, and living in dangerous neighborhoods without safe areas to play. This is the troubled environment in which neglect is most often identified. Other factors thought to be related to child neglect are briefly reviewed next.

Race

There appear to be no differences in the incidence of child neglect across the races after social classs is accounted for (U.S. Department of Health and Human Services, 1996). The disproportionately high representation of minorities in CPS cases probably reflects the association between minority status and lower socioeconomic class as well as professional biases. Poor, minority families, however, may have the added burden of confronting racism in many communities.

Stress

Most of the above problems may be mediated via the stress that impairs the functioning of individuals and families. This may occur particularly when the stress outweighs the available resources and strengths. Prospective studies have found increased stress to be a risk factor for neglect (Pianta, Egeland, & Erickson, et al., 1989; Vietze, O'Conner, Sherrod, & Altemeier, 1991). The impact of poverty and its accompanying burdens is probably mediated via the stress it imposes on parents. It seems intuitive that battling to make sure there is food on the table or dealing with an eviction notice might impede parents' ability to supervise their toddler or to be affectionate. Gaines, Sangrund, Green, and Power (1978) found the most stress, associated with unemployment, illness, eviction, and arrest, among neglecting families compared to abusive and control families. Both acute and chronic stressors may compromise parents' abilities to nurture and protect their children.

Middle-Class Children

There is a question of the adequacy of parental nurturance and supervision in middle-class and upper-class families, but this has not been identified as a significant child welfare concern. Occasionally, a situation evokes great media attention and public outrage, such as when a couple vacationed in Mexico for a week, leaving their two elementary-school-age children locked in their home. A more common concern is the limited time parents in dual career families may have for their children. Although there has been substantial interest in the well-being of infants and young children placed in day care while both parents work, it is not clear that this arrangement is harmful, and these circumstances have not been construed as neglect (see Lamb, chap. 3). Similarly, the harm or risks to latchkey children remains unclear.

Social Policy

There is a need for national policies that seriously support families and enhance the health and development of children. Despite the copious rhetoric about our children being our most valuable national resource, federal policies have not made children and families into priorities. The much touted Family and Medical Leave Act passed in 1993 allows only 12 weeks of unpaid leave to new parents and those caring for a sick relative, but excludes companies with fewer than 50 employees. Consequently, many U.S. citizens cannot benefit from this policy. The welfare reform passed in 1996 dismantles the safety net developed over 60 years for low income families, jeopardizing the well-being of many children (Children's Defense Fund, 1996). An understanding of the highly prevalent problem of child neglect must incorporate this broadest level of societal factors that influence the lives of families and children.

In summary, the social context in which child neglect occurs helps explain the phenomenon of neglect. Poverty is a major culprit. Daunting circumstances impede the ability of many families to nurture their children, and not surprisingly, neglect is identified. Social policies and programs have been woefully inadequate to provide the support many families need. But this picture does not satisfactorily explain all of what leads to child neglect. Indeed, many families in desperate conditions take good care of their children. This leads to a focus on the individual and family levels, recognizing that many of these factors are substantially related to the surrounding community and society. For example, parental conflict, maternal depression, and substance abuse may be major contributors to the neglect of children, and they are strongly influenced by the social context (e.g., acceptance of violence, stress of poverty, use of illegal drugs in a community).

FAMILIES IN WHICH NEGLECT IS IDENTIFIED

There is no simple stereotype of the family in which neglect occurs. There appears to be enormous heterogeneity within neglectful families[1] (Gaudin & Dubowitz, 1997), and research with carefully matched comparison groups has typically found few differences in family functioning. There are a few possible explanations. Families identified as neglectful may share many characteristics with similarly poor families; neglect may not represent very discrete circumstances. Another factor may be the enormous variability among neglecting families, which may mask differences. In addition, neglect is inherently difficult to observe. Research measures of this as well as of family functioning may not be adequately sensitive to detect subtle differences in neglectful families. Nevertheless, some characteristics of these families have been identified and are briefly reviewed in this section.

Interaction Style and Family Stability

Crittenden (1988) found neglectful mothers to have relatively stable relationships with their partners, but there was a "lack of affect" and an "apathetic, passive-dependent" interactive style between parents and children. Their family networks were also seen as stable, but not reciprocal, and members were not supportive of one another. Abuse was associated with swings between passivity and aggression. Kadushin (1988) in his work with neglected children described chaotic families with impulsive mothers who repeatedly demonstrated poor planning. Many neglectful mothers had conflictual relationships with the fathers of their children, many of whom were incarcerated or had deserted them. Both physical and emotional neglect have been found to occur much more frequently in single parent families, with children living with only their father at highest risk (U.S. Department of Health and Human Services, 1996).

A degree of chaos and poor organization of the home characterizes neglectful families (Dubowitz, 1994; Gaudin et al., 1993). Gaudin and his colleagues detected three types of neglectful families: (1) chaotic/leaderless, (2) dominant/autocratic, and (3) democratic. Families described as chaotic and leaderless were less healthy than the other two types in terms of family closeness and cohesion, clarity of expression, mood and tone, empathy, problem solving, and conflict. The dominant and autocratic group occupied an intermediate position, with the democratic families appearing most healthy. Using case record reviews, they found that neglect was associated with family instability, reflected by other adult male and female partners, relatives, and friends moving in and out of the home during the study period. Such instabilitiy and lack of predictability in the home environment may

---

[1]The term *neglectful families* connotes blame and is only used for brevity. Although families have primary responsibility for meeting their children's needs, neglect is seen as resulting from multiple child, parental, familial, and environmental factors.

be distressing to children. It also suggests a climate where children's needs are unlikely to receive the attention they deserve. Dubowitz (1995) found few differences between neglectful families and a high risk comparison group, although healthy family functioning was associated with more positive maternal perceptions of their children and with less emotional neglect. The home environments of neglected children were found to be less well organized and to have fewer toys.

Social Isolation and Poor Social Skills

Several studies have found neglectful families to be socially isolated, lacking social support and sometimes rejected by the community (Giovannoni & Billingsley, 1970; Polansky, Ammons, & Gaudin, 1985; Wolock & Horowitz, 1979). Neglectful mothers have been found to view their neighborhoods as less supportive than did their next-door neighbors and a comparison group (Polansky, Gaudin, Ammons, & Davis, 1985). Gaudin and Polansky (1986) then described *social distancing* in which neighbors reported fewer interactions with neglectful versus nonneglectful families. Neglectful families tend to participate less in social organizations (e.g., church) and shun available support (Gaudin, Polansky, & Kilpatrick, 1992; Zuravin, 1989). As a corollary to social isolation, it appears that neglectful families lack a variety of supports (Polansky et al., 1981), and poor social skills make it difficult for them to develop good relationships. Polansky and colleagues described women with poor social skills who chose ineffectual and unsuccessful partners, thus compounding their problems (Polansky, Borgman, & DeSaix, 1972). In the context of poverty and other stressors, the lack of social support and skills further impairs the ability of families to cope with difficult circumstances, increasing the risk of neglect.

Conflict

Increased conflict in the family is a major stressor and has been associated with neglect (Gaudin et al., 1993). Despite a view of neglect that emphasizes passivity and withdrawal, it appears that aggression and even abuse often co-occur; neglect and abuse share many underpinnings and are not entirely separate phenomena. If conflict is severe, perhaps including violent physical and emotional abuse, a child's exposure to this should be construed as a form of neglect (or abuse). One prospective study found that parental conflict predicted failure to thrive, where infants do not grow as expected due to psychosocial problems—at times a manifestation of neglect (Vietze et al., 1991).

Mother–Child Interaction

Much of the research on neglect at the family level has focused on the relationships between mothers and their children, with several studies examining the mother–child (or infant) interaction in neglectful and comparison families. Aragona and Eyberg (1981) found that neglectful mothers were more critical of their children and paid them less positive attention. In his review of the literature, Gaudin (1994) described the verbal and nonverbal communication between neglectful parents and their children as infrequent and mostly negative, thereby providing little of the stimulation and nurturance children need. Dunst and Trivette (1988) suggested an underlying psychological distancing by neglectful parents from their children. Crittenden found neglectful mothers to be less responsive and sensitive to their children than those in the comparison groups, and the neglected children were often "anxiously attached" (Crittenden & Ainsworth, 1989). A healthy and secure attachment between primary caregivers and young children appears to provide the foundation for developing a sense of trust that is important for interpersonal relationships throughout life. In a small study with extensive observation of 30 mother–infant dyads, Crittenden and Bonvillian (1984) found that the neglectful mothers spoke less, used shorter and less complete utterances, issued more demands, and expressed less acceptance than both controls and abusive mothers. In a similar study, Bousha and Twentyman (1984) found neglecting mothers displayed limited social interaction with their children with few verbal instructions. Burgess and Conger (1978) carefully observed family members in their homes and similarly described neglect associated with reduced parent–child interactions, particularly positive ones; negative interactions were more frequent, compared with abusive and control families. Neglectful families also had the most negative relationships with other family members. Not all studies, however, have found such differences (Gaudin & Dubowitz, 1997). In a high-risk community sample, videotaped interactions between mothers and children were similar in the neglect and comparison groups (Dubowitz, 1995). Despite differing results, overall, these findings indicate problematic interactions between mothers and children in families in whom neglect is identified. From this picture emerges a sense of how some of children's basic needs for affection, warmth, support, stimulation, and nurturance may not be adequately met. The emotional neglect described, however, is not likely to be the reason families were involved with CPS; typically, problems with physical care or supervision are needed for neglect reports to be substantiated.

INDIVIDUAL FAMILY MEMBERS

This section reviews research that addresses individual family members—mothers, fathers, and children—in neglectful families. The section concludes with a brief discussion of the effects of neglect on children, in particular, effects on cognitive and social development.

Mothers

Polansky, Borgman, & DeSaix (1972) and Polansky, Chalmers, Buttenweiser, & Williams (1981) coined the term *apathy-futility syndrome* for many mothers deemed neglectful. They described someone "less able to love, less capable of working productively, less open about feelings, more prone to living planlessy and impulsively, but also susceptible to psychological symptoms and to phases of passivity and numb fatalism" (Polansky et al., 1981). In part, this reflects underlying depression with withdrawal and a sense of hopelessness, and perhaps learned helplessness. Mothers who had difficulty "connecting emotionally with others" were at highest risk for neglect (Gaudin et al., 1993). These maternal mental health difficulties, mostly related to depression, help explain the problematic mother–child relationships and interactions described in the earlier section.

Belsky and Vondra (1989) considered parental personality to be the most important influence on parenting, with an individual's psychological resources helping to determine the choice of a partner, the quality of that relationship, and the amount of social support one receives. In a study of abusive, neglectful, and low-income control mothers, those who were neglectful were the most hostile, impulsive, and stressed, and the least socialized (Friedrich, Tyler, and Clark, 1985). Dubowitz (1996) found mothers in the neglect group were less satisfied with parenting than those in a comparison group.

A number of factors contributing to neglect by mothers are reviewed next.

Mother's History as a Child. An important contributor to a mother's parenting abilities may be the parenting she experienced as a child. In a few prospective studies, women who had poor nurturance in their own childhoods were more likely to neglect their children (Brayden, Altemeir, Tucker, Dietrich, & Vietze, 1992). Kotch et al. (1989) reported neglectful mothers to have experienced absence of or rejection by their own mothers. Nelson and colleagues (Nelson, Saunders, & Landsman, 1993) found that neglect was associated with a maternal history of maltreatment, in keeping with the multigenerational pattern of neglect described by others (Pianta et al., 1989; Polansky et al., 1981). Inadequate care of a child leads to a lack of secure psychological attachment and psychological immaturity, contributing to parents who are inaccessible, unresponsive, or inappropriately responsive to their children (Crittenden & Ainsworth, 1989). Presumably, social learning theory applies so that children who experience neglectful parenting learn this behavior and behave similarly with their children. There is considerable support for the transmission of neglectful parenting behavior from one generation to the next, although there has been little prospective longitudinal research on this issue. In addition, the cycle is far from inevitable; less stress and more support can lower the risk (Egeland & Erickson, 1990).

Depression. Several studies have shown a strong association between maternal depression and neglect. Polansky and colleagues (1972) focused on depressive qualities in describing the "apathy-futility syndrome" as characteristic of neglectful mothers. Wolock and Horowitz (1979) described neglectful mothers as bored, depressed, restless, lonely, and less satisfied with life than mothers in the comparison group. More recent studies have supported these early findings (Culp, Culp, Soulis, & Letts, 1989; Dubowitz, 1995; Dunst, Trivette, & Gowen, 1994; Zuravin, 1988). Gaudin and colleagues (1993), for example, found 60% of neglectful mothers to have clinically significant depression compared with 33% in the comparison group. These findings offer empirical support to the clinical observation that depression compromises parents' abilities to adequately meet the basic needs of their children.

Substance Abuse.   Substance abuse has become a major concern in families involved in the child welfare system (Zuravin & Greif, 1989; DiLeonardi, 1993). Gaudin (1994) summarized several studies showing substance or alcohol abuse to be a factor in up to 80 to 90% of child maltreatment cases. In a study of Native Americans, substance abuse was strongly associated with neglect (Nelson et al., 1994). It appears likely that substance abuse is both a major obstacle to adequate parenting as well as a marker of other problems and overall dysfunction. In addition, prenatal drug use has raised the issue of whether this behavior constitutes child (or fetal) neglect, given the risks to the fetus. As the fetus becomes viable beyond 25 weeks gestation, it is necessary to weigh the needs of the unborn child with the rights of the mother.

Mothers' Cognitive Abilities.   Inadequate knowledge about child rearing and inappropriate expectations of children have been found to contribute to child neglect. The extreme situation is the limited parenting ability of mentally retarded parents (Kadushin, 1988), but the results are similar for parents who are not mentally retarded. Twentyman and Plotkin (1982) found that neglectful parents were significantly less accurate than controls in estimating when children should attain various developmental milestones. Jones and McNeely (1980) also found neglecting mothers to have more unrealistic and negative expectations. This kind of research usually addresses specific milestones, such as "drink from a cup," but does not include important areas such as "when can a baby be left alone in a bathtub?" or scenarios where a parent must decide if medical care is needed. Neglectful mothers have also been found to have poor problem-solving skills (Azar, Robinson, Hekemian, & Twentyman, 1984). Herrenkohl, Herrenkohl, and Egolf (1983) reported neglect to be associated with limited knowledge about parenting, poor skills, and low motivation to be a good parent. Some researchers have found neglectful mothers to be less educated than comparisons (Brayden et al., 1992; Dubowitz, 1996; Gaudin et al., 1993; Nelson et al., 1994) or to have poor intellectual skills (Pianta et al., 1989).

Aber and Zigler (1981) described the influence of parents' own developmental level on how they think and behave in regard to their children. Parents with problems with trust, autonomy, and dependency may have difficulty understanding and meeting the needs of their children and may seek to satisfy their own needs through their children (Pianta et al., 1989). In sum, diminished cognitive abilities may impede the ability of parents to adequately care for their children. Thinking back to the ecological theory explaining neglect, children with special needs (e.g., chronic health problems) are at very high risk for neglect when their parents are cognitively limited. This raises a question of the role of fathers in caring for their children, perhaps compensating for maternal difficulties.

Fathers

Most research on child neglect has focused on mothers, with little attention to fathers. The absence of a partner or spouse has been associated with less income to provide for children's needs and with neglect (Dunst et al., 1994; Polansky et al., 1981). As described earlier, poverty contributes directly and indirectly to the neglect of children. In their study of Native Americans, Nelson et al. (1994) found that neglect was associated with children in the family having different fathers and also with less involvement of biological fathers. Fathers in neglectful families have been found to have few positive interactions with their children and to not comply with their children's requests (Bousha & Twentyman, 1984; Burgess & Conger, 1978). Polansky et al. (1981) also reported that neglecting mothers received less emotional support from their children's fathers compared to controls. Thus, in addition to fathers directly neglecting their children's needs, they may also not provide adequate financial and emotional support to the mothers, indirectly neglecting their children.

There is a good deal of evidence that father involvement in the lives of their children benefits the children in most instances (e.g., National Research Council, 1994; Parke & Neville, 1987; Pleck, 1997). This appears to be mediated via a direct effect on children as well as indirectly via material and emotional support of mothers. To the extent that many fathers participate little in caring for their children, this constitutes a major form of neglect (Blankenhorn, 1995). More than one in four U.S. babies are born each year to unmarried mothers, most of whom are in households without fathers (National Research Council, 1994).

Finally, what is known about the children in neglectful families? The focus here is on child factors that may contribute to neglect, followed by a very brief review of the effects of neglect on children.

Children

Ecological theory posits that children themselves may contribute to their neglect, such as when a child's passivity may lead to limited attention by a parent. Child factors, however, appear to play only a minor role in triggering neglect (Ammerman, 1990). The interaction or fit between parent and child are, however, important. For example, Biringen and Robinson (1991) stressed the influence of a child's responsiveness on the mother's emotional availability. Some mothers are nurturant regardless of their child's response to them, whereas others may be turned off by a child who does not clearly show delight or interest. With regard to physical abuse, infants with a difficult temperament and children with problem behavior are thought to provoke angry responses, contributing to their maltreatment (Pianta et al., 1989).

Unplanned Pregnancy. In a retrospective study of abusive, neglectful, and control mothers receiving assistance from Aid to Families with Dependent Children (AFDC), Zuravin (1987) reported that having had more unplanned pregnancies was associated with neglect more than with abuse. Rohner and Rohner (1980) hypothesized that an underlying rejection of the pregnancy and the child contributes toward child maltreatment.

Birth Weight. One prospective study found a low birth weight to be a risk factor for neglect (Brayden et al., 1992). This could be related to low social class where prematurity and low birth weight are more common and to the physical, developmental, and behavioral problems found in low birth weight babies. Low birth weight is often associated with neonatal problems requiring extended care in an intensive care unit, which may impair bonding and the development of a healthy attachment between child and parents. In addition, prematurity and low birth weight may result from a mother's neglect of her (and her baby's) health during the pregnancy, an example being the use of cocaine prenatally.

Age. Neglect has been identified mostly in young children. For example, one third of substantiated neglect reports are made on children less than four years of age (Jones & McCurdy, 1992). During this period, children are most dependent and understandably viewed as most vulnerable. This might explain an increased likelihood of concern leading to a CPS report and to substantiation. In contrast, the unmet needs of a teenager, perhaps as important, probably would not evoke the same responses. The Third National Incidence Study on Child Abuse and Neglect, however, showed a peak incidence for both physical and emotional neglect in children 6 to 8 years of age, twice the rate for teens, and with preschoolers having the lowest rate (U.S. Department of Health and Human Services, 1996). This might reflect the extent to which schools were a major source of data.

Number of Children. A large number of children, particularly less than 6 years of age, in the home is frequently associated with neglect (Brayden et al., 1992; Gaudin et al., 1993; Kotch et al., 1989; Nelson et al., 1994). The Third National Incidence Study on Child Abuse and Neglect found neglect was identified more than twice as often in families with more than three children compared to those with one child (U.S. Department of Health and Human Services, 1996). It could be that having more children is a marker for poverty and its associated burdens, limiting parents' abilities to cope with childrearing. This could reflect the imposition of caring for several children on limited resources; the demand outweighs the supply.

However, whenever poverty or a related risk factor such as large family size is identified, the possibility of professional bias should also be considered.

Gender. There is no clear pattern of how gender is related to neglect. A study of federal service providers working with Native Americans found that girls were more often identified as neglected (Piasecki et al., 1989). Margolin (1990) reported that boys were more often fatality victims due to neglect, associated with a lack of supervision during a critical time (e.g., drowning), although increased risk taking by boys must be considered. Incidence data reveal no gender differences regarding physical and educational neglect, although boys were more likely to be identified for emotional neglect (U.S. Department of Health and Human Services, 1996). Cultural differences within the pluralistic United States, such as the preference many Chinese families have for males, may contribute to inadequate care of the less favored gender, although this has not been documented here.

Developmental Problems. Belsky and Vondra (1989) concluded that there is an association between prematurity, difficult temperament, and mentally retarded children and the inability of parents to adequately meet their needs. Although this makes intuitive sense, it is also true that these families are often involved with multiple professionals and under far more scrutiny than most other parents. In addition, the increased health care and service needs of some children put them at added risk for these needs not being met. Diamond and Jaudes (1983) found cerebral palsy to be a risk factor for neglect, but another study found no increase in maltreatment among 500 moderately to profoundly retarded children (Benedict, White, Wulff, & Hall, 1990). A child's behavior or developmental problems associated with neglect might lead to further distancing by the parent (Crittenden, 1988) and compound the neglect. Overall, the special needs of some children appear to overwhelm even caring and competent parents, and neglect may result.

The Effects of Neglect on Children

Several reviews have described the harmful effects of neglect on children's development, while also noting the methodological shortcomings in the limited research on this issue (Crouch & Milner, 1993; Gaudin, in press). The longitudinal research of Egeland and colleagues has documented problems with attachment, low levels of enthusiasm, creativity in problem solving, low self-esteem, and increased dependency and anger in neglected children compared to physically abused and nonmaltreated children (Egeland, Sroufe, & Erickson, 1993). Neglected children have been found to have more receptive language difficulties compared to physically abused and nonmaltreated children (Fox, Long & Langlois, 1991). Some have found neglect to impair cognitive development and academic achievement (Eckenrode, Laird, & Doris, 1993; Erickson, Egeland, & Pianta, 1989; Wodarski, Kurtz, Gaudin, & Howing, 1990).

In the realm of social development, neglected children are typically found to be passive and withdrawn (Bousha & Twentyman, 1984; Crittenden, 1992). It is interesting that aggression may also be a problem for neglected children (Herrenkohl & Herrenkohl, 1981). In general, neglect appears to be associated with a variety of behavior problems (Herrenkohl & Herrenkohl, 1981; Aber, Allen, Carlson, & Cicchetti, 1989). Neglected children are also at risk for delinquent behavior. Maxfield and Widom (1996) reported a longitudinal study in which children who had been either physically abused or neglected were at similarly increased risk of arrest for a violent offense compared to controls.

Finally, neglect has also been associated with physical and medical problems (Dubowitz & Black, 1996). Poor growth, for example, can reflect deficits in children's diets and their environments (Drotar, 1992). Almost half the estimated fatalities due to child maltreatment each year have been attributed to neglect (U.S Advisory Board on Child Abuse and Neglect, 1995).

SUMMARY

The portrait of neglectful families in this chapter is drawn from research using substantiated CPS cases of neglect and excludes broader areas where basic needs of children are not met (e.g., exposure to environmental hazards, inadequate schools). Poverty and its burdens are frequently the context in which neglect is identified. Multiple stressors that outweigh the available resources and strengths compromise the functioning of families and their ability to adequately care for their children. There is often a negative relationship between mother and child with little positive interaction, and family conflict, including domestic violence, may aggravate the situation and add to the neglect. Mothers may be depressed and be cognitively limited, impairing their parenting abilities. Mothers' substance abuse is a major factor. The limited role many fathers play in their children's lives has not received the attention it deserves; it appears that both directly and indirectly fathers influence the functioning of families and their children's well-being. The contribution of children to their own neglect seems to be small, although health and developmental problems may be risk factors.

With this portrait in mind, we are faced with the challenge of what can be done to strengthen families to address the serious problem of neglect. Social policies can be very important. The recent federal welfare reform legislation, which includes provisions to improve child support payments by fathers, is an example. Unfortunately, the same legislation dismantles much of the safety net that has been developed for low-income families since the 1930s, and many poor families may face great difficulties. Effective programs to support families, enhance their parenting abilities, and protect children are also needed. Without systemic improvements at the community and societal levels, the challenge for such programs is enormous. We should use our knowledge of families and child neglect as the basis for forceful advocacy to support policies and programs that help families meet the basic needs of their children.

REFERENCES

Aber, J. L., Allen, J. P., Carlson, V., & Cicchetti, D. (1989). The effects of maltreatment on development during early childhood: Recent studies and their theoretical, clinical, and policy implications. In D. Cicchetti & V. Carlson (Eds.), *Child maltreatment: Theory and research on the causes and consequences of child abuse and neglect* (pp. 579–619), New York: Cambridge University Press.

Aber, J. L., & Zigler, E. (1981). Developmental considerations in defining child maltreatment. In R. Rizley & D. Cicchetti (Eds.), *Development perspectives on child maltreatment: New directions for child development* (pp. 1–29). San Francisco: Jossey-Bass.

American Humane Association. (1988). *Highlights of official child neglect and child abuse reporting: 1986.* Denver, CO: American Humane Association.

Ammerman, R. T. (1990). Predisposing child factors. In R. T. Ammerman & M. Hersen (Eds.), *Children at risk: An evaluation of factors contributing to child abuse and neglect* (pp.199–221). New York: Plenum.

Aragona, J. A., & Eyberg, S. M. (1981). Neglected children: Mother's report of child behavior problems and observed verbal behavior. *Child Development, 52,* 596–602.

Azar, S., Robinson, D., Hekemian, E., & Twentyman, C. (1984). Unrealistic expectations and problem solving ability in maltreating and comparison mothers. *Journal of Consulting and Clinical Psychology, 52,* 687–691.

Belsky, J. (1980). Child maltreatment: An ecological integration. *American Psychologist, 35,* 320–335.

Belsky, J. & Vondra, J. (1989). Lessons from child abuse: The determinants of parenting. In D. Cicchetti & V. Carlson (Eds.), *Child maltreatment: Theory and research on the causes and consequences of child abuse and neglect* (pp. 153–202). New York: Cambridge University Press.

Benedict, M. I., White, R. B., Wulff, L. M., & Hall, B. J. (1990). Reported maltreatment in children with multiple disabilities. *Child Abuse & Neglect, 14,* 207–217.

Besharov, D. J. (1990). *Recognizing child abuse.* New York: Free Press.

Biringen, Z., & Robinson, J. (1991). Emotional availability in mother–child interactions: A reconceptualization for research. *American Journal of Orthopsychiatry, 61*(2): 258–271.

Blankenhorn, D. (1995). *Fatherless America—Confronting our most urgent social problem.* New York: Basic Books.

Bousha, D. M., & Twentyman, C. T. (1984). Mother–child interactional style in abuse, neglect, and control groups: Naturalistic observations in the home. *Journal of Abnormal Psychology, 93,* 106–114.

Brayden, R. M., Altemeier, W. A., Tucker, D. D., Dietrich, M. S., & Vietze, P. (1992). Antecedents of child neglect in the first two years of life. *Journal of Pediatrics, 120,* 426–429.

Burgess, R. L., & Conger, R. D. (1978). Family interaction in abusive, neglectful, and normal families. *Child Development, 49,* 1163–1173.

Children's Defense Fund. (1996). Summary of the new welfare legislation. *CDF Reports, 17*(9), 1–7.

Crittenden, P. M. (1988). Distorted patterns of relationship in maltreating families: The role of internal representational models. *Journal of Reproductive and Infant Psychology, 6,* 183–199.

Crittenden, P. M. (1992). Children's strategies for coping with adverse home environments: An interpretation using attachment theory. *Child Abuse & Neglect, 16,* 329–343.

Crittenden, P. M., & Ainsworth, M. D. S. (1989). Child maltreatment and attachment theory. In D. Cicchetti & V. Carlson (Eds.), *Child maltreatment: Theory and research on the causes and consequences of child abuse and neglect* (pp. 432–464). New York: Cambridge University Press.

Crittenden, P. M., & Bonvillian, J. D. (1984). The relationship between maternal risk status and maternal sensitivity. *American Journal of Orthopsychiatry, 54,* 250–262.

Crouch, J. L., & Milner, J. S. (1993). Effects of child neglect on children. *Criminal Justice and Behavior, 20*(1), 49–65.

Culp, R. E., Culp, A. M., Soulis, J., & Letts, D. (1989). Self-esteem and depression in abusive, neglecting, and non-maltreating mothers. *Infant Mental Health Journal, 10,* 243–251.

Diamond, L. J., & Jaudes, P. K. (1983). Child abuse and the cerebral palsied patient. *Developmental Medicine and Child Neurology, 25,* 169–174.

DiLeonardi, J. W. (1993). *Kinship care, permanency planning, and substance abuse.* Bensenville, IL: Lifelink Corp.

Drotar, D. (1992). Prevention of neglect and non-organic failure to thrive. In E. W. Holden & M. S. Rosenberg (Eds.), *Prevention of child maltreatment: Developmental and ecological perspectives* (pp. 115–149). New York: Wiley.

Dubowitz, H. (1994). Neglecting the neglect of neglect. *Journal of Interpersonal Violence, 9*(4), 556–560.

Dubowitz, H. (1995). *Child neglect—Child, mother and family functioning* (Final Report prepared for the National Center on Child Abuse & Neglect, Grant No. 90CA1401). Washington, DC: National Clearing House on Child Abuse and Neglect.

Dubowitz, H. (1996). *A longitudinal study of child neglect* (Final Report prepared for the National Center on Child Abuse & Neglect, Grant No. 90CA1481). Washington, DC: National Clearing House on Child Abuse and Neglect.

Dubowitz, H., & Black, M. M. (1996). Medical neglect. In J. Briere, L. Berliner, J. A. Bulkley, C. Jenny, & T. Reid (Eds.), *The APSAC handbook on child maltreatment* (pp. 227–241). Thousand Oaks, CA: Sage.

Dubowitz, H., Black, M., Starr, R. H., Jr., & Zuravin, S. (1993). A conceptual definition of child neglect. *Criminal Justice and Behavior, 20,* 8–26.

Dunst, C. J., & Trivette, C. M. (1988). Determinants of parent and child interactive behavior. In K. Mayo (Ed.), *Parent-child interaction and developmental disabilities* (pp. 3–31). New York: Praeger.

Dunst, C. J., Trivette, C. M., & Gowen, J. W. (1994). *Intrafamily and extrafamily factors associated with child neglect* (Final report submitted to the U.S. Department of Health and Human Services, Administration for Children, Youth, and Families). Washington, DC: National Center on Child Abuse and Neglect.

Eckenrode, J., Laird, M., & Doris, J. (1993). School performance and disciplinary problems among abused and neglected children. *Developmental Psychology, 29,* 53–62.

Egeland, B., & Erickson, M. (1990). Rising above the past: Strategies for helping new mothers break the cycle of abuse and neglect. *Zero to Three, 11,* 29–35.

Egeland, B., Sroufe, L. A., & Erickson, M. (1993). The developmental consequences of different patterns of maltreatment. *Child Abuse & Neglect, 7,* 459–469.

Erickson, M. F., & Egeland, B. (1996). Child neglect. In J. Briere, L. Berliner, J. Bulkley, C. Jenny, & T. Reid (Eds.), *The APSAC Handbook on Child Maltreatment, 1,* 4–20.

Erickson, M. F., Egeland, B., & Pianta, R. C. (1989). The effects of maltreatment on the development of young children. In D. Cicchetti & V. Carlson (Eds.), *Child maltreatment: Theory and research on the causes and consequences of child abuse and neglect* (pp. 647–684). New York: Cambridge University Press.

Fox, L., Long, S. H., & Langlois, A. (1991). Patterns of language comprehension deficits in abused and neglected children. *Journal of Speech and Hearing Disorders, 53,* 239–244.

Friedrich, W. N., Tyler, J. D., & Clark, J. A. (1985). Personality and psychological variables in abusive, neglectful, and low-income control mothers. *Journal of Nervous and Mental Disease, 173,* 449–460.

Gaines, R., Sangrund, A., Green, A. H., & Power, E. (1978). Etiological factors in child maltreatment:

A multivariate study of abusing, neglecting, and normal mothers. *Journal of Abnormal Psychology, 87,* 531–540.

Gaudin, J. M., Jr. (1994). *Child neglect: A guide for intervention (The User Manual Series).* Washington, DC: U.S. Department of Health and Human Services.

Gaudin, J. M., Jr. (in press). Child neglect: Short and long-term outcomes. In H. Dubowitz (Ed.), *Neglected children: Research, practice and policy.* Thousand Oaks, CA: Sage.

Gaudin, J. M., Jr., & Dubowitz, H. (1997). Family functioning in neglectful families: Recent research. In J. Berrick & N. Barth (Eds.), *Child Welfare Research Review* (Vol. 2, pp. 28–26). New York: Columbia University Press.

Gaudin, J. M., & Polansky, N. A. (1986). Social distancing of the neglectful family: Sex, race, and social class influences. *Children and Youth Services Review, 8,* 1–12.

Gaudin, J. M., Jr., Polansky, N. A., Kilpatrick, A. (1992). The Child Well-Being scales: A field trial. *Child Welfare, 62,* 319–328.

Gaudin, J. M., Jr., Polansky, N. A., Kilpatrick, A. C., & Shilton, P. (1993). *Family structure and functioning in neglectful families* (Final report: National Center on Child Abuse and Neglect, Grant No. 90 CA-1400). Washington, DC: National Clearing House on Child Abuse and Neglect.

Giovannoni, J. M., & Billingsley, A. (1970). Child neglect among the poor: A study of parental adequacy in families of three ethnic groups. *Child Welfare, 49,* 196–204.

Hampton, R., & Newberger, E. (1985). Child abuse incidence and reporting by hospitals: Significance of severity, class and race. *American Journal of Public Health, 75,* 56–59.

Herrenkohl, E. C., & Herrenkohl, R. C. (1981). Some antecedents and developmental consequences of child maltreatment. In R. Risley & D. Cicchetti (Eds.), *Developmental perspectives on child maltreatment* (pp. 57–76). San Francisco: Jossey-Bass.

Herrenkohl, R., Herrenkohl, E., & Egolf, B. (1983). Circumstances surrounding the occurrence of child maltreatment. *Journal of Consulting and Clinical Psychology, 51,* 424–431.

Jones, J. M., & McNeely, R. L. (1980). Mother who neglect and those who do not: A comparative study. *Social Casework, 61,* 559–567.

Jones, E., & McCurdy, K. (1992). The link between types of maltreatment and demographic characteristics of children. *Child Abuse and Neglect, 16*(2), 201–215.

Kadushin, A. (1988). Neglect in families. In E. W. Nunnally, C. S. Chilman, & F. M. Cox (Eds.), *Mental illness, delinquency, addictions, and neglect* (pp. 147–166). Newbury Park, CA: Sage.

Kendall-Tackett, K. A., & Eckenrode, J. (1996) The effects of neglect on academic achievement and disciplinary problems: A developmental perspective. *Child Abuse & Neglect, 20*(3), 161–170.

Kotch, J. B., Browne, D. C., Symons, M., Ringwalt, C., Bentz, W. K., Evans, G. A., Rosenbloom, L., Glenn, W., Cheng, M., & Park, M. (1989). *Stress, social support, and abuse and neglect in high risk infants.* Springfield, VA: National Technical Information Service, U.S. Department of Commerce.

Lamb, M. E., Gaensbauer, T. J., Malkin, C. M., & Schultz, L. A. (1985). The effects of child maltreatment on security of infant-adult attachment. *Infant Behavior and Development, 8,* 35–45.

Margolin, L. (1990). Fatal child neglect. *Child Welfare, 69,* 309–319.

Maxfield, M. G., & Widom, C. S. (1996). The cycle of violence. *Archives of Pediatric and Adolescent Medicine, 150,* 390–395.

National Research Council. (1994). *America's Fathers and Public Policy.* Washington, DC: National Academy Press.

Nelson, K. E., Landsman, M. J., Cross, T., Tyler, M., Twohig, A., & Allen, M. (1994). *Family functioning in neglectful families: Final report* (NCCAN Grant No. 90-CA-1415). Iowa City: University of Iowa, School of Social Work, National Resource Center on Family Based Services.

Nelson, K. E., Saunders, E. J., & Landsman, M. J. (1993). Chronic child neglect in perspective. *Social Work, 38,* 661–673.

O'Toole, R., Turbett, P., & Nalepka, C. (1983). Theories, professional knowledge, and diagnosis of child abuse. In D. Finkelhor, R. J., Gelles, G. T. Hotaling, & M. A. Straus (Eds.), *The dark side of families: Current family violence research* (pp. 349–362). Beverly Hills, CA: Sage.

Parke, R. D., & Neville, B. (1987). Teenage fatherhood. In S. L. Hofferth & C. D. Hayes (Eds.), *Risking the future: Adolescent sexuality, pregnancy and childbearing.* (Vol. 2, pp. 145–173). Washington, DC: National Academy Press.

Parker, S., Greer, S., & Zuckerman, B. (1988). Double jeopardy: The impact of poverty on early child development. *Pediatric Clinics of North America, 35,* 1227–1240.

Pianta, R., Egeland, B., & Erickson, M. F. (1989). The antecedents of maltreatment: Results of the Mother-Child Interaction Research Project. In D. Cicchetti & V. Carlson (Eds.), *Child maltreatment: Theory and research on the causes and consequences of child abuse and neglect* (pp. 203–253). New York: Cambridge University Press.

Piasecki, J. A., Manson, S. M., Biernoff, M. P., Hiat, A. B., Taylor, S. S., & Bechtold, D. W. (1989). Abuse and neglect of American Indian children: Findings from a survey of federal providers. *American Indian and Alaska Native Mental Health Research, 3,* 43–62.

Pleck, J. H. (1997). Paternal involvement: Levels, sources, consequences. In M. E. Lamb (Ed.), *The role of the father in child development* (pp. 66–103). New York: Wiley.

Polansky, N. A., Ammons, P. W., & Gaudin, J. M., Jr. (1985). Loneliness and isolation in child neglect. *Social Casework: The Journal of Contemporary Social Work, 66*(1), 38–47.

Polansky, N. A., Borgman, R. D., & DeSaix, C. (1972). *Roots of futility.* San Francisco: Jossey-Bass.

Polansky, N. A., Chalmers, M. A., Buttenweiser, E., & Williams, D. P. (1981). *Damaged parents: An anatomy of child neglect.* Chicago: University of Chicago Press.

Polansky, N. A., Gaudin, J. M., Jr., Ammons, P. W., & Davis, K. B. (1985). The psychological ecology of the neglectful mother. *Child Abuse & Neglect, 9,* 265–275.

Rivera, B., & Widom, C. S. (1992). Childhood victimization and violent offending. *Violence and Victims, 5,* 19–35.

Rohner, R. P., & Rohner, E. C. (1980). Antecedents and consequences of parental rejection: A theory of emotional abuse. *Child Abuse and Neglect, 4,* 189–198.

Twentyman, C., & Plotkin, R. (1982). Unrealistic expectations of parents who maltreat their children: An educational deficit that pertains to child development. *Journal of Clinical Psychology, 38,* 497–503.

U.S. Advisory Board on Child Abuse and Neglect. (1995). *A nation's shame: Fatal child abuse and neglect in the United States.* Washington, DC: U.S. Government Printing Office.

U.S. Department of Health and Human Services. (1995). *Child maltreatment 1994: Reports on the states to the National Center on Child Abuse and Neglect.* Washington, DC: U.S. Government Printing Office.

U.S. Department of Health and Human Services. (1996). *The third national incidence study of child abuse and neglect.* Washington, DC: National Center on Child Abuse and Neglect.

Vietze, P. M., O'Connor, S., Sherrod, K. B., & Altemeier, W. A. (1991). The early screening project. In R. H. Starr, Jr. & D. A. Wolfe (Eds.), *The effects of child abuse and neglect: Issues and research* (pp. 82–99). New York: Guilford.

Wiese, D., & Daro, D. (1995). *Current trends in child abuse reporting fatalities: The results of the annual fifty-state survey.* Chicago: National Committee to Prevent Child Abuse.

Wolock, I., & Horowitz, H. (1979). Child maltreatment and maternal deprivation among AFDC recipient families. *Social Services Resource, 53,* 175–194.

Wolock, I., & Horowitz, H. (1984). Child maltreatment as a social problem: The neglect of neglect. *American Journal of Orthopsychiatry, 54,* 530–543.

Wodarski, J. S., Kurtz, P. D., Gaudin, J. M., & Howing, P. T. (1990). Maltreatment and the school age child: Major academic, socioemotional, and adaptive outcomes. *Social Work, 35,* 506–513.

Zuravin, S. J. (1986). Residential density and urban child maltreatment: An aggregate analysis. *Journal of Family Violence, 1,* 307–322.

Zuravin, S. J. (1987). Unplanned pregnancies, family planning problems, and child maltreatment. *Family Relations, 36,* 135–139.

Zuravin, S. J. (1988). Child abuse, child neglect, and maternal depression. Is there a connection?

In National Center on Child Abuse and Neglect (Ed.), *Child neglect monograph: Proceedings from a symposium* (pp. 23–48). Washington, DC: Clearinghouse on Child Abuse and Neglect Information.

Zuravin, S. J. (1989). The ecology of child abuse and neglect: Review of the literature and presentation of data. *Violence and Victims, 4,* 101–120.

Zuravin, S. J., & Greif, G. L. (1989). Normative and child-maltreating AFDC mothers. *Social Casework: The Journal of Contemporary Social Work, 70,* 76–84.

Author Index

Subject Index